Eyewitness Korea

Eyewitness Korea

The Experience of British and
American Soldiers in the Korean War
1950–1953

James Goulty

Pen & Sword
MILITARY

First published in Great Britain in 2018 by
PEN & SWORD MILITARY
An imprint of
Pen & Sword Books Ltd
Yorkshire - Philadelphia

Copyright © James Goulty 2018

ISBN 978-1-47387-090-1

Typeset in 11/13 point MinionPro

Printed and bound by TJ International

Pen & Sword Books Ltd incorporates the Imprints of Aviation, Atlas, Family History, Fiction, Maritime, Military, Discovery, Politics, History, Archaeology, Select, Wharncliffe Local History, Wharncliffe True Crime, Military Classics, Wharncliffe Transport, Leo Cooper, The Praetorian Press, Remember When, Seaforth Publishing and Frontline Publishing.

For a complete list of Pen & Sword titles please contact

PEN & SWORD BOOKS LTD
47 Church Street, Barnsley, South Yorkshire, S70 2AS, England
E-mail: enquiries@pen-and-sword.co.uk
Website: www.pen-and-sword.co.uk

Or

PEN & SWORD BOOKS
1950 Lawrence Rd, Havertown, PA 19083, USA
E-mail: Uspen-and-sword@casematepublishers.com
Website: www.penandswordbooks.com

Contents

Acknowledgements vii

Introduction 1

1. Warfare in the Land of the Morning Calm. 5
    The Outbreak of the Korean War, June 1950 8
    The Ground War in Korea, 1950–1953 11
    The Korean Peninsula 15

2. A Lesson in Readiness: Preparing for Action in Korea. 19
    Mobilisation for the Korean War June–October 1950 20
    Conscription and the Korean War 32
    Basic Training: Soldierization for the Korean War 34
    Battle Training: Providing Realistic Combat Training 41

3. Destination Korea 49
    Reinforcements/Replacements and Rotation 49
    Troopship Experience 53
    Flying to Korea 62
    Troops' First Impressions of Korea 64

4. Ground Warfare in Korea: Stemming the Tide 66
    Early Experiences: June–August 1950 66
    Combat in the Pusan Perimeter 73
    Inchon and Seoul 80
    The Breakout and Push North 83

5. Ground Warfare in Korea: From Chosin to Stalemate 93
    X Corps and the Chosin Reservoir Campaign 94
    The Ridgway Effect 102
    Epic Confrontations: the Battles of the Imjin and Kap'yong 111

6. Ground Warfare in Korea: Fighting a Limited War. 121
    Fighting for Limited Objectives 122
    Combat under Static Warfare Conditions: October 1951–July 1953 128
    Patrolling and Raiding 1952–53 140

7. Coping with Active Service. 149
    Surviving on the Battlefield 149
    Motivational Issues 155
    Integration 158

Recreation and Welfare 160
Food and Rations 166
Medical Matters 167
8. Prisoner of War Experiences 175
The Point of Capture or Surrender 177
Journey to the Camps 180
Interrogation, Indoctrination, and the Chinese Lenient Policy 184
Life in the Camps 189
Release and Repatriation 195
9. From Ceasefire to Returning Home 198

Notes 210

Bibliography 242

Index 254

Acknowledgements

I owe a huge debt of gratitude to my editor Rupert Harding, whose encouragement and sound counsel has been invaluable to me. Likewise, I would like to thank Pen and Sword Ltd for agreeing to this book, and I am most grateful for the assistance provided by copy editor Susan Last on this project.

The staffs at the Imperial War Museum; National Army Museum; Tactical Doctrine Retrieval Cell (MOD) provided every assistance. Equally, I am indebted to the curators and staff at the following regimental museums: The Royal Dragoon Guards Museum; The Royal Artillery Museum; The Royal Scots; The Fusiliers of Northumberland Museum; The Royal Regiment of Fusiliers; The King's Regiment (Museum of Liverpool Life); Royal Leicestershire Regiment (Leicester City Museums Service); Durham Light Infantry (Durham County Record Office); The Welch Regiment Museum; The King's Own Scottish Borderers; Duke of Wellington's Regiment; The Black Watch Museum; Regimental Museum of the Argyll & Sutherland Highlanders.

The Imperial War Museum Department of Sound kindly allowed me to quote from their impressive oral history collection on the Korean War, and I am indebted to Anthony Richards for his help regarding checking copyright. Similarly, the National Army Museum allowed me to use their oral history recordings with Korean War veterans.

Dr James Smither graciously granted me permission to use the Korean War oral histories that form a part of the Grand Valley State University Veterans History Project. I am similarly extremely grateful to the Trustees of the Fusiliers Museum of Northumberland, Alnwick Castle, for allowing me to quote from: 'A pretty rough do altogether' The Fifth Fusiliers in Korea 1950–1951.

As a military history student at the University of Leeds I became especially interested in the Korean War. During my PhD research it was a privilege to correspond with/interview a number of British Korean War veterans, and in part this book draws on the material I gathered. The bibliography provides a full list of veterans, but for their special help regarding this particular book, I would like to thank: Keith Taylor and Tony Perrins (Royal Northumberland Fusiliers); Barry Tunnicliffe and John Robottom (Royal Artillery); Tom

Nowell, MM (Duke of Wellington's Regiment); and Barry Whiting (Royal Army Medical Corps). Each in their own way has shown me immense kindness by answering questions, providing photographs, sharing memories of their service in Korea and/or allowing me to quote from their own books.

Likewise, I am deeply grateful to Prof David French for his words of support, and to Dr Meghan Fitzpatrick for kindly supplying a copy of her article on 'Fighting VD in the Commonwealth Division during the Korean War.'

Last, but not least, I am extremely grateful to my family, and Poppy the Boxer, for their unstinting love and support during the writing and researching of his book.

Introduction

Today Korea is often termed the 'Forgotten War,' and in the West has arguably been overshadowed in the popular consciousness by later conflicts such as Vietnam, the Falklands, and the lengthy engagements in Iraq and Afghanistan. Yet, set against a backdrop of global confrontation between communism and capitalism, and with the genuine threat of a nuclear war erupting, the Korean War, when it broke out in June 1950, became one of the major events of the Cold War, the ramifications of which are still being lived with at present.

Initially the Western powers, under the auspices of the United Nations, proved ill-equipped to deal with the threat of the North Korean invasion of her southern neighbour, and faced the real prospect of defeat at the hands of the communists. However, in September 1950 ground forces of the American-led United Nations Command (UNC) were able to break out of the Pusan Perimeter, which in conjunction with an audacious amphibious landing at Inchon changed the course of the war.

Using a variety of sources this book concentrates on the first-hand experiences of American and British ground troops from June 1950 to July 1953. As part of the UNC these personnel belonged to a wider coalition that included sizeable forces from South Korea, and contributions from several other nations including those from the British Commonwealth. Crucially the ground war was not fought in isolation. From an early stage the UNC was able to establish naval and air superiority over most of Korea, effectively enabling the war to be contained on the peninsula.[1] At the battlefront this ensured that ground units could be provided with comparatively high levels of close air support, unhindered by the presence of any credible enemy air threat, not necessarily a characteristic that was liable to be repeated in any future confrontation, particularly with the Soviet Union.[2]

Although some new technologies were used in Korea, much of the fighting employed weapons, equipment and tactical doctrine of Second World War vintage. Likewise, by 1951–52 the front had bogged down into static conditions reminiscent of the trench warfare on the Western Front during the First World War.

Chapter 1 provides historical background on Korea and the Korean War 1950–53, and highlights the physical environment of the country that impacted heavily upon military operations. In particular an underdeveloped road and rail network, rugged mountains and waterlogged rice paddies were a challenge for highly mechanised Western armies. The climate was awful, especially in winter, something few American and British veterans ever forgot. In contrast, spring could be markedly more pleasant, and some soldiers even found themselves appreciating their surroundings at this time of year.

Mobilisation and training is covered in Chapter 2. Alongside regular personnel both the Americans and British were initially highly dependent on re-calling reservists, who although rusty in most cases had plenty of experience to fall back on. As the war progressed, increasing reliance was placed on relatively inexperienced conscripts (draftees and National Servicemen), which emphasised the requirement for effective training. This had not only to impart basic military skills, but also needed to generate a sense of professional pride, and crucially help troops adapt to the demands of active service in an awkward theatre like Korea.

Having been mobilised, troops had to be transported to Korea. Although some flew, the vast majority, as during earlier wars, were ferried to the theatre via some form of troopship, often under unpleasant conditions, particularly when seasickness abounded. Chapter 3 considers what it was like for personnel being transported to Korea, and covers their initial impressions of the country, which often seemed vastly different from their own, and where the war-torn population endured unimaginable levels of poverty.

Combat experience is covered by chapters 4, 5 and 6, and these are arranged broadly chronologically so as to follow the course of the war. However, given the limitations of space, these don't provide a narrative of every action of the war, but rather explain what the fighting was like for ordinary troops during the different phases of the war. They examine key issues, such as enemy tactics and the American and British response to them, and consider how pursuing a limited war impacted on the military at battalion level and below. Readers wishing for more information on specific operations/battles might wish to consult the accompanying chapter notes and bibliography, which outline the main American and British sources.

Chapter 7 is intimately connected with the issues of morale and welfare, and concerns those factors that enabled troops to endure the harsh conditions in Korea. This includes food/rations, mail, religion, leave arrangements and access to alcohol and sex. The importance of medical care is emphasised, along with the pioneering deployment of helicopters in the casualty evacuation role.

The discussion covers self-inflicted wounds (SIW) that were treated by the medical services, and often regarded as a sign of poor morale.

The experiences of POWs are dealt with in Chapter 8. While these men endured many of the hardships familiar to prisoners of the Axis Powers in the Second World War, the communists sought to 're-educate' POWs along Marxist-Leninist lines. Accordingly, they embarked on determined efforts at indoctrination/political subversion, which impacted on all aspects of prisoners' lives, and at the height of the Cold War led to genuine fears of 'Commie brainwashing'. Many POWs died from starvation, neglect or were tortured and executed by their captors. Those fortunate enough to survive their ordeal were often affected psychologically, and many continued to have medical problems into old age that could be attributed to the conditions of their captivity.

Finally, Chapter 9 outlines the experiences of troops on completing their Korean tours, especially those present at the time of the July 1953 ceasefire. This created the present-day conditions, where North and South Korea face each other uneasily across the demilitarised zone (DMZ). Veterans' attitudes towards the Korean War and their participation in it are covered as well. For some the war was worthwhile, or at least fought for the right reasons, whereas others remained less certain, particularly given that from a Western perspective there appeared to have been no clear victory.

Hopefully this book will complement many of the excellent sources that already exist on American and British military involvement in the 'Forgotten War', and introduce the subject to readers who may be unfamiliar with it. In doing so it aims to provide the reader with an overview of the land campaign and a respectful tribute to all soldiers and Marines that served in Korea, especially those who never made it home.

James H.R. Goulty
August 2017

Chapter 1

Warfare in the Land of the Morning Calm

As a jagged, thumb-like peninsula, Korea juts 'out from the Manchurian mainland to within 125 miles of the coast of southern Japan, her northern frontier on the Yalu River was only 500 miles as the crow flies from Peking.'[1] In size she ranges from 500–600 miles long, and from 90–100 miles wide, apart from her broad northern terminus where the Yalu River marks her border with Manchuria that runs for approximately 400 miles west to east, and the Tumen River denotes the shorter border with Siberia that continues for a further ten miles to the east. To the west of Korea, across the Yellow Sea, lies China's strategically important Liaotung Peninsula, including the notable port of Port Arthur.

Korea's geographical position has often seen her become a point of contact and conflict between rival powers. Over the centuries she has served as a battleground for the Chinese, Manchurians, Mongols and Japanese, plus suffered innumerable civil wars. As the eminent American military historian Alan R. Millett comments, 'the Korean people know war. One bit of their lore is that the country has been invaded at least six hundred times in the last three millennia, although the counting includes incidents of piracy, minor punitive expeditions, and naval encounters along Korea's long and island-dotted coastline.'[2]

From about the time of Christ until 668AD, Korea was dominated by the 'Three Kingdoms': Koguryo (north), Paekche (south-west) and Silla (centre). In the late seventh century the Silla dynasty came to an agreement with the Chinese Tang rulers, with the aim of destroying its rivals. A Chinese army was sent to Korea and, combined with a Silla force, overthrew the kingdoms of Paekche in 660, and Koguryo in 668. Subsequently, a Chinese army was defeated by Silla and sent northwards during the 670s, which ultimately ensured that by the mid-700s Imperial China had started to recognise Korea as a single kingdom.

During the thirteenth and fourteenth centuries Mongol invasions occurred, and many Koreans were pressed to help with the abortive Mongol invasions of

Japan in 1274 and 1281, which marked the high point of Mongol power in the region. By the late 1300s the Chinese had started to assert their influence over Korea, and this coincided with the establishment of the Choson (Yi) Dynasty in Korea, which was to last into the twentieth century, thus linking medieval and modern Korea. Under the fourth Choson king, Sejong, the written Korean phonetic alphabet (han'gul) was developed, and there was a decline in Buddhism coupled with the rising influence of neo-Confucian philosophy. Central to the latter was primogeniture, the practice in which the eldest son inherits his father's land, and 'this tradition contributed to a male dominant society that still pertains in Korea.'[3]

In 1592 a Japanese invasion force crossed over into Korea and made swift progress, facilitated in part by their deployment of muskets that had been copied from the Portuguese who landed in Japan during the 1540s. With the assistance of Ming Chinese forces, the Koreans ultimately thwarted the Japanese attempts at conquest, although fighting dragged on until 1598 when the Japanese leader Toyotomi Hideyoshi died. The unusual Korean 'turtle ships' of Admiral Yi Sun-sin's fleet, with their armoured decks, were particularly significant, as they intercepted and sank several Japanese supply ships in the Korean Strait.

During the nineteenth century 'valiant but out-gunned Koreans' opposed French, American and Japanese naval expeditionary forces in 1866, 1871 and 1875 respectively.[4] By the end of the century Russian and Japanese imperialistic ambitions had impacted heavily on Korea, as there was a deep-seated enmity between the two nations over who should hold authority over the peninsula. The rise of Russia and Japan as imperialistic powers also coincided with the declining influence of China in the region.

The Sino-Japanese War (1894–95) largely resulted from a Japanese desire to establish a presence in Korea and China's efforts to resist this. Having landed at Chemulpo, the Japanese seized the palace in Seoul and captured the king, before declaring war on China. The conflict marked the rise of Japan as a significant military power. The Chinese, when they responded, were beaten easily and forced back across the Yalu River by eager Japanese forces that went on to secure the Liaotung Peninsula. Having been severely shocked by their sudden defeat, the Chinese sued for peace and Japan used this as an opportunity to demand sway over the Liaotung Peninsula, plus what was termed 'Korean independence', as part of the Treaty of Shimoneseki. Ultimately, this led to tensions between Russia and Japan spilling over into armed conflict a decade later.

The Russo-Japanese War (1904–05) was in part caused by Japan's desire to deny Russia any influence over Korean affairs. Again it witnessed fighting on Korean soil and highlighted the devastating effectiveness of the firepower of modern weapons, particularly when encountered by attackers assaulting well-defended positions. Japan's navy came to the fore as well, and proved itself to be a modern, highly capable fighting force, including several ships built in Britain. On 8 February 1904 a Japanese naval squadron launched a surprise attack on Russian ships in Port Arthur. Then an army was landed at Chemulpo, which defeated the Russians at the Battle of the Yalu.

Korea's importance 'as a strategic springboard was made manifest when Japan's armies were able to move through Manchuria and blockade the Liaotung Peninsula by land, while Japanese ships, operating from Korea's west coast, blockaded it by sea.'[5] In early 1905 Port Arthur fell after a bitter six-month siege, and a Russian army was subsequently routed at the Battle of Mukden in Manchuria, suffering around 150,000 casualties.

The Russians had sent their Baltic Fleet to the aid of Port Arthur on a long voyage via the Indian Ocean begun in October 1904. In late May 1905 the fleet reached the Tsushima Strait. Here it was spectacularly defeated by a Japanese fleet under Admiral Heihachiro Togo, with only five Russian destroyers and one cruiser managing to escape after being harried through the night by the Japanese. Coupled with their defeats on land, events in the Tsushima Strait forced the Russians to seek peace.

The settlement of the Russo-Japanese War confirmed Japan's authority over Korea. However, she did not impose strict control over the country until 1910, after the Japanese resident-general was assassinated by a Korean national-ist. Japanese rule lasted until the end of the Second World War. Under it the Korean language was proscribed, and Koreans were forced to take Japanese names, while Japanese policies were reinforced by the widespread presence of their military and police. According to the historian Peter Lowe, 'summing up the Japanese impact on Korea, it may be said that efficient but harsh adminis-tration was provided; economic progress was promoted yet in a distorted way, designed to benefit colonial master.'[6]

Crawford F. Sams, a senior American army medical officer involved in the administration of Japan during the 1940s and early 1950s, supported Peter Lowe's assessment of Japanese rule of Korea, noting that they 'literally liquidated the top of the social pyramid' and 'occupied and took over all of the key jobs.'[7] By 1941 around 1.5 million Koreans had been forcibly recruited as labourers in Japan, and many others served in the Imperial Japanese Army as auxiliaries during the Second World War, including as guards in the noto-rious Japanese POW camps in the Far East. As many as 100–200,000 Korean women were forced to become 'comfort girls' for the Japanese military, and as a whole the country was exploited for its mineral and agricultural resources, as well as its manpower.[8] Those fortunate enough to evade the Japanese authorities often fled to China, where many joined either the nationalist or communist armies that were operating there.

The Outbreak of the Korean War, June 1950

Liberation from Japanese rule in August 1945 was understandably greeted with joy and enthusiasm by large swathes of the Korean population. Korean society, however, was markedly divided along political lines, and America and Russia were simply not prepared to relinquish their influence in the region, or allow the Koreans complete freedom to determine their own future.

Broadly speaking, on the right were capitalist modernisers, often Christians, and notably those who were propertied and educated, and who in many instances had actively supported the Japanese. This section of society was opposed to changes such as land reform and tended to tolerate those who had been collaborators. The right could also draw upon the support of less well-educated Koreans who had worked for the Japanese, particularly in the former colonial police force, plus individuals concerned with protecting their own privileged position in society.

On the other side of the political spectrum were various left-wing groups, including students, intellectuals, peasants and workers. Some were Communist Party members, while others were sympathetic to communist ideals. In general they espoused a redistribution of wealth and sought to create a more egalitarian society. Unlike many of those on the right, the left advocated a ruthless purge from positions of power of all those who had worked for the Japanese.

According to the historian Carter J. Eckert, after four decades of Japanese rule the 'colonial policies had shattered the foundations of a remarkably stable nineteenth-century bureaucratic agrarian society and unleashed new forces in conflict with the old and each other.'[9] Yet, as Alan Millett emphasised, this deep-seated struggle within Korean society would have occurred even if America and Russia had not divided the Korean peninsula into separate occupation zones.

Until the end of the Second World War, Korea was of limited interest to the West. In July 1945 the Potsdam Agreement between the Allies let the Soviet Red Army deal with both Manchuria and Korea. The Americans failed to anticipate that the war in the Far East would end as swiftly as it did, and were surprised by the Soviet Red Army's rapid advance through Manchuria and occupation of Korea above the 38th Parallel, the line that was agreed as demarcating the Russian zone from the American.

In the North the Russians installed a puppet government under Kim Il-Sung, who had been a minor commander in the Northeast Anti-Japanese United Army, a guerrilla force controlled by Chinese Communists, before fleeing to Russia where he served with a Korean special operations unit within the Red Army. Similarly, Syngman Rhee, who had the backing of the Americans, returned to his homeland in 1945 and sought to form a government in the South. He had been the leader of a provisional government in exile under the patronage of the nationalist Chinese, and had a long-standing involvement with Korean nationalist politics, having been exiled from Korea in 1905 for fomenting anti-Japanese agitation. He learnt to speak fluent English, was educated in America, converted to Christianity and took a European lady as his wife.

There was nothing balanced about the division of Korea. The South obtained a population that was twice the size of that in the North, and had the choicest arable land. By contrast, the North had all the hydro-electric power, coal and mineral resources, plus industrial complexes established during the Japanese occupation.

In the wake of the Second World War, tensions ran high as both sides desired to establish a single national government for Korea, and went to some lengths to try and achieve this by promoting various forms of intimidation, violence and unrest short of launching a full-scale war. When considering the attitude of Rhee and Kim during the late 1940s, Peter Lowe observed that both were 'intensely nationalistic, ruthless, driven on by a sense of destiny and confidence', aiming to 'unite Korea and lead the nation to a glorious future.'[10]

In 1947 the United Nations determined that elections should be held during the spring of the following year. Accordingly the United Nations Temporary Commission on Korea, or UNTCOK (later UNCOK), was established to observe the holding of free and fair democratic elections across the entire country. This met serious opposition, including from within the UN, and in the South it was viewed as a vehicle by which to give 'a veneer of international respectability for the creation of a south Korean state.'[11] The relationship between UN commission and the American military government of occupation was also far from harmonious. Major-General William F. Dean, who served as military governor and deputy to the commander of American forces in South Korea, highlighted the scale of the challenge: 'the Koreans were completely lacking in machinery and training for holding an election.'[12]

The North refused to co-operate with UNTCOK, and in 1948 elections were only held in the South amid accusations of corruption, intimidation and impersonation. The rightist National Society for the Rapid Realisation of Korean Independence under Rhee, and the Korean Democratic Party, garnered most of the votes. In July a constitution for the Republic of Korea (ROK) was approved and Rhee was elected as its first president. According to the British Official Historian, General Sir Anthony Farrar-Hockley, there was little to commend the new South Korean state, save for the fact 'its government and evidently the majority of its people abhorred communism, but its ability to resist the north was in doubt.'[13]

In response the North proclaimed the establishment of the People's Democratic Republic of Korea (PDRK) under Kim Il-Sung in 1949, and its constitution, which drew heavily on the Soviet model, was in part geared towards promoting nationalism and the desire among ordinary Koreans for a unified country. As William Berry observed, there was a very strong sense of nationalism in Korea, because despite the political divide, as a people they had 'one of the most homogeneous populations with a common ethnicity, language, and culture,' plus 'very few ethnic minorities.'[14]

During 1948 Russia withdrew her forces, but left behind the large and formidable North Korean People's Army (NKPA), trained and organised along Soviet lines. It fielded much equipment of Soviet manufacture, plus a variety of small arms of Russian, Japanese and American origin, many of which had been employed by guerrilla forces during the Second World War. Of particular note were the T-34/85 tanks of the 105th Armoured Brigade. These would prove crucial in the very early phases of the Korean War, as they gave the NKPA 'an unparalleled offensive capability in a region where armoured vehicles were rare.'[15] Similarly, 82mm and 120mm mortars supplied by the Russians proved highly effective in the Korean terrain and were generally handled with some skill by the NKPA.

The North Koreans also possessed limited naval resources and combat aircraft supplied by Russia with which to support any future military action. According to contemporary American and British intelligence assessments of the late 1940s, North Korea would in all likelihood triumph in any future confrontation with the South, so long as other powers did not intervene.

In contrast, the forces protecting the South were comparatively weak. The Americans left behind a constabulary force, although ROK authorities rapidly renamed this an army. There was also a small coastguard intended to act against smuggling, piracy and provide a limited degree of maritime protection.

The ROK Army was trained and equipped with American assistance, but lacked the range and quality of equipment available to the NKPA. Nor did it have any effective air support. As General Matthew Ridgway remarked, 'four of the army's infantry divisions had only two instead of the normal allotment of three infantry regiments and the entire army had only ninety-one 105mm howitzers.' According to contemporary American Army Tables of Organisation, normally there would be 432 divisional artillery pieces supported by non-divisional battalions of the same and heavier calibre guns.[16] Under the Korean Military Advisory Group (KMAG) of around 500 officers and men, the Americans provided advisors down to battalion level in the ROK Army, and by 1949 this was the extent of the American military presence that was left in the South.

During the late 1940s persistent acts of violence occurred, largely stemming from North Korea, and according to the historian Jeffrey Grey as many as 100,000 people may have been killed via this 'vicious civil war through guerrilla activity' before the official outbreak of the Korean War.[17] According to the British Official History in the latter half of 1949 'there were thirty-one incidents of insurrection by communist guerrillas.'[18] These ranged from attacks on police stations to larger operations aimed at seizing entire towns, and there were numerous clashes on the border between uniformed units from both sides. In addition the South was riven by political corruption and economic weakness. Rhee's rule tended to be autocratic and arbitrary systems of justice and policing made conditions worse. The North, in comparison, was well organised and under the control of a particularly ruthless and determined political elite.

As the Cold War intensified on a global scale, the prospects of peacefully resolving the situation in Korea seemed increasingly unlikely. All the ingredients existed for the unrest between the two Koreas to develop into a full-scale civil war. As Alan Millett cautioned, such wars have both 'internal and international dynamics' and their 'own shifting set of political actors, all of whom who have agendas of their own'. The Korean War was 'one of many such wars in the twentieth century in which the "great powers" chose to make a smaller nation a battleground.'[19]

The Ground War in Korea, 1950–53

On 25 June 1950 North Korea launched a major and carefully orchestrated invasion of the South employing eight divisions, supported by its potent armoured forces. The historian Jeffrey Grey stated that Kim Il-Sung largely launched this 'war of conquest and reunification' of his own volition, albeit with the tacit support of Stalin. For contemporary Western observers, however, faced with Cold War tensions in Europe and the extension of what Churchill had dubbed the 'Iron Curtain', it seemed improbable that events in Korea were anything but 'part of a centrally directed Kremlin attempt at world domination.'[20]

Within three days the South Korean capital Seoul had been captured, and although some under-equipped ROK units fought courageously, most were simply outclassed or crumbled and fled the North Korean onslaught. By the time the Americans had committed significant forces to Korea during late summer 1950, the ROK Army had suffered around 60 per cent casualties, but it was later rebuilt and ultimately became a far more effective combat force.

On the day of the invasion the UN Security Council passed a resolution calling for an immediate end to hostilities and described the North Korean action as a breach of the peace. That the resolution was passed owed much to the absence of the Russians, who used their power of veto and boycotted the UN Security Council in protest over its refusal to recognise communist China, and its continued acceptance of the Nationalist Chinese. Another UN resolution was passed on 27 June with the objective of assisting South Korea and restoring peace and stability in the region. Two days later General Douglas MacArthur was ordered to deploy air and naval resources from his Far East Command (FEC) based in Japan, to support the beleaguered South Koreans. Rapidly the American Joint Chiefs of Staff (JCS) pressed for American ground forces to be deployed to Korea as well, after receiving a disturbing assessment of the frontline situation from MacArthur.

To assist the ROK Army American units were sent from Japan and Okinawa, including the 24th Infantry Division, commanded since October 1949 by Major-General Dean. Like the ROK troops, these American units tended to be poorly equipped, undertrained and understrength for the task that lay ahead. Much has been made in the literature on the Korean War of their general lack of combat preparedness, largely as result of their experience of soft garrison life conducting post-war occupational duties in Japan. On the eve of its Korean deployment, Major-General Dean summed up his division as follows:

> The battle-trained veterans of the early occupation days had been whittled down by time and reassignment until they made up only about fifteen per cent of the men and officers now on duty. The division strength was down to about two-thirds of its wartime total. Infantry regiments had only two battalions each; artillery battalions only two batteries.[21]

Likewise, American equipment such as the Second World War vintage 2.6 inch Bazooka and M-24 Chaffee light tank proved of limited effectiveness in Korea.

What was left of the ROK Army, together with those American units rushed to the theatre, was then rapidly pushed down the peninsula by the

NKPA until they held what was termed the Pusan Perimeter. This was a defensive line along the River Naktong that incorporated the south-eastern port city of Pusan, a location that would become familiar to thousands of American and British troops during the course of the war as one of the major entry/exit points to and from Korea.

Fighting in the Pusan Perimeter during late summer 1950 was bitter and desperate. By 13 August, the American 5th Regimental Combat Team (RCT), which played a significant role in holding the perimeter, reported three officers and 35 men killed in action; nineteen officers and 312 men wounded in action; nine officers and 141 men missing; and eight officers and 178 enlisted men classed as non-battle casualties.[22]

However, MacArthur launched an audacious plan which he hoped would restore the territorial integrity of South Korea. An amphibious landing was to be mounted at Inchon on the northeast coast, while simultaneously troops would break out from the Pusan Perimeter. Despite the American JCS having serious doubts about the plan, known as Operation Chromite, the landing at Inchon was successful. It paved the way for an advance on Seoul that would sever the NKPA's lines of communication. During late September 1950 UN forces captured Seoul, before crossing the 38th Parallel in early October. At this juncture MacArthur's aim changed from simply liberating South Korea, to reunifying the entire peninsula under pro-Western Koreans. Consequently, UN forces, including British troops, were sent into North Korea and Pyongyang, the North's capital, was taken on 19 October. The advance then continued towards the Yalu River, the border with Communist China.

The Chinese became extremely concerned about the UN forces' progress, fearing MacArthur might even be contemplating an assault on their homeland. Warnings were issued by the Chinese from late October onwards. American, British and other UN troops then started encountering small numbers of Chinese troops, or at least finding the corpses of soldiers that were definitely not Korean. Ignoring the potential danger, MacArthur ploughed on and put in place plans for a large-scale offensive to the Yalu to be mounted by Eighth Army on 24 November.

While Eighth Army advanced in the west, X Corps was landed at ports in north-eastern Korea. Both were at the end of a long supply chain and vulnerable to counter-attack. In addition the Korean winter was coming, and the rugged terrain was ill suited to the type of mobile, mechanised warfare that the Americans in particular sought to employ. The Chinese stealthily moved thousands of troops into North Korea, and caught Eighth Army by surprise in the flank, forcing it into a hasty, panicked retreat or 'bug-out'. Meanwhile, in the east, X Corps became embroiled in the Chosin Reservoir campaign, culminating in an epic strategic withdrawal. Conducted in the depths of the North Korean winter, the troops involved went through almost unimaginable suffering, during which the cold was as much an enemy as the Chinese.

Pyongyang was retaken on 5 December, and by Christmas 1950 Chinese forces had crossed the 38th Parallel and Seoul was back in Communist hands by early January 1951. However, under General Matthew B. Ridgway (who replaced General Walton H. Walker, who had been killed in a road accident) Eighth Army rallied and morale improved. It was soon deployed in a series of limited offensives intended to restore its fighting efficiency via a series of methodical advances. These would inflict maximum casualties on the enemy by harnessing the superior levels of firepower available to the American ground forces, together with other UN units including those from Britain.

On 3 April 1951 UN forces once again crossed the 38th Parallel, although a spring offensive by the Chinese pushed them back, and involved the titanic stand by the British 29th Independent Infantry Brigade Group at the Battle of the Imjin River. By May the spring offensive was halted. This coincided with the sacking of MacArthur, owing to his constant disagreements with Washington over the direction of the war. In particular President Truman and America's allies were enraged that on 24 March 1951 MacArthur had, of his own accord, issued a lengthy communiqué taunting the Chinese, which was in flagrant breach of the American policy that officials were to abstain from making pronouncements regarding issues of foreign policy. Consequently, he was replaced by Ridgway, with command of Eighth Army going to Lieutenant General James A. Van Fleet, an experienced veteran of the world wars. Subsequently, Lieutenant General Maxwell D. Taylor took over command of Eighth Army for the final phase of the war, and held that post at the time of the Armistice on 27 July 1953.

From mid-1951 the Korean War started to assume a different character as fighting effectively solidified around the 38th Parallel. Neither side was prepared to attempt to seek an all-out military victory. Instead attention was drawn to diplomatic negotiations, while forces were maintained on the frontline, at times engaged in severe fighting. In July 1951 armistice talks commenced and would drag on until the summer of 1953, in part owing to disagreements over significant issues such as the repatriation of POWs. To newspaper audiences back home in America and Britain, reports of the struggles for key terrain features such as Heartbreak Ridge, Pork Chop Hill and the Hook might have sounded exotic, but the fighting was often brutal and bloody, particularly for the infantry.

By 1951–52 the United Nations Command (UNC) included not only South Korean, American and British troops, but also combat and non-combat units from Australia, Belgium, Canada, Colombia, Ethiopia, France, Greece, India, the Netherlands, New Zealand, Norway, the Philippines, Sweden, Thailand, Turkey and South Africa. For these American-led UN forces the aim in Korea became to maintain the status quo, not something that necessarily sat easily with the majority of Western soldiers, including those from Britain, as it appeared that the war lacked a clear purpose. As the military historian Colin McInnes observed, the Americans and British were essentially 'faced with the problem of a lack of meaningful objectives, their freedom of action circumscribed both by the need to minimise casualties and by consideration for the politics of negotiating the armistice.'[23]

By the time of the July 1953 armistice, Korea had proved an immensely destructive war, despite its limited nature. It has been estimated that around four million Koreans perished on both sides of the political divide, a figure that equated to about 10 per cent of the entire population. A further five million became refugees, mainly fleeing from the North across the 38th Parallel. There was also a financial impact, with the ROK suffering around $2 billion of damage, especially in relation to destroyed property. The North suffered only marginally less.

Regarding combatants killed, estimates are as follows: China 900,000 to one million, North Korea 520–600,000. The UNC lost in total around 400,000, mostly from the ROK armed forces, who suffered approximately 70,000 killed, 150,000 wounded and 80,000 captured, many of whom died as a result of mistreatment. At least 37,000 American service personnel were killed during the war, although some sources state the figure was as high as 54,246. A further 103,284 Americans were wounded, many of them seriously, including those suffering from the extreme cold.[24] The total number of British killed during the Korean War has been recorded as 1,078, out of which the army lost ninety-eight officers and 879 other ranks. Likewise, 2,674 service personnel were wounded, the majority (185 officers, 2,404 other ranks) coming from the army.[25]

The Korean Peninsula

The Korean War was pursued in what one historian has termed 'a unique physical environment', which had an impact on the ability of both sides to move men, equipment and supplies, and to deploy their weaponry tactically.[26] Much of the country was hilly or mountainous. Notably the Taebaek Range runs from the Yalu River down towards Pusan, dividing the peninsula into eastern and western sections, and forming a significant natural barrier between the two coasts. The eastern side of the country is narrow and rugged, whereas in the west the terrain broadens out and includes several foothills that merge into flatter areas towards the sea.

As the historian Charles R. Shrader remarked, Korea is also 'well drained by eleven principal rivers, most of which flow generally from northeast to south-west and thus form a series of substantial barriers to north-south movement'.[27] Many of the major urban areas are sited at the mouths or along the courses of these rivers. The strategic town of Taegu and Pusan, the largest port in Korea, for example, both lie on the Naktong River.

Koreans refer to their country as Choson, which literally translates into English as 'morning freshness' or more popularly the 'Land of the Morning Calm', and this resulted from climatic factors. An officer with an American field artillery unit in Korea during spring 1951 noted that it was 'always eerily calm in the early morning'. Even if there had been a storm in the night 'there was certain to be a dead calm following sunrise', with 'every blade of grass and every leaf frozen into absolute stillness'.[28]

The Korean climate is dependent on two factors. Cold air from Siberia travels southwards in winter, and warm monsoon air from the Pacific hits Korea during the summer months. Consequently, winters tend to be cold and dry, with temperatures dropping as low as 45 degrees below freezing in northern areas. However, there can be large amounts of winter sunshine rather than the overcast, grey skies that can characterise winters in northern Europe. A booklet issued to soldiers from 1st Commonwealth Division during 1952–53 warned:

> The Korean winter can be one of the most unpleasant in the world. From November to March there is a damp cold and large variation of temperatures, both from one day to the next and between one day and the following night. This results in rapid changes from thaw to freeze. In addition, owing to the high winds and humidity, it feels much colder that the actual temperature would suggest.[29]

Summers on the other hand were normally oppressively hot (over 100 degrees Fahrenheit at lower elevations) and frequently tended to be unpleasantly dusty. Darrell Thornley, an NCO with A Company 19th Infantry Regiment from the American 24th Division remembered that initially, 'it was so hot. We weren't prepared for it'.[30] Subsequently, the rainy season occurred during July and August, and the southern highlands sometimes received more than 16 inches of rainfall. According to the military historian Brigadier C.N. Barclay, this was probably 'the most unpleasant time of the year' as owing to the monsoon rains 'the whole countryside, including roads, becomes a quagmire, and movement is severely restricted'.[31] High winds were often encountered in late summer as well, because Korea lies fractionally outside the path of the typhoons that frequently plague Japan at that time of year.

By comparison the spring and autumn tended to be far more settled, and the Korean countryside could even appear spectacular during those seasons. Depending on the circumstances they were in, American and British troops were able to appreciate the natural beauty of the landscape, particularly in spring. One Marine noted: 'the mountains had been covered with the fragile colours of wild azaleas, with delicate lilac blossoms, with great white flowers bursting forth amid the vividly green leaves of stately magnolia trees'.[32] Likewise, an officer with the Royal Engineers discovered that the Korean countryside was 'much more pleasant than I expected'. It included a variety of small versions of familiar tree species such as chestnuts on 'the browny-orange hills' and notably ornamental oaks 'with enormous leaves eighteen inches long'.[33]

There was also the wildlife. An American infantrymen who saw action during 1952–53 discovered that when the 'ringnecked pheasants were calling to one another in the grassy fields of no man's land' they 'almost made you forget the war was still going on'.[34] Similarly, General Ridgway was moved to comment on the vivid green of the rice paddies, 'so rich… it can take your breath away'. Yet, he simultaneously summed up Korean conditions by cautioning that the country had 'all the afflictions of the foot soldier… deep snows, viscous mud, very heavy summer rains' and 'bitter biting dust'.[35]

Korea's transport network in the 1950s reflected the country's topography, although its development had also been bound up in the politics of the region. By Western standards port facilities, even at the large port of Pusan, were primitive, and those railways and highways that did exist dated from the Japanese occupation prior to 1945. Typically, communications between the east and west of the peninsula were limited, as most main road and rail routes ran north-south, with the ROK capital city of Seoul being a focal point.

Originally the rail network had been impressive, but by the early 1950s poor maintenance, shortages of rolling stock and trained personnel all had an impact on its overall effectiveness. There were over 3,000 miles of standard-gauge track, of which only around 310 miles was double tracked, plus over 500 miles of narrow-gauge track. Major rail terminals existed at Pyongyang, Seoul and Pusan. As many American and British soldiers would discover during the war, travel by rail in Korea was frequently a tortuous and uncomfortable experience, not least owing to the poorly maintained infrastructure.

Most Korean roads 'were unpaved but well-founded and surfaced with rock and gravel. Few met the 22-foot-wide standard for a two-lane highway, and the best roads were only about 18 feet wide, with numerous bottlenecks at narrow bridges and 11–13 foot bypasses'.[36] Awkward curves and steep gradients, especially in the mountainous regions, further hampered the road network, and in many cases they were little more than tracks. Unsurprisingly in such an underdeveloped theatre, road building and repair became a major task for the Royal Engineers and their American counterparts. As General Sir George Cooper, who served as a troop commander with the Royal Engineers in Korea, recalled, 'ditch clearing, culverting and potholing' were necessary if 'not exciting', particularly to prepare roads as conditions thawed after winter. Similarly, after heavy usage it was important to smooth out the surface on earth roads all year round. Owing to the shortage of mechanical graders, this often entailed towing a metal beam behind a three-ton truck, a process known as 'dragging.'[37]

Clearly the overall conditions in Korea posed a significant challenge for Western mechanised armies. This was particularly pertinent if troops became road-bound and were unable to take to the hills, as was the case with many American units during 1950–51. General Ridgway commented:

> Our ignorance of the terrain and the extreme faultiness of the maps we tried to make use of gave the enemy an added advantage and made his own familiarity with the landscape a sort of secret weapon. Roads we looked for often did not exist, or turned out to be mere footpaths that no wheeled vehicle could negotiate.[38]

Chapter 2

A Lesson in Readiness: Preparing for Action in Korea

On 29 June 1950 President Truman, on hearing worrying updates from the Far East, decided to approve a directive which increased General MacArthur's authority in dealing with the rapidly unfolding situation in Korea. Both men were particularly concerned by the condition of the ROK Army after the North Korean invasion, owing to its heavy losses in personnel and equipment. The directive authorised General MacArthur to deploy American troops in South Korea 'to maintain communications and other essential services'; to use American units 'to ensure the retention of a port and air base in the general area of Pusan-Chinhae'; to use naval and air power against targets in North Korea, while avoiding the frontiers of Manchuria and Russia; defend Formosa ('Taiwan') from the Chinese Communists and prevent the Chinese Nationalists based there from pursuing operations against mainland China; and send any necessary military equipment and supplies to Korea.[1]

Subsequently, General MacArthur was authorised to deploy two divisions to Korea from the American garrison occupying Japan. This was in addition to a regimental combat team (broadly equivalent to a British brigade) that was to deploy in defence of the Pusan-Chinhae area. Lieutenant Colonel Charles Olsen, a former wartime bombardier in the US Army Air Corps, was serving as a captain with 17th Infantry Regiment, 7th Division in Japan. When the North Koreans invaded the South in June 1950, he recalled 'the stuff hit the fan'.[2] This statement readily conveys the turbulent, confused atmosphere in which American units initially mobilised for Korea. Yet, for all the difficulties she faced, America was able to respond swiftly in support of South Korea.

By comparison, Britain at first struggled to mobilise troops in support of the UN effort on the ground in Korea, not least because of the numerous global commitments facing the army during the post-war years. Initially, in August 1950, it was only possible to deploy an understrength infantry brigade that had been hastily patched together from units stationed in Hong Kong. This was joined in October by a full-strength and better equipped infantry brigade group sent directly from Britain. Subsequently, the British Army was pivotal in establishing the 1st Commonwealth Division, which became operational in late July 1951.

To cope with the Korean commitment, both America and Britain relied upon re-calling personnel from the reserves. Typically, these were seasoned veterans of the Second World War, but their deployment was not without its challenges. Eventually, significant numbers of conscripts (draftees and National Servicemen) were deployed. Typically these were young men who lacked significant military experience, and did not necessarily have any natural aptitude for army life. This heightened the requirement for effective training designed to prepare personnel to endure the stresses associated with active service.

Mobilisation for the Korean War June–October 1950

As military historian Peter Kindsvatter outlines, America has tended to fight the wars of the draft era, including Korea, using the following pattern. First regular army and Marine Corps units consisting largely of volunteers were deployed, then federalised National Guard units, again heavily reliant on volunteers. Units mainly comprised of draftees followed, and the majority of individual replacements were also draftees.

In 1950 the American army's strength was around 592,000 and of this, four divisions, the 7th, 24th, 25th Infantry Divisions and the 1st Cavalry Division (also an infantry formation) were scattered across Japan on occupation duty. In addition the 5th RCT was based in Hawaii and the 29th Infantry Regiment stationed on Okinawa. Most had two instead of the officially authorised three battalions per infantry regiment, and other combat units such as artillery battalions were correspondingly understrength. At full strength an American infantry battalion had around 900 men organised into three rifle companies (of three platoons) each comprising around 200 men. These were supported by a heavy-weapons company of approximately 166 men that deployed a variety of mortars, recoilless rifles and machine guns. Consequently, the infantry battalion was potentially an extremely potent force and 'a key manoeuvre element of the regiment and division'.[3]

According to the American Official Historian the divisions in Japan 'averaged about 70 per cent of full war strength, three of them numbering between 12,000 and 13,000 men and one slightly more than 15,000'.[4] Neither did these divisions have their full complement of support weapons, including 57mm and 75mm recoilless rifles and 4.2 inch mortars. Supporting armoured units were equipped with the M-24 Chaffee light tank, as heavier models were deemed unnecessary for an occupation force and too cumbersome to cope with road conditions and bridges in Japan.

Glen Bailey, a regular soldier with 5th Regiment, 1st Cavalry Division, observed that as they crossed over to Korea from Japan, much of their equipment was 'lousy, a lot of World War Two stuff and lousy, it was worn out'.[5] This was far from an isolated case. According to military historian Clay Blair, the equipment in 34th Regiment from 24th Division was in a particularly poor state. Some 25 to 50 per cent of all its small arms were unserviceable. In June 1950 the regiment was also still employing the much-maligned 2.36 inch bazooka, which had already proved of limited value as an anti-tank weapon during the Second World War. Supporting artillery units lacked specialist anti-tank ammunition, many of its .30 calibre machine gun barrels were worn out, and the regiment had only just received an adequate allocation of support vehicles such as jeeps and trucks.

Ironically, as Clay Blair observed, the 24th Division, which was selected to enter combat first, was the least ready of all the formations based in Japan. As the previous chapter showed, not only was it significantly understrength, but it had also lost many of those soldiers with combat experience who would have provided a cadre around which to build on mobilisation. In June 1950 two of its regiments (21st and 34th) were on Kyushu, while its third regiment (19th) was at a training area on Honshu. The individual battalions within these regiments were often dispersed around Japan and this impacted on their ability to train effectively.

Darrell Thornley rapidly became an NCO with the 19th Regiment, after only arriving at Camp Drake near Tokyo on the eve of the Korean War. He had re-enlisted in the army in 1948 after serving as an infantryman in north-west Europe during the Second World War. As he put it 'next thing I know I am on a troop train and back in the infantry' and 'I was probably selected as a platoon sergeant because I held the Combat Infantry Badge'.[6] The CIB, a silver musket on a blue background framed with a silver wreath, was much coveted by American troops as it denoted the wearer had actively engaged in ground combat over a prolonged period with an infantry unit, and soldiers had to be recommended for the award. However, few in Thornley's platoon were well trained infantrymen. Instead they were 'cooks, medics, jeep and truck drivers and clerks and they had no battle experience'.[7] This was fairly typical of units from the 24th Division, and their training had tended to neglect key areas such as night warfare and maintenance of defensive positions that would cause American soldiers problems during their first months in Korea.

To strengthen the 24th Division over 2,000 NCOs were rushed in from the other divisions in Japan during June/July 1950. This in turn weakened those other divisions. For example, the 1st Cavalry Division 'lost 750 senior non-coms, leaving only master and first sergeants in its infantry companies and artillery battalions'.[8] As Lyle Gibbs, a sergeant with 7th Cavalry Regiment, 1st

Cavalry Division recalled, 'we were around 11,000 men as opposed to 18,000, and once the personnel were pulled out for 24th Division I reckon we were only 40 per cent combat ready when we deployed to Korea, whereas we had originally been 85 per cent combat ready before Korea'.[9]

Typically, as American units were readied for Korean service in Japan and elsewhere, uncertainty reigned. After re-enlisting in the army during 1950, Tanjore Splan, a former airborne soldier, was rushed from America to Korea to serve with the 555th (Triple Nickel) Field Artillery Battalion (FAB). He arrived in the field after only 41 days back in the army. His draft was taken by truck from Seattle to 'to Vancouver BC or Vancouver Washington. I never knew which but probably BC, and kept in the dark with the canvas pulled down on the truck the whole time and then we were flown to Japan'.[10]

Many soldiers wondered what might happen in the future, and were understandably concerned about the welfare of their families and loved ones. On 18 July 1950, Boris Spiroff had only recently married. Like Darrell Thornley he discovered that owing to his wartime combat experience and status as a regular soldier he was rapidly ordered to Korea. He became a platoon sergeant with 1st Cavalry Division, and wrote 'this will be a great shock to Cassie, [his wife] and I wonder how the news will affect her'.[11]

Initially some American troops hadn't even heard of Korea, let alone followed the news coverage of recent events. On mobilisation, Corporal Lacy Barnett, a medic with 34th Infantry Regiment, remembered that most of his unit simply wondered: 'Where is Korea?'[12] Other soldiers felt that a Korean deployment would mark a brief distraction from the pleasures of occupation duties in Japan. After all, President Truman had described Korea as a 'police action'. Consequently, many reasoned that they would encounter little serious opposition, and all that was necessary was to give the North Koreans, or 'gooks', a 'bloody nose'. Several were so over-confident that they thought that the sight of American troops would prove enough to make the enemy run. Lieutenant Colonel Charles Bussey, a former Tuskegee airman, led the all-black 77th Engineer Combat Company with distinction during the first year of the Korean War. During early July 1950, as they mobilised, he noted: 'the word was that we would put up a show of force in the field in Korea, and when the enemy quaked and returned across the 38th Parallel – which was inevitable – we would return to home stations'.[13]

In contrast, the situation for members of the National Guard was more strained, as during the Korean War the army adopted a 'piecemeal call-up plan right through February 15, 1952, when the last Guard units were inducted into Federal service'.[14] Consequently, individual Guardsmen and their families lived with the uncertainty of not knowing whether they were going to be mobilised or not. This impacted on decisions affecting their civilian/family lives, such as whether to take a new job or start a family, and was damaging to morale. Typically, National Guard units didn't receive priority when it came to being trained and equipped. Second World War veteran Dave Matteson was re-called in October 1950, together with four other officers, to join 378th Engineer Combat Battalion (North Carolina), shortly after the birth of his second daughter. 'We didn't do extensive engineering training, but did spend some time on the firing ranges. We spent most of the time getting the men and equipment ready for overseas shipment… My platoon needed more training, but they were hard workers, a good bunch of GIs'.[15]

With the onset of the Korean War there was also serious discussion in Washington and Tokyo about mobilising the entire Marine Corps Reserve in order to form a division for service with the United Nations forces under General MacArthur. While a division was furnished later, initially only an RCT of combat-ready Marines was raised for Korea. This entailed 'an air-ground team build around the two main West Coast units, the 5th Marines and Marine Aircraft Group 33', that was designated the 1st Provisional Marine Brigade and commanded by Brigadier General Edward A. Craig.[16] Significantly, among its air element the Brigade included the first helicopter pilots of the American armed forces to be organised into a unit fit for combat service overseas.

As the Brigade readied itself at Camp Pendleton in California and its nearby Marine Air Station, El Toro, frantic activity ensued. 'Weapons and clothing had to be issued, immunization shots given, and insurance and pay allotments made out'.[17] Simultaneously, Marines across America were ordered to report for active duty overseas. Lieutenant Colonel Ray Murray, who commanded 5th Marines, remembered that although the calibre of personnel was high, his unit was understrength:

> Our three battalions were each minus one rifle company and each company was minus one platoon. We were able to scrape together the three missing platoons from troops stationed at Pendleton, but we had to sail minus the three missing companies.[18]

Likewise, the artillery, armoured, engineering and other units supporting 5th Marines were all understrength.

As the war progressed, increasing reliance was put on calling up personnel from the Marine Corps Reserve. As Brigadier General Ed Simons, who was a young major at the time of Korea, noted, Marine Corps replacements from the Reserve who went on to serve in Korea were of excellent quality: 'Most were World War Two veterans. They were experienced combat marines, and that's a fact that can't be made too much of'. This proved a decisive factor in the good performance of the Marine Corps during the war.[19] Yet many who had joined the Marines Reserve did so for the social life and camaraderie, and had not expected to experience active service so soon after the ending of the Second World War. Sometimes within Marine units a divide also appeared to exist between the different types of troops. According to Private First Class Robert Smith, a black Marine with C Company, 1st Battalion, 7th Marines, who served in Korea, 'regardless of colour, the regulars were naturally apt to stick together, as were the reserves'.[20]

The Marine Corps as a whole was characterised by the sort of confidence that comes with being a highly professional, well-trained combat force. However, like many soldiers, Marines initially didn't envisage the Korean situation escalating into a war that would last three years. As Lieutenant Colonel Harold Roise, the commander of 2nd Battalion, 5th Marines recalled, 'Harry Truman said we were going into South Korea to chase the North Koreans back across the 38th Parallel. It was supposed to take two or three months. Then we were to go home'.[21]

Other Marines, like their counterparts in the army, knew little of the Korean situation and even wondered where the country was located. Robert Samuels had enlisted in the Marine Corps in 1948, planning to complete a three-year engagement then go back home to Michigan. Aside from the obligatory high standard of Marine Corps combat training, he received specialist training in water supply work, and was assigned to 2nd Engineer Battalion based at Camp Lejeune. In July 1950 they suddenly 'called everyone back to base and told us we were shipping out. I'd never even heard of Korea'.[22]

Some also viewed mobilisation for Korea with a degree of trepidation. When Private First Class Eddy McCabe from D Company, 2nd Battalion, 1st Marines reported to Camp Lejeune after going on leave he found that the North Koreans had attacked the South and 'no one seemed to know what was going on'.[23] The medic Robert Shoemaker found that the rapid transition from being a 'civilian intern to professional Marine surgeon presented problems of adjustment. How was I to conduct myself? Was I supposed to try to act like a Marine?'[24]

At the time of the Korean War, Britain, like America, had to contend with the run-down of her armed forces after the Second World War. Simultaneously she had to adapt to meet a host of global engagements and deal with the retreat from Empire. Commitments ranged from countering insurgency in Malaya to protecting central Europe as the Cold War escalated. Notably, as part of

NATO during the late 1940s and early 1950s, the British Army of the Rhine (BAOR) had to be reshaped from an occupation force of around two divisions, to a field force of at least four that was prepared to counter the threat of the Russian army at short notice. Despite having an army of around 400,000 men, the level of commitments that existed by 1950 ensured that it was initially difficult to find even a modest force to assist the UN effort in Korea. However, as J.A. Williams highlights, the British Government was swayed by those commitments it deemed to be the most strategically important. It 'chose to give priority to the defence needs of its imperial possessions in South-East Asia,' particularly Malaya, whereas the defence of South Korea, which was outside the sphere of British influence, was thought to be primarily an American responsibility, with the substantial backing of the UN.[25]

In response to General MacArthur's clamour for more troops to defend the hard-pressed Pusan Perimeter, the 27th British Independent Brigade was despatched from Hong Kong in late August 1950. In October it was re-designated the 27th British Commonwealth Brigade when it was strengthened by 3rd Battalion Royal Australian Regiment, and later it was joined by combat troops from Canada and New Zealand, plus an Indian field ambulance unit. As Eric Linklater observed, the Brigade were the first non-American troops to enter Korea, but were soon joined by units from other countries including infantrymen from France and Holland that ensured 'the international purpose of the war was clearly established', although the bulk of the troops involved were American and all came under American command.[26]

As many sources have described, the 27th Brigade was initially severely understrength and consisted of the weakened 1st Battalions from the Middlesex Regiment (Duke of Cambridge's Own) and Argyll and Sutherland Highlanders. These were operating with a special establishment: 'the four rifle companies in each battalion were reduced to three, but each company was thereby raised to about two thirds war strength'. In 1950 the official war establishment of an infantry battalion was thirty-eight officers and 945 other ranks, with nine officers and 176 other ranks acting as first-line reinforcements in theatre.[27] Instead, as the War Diarist of 1st Battalion Argyll and Sutherland Highlanders outlined, they had only three rifle companies, and the support company was abolished with the medium machine gun, three-inch mortar and assault pioneer platoons all being included in the headquarters company. This provided an operational establishment of twenty-seven officers and 618 other ranks.[28]

Nor did 27th Brigade initially have any organic artillery, engineer and medical units, second-line transport or an ordnance field park to support it. These had to be provided from American sources. As one veteran of 1st Battalion Middlesex Regiment put it: 'You will appreciate that consisting of 27th Brigade HQ and two under-strength infantry battalions with no supporting arms whatsoever, the press term 'token force' was most applicable'.[29] Likewise, some writers on the Korean War have referred to it as 'the Woolworth Brigade' on account of it being hastily cobbled together and understrength.[30]

Prior to their deployment in Korea, the Middlesex and Argylls had been part of 40th Infantry Division, tasked with guarding Hong Kong and the New Territories against the threat posed by Communist China. Bob Yerby, an NCO with 1st Battalion Middlesex Regiment, considered that Hong Kong was the type of deployment 'where soldiers could get fat, lazy and idle if allowed'. However, as he noted, 'the Commanding Officers of both regiments had other ideas. Battle schools were opened, climbing mountains under mock attacks, learning how to lay barbed wire, signals and communications between companies, shooting contests and regular cross-country runs were all part of our everyday lives'.[31] Don Barrett, another NCO from that same battalion, provides a vivid impression of what service was like in Hong Kong, and how the comparatively tough nature of the conditions that troops faced there was of benefit to them once they deployed on active service in Korea.

> Our service in the New Territories certainly helped us on entering Korea, for the ground was much as we had operated over in Hong Kong, although the hills appeared far higher and the paddy fields if anything more pungent. Living by the bugle in open fronted stables on bunk beds with a coconut fibre mattress in Beas Stables Camp was comparatively Spartan, plus life in the open when on exercise very little had changed when on arrival in Korea. Dysentery, ring-worm, jaundice, malaria, prickly heat and what we called "Chinky Toe-Rot" were common ailments in Hong Kong and at one time or another most of us would be painted with a rather fetching mauve or green mixture over large areas of our body.[32]

Under 'Operation Graduate' 27th Brigade was mobilised in late August 1950 for service in Korea. Originally it was to be deployed there until a brigade group could be sent from Britain, but as Don Barrett remembered, 'in early November 1950 on the eve of our return posting to Hong Kong, 27th Commonwealth Brigade as it now was, received rather disturbing news that it was destined to remain in Korea indefinitely'.[33]

Mobilisation occurred amid an atmosphere of rumours that units might be bound for action in Malaya, or even posted home. As author Tim Carew observed, most soldiers became aware that 'something was brewing' when they knew that officers were working on Sundays and even orderly room clerks were working late into the night.[34] According to an official report:

> The Brigade had mobilised in five days, a creditable performance, as no fewer than four different establishments were received during this time and, due to secrecy which appeared to be carried to extremes, only Commanding Officers were allowed to be told on the first day and Company Commanders by the evening of the second day.[35]

The no nonsense Commanding Officer of 1st Battalion Middlesex Regiment, Colonel Andrew Man, later confided that they were aware of 'little of the Korean situation apart from the invasion and poor initial performance of American troops'.[36]

There was frenzied activity in Hong Kong as the Brigade gathered together the necessary men, weapons, equipment and stores. In particular, as the Official Historian emphasises, the British required a special shipment of ammunition because the calibre of their weapons was different to that of the Americans. Dr Stanley Boydell, the medical officer with 1st Battalion Middlesex Regiment, recalled the hectic nature of some of the preparations. He had to inoculate his entire unit against tetanus, typhus and other diseases, but was only issued with twenty needles for the job. Consequently, although they could re-sterilise the needles, it was extremely painful for the last troops to receive injections once they had gone blunt.[37]

National Servicemen aged under nineteen had to be left behind, as they were deemed too young for active service, and both battalions therefore had to reorganise and absorb several men drafted in from other units in Hong Kong. These primarily came from the 1st Battalions of the King's Shropshire Light Infantry, King's Own Scottish Borderers, Royal Leicestershire Regiment and South Staffordshire Regiment. This level of rebadging of personnel was fairly typical of the British Army during the Korean War period and, as General Sir Anthony Farrar-Hockley stated, it was 'a necessary expedient to balance and maintain sufficient numbers of (principally) junior officers and soldiers of fighting arms – infantry and armour – in the field. Inevitably this related primarily to those on National Service'.[38]

Both battalions from 27th Brigade comprised a mix of regular soldiers and National Servicemen or conscripts who were eligible for service in Korea. Broadly speaking, those at officer and NCO level typically had significant experience from the Second World War to draw upon, whereas the junior ranks were filled with less experienced troops, notably National Servicemen.[39] Michael Eastap, a sergeant and regular soldier with 1st Battalion Middlesex Regiment, remembered encountering some apprehension in his platoon as they readied for Korea. In particular there was initially 'a sense of professional versus amateur feeling' between the different types of soldiers. However, on active service this rapidly evaporated and by September/October 1950: 'the men were standing up well to active service, including National Servicemen. Everyone felt much happier about it by this stage, knowing that the National Service chaps were as good as anyone else'.[40]

Many soldiers, especially young regulars, were initially enthusiastic about the prospect of experiencing combat, particularly as it was what they had spent their working lives training for. Ronald Yetman, a junior NCO with 1st Battalion Argyll and Sutherland Highlanders, vividly recalled being 'eager as a trained soldier and young man' prior to experiencing action for the first time in Korea during 1950, although his enthusiasm waned once he had tasted combat.[41]

While the military components of mobilisation were met by 27th Brigade, there was still what the Regimental History of the Argyll and Sutherland Highlanders in Korea termed 'the individual heartbreaks inseparable from any war'. The 1st Battalion Argyll and Sutherland Highlanders 'had gone abroad on an "Emergency" scale' to Hong Kong, which was classed as a normal peace-time station. When they arrived, as there appeared to be no immediate emergency, provision was made for wives and families of regular soldiers to follow on. Sadly, as they sailed from Britain their menfolk had already been sent to Korea.[42] As Tim Carew notes, 'the British Army was as hard a taskmaster to the women as it was to the men, and often more so; that whether the husband be general or private, heartbreak, frustration, resentment against the military system, separation and disruption of settled family life are always just around the next corner'.[43]

On 26 July 1950 the British Government pledged to send a brigade group from Britain in support of the UN effort in Korea. In essence a brigade group was akin to a miniature division, although it comprised only 2,500 men. Aside from three infantry battalions, it incorporated its own supporting armour, artillery and engineer units, plus the necessary administrative and logistical organisation to maintain it in a theatre of operations. This included elements such as vehicle repair and mobile bath units, military policemen and a detachment of the Royal Army Pay Corps. In this respect it was a different beast from 'the Woolworth Brigade', with its lack of organic support. However, troops from 29th Brigade lacked the experience of recent service in the Far East that proved so useful to their counterparts in 27th Brigade.

The 29th Independent Infantry Brigade Group had been established in East Anglia during 1949 and was intended to act as Britain's strategic reserve. As its badge it had adopted a white circle on black square background, which had originally been employed by another formation during the Burma campaign of the Second World War. With ribald, soldierly humour the men of the Brigade later inferred that this signified a 'frozen rectum'.[44]

The Brigade had its headquarters in Colchester, a post that was shared with 1st Battalion Royal Ulster Rifles (RUR). However, the other battalions in the Brigade were dispersed with the 1st Battalion Lancashire Fusiliers based at Warminster, and the 1st Battalion Welsh Guards at Wellington Barracks. By January 1950 the latter had been relieved by 1st Battalion Gloucestershire Regimen, which had returned from duty in the West Indies. The Lancashire Fusiliers were then replaced by 1st Battalion Bedfordshire and Hertfordshire Regiment which had returned from Greece.

Units that supported the Brigade were similarly dispersed. The 45th Field Regiment, Royal Artillery was stationed in County Durham; the 55th Field Squadron Royal Engineers at Tidworth; and 57th Company Royal Army Service Corps at Newark. This precluded combined training involving the entire brigade on exercises. Early in 1950 the Brigade moved into Eastern Command when accommodation became available, and it was joined by personnel from further supporting units, including 26th Field Ambulance, Royal Army Medical Corps.

At the end of July 1950 the Brigade was notified that it would be deployed in Korea, and active mobilisation began in August. This resulted in some disorganisation, especially as it was necessary to have a change-over in personnel in most units as National Servicemen were not initially to be sent to Korea with the Brigade. At only three days' notice, 1st Battalion Royal Northumberland Fusiliers (RNF), which was acting as the demonstration battalion at the School of Infantry at Warminster, relieved the understrength Bedfordshire and Hertfordshire Regiment because it had an adequate complement of regular soldiers and NCOs. Most units had to post away National Servicemen who were ineligible, except for volunteers, and arrange to receive large numbers of re-called regular army reservists. In some units the proportion of reservists to regulars was as high as 75 to 25 per cent respectively.[45]

Simultaneously, the Brigade was allocated its full establishment of equipment, although many vehicles were rebuilds from wartime stockpiles. According to Korean War veteran and military historian Colonel Michael Hickey, this mobilisation demonstrated:

> How far the British armed forces had been run down since 1945.
> Vehicles stored in the open for five years had to be restored to

running order; clothing to meet the harsh winter of Korea had to be found and items such as sealskin caps destined for the 1918 Archangel expedition were issued to many units, as were useless boots made for issue to a force which never made it to Finland in the winter of 1939–40.[46]

A short period of intensive training ensued at Stanford Point in East Anglia, before 29th Brigade embarked onto various troopships for the voyage to Korea in late October 1950. According to one official account, 'although there was much wartime experience to be found among individuals in the group, neither the group as a whole nor the units themselves had really settled down as a fighting formation at the date of sailing'.[47] All units of the Brigade had been faced with the tough challenge of attempting to become battle-ready and efficient in a relatively short space of time.

While the period of training in East Anglia was not wasted, it was conducted in far from ideal conditions. On returning from Korea, one company commander from 1 RUR remarked: 'Training in England did not prepare us for what we were to encounter. The period of training the Battalion was allowed in Norfolk before sailing was inadequate and the ground in no way resembled the ground over which we were to fight'.[48] Likewise, Lieutenant L.J. Beavis, a platoon commander with 1 RNF, recalled:

> Before embarking for Korea, the Battalion underwent a six-week refresher course up to Brigade level. Nothing like the required training could be given in marksmanship and fieldcraft with the result that such training had to take place whenever time remained after arriving in the theatre.[49]

Like their American counterparts, many British soldiers from 29th Brigade were uncertain about what the future might hold and initially unsure as to exactly where Korea was. In late July 1950 Digby Grist, a senior officer with 1st Battalion Gloucestershire Regiment, was returning from a tour of the Normandy beaches with fellow officers from 29th Brigade.

> But Korea! Where was it? None in my carload hurrying back to our battalions at Colchester had a clue. We argued ignorantly up the Portsmouth road and bought an atlas at Staines. Even then we were little wiser; we saw where it was but the scale was so inadequate that we still didn't know whether it was flat or hilly, hot or cold, grassland or forest.[50]

Another officer from 1 RNF, on route to Korea in October 1950, confided that: 'We have no further information about our future and there is much speculation about it. I personally think that we will go into the Korean boundary area in an anti-guerrilla role, supervise elections and setting up of an effective Korean government and depart in about a year'.[51] Given the situation in Korea by October, and the routing of North Korean forces after Inchon, this was a reasonable assumption to make, as it genuinely appeared at the time that the UN forces were winning the war.

As 29th Brigade mobilised, the heavy dependency on reservists brought both advantages and disadvantages. Typically the men of the regular army reserve served seven years with the colours and five in reserve, and most of those called-up at the time of Korea had neared the end of their period of reserve liability. Consequently, most were in their late twenties or thirties, and many were married with families and had settled into civilian employment after the Second World War. As Tim Carew noted, they had to take a drop in pay in the order of ten to fifteen pounds per week, and this was deeply frustrating when there were mortgages to be paid, hire purchase commitments to meet, children to be cared for and so on. According to Regimental Sergeant-Major Jack Hobbs of 1st Battalion Gloucestershire Regiment such men 'were ticking like alarm clocks'.[52]

Similarly, Tony Perrins (Intelligence Officer 1 RNF) records that over half the personnel from his unit were reservists, and 'that having such a high percentage of reservists, many if not all somewhat hacked off at being dragged away, yet again, from family and friends, let alone recently acquired wives and children, did make leadership at the platoon, company and battalion level, significantly more difficult'.[53] In October 1950 Colonel Michael Hickey was a young platoon commander with the Royal Army Service Corps bound for Korea with 29th Brigade. He remembered that for junior regular army officers of his generation, many of whom were not long out of Sandhurst, reservists often came 'with welfare problems of hair-raising complexity, pouring their woes to our incredulous ears. Others were clearly so medically unfit that they had to be sent home.' However, he added that 'most bore their unexpected return to the colours with admirable patience; in the coming months I was to learn a lot from them, for they knew their stuff'.[54]

As Colonel Hickey intimated, the experience that most reservists possessed proved one of their greatest assets. In most cases they had been through one or more campaigns during the Second World War, and had rows of medal ribbons to prove it. Lieutenant Colonel Digby Grist noted 'what they brought with them was pure gold; battle experience, a capacity to look after themselves as well as those for whom they were responsible and a huge variety of skills, both civil and military'.[55] Similarly, after experiencing combat in Korea, Major J.W.H. Mulligan (1 RUR) commented: 'Good fire discipline paid dividends every time. Majority of reservist NCOs were excellent in this respect and realised the difficulties of ammunition supply'.[56]

Yet simultaneously the background of reservists could prove challenging. Sam Phillips, a platoon commander with 1 RNF, vividly remembered embarking for Korea with two men in his platoon who had been Japanese POWs from 1942–45. Understandably they were extremely reluctant to be sent to the Far East again, and one of these unfortunate soldiers even suffered a breakdown during the outward voyage.[57] This was far from an isolated case. The War Office made little or no effort to screen reservists prior to selecting them for service in Korea. Colonel Hickey recounted that within his RASC unit they rapidly discovered that some reservists had 'been prisoners of the Japanese, many of them in Korea, and they had unhappy memories of it'.[58]

It wasn't just the junior ranks of 29th Brigade that were swelled by reservists. To bring them up to effective strength for Korea, many units had to rely on reservists at officer level as well. Again such individuals typically brought valuable experience, but there were disadvantages in employing reservists as leaders, particularly given the limited opportunity for training prior to embarkation. Captain Henry Bergin of the Royal Fusiliers was re-called during the summer of 1950 and posted to 1st Battalion Gloucestershire Regiment. Reflecting on his Korean War experiences he commented:

> As a Reservist Officer who was recalled on 28 August 1950 and who sailed on 1 Oct 1950 I feel the nine days training I had at Stanford Training Area was insufficient to adapt me from two years of civilian life to an active unit command, especially as there were several new weapons to be mastered and new theories to be put into practice.

This same feeling was expressed to me on many occasions by the men under my command.[59]

Conscription and the Korean War

Many American and British troops who served in Korea, especially the longer the war went on, were either draftees or National Servicemen, effectively conscripts. In America the Selective Service Act (1948) stipulated that all males aged 19–26 years were eligible for 21 months' military service followed by either 12 months' consecutive active service with the armed forces, or 36 months' consecutive service in the Reserves.

The draft, as it was known, which had originally been introduced in 1917, became a part of life for generations of young Americans. As Carl Ballard, who left high school in 1951, noted:

> You knew you were going to have to join the air force, the navy or be drafted into the army. It was just expected. In fact we had several in my class at high school that were Marine reservists and they didn't even graduate but they took them straight to Korea.[60]

In America the demands of the Korean War also witnessed the passing of the Universal Military Training Act (1951) which lowered the draft age from 19 to 18½ years and increased the period of service from 21 to 24 months. By 1953 over 1,500,000 draftees had been called up to serve with the American military. Selective Service remained effective until the adoption of an all-volunteer force towards the end of the Vietnam War.

As with conscription during the world wars, there was scope for deferrals or exemptions, notably for those men studying at college or in some form of training. As military historian Peter Kindsvatter has shown, this has led to the accusation in America that Korea was 'a poor man's war', because a greater proportion of those killed, captured or missing came from non-white, low income, low educational achievement backgrounds, while those draftees with what were considered to be more highly valued social attributes either didn't serve, or ended up employed in support roles rather than as combat troops.[61]

In Britain conscription was reintroduced in 1947 to cope with the demands of the nation's global commitments as it both retreated from Empire and acclimatised to the conditions of the Cold War. Subsequently, the National Service Act (1948) required that from 1 Jauary 1949 all healthy males aged 17–21 years had to serve for a period of 18 months with the armed forces, followed by four years in reserve. The majority of men served with the army, although the RAF and Royal Navy did take some National Servicemen, as these conscripts were known. Ron Larby, who joined the Royal Signals in November 1950 and served in Korea, was like Carl Ballard, accepting of the need for conscription. He commented, 'National Service was at its height and everyone, friends, relations and the bloke next door, almost without exception, had done, was doing, or was soon to do "his bit" for King and Country.'[62]

Those employed in key industries, notably mining and farming, plus men serving with the Merchant Navy, were usually granted an exemption or 'indefinite deferment' from conscription. Similarly, students in higher education studying for a first degree and apprentices were often able to have their call-up deferred until they completed their courses. Men who opposed conscription on religious, humanitarian, political or other grounds had to appeal before a tribunal. As author and former National Serviceman Tom Hickman observed, they would receive one of four verdicts: 'unconditional registration (acceptance of his case), conditional registration (ordered to do civil work), non-combatant military service, or rejection of his position and therefore normal call-up'. Refusal to agree to any of the above options could result in a prison sentence, and cases of conscientious objection reached 'a peak of 945 in 1952, during the Korea War'.[63]

In response to the outbreak of the Korean War, National Service was extended to two years, but the mandatory period individuals were to spend in the reserves was reduced by six months. By 1952–53 most British units engaged in Korea were heavily dependent on National Servicemen, especially at junior officer, junior NCO and private soldier level. For example, within 1st Battalion Durham Light Infantry, which served in Korea during this period, National Servicemen accounted for around 40 per cent of the unit's full corporals, and six became highly efficient sergeants. Similarly, out of forty-two subalterns that served with the Battalion throughout its tour in Korea, twenty-six were National Servicemen, three of whom were awarded the Military Cross.[64]

However, as in America there were inequalities within the National Service system, notably regarding medical standards. As Tom Hickman explained, these could be adjusted according to circumstances. Consequently, during the period of overstretch at the time of the Korean War standards were lowered so as to take more men. George Younger (later Viscount Younger, Conservative MP and Secretary of Defence 1986–89) was posted to the Black Watch, after passing out of Eaton Hall Officer Cadet School, Chester, and subsequently experienced action in Korea with the Argyll and Sutherland Highlanders. This was 'despite having lost two fingers in a shooting accident', an injury that had he been called up under different circumstances would probably have resulted in his hasty discharge.[65]

Basic Training: Soldierisation for the Korean War

For draftees in America, National Servicemen in Britain, and regular volunteers in both countries who enlisted during the Korean War, their first significant contact with the military was via basic training programmes. These generally lasted from around six to eight weeks, and as the war progressed in many cases men were sent to Korea not long after completing their basic training. As Peter Kindsvatter remarked, in America there was a: 'recognition, based on the experiences of the two world wars, that soldiers could be more efficiently trained at centralized camps by experienced cadre', before they went on to receive specialised training in a particular skill such as an infantryman or truck driver.[66] Likewise, recruits in the British Army usually underwent basic training with the arm that they had joined, such as the infantry or artillery, before receiving further training in a trade.

According to the military historian Richard Holmes, the purpose of basic training was two-fold. As its title suggests, it aimed to provide 'an adequate level of training in such things as weapon handling and minor tactics'. However, of equal importance was its function 'to inculcate the military ethos in recruits, and ensure that the individual values which prevail in most civilian societies are replaced by the group spirit and group loyalties which underpin all military organisations'.[67] In practice there was often considerable overlap between these two functions, even though in theory they might appear to be separate from one another, and this can explain 'aspects of basic training which might otherwise seem stupid, illogical or simply brutal'.[68]

Usually, joining the military entailed travel by train or bus, often followed by a journey in an army truck to some forbidding-looking camp or barracks, and for those men who had never been far from home this was a new and sometimes daunting experience. George Pagan described how, on arriving by truck at Catterick Camp, North Yorkshire, 'tailboards dropped with a crash and a crowd of excited – but also nervous – young men jumped out, to be formed up into loose rows by shouting NCOs'.[69] Walter Adams from Shoreditch was called up to Ballykinla in Northern Ireland for basic training at the North Irish Brigade training centre, before later serving with the Gloucestershire Regiment in Korea. 'I'd never travelled before. I was in London for most of the Blitz, slept down in Moorgate tube station as a matter of fact. As far as we'd ever been was going hop-picking in Kent'.[70] Similarly, when Glen Bailey enlisted with his mother's permission as regular soldier aged seventeen in August 1949, he was posted for basic training at Fort Riley, Kansas, never having 'been out of Michigan' where he grew up.[71]

Depending on their background, army life could be something of a culture shock to some recruits, particularly given the Spartan nature of the living accommodation encountered in the 1950s. Dan Pfeiffer, an American draftee, recalled that during basic training at Fort Riley he was 'so shy that I would use the toilet in the night otherwise I was afraid to go'. This was because 'there were no partitions, the toilets were just lined up'.[72] Alan Carter was called up for National Service basic training under the auspices of the Royal Leicestershire Regiment at Budbrooke Barracks, Warwickshire. He recounted finding 'no hot water' and that others have pinched the electric light bulbs for use in their huts, so we have to make do with a wash in cold water in the dark'.[73] On embarking on his National Service, the film star Michael Caine found that he had to share a barrack room with twenty-seven other men, having previously only ever shared a bedroom with his brother. The stench of unwashed male bodies was overwhelming, but he learned to tolerate 'the mixture of athlete's foot and unwashed armpits'.[74]

Typically, men had also to serve and work alongside others who came from a variety of backgrounds that differed from their own, and who came from different geographical regions. The middle-class Englishman Denys Whatmore, who later became an officer with the Gloucestershire Regiment, commenced basic training at Fort George near Inverness. It was 'bleak' with its mixture of '18th Century fortifications and 20th Century Nissen huts' and:

> My room-mates came from all walks of life, from Scottish city slums to English public schools. Many of the Scots seemed to be hard-bitten, hard swearing characters, foreign to my experience. Our manners differed enormously. For example, only a few of us put on pyjamas at night and were the butt of much ribaldry as a result.[75]

Carl Ballard volunteered for a two-year enlistment rather than waiting to be drafted into the army. At Camp Breckenridge, Kentucky, he found that his fellow recruits 'came from all over the USA. We had men from the deep south and the north and Indiana'.[76]

Food in camps could be stodgy and unappetising. At Catterick Camp, Ron Larby recalled, 'meat pie, mash potatoes and beans' was accompanied by 'very dry bread and no "afters"', which all had to be washed down with tea reputed by many National Servicemen to be liberally laced with bromide in order to dull the male sex drive.[77] Before being selected for officer training at Eaton Hall, Keith Taylor underwent much of his basic training at Budbrooke Barracks with the Royal Warwickshire Regiment. The food was 'pretty foul and hot water on our cereals seems a permanent fixture! For tea we had Toad-in the-Hole – all hole and no toad, just a lump of stodge with an occasional sausage tucked away somewhere! Of course the everlasting "spud"'.[78] During basic training at Fort Riley, Dan Pfeiffer soon learned that it was unwise to complain as after 'querying what was in my mess tin the sergeant put me on KP [fatigues]'.[79]

During basic training men would be required to shed their civilian identities rapidly, so that they could be moulded into soldiers. This included getting rid of their civilian clothes and being issued with a uniform. George Pagan, who joined the Royal Signals in June 1950, recorded something that was familiar to many National Servicemen during the Korean War era: 'Brown paper and string was also issued to each of us, so that we could post home our civilian clothes'.[80] Typically, numerous items of uniform were issued, much of which, especially in the British Army, had to be pressed, polished and 'blancoed'. Some of the items of uniform encountered during basic training were particularly challenging, notably kilts issued to Scottish regiments. As a National Serviceman with the Black Watch in 1952, Derek Halley soon discovered:

> Just wearing the uniform was work. Everything had to be perfect. Our kilts were unique, no belts or buckles, no more than the two pins granny used in her hat. The pleats were not the usual knife-edge, or the box form used by the Argylls or the Gordons, they were barrelled and our kilts had to be hung up with wet cloths and brush shafts to ensure they maintained their shape. When we kilted up before a parade no-one dared sit down for fear of flattening a single pleat.[81]

Along with their military uniform, men were issued with a number which they kept for the rest of their service, even if they changed units. Again this played an important part in removing their civilian identity, although it could also make them feel like nothing more than a cipher, or even a criminal. On joining the army Keith Taylor initially spent a short period as a recruit with the Coldstream Guards at the Guards Depot in Caterham, Surrey. 'Tonight every stich of my clothing and equipment has been numbered – 22405091 so that I feel at the moment like a first class-crook at Borstal'.[82]

Similarly, a severe haircut was normally given to recruits soon after they joined the military. This again reinforced their new identities and the fact that they were to become trained soldiers or Marines. Within twenty-four hours of entering the Guards Depot, Keith Taylor 'suffered at the hands of a merciless barber who, armed with electric clippers, gleefully reduced the top of my head to something resembling a short bristled scrubbing brush'.[83]

Fatigues such as peeling seemingly endless piles of potatoes, and 'bullshit' were another omnipresent part of life for most recruits in America and Britain. At Camp Breckenridge, Carl Ballard recalled, 'us going around on our hands and knees just mowing the grass with our fingers, pulling the grass, weeds. And I remember going out and sprinkling the lawn in the rain'.[84] Such tasks often appeared nonsensical to recruits, and certainly appeared to be devoid of military value. However, they were usually intended to instil discipline, and were part of breaking men down and turning them into soldiers who would obey orders without questioning them. As Carl Ballard noted, 'I guess it was part of the training that you did what you were told whether it made sense or not. If it didn't make sense you went and did it whether you thought it was crazy or what. I guess that's part of it'.[85] Likewise, kit inspections had a role in instilling discipline among recruits by making them conform to authority, and by inculcating them with a sense of pride and the values of the unit which they had joined. They could prove harrowing experiences, particularly for those recruits that failed to meet the exacting standards expected of them. Simultaneously, they could foster corporate spirit among drafts when recruits helped each other to prepare their kit, or encourage a sense of competition between the men of a platoon or the equivalent that helped to motivated them to perform well.

As a National Service recruit with the Queen's Regiment in November 1951, Gordon Butt was subjected to regular kit inspections, and the attendant task of cleaning/preparing his barrack room for inspection.

> Basic training was most definitely 'Brasso, Blanco and Bull'. Beds had to be made with cardboard round the legs so they were all square, spare sheets and blankets were stacked at the head of the bed in order i.e. sheet blanket squared up with cardboard. Wood block floors in the barrack room had to be polished, we acquired an old mattress one lad would sit on it and two others pull it (we did take turns) to buff the floor up.
>
> Saturday mornings it was kit inspection, with the platoon sergeant and adjutant, all kit had to be laid out on the bed, to a diagram with which we had been issued, everything had to be in a certain place, even a tin of Kiwi boot polish had to have all the paint scratched off and just the word Kiwi left, spare laces had to be wrapped up like a Catherine wheel, small pack pouches and webbing had to be cleaned and stacked on your locker, again in a certain order.
>
> To get the kit ready, Friday night till the early hours was spent in preparation to make sure everything was clean and ready for the inspection. A couple of lads found it really hard and would prepare the kit and then sleep on the floor so everything would be ready for the morning. On inspection you had to stand to attention at the foot of your bed with your best pair of boots in your hand, that had been bulled with polish and spit so the toe caps shone like mirrors, if the officer did not think they were good enough he would 'lay' his cane across the toes and knock them out of your hand saying they would have to be done again to be inspected later, as you may have guessed the cane would crack the polish making it even harder to get them back to the required standard. He would then start to poke the kit with his cane finding fault and if you had too much wrong with it

he would say to the sergeant: 'up end it' and the sergeant would get hold of the bed and tip it all on the floor.

They did seem to pick on the same lads all the time. One lad who found it very difficult to get his kit to the required standard and seemed to get picked on, even though we tried to help him, when his bed was up-ended for either the second or third time stood with tears rolling down his face.[86]

Although they may not necessarily have appreciated it at the time, the stressful, intimidating atmosphere of basic training was ultimately intended to condition men into becoming soldiers capable of withstanding the pressures of active service. This paid dividends in an awkward theatre such as Korea. Dan Pfeiffer found his drill sergeants were 'brutal but realised and appreciated the need for it later' on joining 40th Infantry Division on the front line in February 1953.[87] Likewise, William Schrader, who later became a senior NCO in Korea with 9th Infantry Regiment, 2nd Division, found that the climate of fear that existed during basic training was fostered by their instructors, but as a result you learned very fast that 'you did not make the same mistake twice'.[88] Often instructors were Second World War veterans and this too was beneficial. While still at high school, Robert Halle joined the Marine Corps Reserve before later serving in Korea. He remembered that at boot camp in San Diego the instructors 'had pretty good experience and knew some of what we were going to have to put up with and expect'.[89]

Reuben Holroyd joined 1st Battalion Duke of Wellington's Regiment as a 21-year-old, after having his National Service call-up deferred so that he could complete a course at Bradford College of Art. At Wellesley Barracks, Halifax, he found that his instructors were 'a sergeant and two corporals who shout, scream and curse at us from morning till night' and this made for an intentionally tough atmosphere.[90]

Arguably men who joined the Marine Corps in America were subjected to one of the most antagonistic and brutal basic training regimes of the Korean War era. At Parris Island, South Carolina, Howard Matthias observed:

Everyone who survived boot camp had the right to be proud. The physical pressure was tremendous. The emotional harassment was constant. We were demeaned numberless ways. Recent college accomplishments were ridiculed and your 'manhood' was constantly challenged in almost every activity... In addition to normal boot camp routine, we were expected to demonstrate leadership capabilities as officer candidates.[91]

Similarly, Robert Samuels found that as soon as you arrived at Marine Corps boot camp 'you knew they meant business. It's not very good, howling and hollering at you all the time' and soon 'everything would be going double time, go, go the whole time'.[92]

In focusing on what military historian Hew Strachan termed the 'basic grammar of military service', basic training also sought to inculcate recruits with numerous fundamental martial skills.[93] Arguably among the most essential of these was foot and arms drill, which again was related to instilling discipline in recruits and building up their self-assurance. As a British manual published in the early 1950s explained, the principal purpose behind drill was 'to develop in the individual soldier that sense of instinctive obedience which will assist him at all times to carry out his orders'. As a corollary, a high standard of drill could also set the tone for 'the execution of any duty, both for the individual and the unit, and builds up that sense of confidence between commander and subordinate which is so essential to morale'.[94]

Other skills that were routinely taught included: weapon handling and firing range work, exercises in basic infantry tactics and various forms of physical training designed to improve soldiers' fitness and build them up for active service. Fieldcraft was also an important skill that had to be learned, especially when many recruits in the 1950s came from urban areas and so may have been unfamiliar with the nuances that it entailed. As an official British War Office training pamphlet stressed: 'individual fieldcraft may be considered as a man's ability to move himself and his weapon from A, by the best route and method, to an advantageous firing position at B. This ability demands a high standard of visual training, appreciation of ground, initiative, cunning and physical fitness'.[95]

Harold Lotherington did his National Service with 1st Battalion King's Shropshire Light Infantry in Britain and Korea and remembered that his basic training consisted of:

> Road running in PT kit first thing in the mornings then wash and shaved, dressed and down to the cookhouse for breakfast; parading in ranks on parade ground where our marching took place; weapon training consisting of dismantling and putting back together and cleaning weaponry i.e. rifle, Sten gun, Bren gun, [Vickers] machine gun. Then there was the assault course consisting of scaling walls, climbing rope ladders, crawling through pipes, swinging over streams on ropes. Then there was training of throwing and pulling the pin of the 6 second and 8 second hand grenades.[96]

Similarly, Rod Chapman was drafted in 1951 and undertook basic and combat engineer training at Fort Leonard Wood, Missouri, which consisted of 'the firing range, lots of marches' and simulated battlefield conditions. This entailed machine guns firing overhead and 'you had to crawl under barbed wire with dynamite going off', plus lots of the instructors 'were World War Two vets and you learned a lot from guys who'd been over fighting the Japanese'.[97]

Some men adjusted better than others to the overall demands of their basic training, as well as the specific skills that were taught. This was despite American draftee Glendle Callahan reckoning, that 'as long as you did what they tell you, you get along pretty good'.[98] Robert Samuels had a comrade in his Marine intake in the late 1940s who was so poorly coordinated he found marching and drill particularly difficult. 'They'd say left, right and he'd do the opposite. They had to let him go'.[99]

Training with small arms and hand grenades posed challenges too, especially for unwary, clumsy or panicked recruits. As Michael Caine recalled, his platoon had an early experience of coming under live fire when, 'one of the lads' Stens [a notoriously unreliable sub-machine gun] had run away. He turned away from the targets with the gun still spraying to ask the sergeant how to stop it'.[100]

By contrast, on account of their previous civilian or school experiences some recruits proved much better at adapting to the military than others. At Fort Riley, Lamar Bloss coped well with the physical demands of basic training, as he'd previously been a serious 'cross-country and track runner' and this was despite being 'one of the oldest men there'.[101] Another recruit at Fort Riley in the early 1950s, Sherwin Nagelkirk, had spent most of his life as a farm boy in Michigan, and this helped him a great deal on being drafted. 'I had been brought up on a farm and spent most of my life chasing pigs, cows or chickens and so basic training came fairly easily for me and when I had to grab a rope or crawl I had been doing that in the barn for ages so things went pretty well for me. I did rifle training pretty well as I'd been hunting all my life'.[102]

Similarly, in Britain men who had been to public schools where they'd been members of the Officers Training Corps (OTC), or even those who had been members of organisations such as the Scouts or Boys' Brigade, tended to cope better with the pressure of basic training than those who lacked such experience. Many from public schools were also identified as potential officer material while undergoing basic training.

Battle Training: Providing Realistic Combat Training

Another challenge facing the American and British armies was providing realistic combat training for those men destined for service in Korea. This had particular relevance for reservists, who were often rusty, and conscripts, given the heavy reliance that was placed on these types of troops. Experience from the frontlines during 1950-51 highlighted the level of unpreparedness that existed, plus simultaneously illustrating examples of where well-trained and well-led American and British forces had performed with distinction.

The dashing commander of 27th Infantry Regiment (Wolfhound), Lieutenant Colonel John H. 'Mike' Michaelis, initially found that many American infantrymen were too comfort-loving and came too heavily loaded for combat operations in Korea. 'We had to have a general shakedown. We had all kinds of special gear – violins, banjos, God knows what all. There must have been eight carloads of junk shaken out of the regiment before we headed north.' He went on to bemoan the lack of training among the men he was to command, particularly in skills such as 'rifle marksmanship and scouting and patrolling and the organisation of a defensive position.' However, as he put it 'these kids of mine have all the guts in the world and I can count on them to fight. But when they started out they couldn't shoot. They didn't know their weapons' and lacked adequate training 'in plain old fashioned musketry'. Instead, according to Colonel Michaelis, they'd spent far too much time 'listening to lectures on the difference between Communism and Americanism and not enough time crawling on their bellies on manoeuvres with live ammunition singing over them'. As a result they were soft and had to learn in combat what 'they should have known before they ever faced an enemy. And some of them don't learn fast enough.'[103]

By contrast, the Marine Corps at Hagaru in North Korea demonstrated what one war correspondent described as 'the ferocity with which our soldiers can fight when they are well trained, have confidence in their leaders, and have learned to face the brutal fact that they must accept death.'[104] Unlike the army, the Marine Corps insisted on a high standard of infantry training and physical fitness before a Marine undertook training in any specialism. Consequently, it was an old adage that every Marine, even those who went on to become pilots, was first and foremost a rifleman. At Camp Pendleton, California, where numerous Marines trained prior to embarkation for Korea, Martin Russ discovered that 'our entire working day is centred around the M-1 rifle. We rehearse for hours at a time the four positions of fire: prone, sitting, kneeling and off hand, i.e. standing'. And, as he explained, every Marine posted to Korea underwent 'an advanced kind of infantry training' prior to their deployment in which 'the rifle is as much part of that training as are the more complex manoeuvres'.[105]

As the war progressed the American Army, out of necessity, provided better combat training so that troops sent to Korea were not as green as those that had been hastily deployed in 1950. Dan Pfeiffer wasn't drafted until the summer of 1952, and during basic training had to 'crawl on the ground on my belly like a snake with live bullets overhead. One soldier was hit who panicked and stood up'.[106] Similarly, George Hyslop, who completed his basic training at Fort Riley in late 1951, remembered going on marches, doing obstacle courses and dealing with live fire and explosive charges designed to simulate battlefield conditions:

> You crawled with live ammunition firing over your head – don't stand up and look around… As long as you stayed down low you'd be OK, and they'd set off quarter pound charges of TNT in a hole beside you which gives you the idea of what war sounds like – it's quite noisy.[107]

Such training was typically part of what was termed 'battle inoculation' in the British Army, and while it was not a panacea for dealing with all inexperienced troops, it could go some way towards ensuring that men were better conditioned for combat than they might otherwise have been. Colonel Sir James Stirling fought as a National Service second lieutenant with the Argyll and Sutherland Highlanders in the Pusan Perimeter during August and September 1950, where he found that the absence of battle inoculation in his previous training was a drawback.

> As a young officer straight from Eaton Hall [Officer Cadet School, Chester] I had only twice commanded a platoon in schemes. I was not with the Battalion long enough to have a platoon. There was no battle inoculation and I had no idea how near a bullet was or what it sounded like. There seemed to be too much emphasis on platoon training (platoon attacks etc.) and too little on company level.[108]

During the Second World War, the British Army had established battle schools at divisional level that provided soldiers with physically tough, realistic training, with an accent on employing live fire and infantry minor tactics.[109] Training like this could alleviate the problems to which Colonel Stirling alluded, and was used again in Korea. As the War Office manual *Training for War 1950* emphasised:

> The Divisional Battle School, integrated as part of the Divisional Reinforcement and Holding Unit' [was normally] authorized only in a war. It contains a small permanent staff with the object primarily of training the reinforcements held within the division but, by

calling on units for extra personnel and equipment, its scope can be increased to provide centralised training for instructors.[110]

In late August 1950, Number 1 Battle Training Team was formed with the 'task of training specialists and junior leaders both officers and NCOs' of the two British infantry brigades either being deployed or readied for Korea. The unit, consisting of six officers and fifteen other ranks, disembarked at Pusan in early November 1950. From there it proceeded to Taegu and was based in the former Commercial School, from where it ran courses for junior officers and NCOs. As the facilities were deemed inadequate, the unit was transferred to Hiro, Japan in late December, before eventually moving to Hara Mura some 19 miles to the north of Hiro in mid-May 1951. At Hara Mura the facilities were far better than in Korea, and had previously been used by the Japanese military. This included barracks/accommodation, lecture rooms, field firing ranges and access to hilly terrain to train in that was similar to that found in much of Korea. By late 1951, the unit had been expanded to form a fully-fledged battle school that was run under the auspices of 1st Commonwealth Division.[111]

Once it moved to Hara Mura, the Battle School steadily increased the scope of its training so that as well as instruction for infantrymen, it provided courses on the Vickers Medium Machine Gun (MMG); 3 inch mortar; 81mm mortar; plus training for assault pioneers; signallers; Royal Armoured Corps (RAC) personnel and Royal Engineers. Physical and recreational training was also provided, and there were even drill cadres on a few occasions under the supervision of the RSM. As the war progressed the aim of the Battle School was 'to give concentrated training in weapon handling and firing, fieldcraft and patrolling and battle inoculation to: all UK, Canadian and Australian infantry reinforcements, all UK and Canadian engineer reinforcements, and all UK reinforcements for the RAC', for whom a small number of aging Cromwell tanks were provided.[112] In addition, some artillery personnel were posted to the School, and even Royal Marines trained there in infantry skills and the use of explosives.

As a National Service subaltern with the Durham Light Infantry, Tom Hennessy was posted as an instructor to the Battle School during 1952–53. Like many instructors he had gained experience of the frontline in Korea before being posted to Hara Mura. It was vital, he remembered, to try and 'get men fit after six–seven weeks at sea on troopships,' plus provide, battle inoculation, part of which entailed 'skill at arms to achieve confidence in weapons', which included the .303 rifle, Sten and Bren guns, 2 inch mortar, 3.5 inch rocket launcher, and various types of hand grenade. As an instructor you also had to get men used to 'coping with fatigue, ensure they understood how to care for weapons and ammunition, learnt movement techniques, patrol tactics/techniques, fire direction', and ultimately became 'self-confident infantrymen'.[113] Similarly, another instructor recounted that all training was progressive, so that men initially worked on 'individual skills such as weapon handling and firing range work', before eventually being expected to mount 'a company sized attack (all arms) with live ammunition/machine gun and rifle fire overhead'. One ploy sometimes used by instructors was to put the 'tough, older Australians in defence', as unlike the British contingents matched against them most of them were experienced regular volunteers rather than conscripts.[114]

For infantrymen in particular the pace of training was usually frenetic and physically demanding, with regular exercises, route marches and runs in the hills surrounding the camp. Many courses started with a 20-mile march from the holding unit at Kure to Hara Mura. As Denys Whatmore, a National Service officer, found this was tough, especially for a number of older reservists in his draft. He ended up carrying some of their kit and 'at later foot inspections some of the blisters to be seen were really nasty'.[115] On arrival at the Battle School, trainees would often be greeted by the commandant Lieutenant Colonel (later Brigadier) M.R. (Mike) Lonsdale, an experienced Second World War veteran, who held that post until late 1952. He was described as 'a first class soldier with a slightly unorthodox approach to life'.[116] Typically, he wore no badges of rank, and would often oversee training shirtless, wearing only slacks, a beret and gym shoes while carrying his binoculars. However, he also tended to carry a large 'walking stick with which he "thrashes" people who make a bog-up!'[117] He was in many ways an unforgettable officer, who left an indelible impression on most of those young soldiers who came into contact with him. As one former infantry subaltern remembered, he would address drafts along the lines of: 'Welcome to Hara Mura. This is a battle camp. It's not the Ritz. We've got to get you fit... So it's goin' to be rough gentlemen... But when we ship you across, you'll be fit, gentlemen; fit to fight and fit to fuck. You'll be soldiers'.[118]

According to Lofty Large, a regular soldier with the Gloucestershire Regiment who attended the Battle School in 1951, 'we attacked and defended everything in sight the right way and the wrong way to bring out the problems; became accustomed to the crack of bullets passing quite close'.[119] Trainees were also given little or no time to prepare for an inspection. Instead 'staff would wander into a hut at any time and expect to find everything clean and tidy' and similarly 'weapons were inspected at any time of the day or night without warning'.[120] Consequently, soldiers learned to clean their weapons at any available opportunity, even during short breaks on a march.

The training regime attempted to reflect the conditions that soldiers were likely to encounter in Korea. For example, as the war progressed increasing emphasis was placed on patrolling and night warfare in recognition that these were important skills for troops to master as the front line settled down into static mode. As a young regular officer with the Durham Light Infantry, General Sir Peter de la Billière served in Japan and Korea during the latter phases of the war. This included a period at the Battle School, where 'the low, scrub-covered hills were physically demanding, as we constantly ran up and down them; their greatest merit was that they provided total freedom for troops to give each other close fire-support – something which I came to value highly'.[121]

Many soldiers also found that Hara Mura tended to provide more realistic training than they had previously encountered in Britain or elsewhere. As a young National Service subaltern, Keith Taylor attended the Battle School in August 1951, prior to being posted to 1st Battalion Royal Northumberland Fusiliers in Korea. He observed:

> We would receive a lecture (usually short, sharp and in the field) followed by a demonstration which we watched from vantage points. Sometimes deliberate errors were fed in which we had to identify and say what was wrong. Fire and movement allied to the importance of a) intelligence and b) surprise which were paramount... One saw demonstrations that were considerably more realistic than one had seen in the UK of infantry deployment, of tank support and deployment, all based on what we could expect in Korea.[122]

Joe Bailes served as another instructor at the Battle School, and was especially chosen to work there because he was a skilled marksman, previously having served as a sniper corporal with 1st Battalion Duke of Wellington's Regiment in Korea. He recalled training schemes at Hara Mura, particularly with reference to his role in providing battle inoculation that exposed troops to live fire:

> There were three companies A (Australian), B (British), C Canadian. The specialist training was mixed machine gun, mortar and assault pioneers. The infantry were taught section and platoon attacks, recce and fighting patrols, night work including detecting flares and normal platoon weapons: rifle, LMG, grenade and 2 inch mortar and SMG.

The fighting patrol usually consisted of a dash over open ground with obstacles, blow a bunker and race back, all timed to see who was the quickest.

I was often put on the LMG [Bren gun] when the section attacks took place after they discovered I had been a champion Bren gunner at Bisley [shooting ground near London]. This reduced the chance of accidents.

Battle drill and platoon tactics were taught during basic training in England. All we did was to get them to do the same using live ammunition and to get used to fire going over their heads or kicking up the dirt 20 yards in front and hear mortars being fired nearby. The amount of ammo used in England is small whereas at the Battle School there was plenty.[123]

Battle inoculation could be scary, especially for young and inexperienced soldiers. Although efforts were made to prevent it, as during the Second World War there was an acceptance that tough, realistic training that used live ammunition might result in casualties. Jim Lucock, a National Serviceman with the King's Regiment, found that the Battle School 'was a bit frightening at first until you got used to the gunfire. One of our lads got killed there… He was shot while practising at the Battle School. We all stopped knowing something was wrong, but he was dead. But the army just made us get on with it. He is actually buried in Japan. I'll never forget him.'[124]

However, training at the Battle School could also prove enjoyable for soldiers, particularly given the normally generous allotments of ammunition that were available. Keith Taylor noted, 'this morning we saw a platoon attack demonstration and then fired the rifle, Sten gun and Bren gun at targets in the thick undergrowth. Great fun.'[125]

As J.C. Hall, a National Service tank gunner/wireless operator, and many other British soldiers who undertook Battle School courses discovered, 'there was not the "bull" and parades of a camp in, say Germany', something that he put down to the 'presence of other Commonwealth troops with us' that 'led to a more relaxed atmosphere.'[126] An official report even claimed, 'the spirit of integration between officers, WOs, NCOs and men of the different National components engenders a feeling of comradeship and mutual respect which would be hard to find in any other unit, even a unit of the 1st Commonwealth Division.'[127] Similarly, Alan Carter, who mixed with several Australians and Canadians on his mortar course, reflected, 'we all have a great six weeks of learning to be "mortar men" and a good laugh and drink at night together.'[128]

The presence of other Commonwealth troops was also an 'eye-opener' for many young British troops from a disciplinary perspective, as they were used to an atmosphere of 'blanco and bull', which was not necessarily replicated by their Commonwealth counterparts. According to one National Service NCO the Australians'

> Apparent lack of discipline compared to that of us "Pommies" had to be seen to be believed e.g. Aussie platoon lined up for inspection, whilst the officer was inspecting the front rank cigarettes were being lit up in the centre and rear ranks. Hara Mura was a closed camp i.e. nobody was supposed to leave. The camp was surrounded by brothels and some of the Aussies managed to find their way out.[129]

As General de la Billière explained, there was also distinct military value in working alongside Commonwealth troops because it enabled British soldiers to be 'introduced to the concept of the Commonwealth Division' and 'you got to know one another and understand Commonwealth procedures which were not very different to British methods, remember recent Second World War experience'.[130] Likewise, as Tom Hennessy stressed, the presence of Commonwealth troops also fostered an atmosphere of rivalry/competition between drafts that proved beneficial during training.

It is difficult to assess the exact contribution of the Battle School to the performance of the British Army in Korea, as it dealt exclusively with reinforcements rather than entire units. However, between November 1950 and June 1953 over 23,000 all ranks from the British and Commonwealth armies passed through the Battle School, many of whom were conscripts. Undoubtedly these soldiers generally went into action in Korea better prepared than they might have been had they not undergone such training. According to General de la Billière:

> It may sound a bit callous now in peacetime but good quality training and an understanding of combat saves lives in the end. The Battle School gave you the experience of live ammunition, overhead firing, the feel for the impact of weapons whether they were shells, mortars or bullets that you can only get in battle and as you were allowed casualties they came very close to the troops.
>
> The real value of Hara Mura and the impression it made on me in my life was the need for realistic training under fire conditions if you are going to put troops into battle. Start them off with the best possible prospect of surviving that direct fire experience.[131]

Chapter 3

Destination Korea

Throughout the Korean War the Americans and the British were faced with the challenge of transporting troops to the Far East. During the early phases of the war it was possible to deploy troops from elsewhere in the region, notably Japan and Hong Kong, and these became staging posts for operations throughout the campaign. However, as the war progressed drafts of reinforcements were required from further afield, and it became necessary to replace entire units that had completed their tours of duty.

Most personnel were shipped to the theatre, and voyages aboard troopships were long, claustrophobic, uncomfortable and dull, particularly for other ranks. Alternatively others flew to Korea, particularly during the early phases of the war when troops were desperately needed, or if they were part of an advanced party travelling to the theatre ahead of their unit. While flying might seemingly have offered a more pleasant means of transportation than being cooped up for weeks on a troopship, it was not without its challenges. By modern standards the civilian airliners and military transport aircraft of the 1950s tended to be slow, cumbersome, uncomfortable and mechanically unreliable. Once in theatre, most troops usually endured an awkward rail journey aboard rickety Korean rolling stock, and/or an uncomfortable passage by trucks over underdeveloped roads, in order to reach the front line.

Reinforcements/Replacements and Rotation
The Americans employed a points-based system for the replacement of Marine Corps personnel and soldiers. Essentially an individual had to acquire a set number of points (usually thirty-six) to be eligible for rotation on an individual basis. More points went to troops serving in frontline areas than those in the rear. As British Korean War veteran General Sir George Cooper explained, the thirty-six points for rotation were 'based on four for each month in a battalion [forward] area, three per month in a less forward area, two in a place like Seoul or Pusan in Korea and one per month for those stationed in Japan'.[1] Yet, 'changes in the point-awarding process and in the total number of points

required for departure made for an end of tour date that was less firmly fixed' for American troops than would later be the case in Vietnam.[2]

Paul Dunning, a signaller with 7th Infantry Division, recalled, 'when I got to Korea I was in the four point zone for enough to get, well I mean I was north of the 38th Parallel so got 32 points when the armistice was signed. Then everybody went down to one point per month, so I had four more months there and ended up 11 months in Korea'.[3] In contrast, American infantryman Rudolph Stephens reckoned that being in a combat unit was bearable because 'you got four points a month toward rotation and you went home in nine months. Not a bad deal if one managed to survive that long'.[4]

Similarly, as Marine Lieutenant James Brady highlighted, when compared with his Second World War predecessor the Korean War GI had hope:

> No man was to be left in Korea a day beyond what was necessary; there was to be no yardstick of machismo or brute endurance... no marathons as during the last war, when a man might spend thirty-six or forty months in the Pacific with no hope of home until war's end or a bad wound.[5]

Consequently, from a purely morale perspective, the rotation system had much to commend it to individual servicemen. Marine Corps mortarman C.S. Crawford, for example, described how a comrade due for imminent rotation 'got his chance to go down Hill 854 for the last time, a happy man knowing that he had pulled all the time on the line that he was ever going to pull'.[6]

However, there were numerous disadvantages to the rotation system. Notably, it made it particularly difficult to foster a strong sense of esprit de corps in many units because men had to be absorbed as individual replacements rather like a machine being given a new part. As James Carlaw, a wartime airborne veteran who became operations officer of the 8069th 'Repple-Depple' or Replacement Depot at Pusan, stressed, their role was to receive incoming troops, equip them and process them. This included assigning individuals to a specific unit, but the 'Repple-Depple' never dealt with entire units.[7] Consequently, Paul Dunning observed, 'you wouldn't go as a whole company, but there might be two or three men you knew from basic training'.[8] Having joined 9th Infantry Regiment, 2nd Infantry Division, as a sergeant first class in 1952, William Schrader rapidly discovered that, 'at that time there was what we call a pipeline, people coming and going. You didn't create a strong sense of team until you got there. Then one guy would get killed or wounded and another come in so there was a constant turnover'.[9]

While the system might in theory have appeared attractive to individual servicemen, in practice it sometimes failed in its objective of relieving eligible personnel, owing to the strain of active service conditions. Recalling the heavy fighting endured by 32nd Infantry Regiment, 7th Infantry Division, in the Triangle Hill area during September 1952, draftee Rod Chapman noted, 'we had quite a few men that should have rotated. We all stayed and we lost a lot of them'.[10]

Another challenge was that the rotation system tended to encourage what American military historian and former army officer Peter Kindsvatter documents as 'short-timer syndrome'.[11] This entailed troops of all ranks becoming excessively cautious as their date for rotation approached, which could have a deleterious impact on their combat effectiveness and morale, as well as that of the units they served with. Lyle Rishell, a platoon commander with the all-black 24th Infantry Regiment, admitted that as his rotation date approached, 'I became quickly preoccupied with the idea of going home, and the thought of doing anything that might jeopardize my health or my life was primary'.[12]

Symptoms varied from one individual to another, but Marine Corps veteran Howard Matthias recorded some of the most common characteristics exhibited by 'short-timers', based on his experience of leading a platoon in 1952. Short-timers tended to spend more time in their bunkers and eat there 'rather than walking the trench lines back to chow'. They refused to volunteer for anything that might appear risky, and 'conversation about buddies who were no longer around was discouraged'. As their rotation date drew even closer such individuals 'often became more irritable, short-tempered and nervous', and their conversations belied their fear that they might be killed or seriously wounded during the last days or hours of their tour.[13] Similarly, Marine Corporal Robert Hall remembered a fellow NCO machine-gunner in his unit (2nd Battalion, 5th Marines): 'One day after several rounds had hit the hill nearby, he wouldn't even leave [his bunker] to go to the head. He used a ration box and heaved it through the gun aperture'.[14]

Unlike the Americans, the British Army didn't usually replace troops on an individual basis, although at times individuals or small groups of reinforcements were absorbed by units. Instead, as the war progressed, all units that were deployed to Korea went in the knowledge that they would be there for a full 12-month tour. Reinforcements (including National Servicemen) were held at the Joint Reinforcement Base Depot (JRBD) in Kure, Japan, and posted to Korea when necessary, provided they were aged over nineteen. If held for any length of time in Japan, reinforcements often attended the Battle School at Hara Mura to hone their skills and physical fitness prior to deployment.

The regimental system, a distinctive feature of the British Army, continued to provide an effective means of promoting esprit de corps during the Korean War, with each regiment having its own particular traditions and geographical affiliations. After the Second World War infantry regiments were placed together in Brigade Groups structured along geographical lines, and this was intended to improve the drafting process, no matter where individual battalions happened to be serving. Potentially this structure risked weakening esprit de corps. As military historian David French has highlighted, large numbers of National Servicemen in particular were drafted to different regiments from the ones they had originally chosen to join. However, even when much rebadging[15] of personnel was necessary, as was the case during the Korean War, the system appeared to hold up despite being put under considerable strain. Military historian and Korean War veteran Colonel Michael Hickey commented that

> Despite all the turbulence and rebadging, there were enough old hands in the infantry battalions to see that the newcomers learnt the ways of their new units, and I remember the rapidity with which Argylls changed into KOSBs, or Fusiliers into Light Infantry, as proud of their new badge as any of their permanent inmates![16]

However, Colonel Hickey simultaneously highlights the example of 1st Battalion Royal Leicestershire Regiment, which was posted to Korea from Hong Kong in October 1951 with 'a very mixed bag' of personnel. This included 'a mixed gaggle of reinforcements, who were on their way out on the same troopship', plus large numbers of 'National Servicemen and "K" volunteers, who still had some months to serve, from the departing Northumberland Fusiliers'.[17] The 'K' volunteers had specifically enlisted for 18 months' service in Korea with the regular Army, and comprised trained ex-soldiers who had been persuaded to rejoin the colours, in return for having their reserve liability cancelled and a small gratuity awarded if they survived the war. According to Colonel Hickey the diverse make-up of this Battalion may have hindered it operationally, particularly when, after only two weeks in theatre, it was thrown into a full-scale battalion set-piece attack that failed, despite the valiant efforts of many of the individual soldiers involved.

Likewise, the commanding officer of 1st Battalion Black Watch in Korea during 1952–53 considered that despite the merits of the regimental system, 'turnover' was still a significant challenge and deeply felt frustration at battalion level. 'It seemed as though as soon as we had some well-trained corporals to lead out patrols they went off home. It takes a year of very hard work to train a private soldier. The politicians will not understand this.'[18]

Troopship Experience

In the Korean War era, as during the world wars, troopships offered the only viable method of transporting large numbers of American and British military personnel over long distances. While transport aircraft and civilian airliners were used as well, they couldn't carry anything like the same number of troops, and in the early 1950s large jet-powered aircraft had yet to be developed that could efficiently move personnel en masse from one part of the globe to a trouble spot in another. For the British, troopships were an accepted part of life at a time when the country had yet to fully relinquish her Empire. Dan Raschen, a regular officer with the Royal Engineers, left Southampton for Korea aboard the HMT *Empire Fowey* in mid-July 1951, and by then considered himself an 'old hand on troopships. My trips to India and Sumatra at the end of the war had given me the experience of eight of them'.[19]

Typically, voyages aboard troopships were lengthy and uninspiring, especially for British other ranks and American enlisted men. This was despite there often being duties to perform, periods devoted to training, and some stop-overs in foreign ports. A troopship leaving Britain in the 1950s, for example, typically took around six weeks to reach the Far East. One 'K' volunteer recorded that 'the voyage to Japan seemed to go on and on. I was sick of being at sea when we tied up in Kure harbour'.[20] Similarly, on recalling his service as a young subaltern with 1st Battalion Durham Light Infantry in Japan and Korea during the latter phase of the war, General Sir Peter de la Billière cautioned that the 'major problem with troopships was boredom, and the danger of soldiers going stale, running down, switching off and getting unfit'.[21]

Stormy weather and mechanical/engine trouble could also hinder the progress of troopships. The USS *Okanogan*, a Haskell Class attack transport equipped with her own landing craft, was built in 1944, and saw widespread use during the Korean War, including transporting elements of 1st Marine Division from San Diego to Japan in 1950. According to a Marine surgeon who was aboard, 'she was not a speedy ship! We had to detour to avoid a typhoon' and this added an extra twenty days to their journey to Kobe, Japan.[22] Another transport widely used during the Korean War, the USS *Marine Lynx*, developed engine trouble on one voyage, only a few days after leaving America, and limped across the Pacific to Japan. One Marine NCO who was aboard remembered that 'thick, black, oily smoke billowed sluggishly out of her stacks and we were barely making enough headway for it not to settle down upon us'. The Marines were thankful that when they eventually reached the Sea of Japan: 'North Korea did not have any more Yak airplanes. We would have been a sitting duck instead of a lame one'.[23]

The types of vessel used as troopships varied. Although the Americans had several ships specifically designed as transports, others vessels were of a more ad hoc nature. Draftee Robert Mulder was shipped to the Far East in a wartime vintage Liberty ship that had been hastily converted into a troopship, and was thankful that the crossing of the Pacific proved relatively calm. By contrast, artillery sergeant Dave Reeg served in Korea during 1952–53, and was shipped out aboard the *General Howitzer*. Cooped up with around 3,000 other soldiers led him to christen the ship the 'Lousy Howzy'.[24]

The British relied heavily on troopships of the Empire class, of which there were several, and these were mainly converted passenger vessels of inter-war vintage. The *Empire Orwell* was fairly typical. As Barry Tunnicliffe, a National Service subaltern with the Royal Artillery, remembered:

> The *Empire Orwell* (16,662 tons) was built in 1936 by Blohm and Voss, Hamburg, as the passenger ship *Pretoria*, for the North German Lloyd Line's service to East and South Africa. She was taken as a war prize in 1945 and managed by the Orient Line as *Empire Doon*. She underwent a major refit in 1950 and was renamed *Empire Orwell* to carry upwards of 1,500 military personnel.[25]

Ahead of many voyages there was frequently some form of send-off. Although 27th Brigade sailed from Hong Kong aboard warships of the Royal Navy, rather than on troopships, before they departed they were addressed by General Sir John Harding (C-in-C Far East Land Forces, 1949–51) and Malcolm MacDonald, High Commissioner for South-East Asia. The former gave a memorable address in which he urged soldiers: 'Shoot quickly, shoot straight and shoot to kill' and 'don't go away unless you are ordered to do so; stay and fight it out. Even if the enemy gets behind you or round your flank, stay put'. The latter informed troops in no uncertain terms that the North Koreans, backed by the Soviet Union, were the enemy.[26]

Similarly, when 1st Battalion Royal Ulster Rifles embarked on the troopship *Empire Pride* at Liverpool in early October 1950, they were addressed by the Secretary of State for War, Mr Strachey, who wished them well and reminded 'them that their mission would be an important one for the future peace of the world'.[27] Many well-wishers also flocked to the docks to see the Battalion as they set out on their journey to the Far East. Noel Trigg, a National Service-man with 1st Battalion Welch Regiment, left Liverpool later in the war aboard the *Empire Pride*, and remembered that an army band was playing and 'a few of the boys were singing along', plus 'a large crowd of people had gathered on the quayside; some were whistling, some shouting, others frantically waving to their loved ones waiting aboard'.[28]

Such scenes could be very inspiring, but simultaneously emotionally draining. Keith Taylor, a National Service subaltern with the Royal Northumberland Fusiliers, recorded that he felt proud to be British as his troopship left Southampton, as there was

> A large band, which played the Regimental Marches of the Regiments on board, beginning with the RNF's (*British Grenadiers* and *Rule Britannia*) as we were the senior Regiment on board. As we slowly left the quay, dead on 12, they played *Auld Lang Syne* and the men, some 1,800 of them, sang *Now is the Hour*.[29]

On leaving San Diego with a Marine Corps unit bound for Korea in November 1952, Martin Russ recounted, 'The Third Division Band, in dress blues, played a few marches and a blaring *St Louis Blues*... As we began to get underway the band played the Marine Corps hymn... There was not a dry eye among us'.[30]

Soon many troops experienced a degree of trepidation as they set off on their voyage to the Far East. As he sailed into the English Channel and towards the open sea, John Martin, a 'K' volunteer with the Royal Northumberland Fusiliers, recalled 'looking at the faces of the men around me and wondering, how many would be coming back? I was under no illusions that this venture was going to be a picnic'.[31]

Likewise, American Marine Robert Halle found that, after leaving San Diego in 1951, it was 'scary being out on the ocean', plus 'not knowing what we were going to run into when we got to Korea'.[32] Calvin Schutte was drafted in April 1951 and ended up serving for 11 months in Korea with 25th Infantry Division. On the way out he sailed from San Francisco, California, aboard the USNS *General Nelson M. Walker* and, as they passed under the Golden Gate Bridge, there were a 'whole lot of guys on deck of the ship, just looking back at the lights as they faded out... dead silence, nobody said anything and you didn't know if you were going to come back alive and some of them didn't'.[33]

The aura of uncertainty aboard many ships wasn't always helped by the troops' lack of knowledge about Korea. According to Derek Halley, a National Service NCO with 1st Battalion Black Watch, on his troopship: 'there were no direct reports from the war', although they heard enough 'to know that Korea was no healthy place'.[34] In contrast, aboard the *Empire Pride*, 1st Battalion Royal Ulster Rifles maintained a map charting the progress of the war, and 'new symbols began to appear in red' denoting Chinese Communist forces as they approached Korea, and they realised the war situation was changing.[35]

The map was kept in the first-class lounge and presumably could have been used by officers to glean information with which to brief their men.

Conditions aboard both American and British troopships varied depending on a man's rank. As General de la Billière stated, 'the disparity between the living conditions of officers and other ranks was much greater than would be tolerated now', and on British troopships it was starkly reflective of the social class system of the 1950s.[36] Typically, British officers had cabins with portholes, and travelled in comparatively luxurious style, often replete with lavish dining facilities. In July 1951 Keith Taylor sailed to Japan aboard the *Empire Fowey*, a converted Peninsula and Orient liner. He observed:

> We are travelling 1st Class, Warrant Officers 2nd Class and the men 3rd Class. The food, accommodation and all facilities for all classes are excellent. I have never had such lovely food. We go systematically through every course on the menu i.e. we can have all the soups, hors d'oeuvres, all the fish course, meat course, two sweets, cheese, coffee and one can hardly stand at the end of it!... No mess bills. It's too good to be true'.[37]

Similarly, aboard the *Empire Orwell* Barry Tunnicliffe 'shared a cabin up on A Deck with three other subalterns' and

> A cabin steward looked after us and kept us advised of all shipboard gossip. There was waiter-service at properly laid tables for all meals in the restaurant, where the food was always excellent. For those that liked curries, the Goanese chefs and waiters made certain you could breakfast, lunch and dine on an ever-changing selection of spicy dishes; and for the less inclined, the European cuisine could not be faulted. Duty-free drinks were cheap and offered tremendous choice.[38]

American officers and some NCOs tended to enjoy better conditions at sea than private soldiers. Robert Shoemaker, a doctor serving with the Marine Corps, discovered that aboard the USS *Okanogan* there was an officers' mess with three separate sittings for each meal, and that provided you were in one of the first two, there was always 'a decent selection of meats and other fare'. Officers could also retreat to the wardroom of an evening and if they desired participate in games of 'bridge, poker, cribbage, chess, casino and solitaire'.[39] The USNS *General Mann* was used to transport soldiers from the 5th Regimental Combat Team from Hawaii to Pusan in July/August 1950. Sergeant Robert Jamieson was among them, and writing home explained that most of the sergeants managed 'to get a stateroom' rather than being quartered on the troop decks.[40]

By comparison, conditions for ordinary troops below decks were usually characterised by over-crowding, poor ventilation, an absence of privacy and lack of space for kit and personal belongings. On British ships men usually slept in hammocks that had to be stowed away during the morning for 'the ritual of scrubbing down', and generally it was worse at night, especially in wet weather when, owing to the poor ventilation on most ships, the air was 'foetid with the smell of bodies'.[41] Geoff Holland, a National Serviceman with the Royal Artillery, had difficulty getting into his hammock so slept outside on the deck. 'I just couldn't get in the damn thing, everybody was taking the mickey out of me. The ship was absolutely crawling with cockroaches and it didn't help much sleeping on deck'.[42] Additionally, in the tropics the atmosphere could be unbearably hot, leading one National Service subaltern to comment that visiting the troop decks 'as Duty Officer always made me imagine that this must be what Hell was like'.[43]

As a National Serviceman with the Royal Fusiliers, Michael Caine was appalled by the conditions he and his comrades encountered aboard *Empire Halladale*. 'The officers lived quite well, but deep down in the bowels of the ship was an area that out-slummed the Elephant', the area of London where he had grown up in poverty during the 1930s and 1940s. To toughen their skins for service in the Far East soldiers were also ordered to parade on deck to sunbathe, but if they suffered from sunburn it would count 'as an offence and we would be put in the nick for malingering'.[44]

Conditions aboard American troopships for enlisted men were not necessarily much better, and typically they ferried more men than their British counterparts. Private First Class (PFC) Richard Newman served with 1st Reconnaissance Company, 1st Marine Division, and described his voyage as 'hot as hell. You had to stand in line to get a salt water shower. It was one crummy trip'. There were around 5,000 troops on board: 'Our racks were stacked five deep. The lucky guys had the top stack. When we hit rough weather, the Marines with the more squeamish stomachs started to puke… the more they puked, the worse the stink, and the stink would make more guys puke. It was a treadmill going nowhere'.[45] Fellow Marine Martin Russ found that on his troopship, 'the racks – stretched canvas, designed specifically to avoid any support of the sacroiliac, stand four to six high and are so close, one on top of the another, that one's nose, pelvis, knees and toes are partially flattened when the man above moves around'. Despite being inspected and swabbed out twice a day, the troop compartments also had a permanent 'static odour of sweaty feet and vomit'.[46]

Clearly sea-sickness was a significant concern for most troops being shipped out to the Far East, especially during stormy weather. Carl Ballard from Kent County, Michigan, was assigned to 9th Infantry Regiment, 2nd Infantry Division, and vividly recalled his outward voyage from San Francisco to Inchon in 1952.

> I was sick for the first three days. It was terrible, just terrible. If they'd made us stay down in our bunks it would probably have been better but they made us get up and get out on deck and do work chipping paint etc. To keep us busy. And everyone was throwing up on the steps and it smelled and the whole deck was full of vomit and that made it worse. You'd line up for meals and someone would throw up in front of you and it smelled and you would rush to the railings. After about three days you felt a lot better and very hungry. Before that it was just terrible, and felt like you were being sick until you had nothing left to vomit up.[47]

Even if individual troops were fortunate enough not to suffer from sea-sickness, they were usually acutely aware that several of their comrades were affected. Mexican-American draftee Octavio Huerta commented, 'I never got sea-sick but, I saw a lot of guys get sea-sick and they didn't know if they were gonna throw up or run to the toilet, they were really sick'.[48]

On most troopships some form of routine developed during voyages, in an effort to try and keep men busy. As Derek Kinne, a 'K' volunteer with the Royal Northumberland Fusiliers, remarked: 'A troopship's not like a cruise liner, for all the fine pictures you see in the papers when they bring a battalion home. There's never enough room in the canteens to get anything without queueing and there are hundreds of duties'.[49] These often included various forms of fatigues, which varied in their unpleasantness, plus the necessity to routinely practice lifeboat drills in case of an emergency. One soldier spent several hours each day of his voyage 'washing up all the food trays for probably 2,000 men after every meal' in 'a room thick with steam, hot as hell and twice as nasty'.[50] Alternatively, as National Serviceman Alan Carter found, you might be given less onerous tasks, such as ferrying laundry to and from the stores. 'We take the dirty linen to the laundry and bring the clean back, just 1 hour's work between 8 and 9 every morning'.[51]

On most American and British troopships there was some scope for training, although as General de la Billière cautioned this often appeared rather unimaginative. Aboard the *Empire Halladale* in October 1950, an officer from 1st Battalion Royal Northumberland Fusiliers wrote home, explaining that since reaching the Mediterranean they had engaged in 'a certain amount of training', despite there being insufficient space to occupy all personnel simultaneously. 'On the whole I think such mild occupation is a great help to while away the time which usually takes a bit of doing'.[52]

One of the most common military-related activities was getting men to fire small arms at targets off the stern of vessels. Martin Russ noted how he and his fellow Marines engaged in 'prolonged firing of machine guns and BARs [Browning Automatic Rifles] from the fantail'.[53] However, this was not always as effective as it might appear. Recalling the rifle drill he experienced en route to the Far East, National Service NCO Derek Halley described how 'we kept our eye in by firing from the stern at balloons which were floating off haphazardly; it never got any easier to hit the things'.[54] Similarly, John Erickson, who served with 23rd Infantry Regiment, 4th RCT, 2nd Infantry Division, remembered that they 'fired machine guns at balloons from the ship but couldn't hit the target owing to the movement at sea. We spent a lot of bullets out there in the water but never did hit it'.[55]

Onboard training also tended to include periods of physical training, such as runs around the deck, and for British soldiers, when they called at a port, there was often what Bob Walding, a machine-gunner with 1st Battalion Royal Norfolk Regiment, described as 'that traditional route march of about 12 miles'.[56] Often some form of lectures/instruction was given as well, and these could range from covering military topics, such as how to fashion simple booby traps using hand grenades in old cigarette tins, to 'general hygiene and the dangers of the local ladies'.[57] An NCO posted to Korea with 1st Battalion Duke of Wellington's Regiment in 1952 decided that he would provide first aid instruction for the young, inexperienced soldiers in his charge, as he feared they might otherwise panic on encountering wounded troops in the field.[58]

As a young platoon commander, recently commissioned into the King's Own Scottish Borderers from Sandhurst, Lieutenant Colonel J.C.M. Johnston embarked on HMT *Empire Pride* in September 1951, bound for Kure, Japan. He was aghast to discover that a number of the troops aboard were reinforcements destined for units of the Royal Artillery, 'who had no knowledge of the rifle', and immediately set about providing instruction for them on the Mk.4 Lee Enfield.[59] Similarly, Malcolm Frost did most of his National Service with 1st Battalion Royal Fusiliers, having been transferred from the Royal Norfolk Regiment. He recounted that during his voyage to the Far East, 'we were subjected to a fitness regime but very little else as I remember. I was part of a reinforcement group destined originally for Kowloon but eventually to Korea. I do remember having some rifle target practice but not a great deal'.[60]

Some American servicemen discovered that training regimes aboard troopships could be equally haphazard. Private First Class Pedro Behasa, a former military policeman, was posted to Korea with 5th RCT as a second gunner in a 60mm mortar squad, responsible for dropping mortar rounds into the tube. He complained that he had limited experience of the weapon, having only encountered it during basic training. 'After many 'dry' fire missions, we were given eight rounds for 'live' practice. We were also given one clip of rifle ammo to fire into the sea. That was the extent of my combat training'.[61]

However, training was frequently more structured when troops sailed out as part of an entire unit destined for a Far Eastern tour, rather than as a draft of mixed reinforcements. Major Norman Salmon served in Korea during 1951–52, as the intelligence officer with 1st Battalion Welch Regiment, and outlined his unit's troopship training schedule, including some of its less obvious but nonetheless positive aspects:

> On the ship training was mainly Weapon Handling leading up to live firing at balloons from the stern, Fitness Training mainly through gymnastics on board and route-marches at ports of call. There was also Wireless set training, First Aid instruction and various Lectures such as Personal Hygiene especially care of feet (but I don't think frostbite was included because no one knew much about it). Army Bureau of Current Affairs (ABCA) briefs were provided for young officers so that they could explain to their men where they were going and why! As a by-product of the relatively confined sea journey a number of comradeships were formed between individuals, which with the resultant level of trust, proved to be an invaluable asset later when times became tough and reliance on one's 'butty' became vital.[62]

An enterprising officer, who was responsible for training 'D' Company 1st Battalion Gloucestershire Regiment aboard their troopship, included instruction on unarmed combat for all ranks, a skill with which he was familiar as a keen practitioner of judo. Among other topics, instruction was also provided on the American-manufactured 3.5 inch Rocket Launcher, a weapon with which British soldiers were unfamiliar, and would be issued to them in Korea. As none were available on board 'cardboard cut-out tanks (T-34s) scaled to represent the various Ranges and correct sight picture' were deployed, and simulated sights were made from cellophane taken from discarded cigarette boxes marked with Chinagraph pencil. Troops then practiced 'rapid aiming diligently on the cardboard tanks'.[63]

To enliven voyages and keep boredom at bay, various forms of entertainment were normally available. Martin Russ remembered that Marines on his troopship wrote letters during off duty periods or enjoyed reading, including from the Bible, as well as gambling and playing 'Red River Valley or the Marine Corps hymn on harmonicas'.[64] Similarly, British infantryman and conscript Alan Carter recorded that they had numerous 'card games on deck', and although 'gambling for money is illegal in the armed forces... we pay no heed to that!'[65] Alternatively, there were often organised entertainments for large numbers of troops to enjoy, such as film shows and watching or participating in boxing tournaments. As John Martin recalled, on British troopships 'organised games of "Housey-Housey";... the forerunner of Bingo' provided some relief in the evenings from both the tropical heat and the living conditions aboard ship.[66]

Officers also usually had the opportunity to enjoy a wide variety of entertainment. Jilly McNair, who held a regular commission in the Queen Alexandra's Royal Army Nursing Corps, and was posted to Japan, noted that she and her fellow nurses often socialised with army officers when they were free. Many evenings were spent 'with our new friends the subalterns, either playing canasta, pontoon for matchsticks or watching the weekly film show organised by the Entertainment Committee'.[67] As their voyage progressed sessions of Scottish country dancing provided them with further entertainment. National Service subaltern Barry Tunnicliffe, en route to join 61st Light Regiment Royal Artillery in Korea, found:

> The Black Watch were aboard, so Scottish country dancing was a regular stimulus to evening entertainment. Various events typical of Merchant Navy life – horse racing, fancy dress, musical concerts where the performers were not expected to be perfect, betting on the ship's run – all had their place. Ballroom dancing and poker dice sessions also figured. There seemed to be a never-ending list of reasons to hold parties from small to pretty large, to pass the time. And a lot of us counted down the days to the time when even small luxuries would be a thing of the past.[68]

For British troops cooped up for weeks at sea, stopovers in foreign ports often provided a further break from the monotony and claustrophobia of troopship life. As an officer from 1st Battalion Gloucestershire Regiment observed, this could give them a much-needed chance 'to let off steam', such as when his unit docked in Singapore, and the men could 'spend their money and time ashore in bars, dancing most of the night with good-looking young Chinese girl dancers.'[68] In Singapore the Nutfield Centre proved especially popular. As Noel Trigg explained, it 'was a five star club for servicemen where you could sit outside in the gardens, drinking or having a meal, under the palm trees' and enjoy the shopping centre that was part of the complex.[70]

Traditional ports of call for ships sailing from Britain also included Port Said, Aden and Colombo. As a National Serviceman with the Royal Signals, George Pagan fondly remembered the 'Bum Boats' at Port Said, which brightened many soldier's voyages ahead of navigating the Suez Canal. These were traders in small rowing boats who would 'sell their goods to the troops by the method of throwing a rope up the side of the ship, to be caught by the customer on board,' and cash would be exchanged in the same manner.[71] Likewise, Alan Carter and his comrades from the Duke of Wellington's Regiment experienced a few welcome hours ashore in Aden, where they drank beer and haggled with Arab traders to 'strike a deal or two'.[72]

In contrast, there were occasions when troops, frustrated after weeks at sea, became embroiled in trouble ashore. At Colombo Michael Caine records that several Royal Fusiliers, after sight-seeing and enjoying drinking, began brawling with French Foreign Legion personnel, who were on their way back from Dien Bien Phu in Indo-China (Vietnam), and after such a defeat were in no mood 'to be fucked about by anybody', particularly a bunch of British conscripts.[73]

Flying to Korea

A relatively quick method of getting smaller numbers of reinforcements to the Far East, especially during the early stages of the Korean War, was by air. American Marine George Sarros experienced active service during 1950–51, and had the comparatively rare distinction of being 'flown to Korea, but shipped back home to the States'.[74] Similarly, as a regular NCO with the Argyll and Sutherland Highlanders, Ronald Yetman was part of a draft of reinforcements flown out to Korea from RAF Lyneham, Wiltshire, in September 1950. Under such circumstances many British personnel became familiar with the Goodge Street Transit Centre where they were processed. Located at the London Underground station of the same name, it was a 'warren of tunnels – offices and dining rooms and everything, very strange'.[75]

Equally, some troops made the relatively short 'hop' from bases in Japan to Korea by air rather than sea. Colonel John Shipster flew from Hong Kong to Japan en route to Korea with the advance party of 1st Battalion Middlesex Regiment during the summer of 1950. Eventually he touched down in Taegu courtesy of the US Air Force, and surprised many of those around him by alighting from the aircraft with his golf clubs and a tennis racquet while the airfield was under sporadic artillery fire as it fell within the Pusan Perimeter. On leaving Hong Kong he had 'been firmly convinced that our final destination was to be a comfortable location in Japan and was advised to take recreational items'.[76] After serving in Korea he submitted an insurance claim for the loss of his golf clubs and, owing to the unusual circumstances in which he lost them, the insurance company decided to pay out twice the amount he had claimed for.

Flying could prove enjoyable, especially when exotic or interesting locations were factored into the route. Contemporary transport/passenger aircraft on long-distance flights from America and Britain to the Far East lacked the range to make it non-stop without refuelling and had to stop off en route. Edmund Ions was born in Northumberland and undertook a short service commission with the British Army, which included a period of active service with the Royal Ulster Rifles in Korea. In 1951, with a small draft of officers and other rank reinforcements, he flew from Heathrow to Iwakuni in Japan aboard a BAOC Argonaut, a comparatively slow four-engined aircraft. They stopped at Malta, Nicosia and Habbaniya in Iraq, 'where a wall of heat hit the face as we stepped down in the afternoon'. Later they landed at Karachi and then flew to an RAF base in Ceylon (Sri Lanka), where the officers enjoyed swimming in the sea before eating a sumptuous meal at 'the Galle Face Hotel by the harbour in Colombo', with a succession of dishes 'borne by a trail of waiters like bearers on a safari'.[77]

In contrast, Howard Matthias flew from California to Japan and one of the stopping-off points was Johnston Island in the Pacific Ocean, a remote 'dot on the map, an atoll where the US Navy maintained a weather/radar station'. Together with his fellow Marine replacements he was aghast at how lonely a posting it was, and as they left he reflected that 'none of us cared to see Johnston Island again'.[78]

However, although flying appeared to remove men from the oppressive, crowded conditions of a troopship, and was a comparatively rapid means of reaching Korea, it was not necessarily any less stressful or more comfortable. The military transport aircraft that Howard Matthias flew in 'was basically a cargo plane with bucket seats along the side. It was impossible to sit in the seat for more than twenty minutes at a time and sleeping was very difficult'.[79] David Wilson, a senior officer with the Argyll and Sutherland Highlanders, had an equally rough time aboard a beaten-up looking US Air Force transport aircraft in September 1950, along with a small party of soldiers from his unit. They went to war wearing their kilts and immediately suffered the indignity of being dealt with by a brusque Master Sergeant of the US Air Force, who reduced them 'to a state of immobile serfdom by fitting us out with parachute harnesses, which were very tightly strapped up' and proved 'most uncomfortable, and very embarrassing!'[80]

Mechanical problems with aircraft were another potential hazard for troops being ferried by air. During his flight over the Pacific, Howard Matthias awoke to observe that one of the engines on his transport aircraft had given 'one last snort of smoke and stopped'.[81] As they were less than halfway through that leg of their journey, the pilot opted to head back to Johnston Island, which they had previously been so relieved to depart. An even more serious incident occurred during a flight from America to Korea via Anchorage, Alaska. According to one of the passengers, Sergeant Boris Spiroff, moments after take-off 'we got the fright of our lives. The right engine caught fire, forcing us to return to base'.[82] Fortunately they were able to land safely and the threat of an accident was averted.

Troops' First Impressions of Korea

Not only was Korea a war zone, but much of the population was desperately impoverished, and troops were liable to experience harsh climatic conditions and have to deal with awkward topography. Having been processed in California and shipped over to Korea, William Schrader vividly recalled passing through Seoul, which was 'all bombed out and devastated'.[83] Londoner Jarleth Donellan spent most of his National Service with 1st Royal Tank Regiment. By the time he arrived in Korea in the summer of 1952 conditions were static and he couldn't understand: 'Why anybody would want to fight over it. If it was mine I would give it away. It was infested with snakes, crickets, frogs and the hills were blasted by gunfire so that little greenery was left'.[84] Another National Serviceman with the Welch Regiment, who arrived in late 1951, found Korea 'bloody cold and wet'.[85] American infantry officer Lyle Rishell was equally uninspired when sailing into the port of Pusan. 'As far as one could see… the colours were black and grey and olive drab. There was no brightness to light the scene'.[86]

On entering Korea, draftee George Hyslop: 'thought I had gone back in history approximately 300 years. You'd see a popasan out there walking behind a plough in a rice paddy with an ox. Very, very old'.[87] Another American soldier, who landed at Inchon in March 1952, was struck by the numbers of 'little kids that would be running behind us saying "GI bubble gum, GI candy"' and people were so hungry.[88] Likewise, in the winter of 1951, Calvin Schutte, a farm boy from Michigan who had been drafted into the army, was appalled at the plight of Korean civilians, including barefooted children, desperately lighting fires with anything they could salvage in an effort to keep warm. 'It was a sad, sad thing to see these women trying to feed their kids and they didn't have nothing to feed them. I'd never seen anything like it before in my life that suffering and stuff like that.'[89]

Travelling to the front line in Korea was an ordeal for many troops, once they had actually arrived from Japan or elsewhere. Often the British would be reliant on American road transport units to ferry them to where they were needed. Sam Mercer, a regular soldier with the Gloucester Regiment, described what this was like:

> Driven by American negroes and that can be quite hair-raising because they tend to stick a fat cigar in the mouth, foot hard down, and these big 2½ ton GMC, or six bars, six-by-six drive on all three axles and they drive like a bat out of hell and anything that gets in the way, it's just too bad.[90]

Alternatively, some American and British personnel endured lengthy rail journeys in dilapidated rolling stock, as well as travelling by truck. Sherwin Nagelkirk was assigned to Fox Company, 35th Infantry Regiment, 25th Infantry Division, and remembered travelling to the front on 'a rickety train in cold weather' and most 'of the windows were out'. Subsequently, he was driven to a replacement centre by truck and 'the roads were something else, the mountains and the switchbacks you'd look down about 500 feet below and there were smashed trucks. And we were riding on that narrow road.'[91]

Chapter 4

Ground Warfare in Korea: Stemming the Tide

During the first year of the Korean War, American and British troops faced a distinctive array of challenges. The fighting was frequently confused and both the Communists and United Nations Command (UNC) experienced stunning successes followed by equally dramatic reversals. Rugged mountains, sodden, stinking rice paddies and the variable climate added to troops' woes.

Korea was predominately an infantryman's war, although artillery, tanks and aircraft often gave invaluable fire support. Much of the equipment and weaponry deployed came from wartime stock, but there were notable exceptions, including the British Centurion tank and American 3.5 inch Rocket Launcher. Similarly, wartime tactical doctrine proved relevant, especially that forged in the mountains of Italy, alongside experience gained fighting the Imperial Japanese Army (IJA) in the Far East 1941–45, as both the North Koreans and Chinese employed similar methods to the Japanese. Both of these theatres entailed amphibious operations as well, which again had distinct resonance in Korea.

Ultimately troops were thrust into an alien land against a wily oriental foe. Whether in attack or defence the North Koreans and Chinese typically appeared willing to accept high casualties, a phenomenon that was initially disconcerting for many Western troops. For most Americans, the North Koreans were simply referred to as 'the gooks', and to an extent this dehumanised the enemy and made it easier to deal with the more brutal aspects of soldiering. However, as the war developed the derogatory term 'gook' was increasingly applied by American and other UN troops to all Koreans, regardless of their background, leading one veteran to comment that this 'did not augur well for a campaign whose purpose was the salvation of the Korean people'.[1]

Early Experiences: June–August 1950
Shortly after the Korean War commenced, and with President Truman's backing, General MacArthur put forward an ambitious plan (Operation Bluehearts) intended to swiftly halt the onrushing NKPA. Two American infantry divisions (24th and 25th) would be deployed to stem the advancing NKPA,

while a third (1st Cavalry) would be landed at the port of Inchon, thus severing the enemy's lines of communication and trapping them between the American forces advancing from the south. Theoretically, the plan was sound and the amphibious landing at Inchon that was central to it had distinct echoes of the Allied operations at Salerno and Anzio in Italy during the Second World War. In practice, however, in the summer of 1950 the American forces that were immediately available to serve in Korea lacked the training and composure necessary to conduct such a venture. As military historian Clay Blair explained, 'it was a highly complex military manoeuvre that demanded at the very least well-trained, well-led, well-equipped, and combat experienced infantry'. Although the plan was later revived, in July 1950 'Eighth Army was in no way prepared to carry out such a demanding and risky task'.[2]

Contemporary reports, produced by the British War Office, based on data gathered during the first months of the war, highlighted many of the perceived strengths of the NKPA. Its units were equipped with a range of useful equipment, much of which was of Soviet manufacture. This included the PPsh M 1941 sub-machine gun of 7.62mm calibre, often known as the 'Burp gun' by American and British troops owing to the distinctive 'burrrp brrrrp' sound it made on firing. With a high rate of fire (100 rounds per minute) it was potentially formidable, especially at close quarters. Likewise, the 82mm (Model 37 and 41) and 120mm (Model 38) mortars routinely deployed by the NKPA were extremely useful in the Korean terrain, as both possessed good range and rates of fire. The former could fire up to twenty-five rounds per minute to a maximum range of 3,400 yards, while the latter was able to fire up to twelve rounds per minute to a range of 6,200 yards. The T-34/85 tank, famously deployed early in the war, achieved an enviable reputation owing to its powerful 85mm main armament, and because it was comparatively difficult to knock out, especially for relatively poorly equipped American infantry.

It was not just the NKPA's weaponry that proved effective, but also their tactics and mental resilience, especially when on the offensive. According to one contemporary article, 'this led to very determined fighting on their part', plus instances of suicidal charges and 'defence to the last man and round, ending with hari-kiri by hand grenade'.[3] The American Lieutenant Colonel Charles Bussey reckoned 'the NKPA soldier was arrogant, confident, and highly capable' and unlike many UN troops 'he was at home in the heat, the dust, and on the barren mountain sides'.[4] However, an experienced British officer observed, the North Korean was:

> Not unlike the Japanese, in his habits, but I would say that he is not so good. For example I have seen quite a lot of his movement by day (and one never saw the Jap by day), he does not move about at

night so well, and his positions, though good and well concealed are nothing like as good as the Jap positions. But he is very much the same nevertheless, and there is no doubt about it, he can fight very bravely indeed.[5]

North Korean attacks tended to favour infiltration and outflanking movements rather than 'coordinated attacks and pitched battles', and were often assisted by high standards of camouflage and concealment. Major assaults were frequently preceded by 'fighting reconnaissances', which aimed to find the weak spots in any defence. Troops were 'infiltrated who lie up behind the lines until the main attack starts, when they put in a determined attack themselves from the rear', and/or established road blocks behind the defenders. Usually this forced the defenders to withdraw in order to avoid being outflanked, and this could be a highly nerve-racking experience. Enveloping movements using large bodies of infantry supported by armour were another popular approach. Attacks were often 'pressed home relentlessly, regardless of casualties,' as North Korean soldiers had been indoctrinated to believe that they would be tortured and killed if captured by UN forces.[6]

Darrell Thornley, a sergeant with A Company, 1st Battalion, 19th Infantry Regiment, 24th Infantry Division, like most troops from that formation, was rushed to Korea via Japanese ferries in early July 1950. Having landed at Pusan he recalled the task that befell his unit: 'They issued us ammunition and we moved forward. We was then informed the North Koreans had over-run South Korea and was on their way down to us and we were to go up and slow them down'.[7] Although he might not have known it at the time, elements of 24th Division, which was committed piecemeal to the war, had already been engaging the NKPA in an effort to 'slow them down', and throughout the opening weeks of the war the Division was employed in such blocking manoeuvres.

Famously, from 3–5 July, Task Force Smith was sent to hold a blocking position on the Suwon road, approximately fifty miles south of Seoul, the ROK capital, to prevent the North Koreans reaching Osan. Named after its commander, Lieutenant Colonel C.B. Smith, the unit comprised two rifle companies from 1st Battalion, 21st Infantry Regiment, 24th Division, supported by two mortar platoons, six Bazooka teams, a single 75mm recoilless rifle, and a battery from 52nd Field Artillery Battalion (FAB), although this was absent when the action started as it had been delayed in getting into position. According to General Matthew Ridgway, 'it was tragic to picture this handful of poorly equipped men, trained for occupation rather than for battle' faced with T-34/85 tanks with overwhelming infantry support.

They 'soon had to choose between retreat and annihilation. Having held their positions until their ammunition was gone, they withdrew in some disorder, receiving heavy casualties'.[8]

One sergeant who was present complained bitterly to the war correspondent Marguerite Higgins, who covered the action: 'We ran out of ammo. And the enemy infantry moving up way outnumbers us. Besides these damn bazookas [wartime 2.36 inch model] don't do any good against those heavy tanks-they bounce right off'.[9] This situation did improve when American and British infantry were issued the more powerful 3.5 inch Rocket Launcher, and these were rapidly rushed to the theatre. Given the limited threat posed by enemy armour after summer 1950, these proved highly effective in an anti-personnel role and against enemy fortifications.

As the survivors of Task Force Smith withdrew, throwing away equipment as they went, they were tormented by the humidity of the Korean summer, plagues of mosquitoes and the terrain. Given such conditions, the official historian notes that in the early period of the war, 'salt tablets became a supply item of highest priority' and even started to be air dropped to troops.[10] Many men from Task Force Smith were so desperate they were forced to drink from the stinking paddy fields, despite the consequences this might have on their health. The picture that emerges from most accounts of the action is one of panic, ill-discipline and demoralisation, and the complete inability of the Americans to delay the North Koreans for any meaningful length of time. Unfortunately these would be characteristics that were commonly repeated among American units during the first weeks of the war.

According to one officer, who attempted to understand why his platoon had collapsed:

> Out of 31 men, 12 told him that their rifles would not fire. This, he found, was because they had seldom been cleaned and oiled, and the night's rain [prior to the battle] had rusted the mechanisms. Some men had tried to clean their weapons but did not know how to strip them down or reassemble them.[11]

This was symptomatic of the lack of effective military training these troops had received in Japan prior to experiencing active service.

American infantry officer Captain Al Burnett drew attention to another flaw early in the war that he witnessed within his own company. 'I remember the difficulty I had... in getting the men to dig a fox hole to the proper depth. They had not yet learned the first rule of survival in the defence, which is a well-constructed emplacement from which to fight'. However, he did go on to observe that once they came under artillery fire and 'the dirt flew' most troops 'dug in deeper'.[12]

Similarly, when 1st Cavalry Division followed 24th Division into action in late July 1950, it too was badly hampered by inexperience. On entering Korea, Sergeant Lyle Gibbs from 'E' Company, 7th Cavalry Regiment, recalled:

> We had a bunch of green troops, very little training and leadership. They were scared, and on our first night fired at everything they could see or hear, or anything else, and I never saw nothing. Next morning we had two dead lieutenants who had gone to check on something and they were moving so the troops shot them.[13]

Sadly this wasn't an isolated incident, particularly when orders were given to shoot at anything which moved at night or looked suspicious, plus firing indiscriminately gave away American positions all too readily.

The situation confronting American units 'was compounded by almost total lack of communications: telephone wires were repeatedly cut, radios were defeated by distance and mountains between units'.[14] Sergeant First Class Charles Menninger highlighted the problem as experienced by his unit, 3rd Battalion from 34th Infantry Regiment, 24th Division, where communication was virtually non-existent.

> Most of the radios didn't work, and the fact that the enemy was often between our headquarters and the rifle companies made it extremely hazardous to lay phone wires. Almost all communication, therefore, was by runners, and they often simply disappeared.[15]

In addition, maps based on Japanese surveys of the inter-war period often proved unreliable, making it especially difficult to lay on effective artillery support. Second Lieutenant Leroy Wirth served as Forward Observer (FO) tasked with helping to provide artillery support to the Marine Corps during August 1950, and reckoned that they 'were of no use whatsoever'.[16]

As well as a general lack of military training and communication problems, an absence of clear leadership was an issue for many American army units during this stage of the war, not helped by high casualties among officers. Consequently, cases of panicky withdrawals, or 'bug outs', loom large in many accounts of the war. According to the official historian, 'often the unit commanders were new to the units and did not know their officers and men; there were few qualified officer replacements for those lost'.[17] There was a tendency for some senior officers to become involved in fighting their men's battles, including tackling enemy tanks with Bazookas. While extremely brave, this was not the job of battalion or regimental commanders. As SFC Charles Menninger stated: 'When I say that the regiment lacked proper leadership, I can point to the fact that... Colonel Martin [his CO] was killed in the street fighting a T-34 instead of being where he could direct the movement of the troops'.[18]

The fear and tension created by the enemy's use of infiltration tactics, and consequently the absence of any clearly defined front line, provided a further challenge. As Marguerite Higgins observed, 'the enemy simply avoided frontal assault and depended on infiltration and a series of enveloping moves'.[19] This tactic was enhanced by the North Koreans' ability to disguise themselves as refugees, or dress in captured American uniforms so as to appear as friendly ROK troops. General Dean records that by 20 July 1950 intelligence reports indicated, 'that civilians in captured areas had been ordered to make thousands of suits of typical Korean white clothing, in which North Korean soldiers would infiltrate our lines at Taejon'.[20] Equally, refugees could provide a pitiful sight that upset many soldiers. Colonel John Shipster served with the Middlesex Regiment and entered the theatre during August/September. He witnessed thousands of refugees streaming southwards: 'pathetic figures carrying their meagre possessions, tied to wooden frames on their backs or, if lucky, moving their belongings in large wooden ox carts'.[21]

Historian Russel Gugeler emphasised another major impact of the fluid nature of the battlefront, caused by NKPA infiltration tactics, which was that troops in rear areas could be threatened as much as infantry further forward. With specific reference to artillery positions he noted that gun areas 'must be selected that not only will permit accomplishing the primary mission of fire support but will also facilitate local defence against enemy action that might interrupt the fire support'.[22]

During the summer of 1950, numerous atrocities against American POWs were perpetrated by the NKPA, and these fuelled the fear and uncertainty experienced by most American soldiers, although simultaneously they might have helped stiffen the resolve of many GIs to fight when it had been faltering. Equally some American troops were guilty of committing heinous acts, often with the apparent consent of their commanders, as civilians were deliberately targeted, largely owing to the fear generated by the North Koreans' practice of posing as refugees so as to conduct infiltration tactics. Infamously, at No Gun Ri from 25–29 July 1950, a large body of Korean refugees was fired on by American air and ground forces. This included elements of 1st Cavalry Division, who opened fire on refugees that had sought shelter in a railway tunnel after the initial attack, and as many as 400 people may have been slaughtered.[23]

When they did encounter North Korean troops, Americans were often struck by their apparent courageousness and determination. Charles Payne, an officer with 1st Battalion, 34th Infantry Regiment, 24th Division described facing a NKPA mass attack as akin to 'a slow tornado' that 'engulfed everyone and everything', after the Americans had initially had their positions sounded out by 'scouts and patrols'.[24] Darrell Thornley, a combat-experienced NCO who'd previously fought in north-west Europe in 1944–45, recounted:

> I guess they were gluttons for punishment. Their tactics were not like ours, broken into squads and stuff. Instead they'd come in company strength screaming and blowing bugles. I don't know how skilled they was but they advanced right into our fire. They were brave.[25]

Glen Bailey, a regular soldier who fought as a BAR man (Browning Automatic Rifle) with 1st Cavalry Division, considered the NKPA put little value on human life. It seemed as if 'life to them was nothing. It didn't mean anything to them'.[26]

By mid-July 1950, the Americans were attempting to hold a line on the Kum River, north of the strategically placed city of Taejon. Those units involved included the inexperienced 19th Infantry Regiment, 24th Division, famous for its stand at Chickamauga during the American Civil War, which had earned it the title 'The Rock of Chickamauga'. Accordingly, the men of this unit proudly referred to themselves as 'the Chicks'. Darrell Thornley, one of that regiment's NCOs, remembered that it was a highly confused, stressful period:

> We lived on trucks. We'd go from one spot to another in trucks to get off, unload and meet a group because they weren't coming in a straight line at us. Their units would advance miles apart and we would stop them, push them back up the line of the attack, get on our trucks and ride some more. A fire brigade that's all we was.[27]

As the Kum River line disintegrated, American casualties were again heavy, especially within 19th Infantry Regiment. 'Of some 900 men on the river line when the NKPA attacked on 16 July, only half that number could be found the next day', and in 1st Battalion 19th Regiment there was 'a shocking 43 per cent casualties: 388 of 785 men'.[28] The actions along the Kum River paved the way for an assault by the NKPA on Taejon. Again a frontal attack would be deployed, in this case along the Seoul-Pusan highway. This would be launched simultaneously with a bold encirclement from the south-west, where the American defences were at their weakest. By the end of July 1950, the Americans had lost a total of 7,859 personnel, not only through being killed by enemy action, wounded or captured, but also owing to health problems, particularly heat exhaustion in the unforgiving Korean terrain where there was limited water and shade available.[29] Losses in equipment were also high. By 4 August 1950, 19th Infantry Regiment from 24th Division 'had lost 80 per cent of its ¼ ton trucks, 50 per cent of its ¾ ton trucks, and 33 per cent of its 2½ ton trucks,' plus it found it difficult to obtain supplies of clothing, hand grenades and 4.2 inch mortar ammunition.[30]

Defeat at Taejon changed the picture of the war as it forced the decimated 24th Division and ROK forces towards establishing a new front line to the south, towards and then behind the Naktong River. As the author Joseph Goulden put it, throughout July/August 1950 it appeared that 'each day the black line marking the battlefront slipped farther south on the newspaper situation maps'.[31] The prospect of a 'Far Eastern style Dunkirk' evacuation loomed in the minds of UN commanders and soldiers alike. Recalling his initial service as a platoon commander with 27th (Wolfhounds) Regiment from 25th Division, Brigadier General Ent noted that at 'the troop level, there wasn't any sense of a coherent strategy. It seemed like we were continually falling back, and there was no indication where it would end. There was a real fear that we'd be pushed right out of Korea'.[32]

However, General Walton Walker, the commander of Eighth Army, aimed to secure the port of Pusan in south-east Korea and throw up a defensive perimeter around it that would enable enough men and supplies to be landed so the UN could go back on the offensive. To assist the remnants of 24th Division, and 1st Cavalry and 25th Infantry Divisions, during July/August 1st Provisional Marine Brigade was despatched to Korea from California, plus 2nd Infantry Division from Washington, and the 5th Regimental Combat Team (RCT) from Hawaii. These reinforcements were soon joined by a supporting medium tank battalion, hastily re-equipped in Japan, and the British 27th Infantry Brigade which sailed from Hong Kong.

Combat in the Pusan Perimeter

On 1 August 1950 Eighth Army ordered all UN ground forces in Korea to move behind the Naktong River. These defensive positions formed what was termed the 'Pusan Perimeter' by journalists, a broadly rectangular section of land approximately 100 miles south-to-north and 50 miles west-to-east, within which the UN forces established interior lines of communication and held a number of towns blocking key routes to Pusan, through which reinforcements were arriving. According to the author Edwin Hoyt, positions in the north were manned by ROK troops from Yongdok in the east to Naktong-ni, where the line merged with the Naktong River. From there:

> The line ran almost due south, on the eastern bank of the Naktong down to the junction of the Naktong and Nam rivers, where the augmented Naktong turned east and then meandered to the sea at Pusan. At the juncture of the rivers, the line deserted the river and followed the roads, with strong American positions at The Notch, Chungdam-ni, and around Masan.[33]

During August and the first half of September a series of gruelling and savage battles occurred simultaneously at different locations along the Pusan Perimeter. For the Americans this entailed some of the bitterest fighting of the entire Korean War, whether in defensive operations or during counter-attacks. This was evident by casualty statistics and those regarding ammunition expenditure. At Bloody Gulch from 11–12 August, a company from 1st Battalion, 5th RCT, lost 157 out of 180 men, and 90th Field Artillery Battalion (FAB) lost '50 percent of the men of the two batteries present'. On one night in September, 37th FAB fired 2,300 rounds in support of 2nd Battalion, 23rd Infantry Regiment alone.[34] Presented with a good target at the Sachon Pass, artillery officer Addison Terry, serving as an FO, remarked: 'All we wanted to do was kill gooks… kill gooks by the thousand, kill them with hot lead, cold steel, or ripping explosives – but kill gooks. We were accomplished murderers. We were masters of our skilled trade.'[35]

In contrast, at Subok-san, an important area of high ground that commanded the route from Chinju to Masan and onto Pusan, troops from the all-black 24th Infantry Regiment found it tough. One of its officers noted:

> The terrain was rugged. Vehicles were confined to the roads, which were poor. The temperature was 110 degrees Fahrenheit. The tactical plans were inept and poorly suited to the terrain. Barrier and field fortification materiel was in limited supply and often simply not available.[36]

As had been the case with many American units earlier in the war, his troops also proved unprepared to deal with the awkward terrain and shortage of water for drinking and washing.

For many young, inexperienced American troops defending the Pusan Perimeter presented a steep learning curve. According to the Official Historian, it 'gave something approaching a continuous line of troops' and this may have given the American soldier 'a stronger disposition to fight', because unlike earlier on in the fighting reserves became available in the rear and there were known units on either flank.[37] An infantry officer commented that 'one of the things you learn is to put your losses behind you. You can't dwell on losses or you become ineffective. I had the rest of my platoon to lead, and I had to go from there'.[38] Reflecting on his experiences with 5th Cavalry Regiment, 1st Cavalry Division, Glen Bailey noted how he found combat different from basic training when 'you didn't stand and shoot at somebody or try to shoot at somebody, you were just doing the normal thing'. Soon in action 'you learn how to protect yourself some, there was so much stuff going on. It was tough, a hard lesson to learn'.[39] Likewise, Marine George Sarros quickly learned to appreciate that, 'wherever we went we dug holes to protect ourselves. Some sort of hole or another we dug positions'.[40]

However, wide frontages along the Naktong River were still a challenge for the defender to contend with. The American 9th Infantry Regiment from 2nd Division was tasked with holding a front of 20,000 yards.[41] As a report by the British 27th Brigade made clear, it was even more challenging for the numerically inferior British forces. The sector allotted to that formation in early September 1950 'was 18,000 yards, with two weak battalions and 100 South Korean police armed with a miscellaneous collection of Japanese and US rifles', for which the British 'had to provide ammunition, which was a continual problem and a British NCO, otherwise they were liable to fade away'.[42]

Within the above framework 1st Battalion Argyll and Sutherland Highlanders (A&SH) discovered that, 'the 6,000 yards gap in the so-called perimeter to the south of the Battalion, between them and the nearest American unit' was deeply troubling. It called for 'a routine of active patrolling to the south to find out the enemy strength in that area, if necessary by fighting'.[43] Brigadier David Wilson commanded A Company from the Battalion, and recorded that owing to such a wide frontage, 'no company could support each other, and this in some ways applied to platoons... In front of us was a gap of many miles before the nearest US forces (the Marines) coming up from the south', and in the middle was an area that 'a good many North Koreans had infiltrated'.[44]

An account of 5th RCT's experiences in the perimeter cautioned during August/September that the NKPA's infiltration tactics continued to provide a challenge to UN forces. Often they 'dispatched patrols of eighteen or more men, with half dressed as South Korean peasants to assist in infiltration. The remainder took position to provide supporting fires as the infiltrators returned to the unit'.[45] The penchant of the NKPA for such tactics could be unnerving. Tanjore Splan was initially assigned as a loader with C Battery, 555th FAB, 5th RCT. He recalled that during September, 'we would set up a road block and refugees were pouring through our position. Some people were taken out of that group of people as North Korean, and that was done mostly by South Korean people who were assigned to our unit'.[46]

Likewise, Major Penman, a company commander with 1 A&SH, observed that the NKPA demonstrated: 'the ability to disperse and concentrate quite large formations at will, without our intelligence (despite air reconnaissance) being able to keep us informed'. One of his fellow officers reiterated that although 'there was nothing new in the enemy's infiltration methods', the Korean countryside heavily 'lent itself to that type of attack'.[47] Western troops, used to fighting to their front, had initially found that facing the IJA during the Second World War was similarly disconcerting, owing to the enemy's ability to turn flanks and get in behind friendly units. Again in Korea in 1950–51 this was to be a significant challenge for most American and British units.

The NKPA frequently commenced attacks at night so as to negate UN fire and air power, but sought to bring fighting to a close by daybreak. Consequently, in an effort to secure UN positions, attacks were often launched during early evening, so that the ground could be secured by midnight, and the early hours of the morning used to dig in and consolidate, so as to be prepared to beat off any counterattack in daylight. Most assaults were preceded by some form of reconnaissance and launched by widely extended small groups that formed up behind the front line, and approached UN positions stealthily, before rapidly engaging defenders. Frequently, Japanese-style tactics were employed in assaults such as noise, showers of hand grenades and 'Banzai'-type charges at close range. These charges were akin to the brutal frontal assaults routinely employed by Japanese infantry during the Second World War, and could appear unorganised and led by poorly prepared/equipped troops who absorbed enemy fire in an effort to induce the defenders to become short of ammunition. At this stage better-trained troops would rush forward to try and overwhelm a position, and this was often supported by flanking attacks, seeking to utilise gaps in the defender's lines. Major Clayton, 1st Battalion, the Middlesex Regiment (1 MX), reckoned, 'the private soldier was rather surprised at the "Banzai"' type of attack but soon got used to it'.[48]

Many soldiers were initially perturbed by the NKPA's methods of night warfare and infiltration. Tony Kingsford remembered that as a 19-year-old National Serviceman with 1 MX, manning his slit trench at night he heard rustling, 'which got nearer and nearer and at night your imagination plays tricks and I was quite convinced that the "gooks" were coming for me'. It turned out to be 'an enormous toad', but his experience was indicative of the sort of jitteriness that the enemy's tactics could induce.[49] As a young subaltern with 1 A&SH, Colonel Sir James Stirling was struck by the North Koreans' 'use of numbers with very little regard for covering fire or preservation of lives'. Years later he confided that it did feel as if 'the NKPA were superhuman and could climb up and attack whatever the difficulties. Keeping your finger on the trigger all night and pressure from loss of sleep' added significantly to the strain that soldiers were under.[50]

However, the 'gook' was not unbeatable, as a patrol from 1 A&SH demonstrated on 18–19 September when it scored a notable tactical victory. The North Koreans attacked a machine-gun position, not realising the British had already deliberately vacated it. This was observed by a patrol commanded by Sergeant Robertson, who remained still and held their fire and waited until there was enough daylight to engage the enemy, who were subsequently caught by surprise. While sustaining no casualties, Sergeant Robertson's patrol was credited with killing ten and wounding three enemy troops, ensuring that 'the gooks did not try again to infiltrate patrols in that sector'.[51]

During this period, many of the NKPA's weapons raised concerns as well. Despite the terrain, self-propelled guns (SPGs) were brought into commanding positions from where they could potentially inflict serious damage and demoralise UN troops. According to one British officer: 'the accuracy and flexibility' with which the NKPA deployed these weapons with their high velocity, flat trajectory fire 'was a surprise', and they proved 'difficult to pinpoint and consequently to neutralise', which 'combined with their extreme accuracy' made them a bugbear to troops. Similarly, in close combat 'the peculiar sound caused by the high rate of fire of the Burp-gun at first had an adverse effect on morale', although with exposure to this weapon the effect gradually wore off.[52]

The enemy's use of mortars was another feature of the fighting. For the British particular frustrations were felt with regard to these weapons. As Lieutenant P. Mackellar (1 A&SH) explained, NKPA mortars 'had greater range than our own 3 inch mortar and were also more accurate' although their bomb appeared less effective.[53] Likewise, an American infantry officer noted how effective the NKPA could be with their mortars. 'They generally dropped a round in front of the position they were firing on, then one to the rear, and finally adjusted their fire to the centre and laid down a barrage'.[54]

Equally, artillery was frequently handled with some skill by the enemy, despite the threat posed to it by UN air power and counter battery fire, and the difficulty in finding suitable gun positions owing to the terrain. Field artillery, notably Soviet-manufactured 122mm howitzers, 'at Taejon Airfield on 16 July 1950, and on the Kum River, generated firepower comparable to that of Second World War battles'.[55] Similarly, anti-tank guns were often deployed with a degree of cunning that made use of well-camouflaged positions in the awkward terrain, even sited on high ground from where they could penetrate the weaker top armour of UN tanks. Artillerist Addison Terry experienced significant combat in the Pusan Perimeter, and recounted coming across 'two elephant guns (51mm anti-tank guns) and their dead crews, only a few feet off the road where they had been ingeniously concealed'.[56]

For the defender it proved vital to seize and hold areas of high ground. The British attempted to do this 'by means of Company defensive localities, which owing to the wide front that had to be held were often well over a mile apart, and not mutually visible, although sited to be able to cover the intervening ground by day'.[57] Ideally all positions needed to be well concealed, mutually supporting, and capable at all times of being controlled by wireless/radio. However, as indicated by Brigadier Wilson's comments above, this was sometimes difficult to achieve in practice owing to the wide frontages held, and the nature of the terrain. Most ground was rocky 'rather like the North West Frontier of India', which could hinder the construction of defensive positions, and at lower levels scrubby 'stunted growth… offered good concealment for infiltrating enemy'.[58] As an infantryman with 1st Cavalry Division put it: 'the North Koreans had a habit of hiding in the bush'.[59]

The Americans also found maintaining adequate defensive positions a challenge. Glenn Ellison, a soldier with 27th Infantry Regiment, observed that within his unit it became common practice to use two-man fox holes. 'This served two purposes; it provided a buddy system of defence and allowed for a two-shift security system at night'.[60] Under such conditions early warning devices were useful, and could consist of old ration cans containing stones or metal fragments that were strung up on the approaches to positions and rattled when they were disturbed. Corporal Richard Benedict of 8th Cavalry Regiment, 1st Cavalry Division, discovered that these enabled defenders to direct fire against North Koreans before they reached American positions.[61]

Similarly, 'grazing fields of fire' from the sides of hills or forward slopes could be useful, but equally infantrymen had to appreciate the value of plunging fire from areas of high ground.[62] As in the Second World War, especially in the mountains of Italy, the benefit of reverse slope positions was again apparent in Korea. These made it harder for the enemy to attempt to neutralise defences with observed fire, and ensured that enemy attacks were launched with a less clear impression of what they were facing. However, this was not lost on the NKPA either, who typically employed well-concealed defensive positions that 'held long frontages, the top slopes of hills and often reverse slope positions'.[63]

Typically, the North Koreans were stubborn in defence, and invariably made life difficult for the attacker, assisted by the terrain. An officer with 24th Infantry Regiment recalled an assault on an enemy hill, shortly after breaking out from the Pusan Perimeter: 'it required herculean effort to push ourselves forward to reach the top. The enemy didn't give up easily, and the men had to be prodded forward to take the hill'[64] During an assault on Obong-ni Ridge, Marine units had to contend with 'sniping fire from the crest and forward slopes', before finding that 'the summit suddenly came alive with Communist machine guns', so that 'intense fire poured down on the attackers'.[65] Despite the difficulties and dangers in such situations, Marines, as one veteran explained, were motivated by 'the fear of letting your buddies down. There's an almost unbelievable loyalty among men in a rifle company, and you don't want to be the guy to break that bond. You didn't want to die, but you also didn't want to embarrass yourself by failing your buddies'.[66]

Conversely, other soldiers found that NKPA units didn't linger to offer much in the way of defence. Instead, much like the Germans in the world wars, they favoured fierce and rapid counter-attacks, before UN forces had time to consolidate a position. A captured North Korean soldier under interrogation stressed, 'our troops make strategic withdrawals when the enemy attacks. Our troops then attack from the flanks and encircle the enemy with superior numerical strength'.[67]

A sergeant leading a patrol from 1 MX on the Naktong River recounted:

> Having ordered the platoon to fix bayonets in preparation for an assault on the lightly held trenches, I rapidly changed my mind, when a North Korean wearing a very thick leather coat suddenly appeared... on the skyline of the crest, facing the reverse slopes and frantically waving his arms. Almost immediately, about 150 men appeared over the crest and occupied the near empty trenches. Realising we were in very serious trouble, I ordered the platoon to withdraw, and fortunately we were soon out of sight of the enemy due to the convex nature of the ground..., which protected us from any fire from the trenches.[68]

Ultimately, whether in defence or attack, there came a time when hand-to-hand combat might be necessary, especially given the NKPA's propensity for 'Banzai'-type charges in order to close with the enemy. At such close quarters any available weapon or even entrenching tools and bare fists might have to be deployed. One American private soldier from 29th Infantry Regiment commented that under such conditions: 'When your weapon went empty there was no time to reload; you just had to use it like a baseball bat', and fight with 'your bayonet, fists, teeth, or anything else you could get your hands on'.[69]

Inchon and Seoul

On 15 September 1950, the pattern of the Korean War changed radically when Operation Chromite, an amphibious landing, was launched at Inchon around 150 miles behind enemy lines, and only 20 miles west of the ROK capital Seoul. It cut the NKPA forces in the south off from their supply lines, and trapped them between the Pusan Perimeter and the Inchon landing force. Lieutenant Colonel Ray Murray commanded 5th Marines, 1st Marine Division, during the operation and later stated, 'I can't think of an important part of Inchon that went wrong… it went like clockwork'. Likewise, another senior Marine officer, Harold Roise, reckoned the landing 'was almost a complete surprise. Just about the only casualties my battalion suffered occurred in the weapons company [equivalent to a British support company] and were inflicted by friendly fire'.[70]

The impression given in much of the literature on the war is that Operation Chromite was a master stroke, an event that highlighted General MacArthur's genius and strategic vision. Although extremely bold, if it failed it risked turning into a latter-day Anzio-type situation, where an ambitious landing behind German lines in Italy during 1944 became a protracted battle of attrition. Effectively it was a reworking of the 'Bluehearts' idea, and according to military historian Clay Blair was based on 'a plan known as SL-17, which assumed a NKPA invasion, a retreat to and defence of a perimeter at Pusan, followed by an amphibious landing at Inchon' that had been approved by the Pentagon prior to the Korean War.[71]

Even so, numerous difficulties had to be overcome by General MacArthur, ranging from objections by the Joint Chiefs of Staff, who favoured a landing that was nearer to Pusan, to the practical difficulties of landing at Inchon where 'extreme tides, mud flats, and high sea wall made amphibious operations exceptionally risky'.[72] In addition, the coastline around Inchon and the island of Wolmi-do appeared to be well covered by various types of artillery and defensive emplacements, although it was not thought that all these positions were occupied.

In the weeks preceding the landings, American naval officer Eugene Clark bravely led a covert mission ashore that gathered much valuable intelligence on the area. General MacArthur was also fortunate in that he could rely on the professionalism of the Marine Corps and US Navy, ably supported by ships from the Royal Navy. It transpired that despite pockets of fierce resistance, the general quality of the North Korean units defending the area was less formidable than those fighting the UN in the south. Within the Marine Corps in 1950, particularly at officer level, were numerous veterans of the Pacific campaign during the Second World War. Such personnel had an abundance of knowledge of opposed amphibious landings on which to draw. Historian Max Hastings noted: 'These men understood from experience every subtlety of tides, beach gradients, unloading capacity, and fire support plans'.[73]

Initially Wolmi-do had to be seized as it commanded the seaward approaches to Inchon and was linked to the city via a causeway. If it was it ignored, any invading force ran the risk of being exposed to heavy, close-range enfilading fire from the island. Here the assault by 3rd Battalion 5th Marines at Green Beach was dependent on the early morning tide, and the idea was to storm the island as rapidly as possible. One Marine platoon commander who took part remembered: 'There was some tension and a lot of excitement. Every rifleman knew what the plan of fire would be: naval gunfire, air, rockets, air. The Corsairs [fighter-bombers] would be working over Wolmi-do seconds before the first wave landed'.[74]

In contrast, Marine Captain Francis Fenton landed at Red Beach in front of the city where there was no natural beach at high water, only a high sea wall, and at low tide extensive mud flats would have to be negotiated which would be awkward and dangerous. His unit landed against the sea wall, which was around 15 feet above the water level, and in many cases this necessitated the deployment of scaling ladders from their landing craft. This 'meant that only two men at a time could get out of the boats and climb up onto the sea wall. Equipment had to be lifted by lashing and lowering lines'.[75]

Another complication of Operation Chromite was 'the necessity to deliver two widely separated simultaneous regimental assaults'.[76] While 5th Marines secured their objectives at Red and Green beaches, 1st Marines were tasked with landing to the south of Inchon at Blue Beach, the aim being that this two-pronged approach would secure the port of Inchon as rapidly as possible so as to support the campaign for Seoul. The Marines at Blue Beach were followed up by the American 7th Infantry Division that was to link up with General Walker's forces as they broke out from the Pusan Perimeter and advanced northwards. Blue Beach had the advantage that it offered the Marines more room for manoeuvre, and unlike the other beaches it was free from the constricting urban space of Inchon in which to fight. However, to take advantage of this it proved essential to bombard the land either side of the beach, so as to prevent the defenders from dominating the lengthy approach to the beach over mud flats. Despite these challenges, American casualties during the entire operation were slight. According to one account of the Inchon landings, twenty-one servicemen were killed, one was recorded as missing and 174 were wounded.[77]

The capture of Inchon paved the way for the Marines and elements of 7th Division to advance on Seoul, the battered remains of which were liberated on 28–29 September 1950. Compared with the army, the Marines tended to take a more direct approach in the fighting during this period, and drew some criticism for it. One army officer claimed:

> On that march to Seoul, I saw Marines doing things no army unit would think of. I watched them crossing that great sweep of wide open ground in front of Kimpo airfield, hundreds of young men rising up and starting across the flats in open order. They took far more casualties than we considered appropriate.[78]

The fighting for Seoul was bitter as Marines sought to wrestle it street by street from the North Koreans, while simultaneously attempting to preserve as much of the city as possible, particularly its historical monuments. General Almond, who commanded X Corps, understandably infuriated Marine commanders by resenting their methodical approach, and pulling resources away from them to support 7th Division. However, the troops on the ground were more concerned by the difficulties immediately facing them. According to British war correspondent Reginald Thompson, what greeted American troops at Seoul was:

> An appalling inferno of din and destruction with the tearing noise of Corsair dive bombers blasting right ahead, and the livid flashes of the tank guns, the harsh, fierce crackle of blazing wooden build-ings, telegraph and high-tension poles collapsing in utter chaos of wires… it seemed indeed that 'all hell was let loose' upon this city.[79]

For young Marines and soldiers alike, the Inchon Seoul campaign was an introduction to the harsh realities of war. Leroy Schuff joined the Marine Corps as an 18-year-old in February 1950, and landed as a machine-gunner with Dog Company, 2nd Battalion, 5th Marines, at Inchon. He recalled it was burning like an inferno and the city appeared to be a pile of rubble. The lead-ing rifle platoons that he was supporting met resistance and the enemy was surprised.[80] Similarly, during the fighting for Seoul, William Wood from B Battery, 49th FAB, 7th Infantry Division, first witnessed the death of comrades. He didn't know what to do, but fortunately an experienced sergeant grabbed him and told him that he would cope, and they stuck close by that night, although nobody had any sleep.[81]

The Breakout and Push North

Simultaneously with the Inchon landings, Eighth Army was tasked with breaking out from the Pusan Perimeter, despite being under continued pressure from the NKPA. On 16 September 1950 General Walker was ordered to thrust northwards, destroy what remained of the NKPA and link up with X Corps. This was not as straightforward as it sounds, as the enemy, despite heavy losses, were not as demoralised as General MacArthur and his staff presumed. Battles during mid-September in the north-west sector of the Pusan Perimeter bore this out. These centred on American assaults against NKPA hilltop positions, including Hill 174 where one infantry unit launched eleven separate attacks before it finally succeeded in securing the feature. Victor Fox, a soldier who was present, recorded

> Around our positions the enemy dead lay in terrible positions...
> Most had been badly mangled by artillery fire... the stench...
> became stifling... In all the time I spent on Hill 174 there was never
> an opportunity to remove the corpses that surrounded us. The con-
> stant, "deadly firefight" made this impossible.[82]

For the breakout Eighth Army, newly reinforced via Pusan, was split into two corps: I Corps under Major General Frank W. 'Shrimp' Milburn, and IX Corps commanded by Lieutenant General John B. Coulter. The former was to drive north-west as the main attack, while IX Corps was to advance to the south-west, and clear the area of guerrilla forces that had been strengthened by troops from the NKPA who had been cut off in the mountainous terrain of western Korea. As the author Joseph Goulden stressed, 'major portions of the NKPA managed to escape to the north or melt into the South Korean countryside as guerrilla bands'.[83] At the same time ROK divisions that had performed with mixed results were expected to advance up the east coast, where enemy resistance was thought to be minimal.

As Seoul was being liberated, with the approval of the President, the Joint Chiefs of Staff also authorised General MacArthur to pursue operations north of the 38th Parallel. In early October 1950 ROK infantry crossed the line, shortly to be followed by elements from 1st Cavalry Division that headed towards Kaesong. As Colonel Robert Heinl (USMC) remarked 'no one yet knew that Red China had determined that the crossing of the 38th Parallel by US troops – made possible by Inchon – was the contingency which would precipitate Chinese intervention in Korea'.[84] With the NKPA on the run and reeling from the effect of Inchon, it did genuinely look to troops and their commanders as if the war might possibly be over by Christmas.

Michael Eastap, an NCO with 1 MX, recorded the conditions facing his unit as they pursued their North Korean adversary up the peninsula.

> We appreciated that they had fought well... we had no illusions about their capabilities in that respect, but we at this time did realise that they were on the run, were somewhat disorganised. We tried not to get too complacent about it, perhaps some UN units did. They were certainly good at tactics, they could certainly hide their artillery and their supporting fire, and that type of North Korean was giving us trouble right from the beginning of the advance... hidden artillery support or support weapons, just putting a few shots down at us at different times of the day. And they took quite a lot of time finding and eliminating, but we didn't come across any more full size NKPA units after the initial advance across the River Naktong.[85]

During the breakout and pursuit northwards, leadership remained an important issue, particularly for American army units. Historian Russell Gugeler asserted that:

> While the American soldier is typified by courage, he is at the same time, universally marked as an impulsive, intelligent individualist. Thus it is that strong leadership and guidance are necessary to weld a group of American soldiers into a singular unit of specific purpose.[86]

In contrast, in the British Army, although strong emphasis was placed on officers as leaders, the regimental system was prized as an essential ingredient in instilling esprit de corps.

As they advanced, UN forces simultaneously had to be prepared to return to the defensive when necessary, particularly when dealing with bands of North Korean guerrillas, often regular troops who had dispersed to the hills. An officer from 1st Battalion Gloucestershire Regiment (Glosters) stressed 'a drill in case of ambush is... essential. Such a drill must be prepared whether moving on foot or in motor transport'.[87] At Sibyon-ni, 1st Battalion Royal Northumberland Fusiliers (RNF) countered significant guerrilla activity on 30 November 1950. Although the enemy were dubbed guerrillas, they proved highly capable. For three hours two companies from the RNF faced 'continuous and determined attacks, and infiltrations by snipers' by around 1,200 enemy troops.[88]

American and British infantry increasingly also had to contend with hill/mountain warfare, which again had tactical implications. Often some form of fire support was available for the infantry. In late September 1950 elements of 1 A&SH were assisted by M-24 light and Sherman (76mm and 105mm) medium tanks from the Reconnaissance Company of 24th Division near Songju. 'The tank shooting was quite excellent', enabling the infantry to seize their objectives, and 'company battle drill worked well', including communication between tanks and infantry.[89] However, as a senior British officer emphasised, while artillery, tanks and aircraft could 'always assist', ultimately the 'enemy on hilltops could only be successfully removed by infantry assaulting their positions', often at bayonet point.[90]

Sergeant Boris Spiroff (1st Cavalry Division) commented that

> Going up-hill against a dug-in enemy is slow and difficult. The best way to advance is by leapfrog method, one platoon at a time… It's so difficult firing weapons while moving uphill, especially so on an unseen, well-camouflaged, dug-in enemy.[91]

One method of dealing with this challenge was to employ what the British Army termed 'pepper-potting'. As an officer from 1 A&SH explained, it was based around fire and movement

> And requires much training and skill to execute properly. In essence it is that while some men dash forward, others give them covering fire before they themselves advance under cover of fire from those ahead. It appears haphazard and it is confusing to the enemy, who is offered no good targets and probably cannot even estimate the number of soldiers against him.[92]

Another method of attacking hill positions was developed by the Glosters known as the 'Winkle Group.' Brigadier M.G. Harvey served as a captain with D Company, and outlined this approach. Typically, Winkle Groups had:

> Four Stens, man-pack flame throwers, two grenade men and two flank Brens. The supporting fire keeps the [enemy's] heads down ahead, but when this lifts the Stens fire into the immediate bunkers and prevent [enemy troops] lobbing grenades down on you, and the grenadiers dash in and throw into the bunker. The flame quietens down the next bunker and the Brens keep the enemy heads down and provide immediate flank protection and close support. Although your advance is on a very narrow front, perhaps only five or six yards wide, this method permits you to deal with the enemy

piecemeal, and your concentration of automatic fire in the 'Winkle Group' kills the other fellow before he can throw his grenade.[93]

The hills and mountains in Korea also proved a burden for most troops that encountered them. As Captain A. Fowle, from 170th Independent Mortar Battery, Royal Artillery, admitted, 'as with nearly all new arrivals in the battle area I felt physically untrained for the first few weeks'.[94] Curtis Morrow joined 24th Infantry Regiment, 25th Infantry Division, as a rifleman in late 1950. A 'difficult task we foot soldiers had to deal with in Korea was those damn mountains. We fought our way up and down them, up and down... Usually when we reached the halfway point we'd be exhausted'. Typically they would have marched several miles before even embarking on an assault.[95]

Ronald Yetman, a Regular Army NCO with 1 A&SH, found the terrain awkward to deal with, especially as at this stage whatever troops needed had to be carried. It was

> Nothing like I'd been trained for, my army training for normal 'battle conditions' was in flat countryside. In Korea there was no such thing as flat countryside, not for long, just hilly country. You walked up the road to your battle position went up a hill and came down it the next day. Everything had to be carried... The hills were quite big in some cases and by the time your halfway up you'd be out of breath.[96]

A corollary of this strenuous existence was that, in the infantry at least, there were seldom any fat soldiers, and many veterans recall losing weight on operations.

British soldiers often tried to fight while lightly equipped, but this created a requirement to bring up defensive stores and bedding later on, if they were to hold a position. A company commander from the Glosters reckoned that in November–December 1950, 'the infantry could go anywhere', but 'the necessity of taking with them warm bedding undoubtedly made movement to a defensive position slow. Reserve ammunition and rations also have to be carried to the tops of the hills, a most laborious undertaking, but there was no alternative. Similarly, when moving downhill again time had to be allowed for moving the kit'.[97] The situation was less severe in warmer weather, and as the war progressed, both the Americans and British made increasing use of Korean labourers to assist troops by transporting supplies in the hills.

During October and November 1950, it became clear that the Americans and British were no longer simply facing the NKPA. At Unsan in North Korea during this period Sergeant Boris Spiroff became aware of Chinese soldiers who appeared 'to be much better and more disciplined than North Koreans', and would shortly put in a massive counterattack against American units in that area.[98] BAR man Glen Bailey remembered that the Chinese entry was a

> Big surprise. We had heard they were coming from other outfits but they had no feeling of life either. They were just masses of soldiers. 1 out of 3 did not have a weapon. One guy got shot he would grab his weapon and keep right on coming and we had barbed wire out in places but the first wave would lay on it and second wave go over... we had to fight our way out to withdraw, it was chaotic.[99]

In November and December 1950, and in their subsequent offensives against the UN forces, the Chinese tended to favour mass-attack tactics. These were steeped in Mao's 'man over weapons' philosophy, and often followed what was termed the 'one point-two sides method'. This was:

> A frontal fix at the base of the V with simultaneous double envelopment executed suddenly and precisely. The attack was characterised by its intensity, a quality the Chinese describe as *san-meng kung-tso*, or 'the three fierce actions', i.e., fierce fires, fierce assaults, fierce pursuit.[100]

Such tactics were initially a shock, and challenging for American and British units to counter. In the winter of 1950 Eighth Army was forced into an ignominious long retreat from North Korea in the wake of the Chinese intervention. As Colonel Michael Hickey put it, 'panic was setting in' and 'Bug-out fever had gripped the Americans and seemed incurable'.[101]

One American infantry officer later remarked:

> This was the great bugout. In ten days I believe the Eighth Army retreated one hundred and thirty miles. It was not an orderly retreat. I hesitate to call it a complete rout, because some units did hold their ground under the most appalling conditions. But just about everybody had only one thing in mind, and that was to get out of the trap the Chinese had sprung on us.[102]

Similarly, First Lieutenant Charles Payne from 19th Infantry Regiment vividly recalled the tension of this period: 'Seems as though we were almost in sight of the Yalu when out of the blue came orders to get south fast, no questions... We had learned the Chinese were over the river and running around North Korea'. Ahead of his unit lay a convoy that had been ambushed by the Chinese, and it emphasized how vulnerable they were to such 'hit-and-run'-style tactics as they attempted to head for a new position further south.[103]

According to military historian S.L.A. Marshall, who studied US Army combat performance in 1950–51, the Chinese didn't 'characteristically employ mass... in the way that the Red Army used it against the Germans in operations in the Ukraine during World War II, coming in such numbers that the human sea absorbed and ultimately smothered the fire volume'. Rather they 'tend to move against our works in multiple, thin lines, well-spaced each from the other, after having deployed out of column in the last phase of the approach'. Ground was also significant, as it encouraged dispersion, plus 'the ridges are not evenly bottomed or sided. There are frequent bulges, out-croppings, draws, and small ravines', so even if 'the attacking line advances uniformly, no defending weapon is likely to have a clear field of fire against any significant number of the enemy'.[104]

Similarly, based on his experiences with the Glosters, Brigadier Harvey maintained that the Chinese invariably attacked at night so as to negate UN firepower, and small, lightly equipped patrols would 'move with great speed up every ridge.' These would 'feel the extent of your perimeter, and sound out the "widest approach" and your "weakest fire".' During this 'feeling out' process they would 'carry out this principle on every piece of high ground in the area. Any ground not held will immediately become a MMG or mortar position', held by just enough men to maintain the weapon. The 'sounding out' was

> Now complete, and the MMG has located your positions very accurately from your fire at the 'feeler groups'. They now have your positions under heavy MMG fire from six to twelve places at once. Under cover of this, a great mass will have worked their way up under the lee of your weakest flank... Whistles and horns will herald a mass assault.[105]

The latter were used for communication by Chinese units, but in keeping with Chinese tradition the use of noise sought 'to encourage the ardour of the attackers and paralyse the defenders with fear'.[106]

A company commander with 1st Battalion Royal Ulster Rifles (RUR) admitted that 'quite a large number of the men were definitely surprised at the Chinese night warfare and their methods of infiltration and "noises off" trumpets, whistles, gongs, slogans etc.'[107] Similarly, one of his fellow officers considered that the Chinese use of mass was a surprise, because 'the concentration of enemy at the point they were going to attack ensured that they had at least a 10 to 1 superiority'. In his opinion they were also 'most excellent at night work' and the 'lightness of his equipment and simple way of feeding and living made him very mobile over the mountainous country'.[108] Another British officer reckoned that Chinese infantry appeared to cover ground by night with 'amazing speed'. He also considered that his company was shocked by

> The speed with which his main body would follow up a probing patrol... and dig individual shell scrapes under cover of confusion caused by his patrol. Major attack would follow within an hour of the patrol's withdrawal. This method did in the early stages find us short of ammunition, and slightly relaxed, feeling that the patrol was all that would come that night.[109]

Corporal Bertram Sebresos from the American 7th Infantry Regiment remembered the Chinese launching an attack near midnight during November 1950, with 'a wailing bugle call' that 'was real eerie... It gave me goose bumps'. Subsequently, tanks and mortars supporting his unit 'got the range but the human mass continued forward' before eventually 'our entire line erupted in a firing frenzy'.[110] Similarly, a British artillery officer, who served in theatre during 1950–51, recorded that the Chinese use of noise at night 'was unusual, you didn't know what to expect, except that an attack was coming. It seemed to give the impression of ghost-like remote control of the battle'.[111]

Under such conditions trigger fatigue could be a problem, as although support weapons had an important part to play, ultimately mass attacks forced infantry to mount a defence using their own resources. One British company commander explained: 'the trigger finger became exhausted with killing, and his men finished up by pulling the triggers of their weapons with the third, fourth and little fingers'.[112] Faced with such mass-attack tactics, Sam Mercer, a regular soldier with the Glosters, thought that 'in retrospect... greater firepower would have been beneficial [to British infantry that lacked automatic firepower, especially at company/platoon level] but fire control with bolt action [Lee Enfield] rifles was effective when done properly and there was less ammunition to carry than with automatic weapons'.[113]

The potential dangers of trying to provide extra ammunition to ward off mass attacks were demonstrated by an anonymous American NCO who spoke to S.L.A. Marshall. Although troops were not supposed to take loose ammunition into 'an active position', many did so, and at night, coupled with the nervous tension of battlefield conditions, they often found it difficult to fill clips for their weapons. 'Though I have had many nights in combat, this sweat of having to deal with loose ammunition in the dark was the most demoralizing experience I have known'.[114]

If weapons failed to function effectively this could have serious consequences. Failure might result from negligence if a weapon had not been maintained and cleaned properly, especially in the dust of a Korean summer. Equally, winter conditions could result in mechanisms freezing, despite the best efforts of soldiers to use lubricants intended to prevent this. However, given that much of the ammunition deployed came from aging Second World War stockpiles, faulty ordinance was a significant issue. In particular, the British two-inch mortar, a light weapon deployed at platoon level, suffered problems. Potentially it could have been very useful at night, because it fired an illuminating round, but these often failed. An officer from the Glosters observed during one action:

> To our frustration, 50 per cent of the bombs failed to be accepted in their mortar barrels! The brief flickering illuminations revealed nothing... I inspected the... 'bomb' failures and was surprised to see Ordnance Quality Control had already rejected them, by putting red paint along the edges of the tail-fins.[115]

However, for all the problems that they presented, Chinese offensive tactics, like those of the NKPA, could be countered with a degree of success, especially if troops held their nerve and maintained their discipline. Lieutenant L.C. Sharpe served with 1 MX in Korea from late September 1950 until April 1951, and afterwards contended that 'the enemy were fanatical but not unbeatable.'[116]

Several means of thwarting Chinese attacks were suggested by Brigadier Harvey. 'Rigid fire control, or the use of grenades only' to engage enemy 'feeler groups' was essential, as it could 'fool the covering groups as to your exact location and leave them guessing as to your exact location and fire plan.'[117] This was because, unlike small arms, grenades didn't give away the defenders' position at night, especially in mountainous/hilly terrain where they could be 'rolled' down slopes. Likewise, hand grenades (British No.36 Mills Bomb) made primitive but nonetheless effective booby traps/early-warning devices that could protect positions when placed inside an old cigarette tin. 'By punching two holes in [the base of tins] and looping signal wire through them; these were then tied to the branches of small trees and bushes, simultaneously drawing the pin when the lever was restrained, and balancing the tin in a fork in the branches.' Any disturbance of the tree/bush would tip up the tin and release the grenade so that it exploded.[118]

According to Brigadier Harvey, automatic firepower needed to be handled flexibly. Each infantry section position needed 'an extra two automatic pits and when the Chinaman has committed his force a rapid re-adjustment of firepower should take place', so that 'he is now fighting a platoon which has six Bren guns'.[119] Defensive positions had also to 'contract at night like a deflating platoon', to prevent penetration by the enemy, who would overwhelm any breach 'by weight of numbers'. Subsequently, day positions should 'extend outwards' to incorporate/command all approaches and dead ground:

> This concentration at night is the only sure way of seeing the light of the next day as a complete company... Be prepared to fire over any of your own platoon weapon slits. Even when overrun, this drill will give you the surest chance to knock him off.[120]

Similarly, an aggressive counterattack drill was essential in Brigadier Harvey's opinion:

> The Chinese will use every crease and fold in the ground; he will be waiting, 'just out of sight', for the next night attack. One of your groups must go and knock him off these positions. Good DF [defensive fire from artillery] may partially do this for you. Re-establish your perimeter and your extensive observation and domination.[121]

In defence the Chinese frequently proved a stubborn opponent. Although they had limited artillery available at this stage in the war, Chinese troops typically proved skilful and accurate in their handling of mortars. Invariably objectives were on high ground, so that American and British attacks had to be mounted up ridges. Brigadier Harvey cautioned:

> Re-entrants are all dominated from two sides and the last stage of the climb, the vital last twenty yards, may be impassable. Your advance up the ridge will be supported by close supporting arms, artillery, tanks etc; and the nature of the ground will allow very close support indeed. A short rest before the last dash to the top is vital. Forward elements must cross the crest together and not in ones and twos which can quickly be mopped up piecemeal.[122]

As another officer from the Glosters discovered, typically 'in defence the Chinese would... remain in their fox holes throughout heavy air and artillery concentrations, showing themselves only when assaulting infantry were close upon their positions.[123] This skill at concealment was remarked upon by several other UN soldiers, including Lieutenant (later Brigadier) J.M. Cubiss of 1st Battalion Royal Northumberland Fusiliers (RNF): 'In defence he did not mind being by-passed and would fire when main body had passed. Automatic weapons cleverly sited and fire withheld until attacking forces fifty yards away'.[124] Similarly, Herbert Ikeda, a platoon commander with 5th RCT, noted that during one attack he, 'moved to the left side of the hill and almost stumbled into a Chinese machine gun pit no more than 20 yards away, firing down into my attacking platoon', which had been well camouflaged, and he was able to kill the machine-gun crew with his .45 pistol before they turned their weapon in his direction.[125]

Much like the Japanese during the Second World War, the Chinese made proficient use of bunkers, which posed innumerable challenges to the attacker. According to the commanding officer of Y Company, 1 RNF, Major (later Lt Col) Robert Leith-Macgregor, these were 'held by a small number of men armed with automatics' and:

> Would be obvious at 150 to 200 yards range and proof against field artillery. Each bunker was covered on all sides by very well sited LMG [light machine gun] pits. The bunker drew fire and was the focus of the attack, and was difficult to take until all LMG pits were silenced. Immediately this occurred enemy counter attacked'.

If successful, this ensured he reoccupied these positions. Also,

> In all defensive positions, the reverse features were most strongly held, and in undulating country the base of the forward slopes which covered the reverse and crest of the main feature. The high ground and tactically important features were always defended.[126]

By the end of 1950, Eighth Army had been forced back to broadly the line of the 38th Parallel, the pre-war dividing line between the two Koreas. Matters were not helped by the death of General Walker in a road accident. He had been a pugnacious commander who had succeeded in holding then breaking out of the Pusan Perimeter. Command of Eighth Army was given to General Matthew B. Ridgway, who had distinguished himself as the commander of 82nd Airborne Division and later XVIII Airborne Corps during the Second World War. His revitalisation of Eighth Army as a combat-effective force during spring 1951 must rank as one of the most notable achievements in twentieth-century military history, and will receive more attention in the next chapter. Throughout this period the British forces were generally regarded as professional and highly competent, as indicated by American commanders' repeated use of them to perform difficult tasks, such acting as rearguards during withdrawals.

Chapter 5

Ground Warfare in Korea: From Chosin to Stalemate

After the success of the Inchon-Seoul campaign, General MacArthur was given permission by the President and JCS to cross the 38th Parallel, provided there was no indication of Soviet or Chinese intervention. Large numbers of NKPA troops were escaping through the mountains of central Korea, so it could justifiably be claimed that the enemy had not been completely destroyed. A move into North Korea would create the opportunity to achieve this, as well as unifying the entire peninsula, supported by free elections. Eighth Army advanced on the western side of Korea, and during early October 1950 ROK forces crossed the 38th Parallel, to be rapidly followed by American, British and other UN troops. This had the backing of the UN, which had passed an ambiguously worded resolution effectively urging that all should be done to ensure stability throughout the entire peninsula.

Once Seoul was liberated in late September 1950, Eighth Army was joined by X Corps under Lieutenant General Edward M. Almond, often portrayed as an ambitious or thrusting commander who desperately sought success, as during the Italian campaign in the Second World War he'd proved an undistinguished commander of 92nd Division. Instead of the two commands being combined as one force, X Corps was deployed as a separate entity on operations in northeast Korea. General MacArthur's decision to split his forces in this way has received much attention, and the popular view is that it was a mistake to open up such a gap between his forces, particularly given the impact of the subsequent Chinese offensives. Historian Clay Blair stated:

> Contrary to the standard Army doctrine, it would divide the major elements of the American ground forces in Korea into two separate and non-interacting commands. Like two different armies, they would be directed by MacArthur or GHQ in Tokyo. Many believed MacArthur and GHQ were too distant from the battlefield to manage these disparate forces properly.[1]

However, the mountainous terrain and poor communications in North Korea made an advance on a broad, well-defined front difficult to accomplish.

Additionally, as Lieutenant Colonel Roy Appleman stressed, General MacArthur could not have attempted to reach 'the border over its whole distance and held the places needed to secure and unify the country', if he had not split his forces in this manner.[2]

X Corps and the Chosin Reservoir Campaign

After some wrangling a plan was thrashed out by General Almond and his staff that saw X Corps shipped to various ports in northeast Korea during October 1950. This was not without some discomfort to many of the troops involved, as they waited for their mission to be finalised while cooped up aboard transports at sea. A journey that might normally be expected to take only a matter of days took upwards of three weeks. Matters were further complicated by the need to clear mines around Wonsan. This led many to christen proceedings 'Operation Yo-Yo', and, as Marine officer Joseph Owen explained, 'our three-night boat ride' became instead 'a three-week ordeal of misery and sickness' during which the holds of his Landing Ship Tank 'stank of unwashed bodies and sweaty clothes'.[3]

Initially it was envisaged that elements of X Corps would move westwards to cut the supply lines of Chinese troops expected to cross the Yalu River and threaten Eighth Army, while the remainder headed towards the Manchurian border with a view to controlling Korea. In the event neither objective was attainable because the Chinese launched a massive surprise attack on 1st Marine Division and elements of 7th Division in the Chosin Reservoir area, which eventually forced surviving units to fight a monumental strategic withdrawal before being evacuated from Hungnam.

Elements from 7th Division started to land at Iwon during late October, and were to position themselves on the distant right flank of the Marines and advance northwards towards the Manchurian border. Chet Kesy landed with 7th Division at Iwon, which he found a beautiful beach. Subsequently, they were loaded onto trucks for the journey north, and came across little towns where local children waved American flags, and it was difficult to imagine that there was war happening.[4]

By 1 November 1950, 7th Division had landed over 18,000 troops, and would shortly engage in its first actions in northeast Korea. Having fought off a North Korean attack with his unit, Chet Kesy encountered a grisly sight in a recently liberated town. What looked like a pile of rice straw proved on closer inspection to be hundreds of frozen corpses stacked together. Before retreating the NKPA had slaughtered the entire town.[5]

During the rest of November heavy combat was experienced by the Division. Richard Gruenther, a junior officer with 17th Infantry Regiment, recalled facing a typical outflanking manoeuvre by North Korean infantry intent on mounting an attack on their rear area. B Battery, 49th Field Artillery Battalion (FAB), was providing support.

> In order to ward off the intruders, the 105mm howitzers were forced to level off and fire point blank into the attacking horde, which was less than 200 yards away. The result was devastating. As shells burst, I could see arms, legs and mortar tubes flying through the air.[6]

On 19 November, the 1st Battalion, 17th Regiment, seized Kapsan, a town approximately 30 miles from the Yalu, in a combined and skilfully coordinated infantry, tank and artillery attack. Heavy fire from the 15th Anti-Aircraft Artillery (AAA) Battalion, using M-19s armed with dual 40mm guns, mounted in revolving turrets on a Chaffee light tank chassis, proved especially devastating in the ground support role. These 'fired a bursting shell and, on automatic, resembled in killing and maiming power 240 fragmentation grenades dropping every minute among an enemy'. The 40mm shells were ideal for 'hard-hitting flat trajectory fire at specific enemy emplacements or weapons up to a distance of two or three miles'.[7]

By late November X Corps 'was scattered across an area of more than four thousand square miles of bare, bleak and rugged mountains', and 17th Regiment had even penetrated as far as the banks of the Yalu River, the border with Communist China.[8] General Almond sent a special message of congratulations to Major General David G. Barr, the commander of 7th Division, stating:

> The fact that only twenty days ago this division landed amphibiously over the beaches at Iwon and advanced 200 miles over tortuous mountain terrain and fought successfully against a determined foe in sub-zero weather will be recorded in history as an outstanding military achievement.[9]

Senior American officers came to witness this event and famously posed for an official photograph. It was also marked by the 'hallowed ritual' of urinating in the Yalu.[10] As Charles Olsen, assistant operations officer to the commander of 1st Battalion, 17th Regiment, recorded:

> One company I was with was the first company to get to the Yalu River, and in that company was a pioneer platoon and we received an order from HQ to blow a hole in the ice on the Yalu River by eight

the next morning as some generals were coming and they wanted to pee in the Yalu River.[11]

Like their counterparts in Eighth Army in the west, during mid-late November 7th Division started making contact with Chinese troops. William Wood, a soldier with B Battery, 49th FAB, recalled seeing tracks in the snow near the Yalu that must have been left by numerous Chinese troops moving into the area and that appeared just as if a herd of buffalo had passed through. When he returned to his unit's communication outpost orders were issued to fall back, and he heard that the 31st and 32nd Regiments were being 'clobbered'.[12]

The fighting to which William Wood alluded presumably referred to the desperate actions in late November conducted by Task Force Faith, as the 32nd RCT became known, after Lieutenant Colonel Don C. Faith (OC 1st Battalion, 32nd Infantry Regiment, 7th Division). The Battalion had been tasked with moving from Hamhung to relieve a Marine unit on the east of the Chosin Reservoir, before continuing to advance towards the Yalu. On 26 November the Battalion was joined by 31st Infantry Regiment (Colonel Allan D. MacLean). He took command of troops on the east side of the reservoir, until he went missing in action, when overall command of the combined force fell to Lieutenant Colonel Faith. It was later confirmed that Colonel MacLean had been captured, only to die of wounds a short time later.

The 31st Regiment brought numerous supporting units with them, including a battery from 15th AAA Battalion, equipped with M-19 and M-16 half-tracks. The latter mounted quadruple calibre .50 machine guns and were originally conceived as anti-aircraft weapons, but in Korea proved invaluable in the ground support role. They fired 'on automatic at the rate of 1,800 rounds a minute' and swept 'a front like a scythe cutting grain', making them potentially devastating against relatively lightly equipped Chinese infantry engaged in mass attacks.[13]

The Chinese initially probed American positions, seeking to draw fire before disappearing. Having established the extent of American defences they later put in heavy attacks and attempted to seize key high ground that threatened the integrity of the Americans' defensive perimeter. By 28 November the various units of 7th Division were hemmed in on all sides, and Lieutenant Colonel Faith's Battalion was separated from Colonel MacLean's forces by around three miles and a frozen inlet of the Chosin Reservoir. Subsequently, air drops were used to resupply troops, despite the proximity of the enemy making this awkward. Kansas farm boy Don McAlister enlisted as a regular soldier during early 1950, and served with 1st Battalion, 32nd Infantry. He remembered, 'receiving them [air drops] was difficult, because the Chinese wanted them as much as we did, and some were dropped far out of reach'. When they did reach American lines often 'belts and clips [of ammunition] were damaged and we had to work in the cold refilling the BAR magazines'.[14]

Private First Class James Ransone vividly recalled the grim conditions facing troops in the perimeter:

> You couldn't leave your hole to use a latrine. We used our helmets instead and threw the human waste outside the holes. Supplies were short. Planes dropping things would miss the perimeter and the Chinese would end up with them. Nothing was working out. We were being shot up bad. We were just in a terrible situation. We were being annihilated.[15]

Facing mounting pressure from the Chinese and with little prospect of relief during November or December, Lieutenant Colonel Faith decided to break out and attempt to reach Hagaru-ri. Here 1st Marine Division held a perimeter that included an airstrip for resupply, evacuation of casualties and the flying in of reinforcements. When the survivors of TF Faith reached Hagaru-ri, the extent of their losses became apparent. According to historian Russel Guegler the casualty figures for 1st Battalion, 32nd Regiment, were representative of the suffering endured by most units. Out of 1,053 troops from that battalion who had started the operation in North Korea, only 181 officers and men remained on 4 December.[16]

The break-out, on foot or by vehicle, was desperate: troops were often hounded by the Chinese, and in some cases suffered from friendly fire, particularly when supporting aircraft dropping napalm missed their intended targets. PFC Ransone witnessed American troops with horrible burns 'as though the skin was curled like fried potato chips', many of whom were in such agony that they begged their comrades to shoot them.[17] Another soldier who survived TF Faith was NCO Chester Bair. He described conditions on reaching a Marine outpost on the southern end of the Chosin Reservoir:

> I was disorientated, exhausted, nearly frozen, hungry and vomiting blood. The temperature at night was 20 or more degrees below zero. The wind was so strong it was hard to stand or walk on the ice.[18]

Simultaneously with 7th Division's operations, 1st Marine Division was landed further south at Wonsan. As William Hopkins, a company commander with 1st Battalion, 1st Marine Division, emphasised, they were effectively akin to 'a small army', replete with their 'own tanks, air force, ground transportation, artillery supply and medical battalions, plus an engineering battalion with the ability to build bridges, roads, airfields, water purification plants, and so forth'.[19] Major General O.P. Smith, who commanded 1st Marine Division, began a methodical advance that may have irked General Almond, but proved eminently sensible given that it appeared that X Corps was in danger of being sucked into the mountains where it could be dealt with piecemeal by the enemy. As his chief of operations, Colonel Alpha Bowser later commented:

> We pulled every trick in the book to slow down our advance, hoping the enemy would show his hand before we got even more widely dispersed than we already were. At the same time, we were building up our levels of supply at selected dumps along the road.[20]

General Smith concentrated his Division in the Hagaru-ri area to the south of the Chosin Reservoir, approximately 64 miles from the port of Hungnam. Work included constructing an airfield that was capable of handling C-47 transport aircraft. Stores were stockpiled, and an operational base established with the necessary headquarters, medical and administrative units. Outposts were also located on high ground covering the road that might be necessary if the Marines found they had to retreat. During late November the 5th and 7th Marine Regiments were ordered to Yudam-ni, around 12 miles from Hagaru, from where they were to establish contact with ROK II Corps on the right flank of Eighth Army. Before this could occur news reached the Marines of a massive Chinese counter-offensive and the collapse of ROK II Corps. By the end of the month 1st Marine Division was also under heavy attack from the Chinese. In response General Smith ordered his troops to form defensive perimeters around Yundam-ni, Hagaru-ri and at Koto-ri, some 10 miles southwards down his Main Supply Route (MSR) near the Funchilin Pass.

Typically, the Chinese sought to employ frontal assaults while simultaneously cutting the MSR behind the Marines' positions. They also held dominating positions along the road back from Yundam-ni, which prevented American troops from easily escaping the Chosin Reservoir area. In doing so the Chinese People's Volunteers (CPV) were harking back to tactics that had proved successful for the Communists during the Chinese Civil War. Notably, this included 'outnumbering the enemy whenever the situation permitted, in order to wipe out entire enemy units… rather than simply repelling the enemy', plus 'achieving surprise as much as possible'. This was done via night warfare and close-range actions intended 'to offset superior enemy firepower'.[21]

However, as against Eighth Army, the 'human wave' or 'human sea' tactics that have predominated the popular image of the Korean War have been mythologised. Rather as Korean War veteran and military historian Lieutenant

Colonel Appleman outlined, the Chinese normally attacked 'in small groups, fire teams of four or five men, or in squad size, or sometimes platoon-sized skirmish parties'. If one squad perished, another was close at hand to continue the assault on the same axis, and yet another if required. This way the Chinese tended to hit the same spot repeatedly 'until they had worn down the defenders of a small sector', who may have run low on ammunition and suffered several casualties in beating off repeated assaults by 'squad sized skirmishers'. Consequently, a larger Chinese group would often be ready to exploit such situations by penetrating the defences at this point and fanning out towards the flanks, generating alarm and confusion as it did so. The Chinese also sought to block escape routes by infiltrating rear areas, which could cause further panic and casualties. Although awkward for 1st Marine Division to deal with, ultimately these tactics were not as successful as they might have been, because unlike Eighth Army the Marines 'did not have an open rear' and could not be readily forced into a hasty, panicked retreat.[22]

Even so, the combat was typically intense, with mounting casualties on both sides. Before shipping out from San Diego to Korea, Marine Robert Samuels from Grandville, Michigan, was designated a BAR (Browning Automatic Rifle) man. He remembered that at the Chosin Reservoir 'everything broke loose… We didn't know it then but we were outnumbered 15 to 1. And it was pretty hectic, they came at you like flies'.[23] Similarly, Corporal Patrick Stingley, a machine gunner attached to Easy Company, 5th Marines, vividly recalled that at dawn after one Chinese assault 'there were so many [enemy] corpses they actually changed the contour of the terrain'.[24]

During the campaign, 1st Marine Division was joined by 41 Commando Royal Marines, which had originally been deployed to Korea as a specialist amphibious raiding unit to mount operations behind enemy lines. All of its 300 personnel were volunteers and highly trained. On 27 November 41 Commando reached Koto-ri, and was subsequently tasked with breaking through to Hagaru-ri under its commander Lieutenant Colonel D.B. Drysdale, together with American units. Once there the survivors augmented the garrison at Hagaru-ri, and were involved in the bitter fighting that saw the defenders break out southwards in freezing conditions. Dave Brady, a 26-year-old Royal Marine, took part in these operations, and particularly remembered the confused conditions encountered during night close-combat.

> Out of the darkness, I saw running shadows heading towards me and in the sporadic light of fires and bursting grenades, I saw they were a line of quilted-jacketed Chinese. As one stumbled into me, I

shouted, and bayonet in hand, I lashed out at the dark shape, stab-
bing him in the face.[25]

The Marines and RM Commando personnel formed a close bond, and it
was the first time since the Boxer Rebellion (1899–1901) that RM personnel
had fought alongside the USMC. Notably, the RM Commandos tended to be
admired by the Americans, not least because, as one Marine officer stressed,
despite the conditions, 'they looked so neat and clean and militarily ship-
shape'.[26]

As the fighting continued during November and December 1950 it became
clear that the Hagaru-ri perimeter could not hold out for ever. General Smith
was ordered to march south towards Koto-ri, and it became a matter of honour
to him and his Marines that they would take out their wounded and as much
equipment as possible. Famously he announced that it was not a retreat, but
'an advance in a different direction'. Technically and tactically this was correct
'because you couldn't withdraw when you are completely surrounded'.[27]

Both in holding the Hagaru-ri perimeter and in the subsequent epic
breakout operation, when hills flanking the road had to be seized and Chinese
roadblocks negotiated, American firepower played a decisive role. During
the campaign it made the tactical approach of the enemy less effective than
it might otherwise have been. It wasn't just the heavy weapons that Marine
units possessed that proved valuable, but also their ready access to effective
artillery and close air support (CAS). A forward observer (FO) at Fox Hill
at the Toktong Pass, for example, transmitted the map coordinates of four
Chinese machine guns that were causing Marines a problem to a battery of
105mm howitzers seven miles away at Hagaru. With the shells on the way,
PFC Lloyd O'Leary (mortar chief) was then ordered to send up two illuminating rounds from his mortars, so that gunners could make adjustments for
a second salvo. His mortar rounds 'lit up the sky just as the [first] 105mm
rounds impacted on the ridge. No adjustment was necessary'. The enemy
machine guns were obliterated along with their crews.[28]

Air-drops were also significant in keeping 1st Marine Division resupplied,
especially with ammunition, as although some was damaged on landing or fell
into enemy hands, the amount recovered in the Hagaru-ri perimeter might
have 'made the difference in firepower capability that enabled the defenders
to sustain their margin of superiority over the Chinese sacrifice attacks'.[29] A
Marine officer observed that 'to nullify Chinese night tactics, regardless of
how large the penetration or infiltration, the defending Marine unit had only
to maintain position until day break'. Subsequently, with 'observation restored',

American fire and air power 'would invariably melt the Chinese mass to impotency'.[30]

Several other practical points were raised by the fighting as well. Marines swiftly learnt that it was tough carrying ammunition up the hills, so when using mortars, for example, it was seldom common practice to bracket a target because it 'was too valuable to be wasted on the niceties'. Chinese ammunition seldom emitted smoke on firing, meaning that troops found it virtually impossible in daylight to detect the muzzle flashes of enemy weapons. Consequently, emphasis was placed on locating enemy positions by sound rather than sight. Importantly, troops learnt never to be silhouetted on the skyline (something applicable to most Korean fighting) where they became 'perfectly outlined targets', and potentially unnecessary casualties.[31]

The 3rd Division played a significant part in the campaign as well, after it deployed to the area during November 1950. It was understrength and augmented by over 8,000 South Korean draftees, so that some 'squads consisted of two American enlisted men and eight Koreans'.[32] Notably, 65th Infantry Regiment, a Puerto Rican outfit, was part of the Division, and comprised: 'white Puerto Ricans, Virgin Islands Negroes, white soldiers from the United States, Negroes from the United States (tank company), Americans of Japanese descent, and finally, integrated South Koreans'.[33]

Initially 3rd Division's task was to relieve 1st Marine Division in the Wonsan area and south of Hamhung, and to protect the southern part of X Corps' zone against guerrillas and the remnants of NKPA units moving up from the south. However, 3rd Division's major action was at the end of November during the Battle of Sachang-ni, when it fought desperately to protect the lower end of the road needed by the Marines if they were to escape entrapment at the Chosin Reservoir.

George Zonge, a regular soldier from 7th Infantry Regiment, recorded how his unit held a series of low hills covering the road, and proved able to successfully adapt their tactics against the Chinese. Soldiers learnt to listen out for enemy whistles or bugles heralding another assault. Then 'we'd pile all our grenades in the empty ammo boxes and hold our fire until we heard the whistles, and then we'd shift positions so that all our firepower was concentrated in the direction of the whistles'. Consequently, the Chinese would target a new part of the line, only to discover 'it would be as strong as the place they'd hit before. They'd try spot after spot, and we'd beat the hallelujah out of them'.[34]

After its ordeal X Corps was eventually evacuated from Wonsan and Hungnam during December 1950. This was a monumental operation, heavily reliant on the US Navy, and throughout it Marines and soldiers held a defensive perimeter. One Hawaiian soldier from 7th Infantry Regiment described how at Hungnam, 'all day and night shells [from warships] whistled overhead without any let up' to prevent the Chinese from attacking.[35]

At Wonsan 'the 3rd Division task force and a Marine shore party group totalling some 3,800 troops loaded themselves, 1,100 vehicles, 10,000 tons of other cargo, and 7,000 refugees aboard transport ships and LSTs provided by Admiral Doyle's Task Force 90'.[36] Likewise, around 105,000 combat personnel, 17,000 vehicles and 35,000 tons of stores, plus 98,000 Korean refugees, were shipped out from Hungnam.[37] John Connor, a member of 1st Raider Company, which like the RM Commandos had been activated to conduct operations behind enemy lines, witnessed the evacuation while covering the withdrawal of the Marines and 7th Division. Huge amounts of supplies were piled up, and what couldn't be evacuated had to be destroyed. '...you could help yourself. You could live on nothing but chocolate bars if you so desired'.[38]

By the end of December X Corps units had all been shipped to South Korea, and the following month were integrated into Eighth Army. Although seen as a strategic defeat, the campaign was viewed by many as a tactical victory for the UNC, not least by troops who took part. As one Marine officer emphasized: 'We kicked shit out of the Chinese first time we met them, which was at Sudong, we were still kicking shit out of them when we crossed the Treadway bridge [Funchilin Pass]. They were surrendering to us not the other way around'.[39] In opposing the Marines, the Chinese Ninth Army Group suffered at least 25,000 killed, in addition to thousands wounded in action or by frostbite.

The Ridgway Effect

In late December 1950 General Matthew B. Ridgway, who had distinguished himself as the commander of 82nd Airborne Division and later XVIII Airborne Corps during the Second World War, replaced General Walker as commander of Eighth Army when the latter was unfortunately killed in a road accident. Justifiably credited as the man 'who rescued Korea', his first task was to meet the Chinese and North Korean's New Year offensive, before leading Eighth Army back onto the attack. In doing so he restored both the morale and combat efficiency of American army units. Key to this success was his rejection of the highly mobile operations that had so far characterized American military involvement in Korea, in favour of methodical advances on broad fronts. These were designed to coordinate the superior firepower at the disposal of UN units (especially the Americans) to inflict heavy casualties on the Communist forces, while maintaining friendly forces intact. General Ridgway referred to this approach as 'good footwork combined with firepower', whereas many of the troops in the line simply termed it 'the meat grinder'.[40]

According to one account, Ridgway:

> was known for his leadership qualities, and as an officer greatly concerned for the welfare of his men. In his command leadership during combat, Ridgway insisted on being up near his front lines; he felt a commander must see with his own eyes what was happening in a critical area and be there to assume personal command of a critical situation if it developed.[41]

When Ridgway arrived in Korea, he promptly donned his trademark airborne webbing with a grenade on the right side and first aid pack on the left, and set about touring the battle area. He was dismayed to find that although Eighth Army units were not lacking in courage, most appeared extremely dispirited. They:

> were simply not mentally and spiritually ready for the sort of action I had been planning... there was too much of a looking-over-your-shoulder attitude, a lack of that special verve, that extra alertness and vigour that seems to exude from an army that is sure of itself and bent on winning.[42]

Militarily this ensured that many units were not patrolling effectively to gain information on the enemy's location and strength. The army was too roadbound. 'It forgot to seize the high ground along its route', or 'maintain contact in its front', and take advantage of the terrain. In other words it was reluctant 'to get off its bloody wheels and put shoe leather to the earth, to get into the hills and among the scrub and meet the enemy where he lived'.[43]

Harry Summers, a young enlisted man in Korea during 1951, observed: 'What Ridgway did primarily was get us off the roads and up into the hills'.[44] In doing so he set about restoring the fighting spirit of Eighth Army, repeating to commanders the old army mantra: 'Find them! Fix them! Fight them! Finish them!'[45] As a leader he was just as good at dealing with subordinate commanders as with the lowliest infantry private, and had a knack for remembering the names and faces of the ordinary soldiers he met. In touring units he sought to put his stamp on them, and his addresses to troops seem to have been effective, and contained what they wanted to hear. On a cold morning in late January 1951, for example, a small detachment of gunners and tank crewmen from the British 29th Brigade were informed by Ridgway:

I want you to know that I am not going to fight for a particular piece of Korean real estate. If they attack us before we are ready, we shall roll with the punches. But then we shall attack them when they are extended. They may have numbers but we have firepower.[46]

Initially Ridgway had hoped to go onto the attack as soon as possible, but his army was not ready, plus the Chinese launched an offensive over New Year 1951. This 'Third Phase Offensive' sought to drive the UN forces below the Han River and set up the conditions for a further 'Spring Offensive' designed to expel UN forces from the peninsula. Consequently, Ridgway was compelled to mount a phased withdrawal beyond the Han and take up defensive positions to meet the Chinese offensive. There was to be no 'bugging out'; rather units performed an organised mutually supporting withdrawal, which resulted in 'minimal loss of equipment and lives and building confidence within units, leaders and soldiers'.[47] The ability of Eighth Army to harness and coordinate its firepower during the withdrawal was similarly significant, and caused heavy losses to the enemy. Meanwhile, in defence the number of field artillery pieces in Eighth Army was tripled 'from four battalions consisting of 78 tubes to sixteen battalions consisting of 240 tubes'.[48]

Another facet of the fighting during January 1951 was that Seoul had once again to be relinquished to the Communists. According to one British soldier '…its once majestic buildings battered into mere shells, stood as grim and silent witness to the passage of defeated armies'. Even worse was the heart-rending sight of desperate Korean refugees, who on leaving Seoul were throwing dead or newborn babies into the icy waters of the Han, bringing 'instant and decisive relief from a burden that could not be buried in the iron hard ground or which the poor mothers were unable to feed'.[49]

Despite efforts to mount a phased withdrawal, conditions were awkward for Eighth Army. Harry Summers reckoned 'morale went so low it dropped off the scale'.[50] Among the hardest hit in early January were ROK units that typically wilted under the pressure. General Ridgway recounted how a few miles north of Seoul he witnessed the terrible sight of elements of 6th ROK Division fleeing in panic, desperate to evade the much-feared Chinese.

They were coming down the road in trucks, the men standing, packed so close together in those big carriers another small boy could not have found space among them. They had abandoned their heavy artillery, their machine guns – all their crew-served weapons. Only a few had kept their rifles. Their only thought was to get away…[51]

To help cover the withdrawal, British units were deployed and became engaged in awkward fighting. Covering any withdrawal can be tricky, and in Korea it was seldom possible to reconnoitre the ground from which rear-guards were to be mounted. Owing to the state of ROK 6th Division, which was virtually combat ineffective by 3 January, the British 27th Brigade was ordered to replace it in the IX Corps sector, and soon deployed covering the Uijongbu–Seoul road. Its commander, Brigadier Basil Coad, later remarked:

> We had now done two rear-guards in three days. The 24th Divisional Commander naively told me that he liked the British troops to do this, as they were a steadying influence on the American soldiers. A nice compliment, but a repetition of anything becomes tiring. Another American commander who passed through us told me his troops would not like to have been left behind in Seoul as we were and seemed quite surprised when told we did not particularly relish it either.[52]

As a junior NCO with 1st Battalion the Middlesex Regiment (1 MX), from 27th Brigade, Bob Yerby gained much experience covering withdrawals during 1950–51. He recalled the kind of close combat that could ensue when contact was made with the Chinese. Typically, they 'came at us in droves, wave after wave came and as fast as we cut them down still more and more came. Because our location was temporary there were no barbed wire defences, just one-man fox holes dug in the soil'. If the enemy broke through,

> Out of our holes we climbed to meet them. You fire your weapon from the hip until the ammunition runs out, you have no time to reload or you would be dead. You jab your bayonet at the man before you and with a sickening crunch you feel it rammed into his body. He cries out, his eyes are wide open in fear, but you are scared too and basic training again helps, you pull your bayonet out and ram it back in again, pulling it out only when he slumps to the ground.[53]

The British 29th Brigade was effectively 'rushed into the void caused by the near destruction of the ROK 12th and 15th regiments' during the early phases of the Chinese offensive.[54] Subsequently, the brigade became embroiled in heavy fighting when attacked near Koyang by 149th Division, Chinese 50th Army, which simultaneously targeted 1st Battalion Royal Ulster Rifles (RUR) on the left flank, and 1st Battalion Royal Northumberland Fusiliers (RNF) on the right. A company commander from the RUR recalled,

> Initially I had a platoon overrun by Chinese pretending to be South
> Koreans – this is always likely to happen when one's allies look and
> act like the enemy, and particularly when one has had so many false
> alarms as we had up to our action North of Seoul 3/4 January 1951.'[55]

Fortunately, the RUR were able to counter-attack and restore their position
relatively rapidly, supported by field guns and mortars from the Royal
Artillery, plus air strikes.

The RNF had a tougher time when their company localities were penetrated by the Chinese, and snipers who had infiltrated in between companies
caused numerous casualties, firing from high ground. A counterattack had to
be launched by W Company, which was in reserve covering crossings on the
Han River, and Churchill Mk VII tanks from C Squadron, 7th Royal Tank
Regiment. Originally intended to be deployed as Crocodile flame-throwing
tanks these proved more useful in Korea as conventional gun tanks.

> The attack, which started at 14:15 hours went very well, and with
> the support fire from the flanks the Chinese rose and fled in large
> numbers, those that did not run gave 'W' Company the opportunity
> of going in with the bayonet and by 16:00 hours the situation was
> completely restored.[56]

However, there were difficulties that had to be overcome, including how
best to handle tanks on narrow, frozen roads. The War Diarist of C Squadron,
7th RTR, noted that after the attack: 'Tank troops withdrew after dark' when
there was 'severe ice' ensuring 'each tank was led by hand, a hazardous operation – it took 3 hours to cover 6 miles'. Simultaneously, the remainder of the
squadron covered the withdrawal of the infantry.[57]

The RUR were supported by Cooper Force, an ad hoc armoured unit
commanded by Captain D. Astley-Cooper (8th King's Royal Irish Hussars),
which comprised the 8th Hussars reconnaissance troop equipped with
Cromwell tanks, plus a further six Cromwell tanks used by 45th Field
Regiment Royal Artillery as observation posts. Given the terrain and narrow
roads with poor bridging, the heavier Centurion tanks of 8th Hussars had
been kept back behind the River Han.

During 3/4 January Cooper Force and elements of RUR were ambushed
by the Chinese, while trying to extricate themselves from the Chaegunghyon
area.

> Vehicles slid off the track in the confusion and blocked the way of
> those behind. The Battle Patrol section, returning from its standing

patrol, found the tanks of Cooper Force engaging the enemy on the hills with their Besa machine guns and with their 75mm guns.[58]

The Battle Patrol was comprised of men from the RUR's Support Company, and regularly transported in Oxford Carriers, a tracked vehicle similar to the Bren gun or Universal Carrier.

Bitter combat ensued against tenacious Chinese infantry, many of whom were prepared to confront the tanks. As the War Diarist of 1 RUR observed, 'confused and close fighting took place, the enemy assault troops being armed with grenades and pole charges'.[59] Edward (Ted) Beckerley, a former wartime tank driver, was re-called from the reserve for Korean service in 1950 with the reconnaissance troop of 8th Hussars. He was astounded that the Chinese seemed prepared to board British tanks and had not encountered such fanaticism before.[60]

Major Howe (45th Field Regiment RA) recorded many of the problems that were confronted during this action, particularly when deploying tanks in the awkward terrain against a determined enemy. This was not something for which 29th Brigade was ideally prepared, having conducted its limited pre-deployment preparations in the flat landscape of Norfolk, which bore little resemblance to Korea.

> At 17:00 hours Battalion HQ had orders to withdraw south of Seoul that evening. The enemy had been quiet all day and it was not anticipated that there would be any difficulty in breaking off contact. Soon after 19:00 hours the marching infantry and the echelon vehicles started back. It was decided that the tanks and infantry carriers should tie in at the end of the column and the infantry should be carried on the tanks... About 21:30 hours when there was still about four serials to pass the start point, enemy machine guns opened up on the column to the left rear of the position. The column was forced to halt and the tanks asked to neutralise with Besa [machine gun] fire. This was achieved to some extent but the enemy kept opening up from fresh localities.
>
> Later it became clear that the enemy were in considerable numbers and that casualties were being caused to our own troop by the enemy mortar and machine gun fire. The tanks fired from their positions for some 20 minutes but by this time the enemy had come in closer and one could not distinguish them from our own troop, many of whom had moved forward on foot. It was then decided to break through up the valley [dubbed 'Happy Valley' by British troops] and over the

pass. This might have been achieved but for the fact that the enemy appeared to have been ready for this and were carrying pole-charges and sticky bombs and also had arranged little heaps of sticks and straw which could be lit to give a silhouette effect.[61]

When the RUR assembled at Suwon it was feared that over 200 casualties had been suffered. This later proved false as stragglers made their way back, 'either from American hospitals where they were given treatment, or even from the area of Pulmiji-Ri, where an American helicopter pilot most gallantly landed… and brought out a total of seven survivors'.[62]

Having observed the progress of the New Year's Offensive, Ridgway was convinced that Chinese tactics had certain weaknesses, despite their advantage of 'sheer numbers'. They tended to probe on a wide front and on meeting resistance 'flow round both flanks and meet in the rear'. The Chinese lacked air support and modern communications, had only limited amounts of armour and artillery, and their other armaments were 'inferior quantitatively and qualitatively' to those of the UN forces.[63] Consequently, Ridgway was determined to get Eighth Army onto an offensive footing, and restore confidence and reinstil aggressiveness, particularly among American units.

A series of limited counter-offensives were launched by Eighth Army: operations Thunderbolt (25–31 January); Roundup (5–11 February); Killer (20 February–6 March); and Ripper (6–31 March). On 14 March Seoul was recaptured by UN forces, and by the end of the month the front line had stabilised roughly along the 38th Parallel, prompting President Truman to seek opening armistice negotiations with the Communists.

These operations tended to be extremely methodical in contrast to the motorised push towards the Yalu earlier in the war. As an NCO with L Company, 35th Infantry Regiment, who took part in Operation Thunderbolt, explained, 'each day meant a foot march' complicated by mountainous terrain. Every night when an objective was reached the commanding officer had to 'locate his sector, boundaries, and defensive line, and apportion these among his platoons'. Each platoon sector then had to be 'apportioned among its squads and occupied by them'. Subsequently, squad leaders had to designate and position two-man fox holes, so it could be an hour or more before a unit dug in. There also had to be 'co-ordination to ensure against being fired on by friendly troops' and sites selected for supporting weapons.[64] PFC Jerry Emer from 5th Cavalry Regiment discovered that during Operation Killer the days 'were like a bad dream. We advanced slowly, ridge by ridge. Patrol, assault, patrol again, assault again – and again, and again. The weather was miserable, and we were often soaked to the skin by cold drizzle or sleet.'[65]

Lieutenant R.M. Cain (1MX) north of the River Han during February–March 1951, typically found Chinese defensive positions a tough proposition to deal with. They were 'well dug with timber and earth cover, even sleeping pits near villages'.[66] Another officer from that same battalion recalled that the enemy 'were very patient when making an ambush' and would employ 'pill boxes… almost invariably covering re-entrants', although these 'had a very limited field of fire.' Like many UN soldiers he noted that the enemy 'appeared to have no concern for their own lives, and many appear to be drugged. They were very frightened of being taken prisoner, and some committed suicide if wounded'.[67]

During these offensives American firepower proved invaluable, and was deliberately employed in an effort to maximise enemy casualties, while maintaining friendly forces intact. Boston-born Edmund Krekorian commanded a platoon with the 3rd Anti-Aircraft Artillery Battalion, 65th RCT, equipped with the M-16 and M-19 half-tracks, deployed in the ground role. During Operation Ripper, these fired onto an enemy position, 'into an area of about twenty yards by twenty yards… Black smoke from the rapid-firing forties began to cloud over the hill as the tracers leaped for cracks, crevices, caves, emplacements – anywhere that a man could hide', enabling the infantry to secure their objective without loss.[68]

Conversely, given that UN forces were advancing methodically, and the enemy were in retreat, it was sometimes possible for troops to have limited, or even no contact with enemy forces. As a young National Service subaltern attached to the Argyll and Sutherland Highlanders, A.C. Gilmour recounted that during Operation Killer: 'I hardly saw any enemy personnel as they had always retreated from the objective by the time I arrived'.[69]

Some of the heaviest combat during this period occurred at Chipyong-ni, where during mid-February 1951 the 23rd RCT under Colonel Paul Freeman was surrounded by the Chinese, who attempted to eliminate it. Had this happened earlier in the campaign then it might have been expected to mount a hasty withdrawal and run the gauntlet of the on-rushing enemy. However, instead they were ordered to hold their positions around Chipyong-ni, and relied on C 119 'Flying Boxcar' aircraft dropping supplies, especially artillery ammunition. Gaps between the battalions holding the area were mined, blocked by wire and systematically covered by fire.

According to one account,

> The tanks and the gun carriages bearing the quad-50s and twin-40s were carefully sited to add their direct fire to the defence. Indirect fire was provided by the 37th FAB, the organic 105mm howitzer

outfit, and a battery of 155mm howitzers provided by B Battery, 503rd Artillery, the segregated unit assigned to 2nd Division. Additionally, the regimental 4.2 inch mortars, and the 81mm mortars of the battalions, plus the 60mm mortars in each rifle company lent their weight to the fire plan.[70]

Alongside the American infantrymen were the volunteers of the 'French Battalion,' commanded by General Ralph Monclar, who had taken a drop in rank to command the unit. For some Americans these French troops, most of whom were hardened regulars, provided something of an 'eye-opener', particularly in relation to their tactics. One favoured French method of dealing with Chinese attacks was to deploy a double line of trenches. When facing an assault the French would withdraw into the second trench, allowing the Chinese to occupy the first, where they would subsequently be trapped as the French launched a savage counterattack with the bayonet.

Close air support was available, and welcomed by the besieged troops. As one soldier explained, it gave you a 'tremendous lift' to witness 'bombing and strafing runs on the surrounding hillsides. Apparently their method was to have the jets drop the napalm to flush the enemy and then the following plane would be a propeller driven unit for strafing'.[71] The tension of the fighting was captured by PFC Ben Judd from F Company, 23rd Infantry Regiment, while facing seemingly endless Chinese attacks.

> Had I enough ammunition? Would I shoot fast enough? Straight enough? Would my fingers move with speed and ease in the below-zero cold while I reloaded a clip? ...There could be no loss of movement, no slack in doing my job.[72]

In an effort to relieve Chipyong-ni, Task Force Crombez was formed, taking its name from its commander, Colonel Marcel G. Crombez. It consisted of the three infantry battalions from 5th Cavalry Regiment, 1st Cavalry Division; plus two FABs and a company of combat engineers, and armour from D Company, 6th Tank Battalion, equipped with M-46 Patton tanks mounting powerful 90mm guns, and two platoons from 70th Tank Battalion that fielded Sherman 'Easy Eights' equipped with 76mm guns.

According to one former American army officer who has studied the battle, the arrival of TF Crombez helped save the position, rather like the Prussian Army's contribution to victory at Waterloo late in the day. However, the numerous enemy assaults also suffered from a lack of coordination, as once battle was launched Chinese commanders possessed little 'ability to command, control, and communicate with their forces'. Similarly, Chinese intelligence-gathering could have been better, as they appeared unaware that the ammunition supply for 23rd RCT was becoming increasingly desperate, and that air drops required improved co-ordination with the besieged ground forces. The American and French troops were also inspired by their leaders, and this bond of trust generated morale among the defenders, and ensured that 'orders would be unquestioningly carried out'.[73]

While the action resulted in victory, casualties were relatively high as 23rd RCT suffered sixty-six dead and 179 wounded, although some returned to duty promptly. The artillery units suffered less – five killed and twenty-two wounded.[74] Likewise, when TF Crombez broke through into the perimeter, only twenty-three soldiers were still on the tanks they had been riding, and many of these were wounded. Another 141 'who had started riding tanks in the column were strung out along the five-mile road over which the TF had raced to the relief of the besieged 23rd Infantry Regiment', many of whom were dead or dying.[75]

One of the significant consequences of the operations outlined above was, as Ridgway hoped, the restoration of the fighting spirit of Eighth Army. Some fifty-four days since he had taken command, it had manged to push the Communist forces across the 38th Parallel and inflict enormous losses on them. One British war correspondent commented:

> Exactly how and why the army was transformed in a few weeks from a mob of dispirited boobs still thinking in terms of a 'press-button war' to a tough and resilient force is still a matter for speculation and debate. I think most of the credit is due to General Ridgway, who had decided there were to be no more 'bug-outs'.[76]

Epic Confrontations: the Battles of the Imjin and Kap'yong

As a result of General Ridgway's limited offensives, not only was Seoul liberated, but the UN forces were in a position to contemplate establishing a defensive line roughly covering the line of the 38th Parallel. However, on 22 April the Chinese Spring Offensive commenced, and put pressure on almost all of the UN front line. In many cases, under its new commander General James Van Fleet, ground was 'given up voluntarily by the Eighth Army, who were concentrating on maintaining their line intact by "rolling with the punch"'.[77] However, serious penetrations occurred at the boundary of the American I and IX Corps near Chorwon; in the vicinity of Kap'yong which was contained by 1st Cavalry Division and 27th British Commonwealth Infantry Brigade; and at the Imjin River at the junction between 1st ROK Division and British 29th Brigade.

On 1 April, 29th Brigade had 'moved up to the line of the River Imjin, known as the Kansas Line, to occupy a frontage of 13,000 yards' with 1st ROK Division on their left and 3rd American Infantry Division on their right.[78] The Belgian Battalion, described by one British officer as 'bearded, wild-looking men', had come under British command and was positioned north of the Imjin, blocking the most likely approach route.[79] South of the river, on the left, was 1st Battalion Gloucestershire Regiment (Glosters), and on the right 1 RNF, with 1 RUR in reserve.

Initially conditions holding the Kansas Line were relatively congenial by Korean standards, as spring weather made soldiering more bearable than during winter. Major John Winn (OC Z Company 1 RNF) found it 'agreeably warm and sunny by day with a fresh wind most of the time' and although nights were 'a trifle chilly... it seldom freezes'. Moreover, wildlife and fauna could enliven the soldiers' lot, including 'little scrubby azaleas' that turned the hillsides 'bright purple' with their small flowers.[80] There was 'no shortage of food, beer or cigarettes', and men returning from patrols/listening posts could be safely held in reverse slope positions and enjoy snatching moments in the April sunshine.[81]

Although many troops in 29th Brigade attempted to dig slit trenches, there were no elaborate defences, such as minefields or barbed wire. David Green, a National Serviceman with C Company from the Glosters, recalled, 'it was believed that we would not be in the position for long, before moving forward to join the new UN line in the general area of the 38th Parallel'. He was surprised to find the River Imjin 'was fordable in most places, so it did not constitute a serious obstacle to any advance from the north'.[82] Similarly, regarding the general lack of defensive preparations, the Intelligence Officer with 1 RNF commented,

> I think it was probably a case of no one knew how long we were going to be there, and they assumed at Brigade level that no one was going to stay there very long. And I can't remember anyone using wire (except trip wires with flares) until after the Imjin.[83]

At this stage in the war the fighting had been fluid, and UN troops had yet to experience the kind of static, defensive warfare that predominated from late 1951 onwards. According to the *St George's Gazette*, 'it was not intended to hold the river line but to destroy such enemy as might cross between line Kansas and the river by armoured sweeps, the while keeping all fording places under constant artillery fire'.[84] Under its commander Brigadier (later Major General) Tom Brodie, a former wartime Chindit, 29th Brigade was imbued with an aggressive outlook, not necessarily a bad characteristic for any military formation to hold, depending on tactical circumstances. As the commanding officer of the Belgian Battalion observed, as UN units moved towards the 38th Parallel, it was 'forbidden to speak of or prepare for defensive action'.[85]

However, it was realised that an enemy offensive was likely, and in order to gather intelligence several probes or patrols were mounted across the Imjin into what was considered 'no man's land'. Invariably these had limited results. Several combined Centurion tanks from 8th Hussars with infantry. Digby Grist, second-in-command of the Glosters, recounted leading an infantry contingent aboard tanks and being ferried across the Imjin on 20 April 1951. 'We were to "swan" for twelve miles into enemy held territory and hunt the elusive enemy out. There were even sappers with us in case the tracks had been mined'.[86] They found no trace of the enemy.

At other times crude Chinese propaganda was discovered, consisting of

> naively worded leaflets... urging the United Nations' troops to give up the fight, and telling them this was a war for the blood-soaked profits of Morgan, Dupont and Rockefeller. Safe conduct was guaranteed to those who surrendered in possession of the leaflet.[87]

David Holdsworth, a platoon commander with D Company, 1 Glosters, recalled that on discovering such notes 'everybody laughed, little did they know in a few weeks they would get their comeuppance'.[88]

Other units had similar experiences, despite the hard work 'by all ranks to see that the patrols have the very best chance to achieve the required results'.[89] Derek Kinne volunteered for Korea and served with 1 RNF. He remembered that his unit would send out patrols with tanks, 'to see if there were any Chinese in the long, ribbon-like trenches that ran around every hill'. Few were ever found and those that were 'never offered us a fight'. At night 'we sent down listening-posts to the river bank but they heard very little'.[90] The Battalion's Intelligence Officer admitted, 'we did not know where the Chinese (enemy) were'. He even overflew the area north of the Imjin in a light aircraft shortly before the battle. 'Our sole purpose was to get some sighting of the enemy... we did not see anything and we were flying low and searching', although one rifle round whistled past the aircraft, they never saw who fired it.[91]

The main reason enemy troops were difficult to detect was that they employed numerous simple but highly effective methods of concealment, particularly from aerial observation. As an officer from 1 RUR emphasised, the Chinese demonstrated

Really first class camouflage and track discipline... South African pilots, whom I have spoken to, stated that they very rarely saw anything worthwhile to shoot at, and that the country side looked absolutely dead after they crossed our lines into North Korea.[92]

Lieutenant Colonel Robert Leith-Macgregor commanded Y Company 1 RNF in Korea. The enemy competed against UN air superiority:

by excellent air and ground camouflage; and by movement at night. It was recorded that if moving by day they carried small bushes, and when aircraft were heard spread out and took cover underneath, similarly in snow each section carried a sheet and hid under it when aircraft were near.[93]

Events during the famous Battle of the Imjim (22–25 April 1951) have been well covered, notably by General Sir Anthony Farrar-Hockley, who served as Adjutant to the Glosters, before bravely leading the remnants of A Company prior to being captured by the Chinese.[94]

A vivid sense of the intensity of the combat can be gleaned from the records of 45th Field Regiment RA. As the organic field regiment to 29th Brigade, it provided invaluable support to infantry, despite having its gun area targeted by the enemy during the battle. Equipped with the reliable 25-pounder Field Gun, which had seen widespread use during the Second World War, the unit fired in excess of 17,000 rounds in support of 29th Brigade, plus a further 12,000 for the American 3rd Division shortly afterwards.[95] The regiment was instrumental in maintaining efficient communications, as its standard wireless procedure was adopted through-out 29th Brigade. Essentially 'every wireless set in the Regiment' was 'on the same net' so that 'everyone could hear what was going on across the whole front', which 'demanded a very high standard of wireless discipline if the net was not to get clogged'.[96]

Extracts from 45th Field Regiment, RA War Diary:

22 April At Chogam-ni: Enemy were seen moving down to the river on the Brigade front during daylight hours. Opportunity targets were engaged. DF [Defensive Fire] SOS for 1 RNF, 1 Glosters and Belgian Battalion in evening as well as many DF tasks.

23 April Firing in support of infantry all night. Enemy got through hills overlooking gun position. 'P' Battery at dawn was firing over open sights at enemy. Gun position was mortared and sniped throughout the day. Continued to fire in support of 29th Brigade. Afternoon pulled back to Sangbi-ri. Sustained heavy enemy attacks, continued throughout the

evening which were fired on by the Regiment and supporting artillery. 1 Glosters cut off. Total rounds fired in 24 hours 4541.

24 April Enemy continue to attack and infiltrate throughout the day. Regiment continue infantry support. Orders issued for general withdrawal.

Total rounds fired in 24 hours 4957.

25 April 1 Glosters held out through the night calling for artillery fire, as much as possible placed in support. Capt. Newcombe MC, RA OP officer with 1 Glosters KIA. 1 Glosters ordered to break out. [Eventually only around 40 survivors from 'D' Company made it safely back to UN lines]. No further artillery support for them after 10.30 hrs. Gun positions again fired on but situation dealt with quickly. Regiment pulled out Battery by Battery as battalions came back. 70th and 116th Field Batteries RA move to Saengol. Final gun area for the night was Majon-ni in support of U.S. 15th Infantry Regiment.

Total rounds fired in 24 hours 7570.[97]

Contrary to the popular and emotive view of the battle, 1 Glosters were not in fact 'annihilated' or 'wiped out', despite failed attempts to rescue them. Once cut off and overrun by the enemy they 'courageously and grimly held on to their position for several days, until their ammunition was exhausted'.[98] Consequently, as Colonel Michael Hickey, a veteran of 29th Brigade, astutely points out, the majority 'sensibly laid down their arms when further resistance was clearly out of the question'.[99] After the battle numerous honours and awards were conferred on members of 1 Glosters, including two Victoria Crosses, and the battalion received the United States President's Distinguished Unit Citation.

However, the legend of the 'Glorious Glosters' has tended to overshadow the fact that the Imjin was fought by the entire 29th Brigade, and not just that illustrious battalion. As the Official Historian commented, 'The other members of the brigade fought no less well. Neither they nor the Glosters sought to be heroes; only to acquit themselves honourably and competently, one among the other'.[100] According to one of the more recent accounts of the battle, total British casualties were 1,091, including 141 who were killed in action.[101]

The fighting at the Imjin raised several issues that were pertinent to British troops that had resonance beyond the battle. The Chinese employed their familiar mass-attack methods, although there was less 'sounding out' prior to their main assault, mounted in at least divisional strength. One reason for this was the enemy were later thought to have a good idea of 29th Brigade's dispositions from 'local civilian sources'. The Imjin was successfully crossed at several points, and rapid infiltration followed. 'The Gloster Echelon area five miles behind their main position was attacked and scuppered the same afternoon.'[102] A platoon commander with 1 Glosters observed, 'mass infiltration' occurred 'through any weak spots… in order to isolate strong points. Then mass attacks on isolated strong points'.[103]

Additionally, areas of high ground were seized, and often became heavy machine-gun positions. An officer with 1 RNF commented:

> The enemy used automatic fire to good effect. Mobile teams of two or three Chinamen boldly manoeuvred these weapons firing tracer and covering the advance of the main body. There were many of these teams and the firepower engendered was tremendous, more particularly when fire was opened from flank or rear which frequently occurred.[104]

General Farrar-Hockley described how this enabled entire company frontages to be engaged by the Chinese 'from ranges in excess of two thousand yards'. Subsequently, if tackled by artillery these well-sited heavy machine guns would divert gunners from more pressing tasks. At closer range mortars and light machine guns were deployed to support Chinese attacks and infiltration. Eventually, it became apparent to the defenders that it was 'not a battle in which courage, tactical and technical superiority will be the means to victory: it is a battle of attrition'. As elsewhere in Korea, the enemy pressed on seemingly regardless of casualties. Ultimately at the Imjin this ensured the defenders were steadily reduced, until the Chinese 'rush in upon the few survivors-and the ground is lost'.[105]

This was despite the fact that in Korea a shooting technique was employed that enabled a well-trained British infantryman to fire thirty rapid shots a minute with the Lee Enfield rifle. To do this the bolt was 'worked with the little finger extended' and this used to pull 'the trigger as soon as the round was chambered, while the others continued to grip the bolt'.[106] After the Imjin, units started employing an extra Bren gun per section in defence and were issued or acquired American manufactured .30 calibre Browning machine guns that again boosted defensive firepower.

For younger, less experienced soldiers, combat at the Imjin represented a steep learning curve. Lofty Large had only joined the Glosters days before the battle, and during one assault acted as a Bren gunner, having offered to carry the weapon for another soldier. 'I ran forward to a position where I could see the top of the hill, hit the deck and prepared to give covering fire as required'. He was immediately rebuked by his platoon sergeant, because all the Brens were wanted in an assault line that would rush uphill to get safely under the expected shower of grenades and close with the enemy. This tactic was completely foreign to Large, although 'the Glosters had obviously done it this way before, as everyone seemed to know what to do'.[107]

Similarly, Lofty Large learnt to appreciate an old soldiers' lesson that if an enemy didn't 'get you with the first shots-when they think they have everything right – then it's unlikely the shooting will improve'. Simultaneously, there was the mixture of 'anger, fear, excitement and exultation' felt when trying 'to hit the right targets', without any sense of hesitation, remorse or pity.[108] Soldiers who experienced hand-to-hand combat during the battle tended to have similar emotions. John Dyer, a National Serviceman with 1 RUR, remembered that it was a case of: 'This guy against me. I don't really want to dispose of him, kill him, take his life, but if he's prepared to take mine, nobody wants to die so it's a matter of defend yourself, so it was really scary'.[109]

There was also the confusion and noise to contend with. The chaplain to the Glosters described an air strike during the battle as 'an inferno of tearing, screaming sound'.[110] This was in addition to sounds such as the rattle of small arms, explosions from grenades, mortars and artillery, plus calls of Chinese bugles. As a private soldier – a fusilier – Derek Kinne 'had no maps, no detailed briefing to tell me what was going on all about me – to the other companies, to the other battalions to the left and to the right of us'.[111] Under the stress of battle soldiers could also lose their sense of time. General Farrar-Hockley recounts how at Hill 235 (Gloster Hill) 'what seemed an hour's action took but three minutes of the morning'.[112]

Crucially, the battle demonstrated that there wasn't enough artillery to perform all the tasks required of it. The military historian Bruce Gudmundsson highlights that 29th Brigade, 'found that its one field regiment of twenty-four 25-pounders, supplemented by a single battery of 4.2-inch mortars, was not up to the job of cooperating with four infantry battalions attacked by Chinese infantry in division strength'. The problem was not one of coordination, as the British practice of employing battery and troop commanders with forward units proved effective, but rather a matter of scale. 'The seven-and-a-half-mile front' held by 29th Brigade 'was too large to be held continuously'. Consequently, the infantry were divided among a number of hill-top positions, and the enemy was able to exploit the gaps in between these, despite suffering from artillery fire from single batteries and threaten gun positions. Moreover, there were not sufficient guns available to 'stonk' areas of low ground between battalions as would have been done during the Second World War. Without the guns the brigade's 'defence was deprived of its glue' and ultimately forced to withdraw.[113]

Similarly, there were implications for the employment of armour. By spring 1951 the Centurion tank had 'showed its remarkable cross-country performance and the deadly accuracy of its gun'. However, C Squadron, 8th Hussars, had to employ their tanks as makeshift armoured personnel carriers to ferry out wounded and survivors from the brigade during its withdrawal. This was only achieved 'with the greatest difficulty and the loss of five tanks'.[114] As one report highlighted:

> Two Centurions covering the exodus had the greatest difficulty in stemming a tide of some 2,000 Chinamen running down the road and through the paddy fields at them. That they held them off long enough for our own infantry to get clear was due far more to their brilliant handling than any unwillingness on the part of the Chinamen, despite enormous casualties, to come on.[115]

While the Battle of the Imjin raged, 27th Brigade was engaged in a similarly desperate struggle near the village of Kap'yong, situated at the confluence of that river and 'a smaller stream where the valley curved around from the northwest to the southwest toward its junction with the Pukhan River'.[116] Again comparatively few UN troops were tasked with holding a wide frontage against a determined and more numerous enemy. The Chinese 9th Army Group sought to destroy 27th Brigade in order to 'open a means of cutting in behind American forces on its flank' – in this case 24th Division.[117] Unknown to the Chinese, at the time of their offensive 27th Brigade had been replaced in the line by 6th ROK Division, and sent to a reserve position near the strategically placed village of Kap'yong.

Subsequently, Australian and Canadian infantry bore the brunt of the fighting, ably supported by New Zealand gunners, plus American armoured and artillery units. Notably, Sherman tanks from A Company, 72nd Tank Battalion (US Army), commanded by Lieutenant Kenneth W. Koch, cooperated closely with Australian troops during 23–24 April, and were thought to have been influential in repelling numerous Chinese attacks, even destroying an entire enemy platoon at point blank range who had unwisely sought cover in a farmhouse. Despite being nearly at the end of its Korean tour of duty, 1 MX was ordered to send a company to assist and reinforce 3rd Battalion Royal Australian Regiment. Moving under overhead tracer fire, D Company (1 MX) were to hold a ridge to the northwest of the Australian position that if it were taken by the Chinese would enable them to swiftly encircle the Australians.

Major Barry Reed recalled the action, in which, as a National Service subaltern, he led a platoon from D Company and was awarded the Military Cross for his bravery, as well as for his overall leadership in Korea from November 1950–May 1951.

> D Company was suddenly asked to go forward at about 4 o'clock in the morning [24 April, 1951] to try and help the Australians, and we marched up along the Kapy'ong Valley – in the dark – and got to a point where the Australian battalion was a bit ahead of us and on the right, and there was sort of Canadians [2nd Princess Patricia's Canadian Light Infantry] back there, and there was a low feature – well, it wasn't that low, but it was a hill, not too high, and Clinton Nolda [OC D Company 1 MX] met the Australian battalion commander, actually, who for some reason had his command post rather low down near the valley than up with his soldiers. [According to one Australian officer the OC 3 RAR always liked to position his Battalion HQ in isolation away from his rifle companies]. And he asked Clinton to take us up onto this feature and try to hold back the Chinese on that side.
>
> Well, of course, when you got up there, it was a very much bigger feature than you could possibly imagine for one company, and already the Chinese were moving around it, and we were no sooner, sort of, we were atop of his, where there was a re-entrant, a knoll, and we sort of set ourselves out – there was no time to dig in – and the Chinese appeared on the opposite side of the knoll, you know, almost immediately, and were clearly in some strength, and it was my Sergeant Bartholomew, an Australian, who'd taken over as my platoon sergeant – at that point... he used the bazooka [3.5 inch Rocket Launcher] rather effectively – but we also got an incoming one which knocked out about five chaps in one of my sections – we had to rally them round – and then in fact Nolda got an order on his radio to withdraw, because it was realised the whole thing was untenable, really... So we managed to get the wounded out, with us, and we had to cross fields, and then cross a river, and then get up a very steep hill; and on the way up this hill we were quite heavily machine-gunned, because the Chinese got up there and captured an American heavy machine-gun which was mounted on a jeep... We got out and eventually late that morning we joined the battalion.[118]

The stand at Kap'yong, in which the Middlesex Regiment had played a part, ensured that 27th Brigade remained intact, and that neighbouring units were protected. As the New Zealand Official Historian remarks, had 'Kap'yong fallen immediately, the Chinese would have been presented with a great opportunity because of its position on the main east-west communication axis', and troops held back by the enemy could have been used to exploit the situation, potentially endangering the entire UN front. Moreover, 'the fluidity and uncertainty of the situation had demanded cool nerves and a determined performance' from the troops that were involved, despite many of the ROKs having 'bugged out'.[119]

By mid-1951, with the failure of the Chinese Spring Offensive, the war started to assume a different character. The front line stabilised roughly along the line of the 38th Parallel, and during the ensuing months neither side proved willing to risk seeking an all-out military victory, particularly the UN owing to the likelihood of suffering unacceptably high casualties. Instead attention started to focus on diplomatic negotiations while fighting continued, eventually leading to static conditions developing, highly reminiscent of the trench warfare on the Western Front during 1916–18.

British and Commonwealth troops undergo training on the 3-inch mortar at the Battle School in Hara Mura, Japan.

Korea witnessed the first widespread military employment of helicopters in a variety of roles, including air-lifting troops.

A Korean house observed by British troops. In the early 1950s Korea was very much an agrarian/peasant society.

The stress of battle is clearly evident on this American officer's face. Korea was far from a simple 'police action'.

Many American troops captured by the North Koreans were executed, especially during 1950–51.

North Korean POWs, or 'gooks', being rounded up by US Marines.

In September 1950 US Marines engaged in bitter urban warfare as Seoul was liberated.

The Chosin Reservoir Campaign was fought under almost unimaginable conditions, with the cold as much an enemy as the Chinese.

A view of positions employed by 61st Light Regiment, Royal Artillery, under static conditions – note the typically hilly Korean terrain.

American positions near Pork Chop Hill – during 1953, numerous enemy attacks were resisted before the hill was eventually abandoned.

A sergeant from the Duke of Wellington's Regiment relaxes at the 38th Parallel, the political frontier between the two Koreas.

A KATCOM (Korean Augmentation Troops Commonwealth Division). Like the Americans, British and Commonwealth units utilised Korean manpower, with mixed results.

Korea was very much an engineers' war, and road-building was one of many vital tasks they performed.

Members of HQ Company (1st Battalion Duke of Wellington's Regiment) wearing cap comforters, a popular item of clothing with the British.

The .30 calibre Browning machine gun was belt-fed, easy to operate and employed by both the Americans and the British.

The 3.5-inch rocket launcher, seen here in action with American troops, was a marked improvement on the Second World War bazooka.

The standard American infantry support weapon was the M20 75mm recoilless rifle, particularly useful against enemy defences.

An Australian soldier demonstrates the sniperscope, a first-generation infra-red night sight, fitted to an American-manufactured carbine.

A 4.2-inch mortar of the Royal Artillery. It proved an effective 'man killer' in Korea, providing support to infantry.

Black American troops prepare a 105mm howitzer for high-angled fire. Crest clearance was a challenge for field artillery during 1950–51.

Royal Artillery personnel receiving sound-ranging data from microphones as part of the counter-bombardment effort against Communist guns/mortars.

The M-40 self-propelled gun mated the 155mm howitzer with a Sherman tank chassis and proved extremely versatile in Korea.

Prodigious amounts of ammunition were stockpiled from 1951–53, when artillery duels occurred under static conditions.

The M-16 half-track or 'quad fifty' was formidable even against troops under cover, and capable of providing prolonged saturation fire.

A British truck-mounted 40mm Bofors light anti-aircraft gun. Like the M-16 it proved useful in the ground role in Korea.

A Marine Corps M-46 tank. In Korea, armour was predominantly employed in support of infantry.

Psychological warfare: to scare supposedly superstitious Chinese troops, many American armoured units painted 'tiger faces' on tanks during spring 1951.

UN ground forces frequently had significant close air support. This included use of napalm, rockets and conventional bombs.

The Korean terrain ensured that evacuating casualties by stretcher was usually a lengthy and awkward business.

American troops receiving treatment at a Regimental Collecting Station, before being evacuated further from the front line.

The H-13 helicopter was the military counterpart of the Bell 47, and radically improved casualty evacuation in Korea.

National Service medic Barry Whiting stands by a direction post employed by 26th Field Ambulance Royal Army Medical Corps.

Conditions were rough in Korea, even for support units. Tents belonging to 26th Field Ambulance (RAMC) are laid out in typically rugged terrain.

Water purification was essential in Korea, and much of the medical effort was directed towards preventative measures against disease.

Chapter 6

Ground Warfare in Korea: Fighting a Limited War

With the relief of General MacArthur on 11 April 1951, his position as UN C-in-C was filled by General Ridgway, and command of Eighth Army went to General Van Fleet. Initially operations centred on the 38th Parallel as the UNC and Communists battled it out for key terrain features. Yet as the year progressed the war increasingly drifted towards static mode. From a military perspective the aim ultimately became maintaining the status quo on the battlefield while armistice talks were held. By late 1951 both sides employed entrenched defensive positions, backed by significant levels of artillery. An American artillery officer highlighted that the 'US Army had been forced into a general revision of its standards for ammunition requirements', particularly as slogans such as Van Fleet's: 'Shoot twice as much artillery; kill twice as many enemy' were used to reinforce army policy.[1]

Likewise, the increased use of artillery by Communist forces, including mortars and rockets, came as a shock, especially to British troops, given that previously combat had been characterised by its comparative absence. Officers reckoned enemy mortars were 'uncannily accurate', appearing to 'follow you around as you moved' and 'had the greatest adverse morale effect', because 'even one bomb can cause so many casualties and cannot be heard coming'.[2]

Battles for key terrain features during 1951–53 were usually costly, and their intensity rivalled combat experienced by Allied personnel during the world wars. Increasing emphasis was placed on patrolling and raiding, which had further overtones of the First World War. In May 1952, the charismatic General Mark Clark, who rose to prominence in the Second World War during the Italian campaign, succeeded Ridgway as UN C-in-C. He highlighted the frustration that fighting a limited war caused UN forces.

> Since it was not our Government's policy to seek a military decision, the next best thing was to make the stalemate more expensive for the Communists than for us, to hit them where it hurt, to worry them, to convince them by force that the price-tag on an armistice was going up, not down.[3]

Fighting for Limited Objectives

Within the context of fighting a limited war, Eighth Army was determined to resist attempts by the Communists to penetrate its lines, and when practicable chose to mount its own local offensives and limited attacks. After the failure of the Chinese Spring Offensive in April 1951, Eighth Army conducted an offensive (Operation Piledriver) all along the line, and eventually regained all the territory lost. This led to the establishment of a defensive line slightly north of the 38th Parallel, dubbed the Kansas-Wyoming Line. Another important facet of the operation was targeting the Communist logistics/communications network centred on what was termed the 'Iron Triangle' of Chorwon, Kumhwa and Pyongyang. This proved to be the last large–scale operation mounted by the American-led UNC during the war, and was undertaken in difficult circumstances. It rained incessantly, troops became exhausted, and increasing enemy resistance was met the longer the operation progressed.

The Kansas Line was intended to act 'as the main line of resistance with defensive positions in depth and elaborately fortified', whereas on the Wyoming Line troops were expected to hold 'hasty field fortifications from which to blunt and delay enemy attacks' prior to withdrawing to their allocated main line positions. North of the Kansas—Wyoming Line patrol bases were established to cover likely enemy approach routes, and Korean civilians were cleared from the area in an effort to prevent enemy agents from mingling with the local population.[4] By June 1951, around 554,000 troops from Eighth Army opposed approximately 569,200 soldiers of North Korean People's Army (NKPA) and Chinese People's Volunteers (CPV), and both sides had received fresh units.

Over the summer, even more limited offensives were launched from the Kansas–Wyoming line in an effort to push the Communists off significant features, notably the Hwachon reservoir, on the central front. This was to improve the overall position held by Eighth Army as peace talks commenced. Sergeant Boris Spiroff (1st Cavalry Division) found that in July 1951, 'minor patrol battles and skirmishes are taking place. Each side is attempting to seize key hill and terrain positions, particularly OPs [Observation Posts]. This is in the event the negotiations break down'.[5] Similarly, reflecting on the fighting he experienced during that summer, a British soldier from 1st Battalion King's Shropshire Light Infantry (KSLI) stated,

> The advance to the North was pure infantry work, marching, climbing and digging – very much like the training the Battalion had practised on the hills of the New Territories [Hong Kong], except now and again the 'exercise' was enlivened by small parties of Chinese who had to be chased from the hilltops.[6]

However, limited operations still proved awkward and resulted in casualties. During August/September 1951, British and Commonwealth units embarked on Operation Minden. This involved crossing the River Imjin to prevent enemy units from improving their defences, denying them the space in no man's land to launch another offensive. Brigadier George Taylor (OC 28th Brigade) commented that during this period 'sudden squalls of hostile mortar and artillery fire reminded one of sterner contests in France', where during summer 1944 after D-Day he had distinguished himself as a battalion commander.[7]

Some of the bitterest fighting occurred from August–November 1951, as both sides attempted to improve their defensive positions around a feature known as the Punchbowl, a large circular valley 'rimmed by hills rising sharply to heights of 1,000 to 2,000 feet above the valley floor'.[8] While the valley itself had limited military significance, the 'high ridges that rimmed it provided direct observation of the UN defences and supply routes in that sector of the "Kansas" front'.[9] Consequently, X Corps was tasked with clearing these, which entailed heavy fighting by ROK units and 1st Marine Division, combined with direct assaults by the American 2nd Infantry Division on Bloody Ridge, where artillery bombardments reduced much of the area to a barren wasteland, devoid of vegetation, and in which lurked a well dug-in and fanatical enemy. One American draftee, who was posted to the area in late 1951, vividly remembered that the trees were 'riddled like kindling' owing to the amount of shelling that had occurred.[10]

It required a solid month of intense fighting to wrestle Heartbreak Ridge, northwest of the Punchbowl, from determined North Korean and Chinese troops, who had been ordered not to yield any ground. Consequently these ridgeline battles were costly in men and materials. Later in 1952, Sherwin Nagelkirk was sent to Heartbreak Ridge with 35th Regiment, 25th Infantry Division, and found:

> A mess there was a foot sticking out the ground here, a hand sticking out the ground there. They must have had a terrific battle there. And we took a lime bucket every morning and sprinkled lime on these body parts. They had sneakers on [Chinese corpses] and they just bulldozed them.[11]

However, ultimately this fighting prevented 'renewal of Communist offensive operations and secured a strong defensive line for the UN Command while the armistice negotiations continued'.[12] By mid-October 2nd Infantry Division alone suffered approximately 3,700 casualties, and most accounts state that enemy losses for the same period were around 25,000. The brutal nature of the fighting led to these ridges being given their dramatic names by the press. Bloody Ridge reflected 'the true nature of battle between armies deeply emplaced on heavily defended main lines of resistance'.[13] At Heartbreak Ridge, as an American infantry officer explained, it was literally heart-breaking to watch soldiers from his unit, 'clusters of little figures', desperately scrambling about on the slopes, 'trying to fight their way up these steep ridges', amid the explosions of enemy mortar rounds and artillery.[14]

American firepower was vital to these ridge-line battles. One field artillery battalion (FAB) fired 'a record 14,425 rounds in twenty-four hours'.[15] The Official Historian highlights that during 13–15 September 1951, when the 23rd Infantry Regiment, 2nd Division, assaulted positions near Heartbreak Ridge, it received 'direct support from the 37th FAB, under Lt Col Linton S. Boatright, and its 105mm howitzers', while the 503rd FAB and 96th FAB (both equipped with 155mm howitzers), plus '38th FAB (105mm howitzer) and Battery C, 780th FAB (8-inch howitzer) provided general support'.[16]

Even with such support, it was still difficult to force Communist troops off their hill-top or ridgeline positions. Typically, well-constructed enemy bunkers proved awkward to deal with, even when held by only a few men with a machine gun. Often 'only a direct hit by the heaviest-calibre artillery was able to destroy them', and this was hard to achieve, because it was difficult to locate bunkers in ground 'chewed up' by artillery. Neither could heavier guns, notably the 155mm Howitzer 'Long Tom' with a rifled barrel, always be positioned to 'snipe' bunkers with the necessary 'direct, low-trajectory fire' capable of destroying them.[17] Like artillery, the infantry's own support weapons, such as mortars and recoilless rifles, could not be relied upon to dislodge such a determined enemy. Accordingly, bunkers often had to be tackled by infantry platoons/squads at close range using grenades and flamethrowers. There was also a danger that infantry might come under friendly fire from their own support weapons, as the white phosphorous grenades (Willie Peter) they carried were employed as markers for tank and recoilless rifle crews, meaning troops had to move away fast when using these on bunkers.[18] American troops started to deploy bunkers on their positions during the ridgeline battles as well. Corporal Benn Judd from F Company, 23rd Infantry Regiment, was pleased to have as his assistant a former hillbilly from the mountains of Kentucky, well versed in the construction of log-cabin chimneys from stone, who built them a good bunker.[19]

Another distinctive feature of the fighting during this period was its sheer physicality. Elroy Roeder was drafted in January 1951 and trained as combat engineer before serving as an infantryman with Easy Company, 23rd Infantry Regiment. As part of a 60mm mortar team he experienced the tail end of the battle for Heartbreak Ridge. Carrying ammunition and grenades up hills was exhausting, even when at the steepest points there were ropes tied to trees to help soldiers pull themselves up. The to-and-fro nature of the fighting was also fatiguing, as they would take a hilltop, only to be rapidly forced off by the Communists, before having to recapture it.[20]

As with most phases of the war, where 'brutal, dirty, fear inspiring' close combat was required, there were examples of extreme bravery during these ridgeline battles.[21] PFC Herbert K. Pililaau, one of fourteen children from Waianae, a working-class suburb of Honolulu, was a gifted musician who under different circumstances probably wouldn't have joined the military. He was drafted, and posted to Korea in March 1951, where he served as Browning Automatic Rifle (BAR) man with C Company, 23rd Infantry Regiment, 2nd Division. His squad was designated to cover a withdrawal by the rest of his unit during fighting for Hill 931 at Bloody Ridge on 17 September. Having refused to vacate his position, and used up all his ammunition and grenades, he eventually threw rocks at the on-rushing North Koreans, before charging them with his bayonet. In the ensuing struggle he was killed. Next day forty dead North Koreans were discovered around his body. Pililaau was later posthumously awarded the Medal of Honour.[22]

From 2–15 October 1951 on the western front in Korea an offensive was launched by I Corps, described as 'quite a battle' by one senior British officer.[23] Known as Operation Commando, it was heavily reliant on 1st Commonwealth Division, especially 28th Brigade, which had arrived during the spring. The division was tasked with mounting an advance of 6,000–8,000 yards along its entire frontage to a new position, referred to as the Jamestown Line. This, in conjunction with action on its flanks, would deny the enemy ground that gave them direct observation over crossings over the River Imjin and roads serving I Corps' defences. Consequently, the division was required to assault and fortify numerous key features, including Maryang-san (Point 317), Kowang-sang (Point 355), and a series of smaller hills running southwest from Point 210 to Point 187, with each of these numbers referring to the height of the feature in metres above mean sea level.[24]

The operation was planned so that each assaulting brigade could in turn call upon the support of the entire divisional artillery (seventy-two 25-pounder guns), along with its organic 4.2-inch mortars, plus American batteries of medium and heavy artillery. This was in addition to air strikes in support of the operation and fire from the various infantry battalions' three-inch mortars and Vickers machine guns, which at times produced 'a continuous sheet of fire.'[25]

Even so, as one soldier from 1 KSLI who took part warned, the Chinese proved 'experts at the art of digging in and are not to be driven off their positions as easily as some appear to imagine.'[26] At Hill 227, which flanked Kowang-sang, troops from A Company 1 KSLI found the position 'very heavily fortified with bunkers and communicating trenches. Support was given by 8th Hussars [Centurion tanks] from Point 210 but nevertheless heavy fighting took place.'[27] A report produced by Staff College afterwards highlighted that, 'deep bunkers with overhead cover' typically gave the enemy 'complete immunity against air and artillery bombardment'. Echoing experience of the First World War, when the barrage ceased Chinese defenders had 'plenty of time to emerge from these shelters, man… weapon pits and inflict severe casualties on our infantry as they climbed towards their objective.'[28]

The nature of the terrain proved challenging. Soldiers from 1st Battalion King's Own Scottish Borderers (KOSB) discovered on 3 October when assaulting a feature near Point 355 that the steepness of the ground and densely wooded areas slowed their rate of advance, making 'keeping direction and control' difficult. After crossing the start line, heavy artillery and mortar fire and snipers added to their problems. The latter had remained hidden in dense undergrowth, holding firing, until leading platoons had passed'. Similarly, the KSLI encountered a determined enemy in 'well sited and ingeniously dug positions', who 'had to be rooted out post by post.'[29]

The terrain also hampered efforts to provide effective cooperation between infantry and their supporting arms. Despite the lavish artillery support available, it was difficult for gunners to estimate the time it would take for infantry 'to reach their objectives', making it virtually 'impossible to arrange' a set-piece timed programme.[30] The 'wooded country' made it impossible for tanks 'to see or have any field of fire,' plus heavy rainfall made 'the going' treacherous in valley bottoms.[31]

Despite these difficulties, when Centurions could get into position, they provided invaluable close support to infantry. At Point 210, A Squadron, 8th Hussars, assisted D Company, 1 KSLI, even though it was reduced to only three tanks, because others had become bogged down. These – *Allenby*, *Abbott's Pride* and *Artist's Dream*, 'crashed their way along heavily wooded ridges' until only around 200 yards from the objective. Then:

> As the infantry descended into low ground for the final assault, they poured HE [high explosive] into the enemy positions, until the infantry entirely confident in the rage of fire passing over their

heads, called for the change to Besa [machine-gun fire]. With this fire support 'D' Company were able to sweep onto the hill with bayonets fixed, and the presence of the tanks virtually erased any prospect of an enemy counter-attack. Around 50 enemy soldiers were killed, and a handful captured, whereas 'D' Company received 15 casualties during the entire assault, a figure kept to a minimum as a result of the effective tank support.[32]

Arguably some of the worst fighting during Operation Commando involved 1 RNF, which had been held in reserve, but during 5–8 October was brought forward to support 3rd Battalion Royal Australian Regiment (RAR) in an attack on Maryang-san. As the commander of Z Company recalled, 1 RNF had 'to take three objectives on a frontage of nearly a mile, including a commanding feature, Hill 217, which overlooked an extensive area of lower ground already in our possession'.[33]

According to 1 RNF's War Diary, the operation commenced 'with a thick ground mist', which was of some benefit to the attacking troops and initially allowed Y and Z Company to make good progress, unobserved from Maryang-san. However, once at Hill 217 (code-named Newcastle) attempts by Z Company 'to make headway and enemy counter-attacks to dislodge us' ensured that 'grenade-throwing battles at hand-to-hand range' occurred. Eventually, shortage of grenades and ammunition forced the company to withdraw, having suffered around 50 per cent casualties. A further assault, but from an alternative angle, followed using W Company, with one platoon attacking frontally while the remainder attempted to work their way through dense undergrowth on the left flank. Again the enemy's tendency to use clusters of grenades, coupled with the fact he was well dug-in, and that the undergrowth aided his concealment, caused problems for the attackers, leading to X Company being ordered up to cover the evacuation of the wounded. That company subsequently attempted another attack, but placed Number 4 Platoon, giving fire support, on the left flank, while Number 5 Platoon assaulted frontally. The terrain and undergrowth again posed a problem, and 'the assault was met by undiminished fire', prior to the Chinese launching another determined counter-attack.[34]

During this period 1 RNF suffered sixteen killed, ninety-four wounded, and three missing, which was particularly tragic and galling given that the battalion was on the verge of being rotated out of the theatre. As a 19½ year-old National Service subaltern, recently commissioned from Eaton Hall OCS, Keith Taylor served as the assistant to the second-in-command, Y Company, 1 RNF, during Operation Commando. He vividly remembered,

It was the first time I had seen dead bodies of people that I knew. I shall never forget that after the battle the RSM invited all the officers in small groups to simply view and say goodbye as it were to officers and ORs who were laid out in a clearing. That was the most incredibly moving experience, which I have never forgotten, and never will. It brought home the reality of war and how ghastly it really is.[35]

Overall the Commonwealth Division suffered around 400 casualties in the operation, comparatively few by Korean War standards. Despite the challenges alluded to above, it was successful in establishing the Jamestown Line. Significantly, after the operation members of the division were bound by 'a common experience of danger, endurance, dependence on one another, and accomplishment', as the second winter of the war beckoned.[36]

Combat under Static Warfare Conditions: October 1951–July 1953

During late October, the stalled peace talks resumed, having been moved at Ridgway's insistence from Kaesong to the small village of Panmunjom, which consequently became famous overnight. One of the major items under dispute was the line of demarcation, which assumed increasing importance at the battlefront. The UNC and Eighth Army operated on the principle that 'if the negotiations broke down or became hopelessly ruined, then an offensive might be launched'.[37] However, despite plans being drawn up, Ridgway considered that proposed offensives would not be worth the casualties likely to be suffered. On 12 November he ordered Van Fleet to adopt what was termed an 'active defence', and limit offensive operations to the capture of outposts, 'while being prepared to exploit opportunities to inflict heavy casualties on the enemy'.[38] The JCS supported Ridgway's approach, and from a UN perspective this set the future pattern of the war, with operations in 1951–53 largely being characterised by small-scale actions and patrolling, coupled with the maintenance of permanent defensive positions against Communist attacks.

In contrast, the Chinese Communist forces, when practicable, were prepared to launch large-scale attacks during this period, chiefly aimed at regaining lost territory and thereby influencing the armistice negotiations. This was despite, from the summer of 1951, facing unprecedented demands in their military history, 'including fighting a positional defence' as conditions moved towards stalemate, and 'protecting logistics from devastating US/UN air interdiction efforts'.[39]

Notably, during November 1951 the Chinese sought to recover positions lost during Operation Commando, including Maryang-san (Point 317), and features held by 1 KSLI, where the Commonwealth Division's frontage seemed over-extended. This was done via daylight assaults, rather than their more common night warfare, and used significant artillery support. During these operations the accuracy of this artillery, and the enemy's apparent 'acceptance of very heavy casualties by marching through minefields in attack and by attacking among his own shells' was unexpected.[40] Clearly it was extremely challenging to defend against a numerically superior enemy prepared to use such 'suicidal tactics', rather than a more orthodox creeping barrage, or even a 'heavy concentration on one's objective just before' an assault.[41]

On 3 November it became clear that something was happening, as despite the Commonwealth Division's DF a trench was being dug towards 1 KOSB positions on the Point 217–317 ridgeline, where a banner appeared reading: 'Go home Britishers or this hill will be your graveyard'.[42] Airstrikes were called using napalm, but the enemy still massed for an assault and deployed artillery methodically and skilfully against select points. On 4 November an intense bombardment developed, 'with shells of all natures falling at the rate of 6,000 an hour'.[43] Under such conditions, defences were destroyed and communications heavily disrupted. An officer who witnessed the attack on 1 KOSB from a neighbouring position commented, 'the enemy control and use of artillery was quite excellent. Approximate length of time between commencement of bombardment and use of short range weapons was 30 minutes'.[44]

Forward elements of the KOSB were subsequently overrun in the ensuing mass infantry attack, and according to one account they 'lacked the close-quarter firepower needed to stop such a determined' enemy assault.[45] Frequently vicious hand-to-hand combat occurred as Chinese infantry made it to the forward slopes of the British positions. At Point 217, for example, every effort was made to clear the crest of the hill from reverse slope positions using 'LMGs [Bren guns] fired from the hip and [Number] 36 and [Number] 80 grenades thrown by parties of men'.[46] Famously, Private Bill Speakman from Cheshire was awarded the Victoria Cross during this fighting. He made numerous grenade charges against the enemy, despite being wounded in the leg, which ultimately helped his B Company to withdraw successfully, as well as inflicting numerous casualties on the enemy. The episode, along with 'the legend of the alcoholic stimulus that played some part in it – passed into the history of the British Army'.[47]

Similarly, at Hill 227 a battalion from the Chinese 569th Regiment sought to eradicate 1 KSLI, starting on 5 November and persisting with attacks that month. The regimental signal officer with 1 KSLI (Lieutenant G.H. Benson) gained an overview of Chinese methods. Their

assault tactics were quite astounding. It would appear as if a
Wembley football crowd was bearing down on one. The 'crowd'
being formed up into waves, each wave assaulting in rapid
succession, but not before the signal of a green Verey light had been
given. This signal had the effect of lifting the enemy shell fire and
starting the attack. The attacks were always forceful and continued
regardless of casualties. The enemy did not like to leave his dead
lying about often and would often remove them with remarkable
rapidity and under heavy fire.[48]

The British attempted to take back ground from the Chinese, especially
at Point 217, where an attack by 1 R Leicesters failed, possibly, according to
Colonel Michael Hickey, because of lack of confidence and the inexperience
and youth of many of the soldiers who took part.[49] This is not to detract from
the individual determination and bravery of many of the soldiers present, but
as the regiment's War Diary and history make clear, it was difficult for assaulting
companies to secure their objectives, given the weight and accuracy of
Chinese shelling and mortaring that caused mounting casualties.[50]

Maryang-san remained in Chinese hands, but other positions were
fortified by the Commonwealth Division, including Hill 227, which had wire
laid 'over 100 yards deep' in places.[51] Historian Max Hastings claims these
defensive battles were representative of 'the kind of local action that [UN]
units up and down the front found themselves compelled to fight at regular
intervals through two years of positional war'. While of significance to those
taking part, they therefore had less relevance to the wider context of the
war.[52] However, these actions, and those fought by American and other UN
contingents during November 1951, might have influenced the peace talks,
owing to the cumulative effect of casualties suffered by the enemy. Later
that month bloody fighting occurred for other hills, including 355 or 'Little
Gibraltar', vital to Eighth Army's defensive system on the Jamestown Line,
which had to be retaken by the American 7th Division, reinforced by 15th
Infantry Regiment and the attached Belgian battalion.

On 27 November Communist delegates at Panmunjom agreed to the principle of having a demarcation line based on the current battlefield situation.
However, the winter ahead 'promised to be filled with frustration' for troops
unless 'agreement at Panmunjom followed swiftly on the heels of the drawing
of the line of demarcation'.[53] Marine John Breske recalled that his unit held a
hill overlooking Panmunjom, so they had a clear view of the activity of the
delegates at the peace talks. If ever they met for a lengthy period the troops
had their hopes raised that an end to the war might realistically be in sight.[54]

Talks dragged on until summer 1953, partly owing to Communist negotiating tactics that routinely distorted the truth and facts, making it very difficult for Western delegates to cope. Static conditions now predominated at the battle front. American infantryman Tom Clawson recorded, 'you spent hours every day digging improving your position'. During his entire active service he was always manning positions along the same ridgeline, on a hill known as Old Baldy, owing to artillery fire that had denuded the area of vegetation.[55] The naming of hills in Korea was 'mysterious', according to Sherman Pratt, an experienced American officer, and catchy names such as 'Chinaman's Hat' or 'Old Baldy' tended to be used rather than the designated number, and these found their way into the newspapers.[56]

Draftee Rod Chapman was trained as a cook but ended up as a rifleman in Korea in 1951–52, where he was posted to 32nd Infantry Regiment, 7th Infantry Division. Initially deployed at Heartbreak Ridge, he later served at Henry Hill, which his unit held for six weeks. Much of their time was spent simply keeping an eye on the enemy. As he put it, on a typical day:

> We were just sitting there watching you know. We had three men in a bunker and you pull your guard and everything during the day and at night Leroy [his corporal] says you don't just pull two hours if you can pull longer stay there as long as you don't sleep or anything. Two hours is a lot if staring out into the dark and everything. We had barbed wire out and we had cans tied to the wire [early warning system] and you did a lot of listening at night and during the day you could see quite a ways but at night you couldn't see your hand in front of your face.[57]

Units operating in support of the infantry developed a routine during this static warfare as well. As a National Service subaltern with 61st Light Regiment Royal Artillery, Barry Tunnicliffe arrived in theatre during June 1952, and was initially employed as a Troop Leader before swapping jobs with the Regimental Intelligence Officer, who as a regular lieutenant desired first-hand experience of a mortar position. Consequently, Barry Tunnicliffe became responsible for running the Regimental Command Post based in an American 2½-ton truck.

> In a mortar regiment this is not as demanding as in a field regiment. The limited range of the 4.2 inch mortars (4,200 yards) meant that a mortar battery's targets were limited to the area in front of the infantry brigade to which the battery was assigned… Targets ordered by HQRA were passed on to the appropriate mortar troop.

These were almost always counter- bombardment (CB) targets. For pre-planned sorties, HQRA sent their barrage plan for me to decide which troop or troops had the range to hit the specific targets and instruct the relevant troop to include that target on their list, with details of times, ammunition type, fuses etc. On duty from 08h00 to 19h00 every day with a break for lunch, night duty was required every fourth night, with no time off to catch up on lost sleep.[58]

Another artillery officer noted that by mid-1952, the enemy typically

held/dug positions on hills 1,000 yards or more from our own forward defensive lines (FDLs). Normal activity was limited to artillery harassing fire (HF) on forward companies by day and patrolling no man's land by night. Occasional night raids on our own positions using numbers with the object of inflicting casualties and withdrawing before dawn.[59]

When Louis Baldovi from Hawaii was assigned to Able Company, 180th Infantry Regiment, during May 1952, he discovered that from his position at Hill 347 he could see into a valley where there were dry rice paddies and smaller hills. This was no man's land, beyond which the Chinese similarly held defensive positions. From his platoon's position he observed that the defences consisted of a continuous trench about 5–7 feet deep, and around 3–4 feet wide, which 'cut across the forward slope of hills, crests and ridges, and ran as far as the eye could see'. Heavy use of sandbags made these trenches appear even deeper, and fighting positions were incorporated into the trench line at irregular intervals, while sheltering on the reverse slope were bunkers or hootchies.[60]

By 1952–53 increasing use was made of barbed wire, trip flares and minefields, including the notorious 'bouncing betties', anti-personnel mines that would 'jump out of the ground to go off about waist high'. Sometimes large barrels of napalm were even deployed, which when ignited sprayed 'jellied gasoline in a big ball of fire' at the enemy.[61] However, such defensive measures were not necessarily as effective as they might appear. A company commander from 1 R Leicesters found the enemy's 'ability to get through large belts of wire was surprising'.[62] They proved adept at negotiating minefields as well. As one British officer observed, it was 'surprising how clever the enemy was at infiltrating through our anti-personnel minefields. On one occasion the enemy replaced detonators of our own mines with small pieces of wood to render them harmless.[63]

Most mines deployed were of American manufacture, and regarded as something of a mixed blessing, especially if owing to carelessness or the confusion of war minefields had been marked inaccurately, and threatened to cause unnecessary fatalities or serious injuries to friendly troops. Serving with the National Guard, Don Stafford had to lead his men in the awkward task of lifting a minefield left by an ROK unit that had been recorded incorrectly by headquarters personnel who weren't even present when it was laid.[64] As indiscriminate weapons mines were also widely feared. A Marine officer remembered that the first thing many new arrivals learnt, when walking about a position, was to always check where they placed their feet, in order to avoid 'the nasty, unexpected blast of a mine'.[65]

In coordination with heavy artillery bombardments, the Chinese continued to prove adept at launching infantry attacks on key UN positions. Notably, the Hook that dominated the Samichon Valley was held successively by the Marines and British units from October 1952–May 1953 when severely attacked.[66] During the Third Battle of the Hook on 28 May 1953, the position was manned by 1st Battalion Duke of Wellington's Regiment (DWR). According to one soldier, leading up to their assault the Chinese were 'throwing everything' at them, and 'the shelling and mortaring was indescribable'.[67] Subsequently, Chinese infantry, accompanied by assault pioneers, rapidly followed up their barrage and were onto the British forward positions within minutes.[68] The ferocious nature of the fighting can be gauged by the ammunition expenditure for 20th Field Regiment, Royal Artillery (RA), which supported 1 DWR. On 28 May it fired 13,609 rounds, and, according to one young gunner officer, 'next morning, the piles of empty ammunition boxes were an unforgettable sight'.[69]

Elsewhere, artillery was equally vital during other major battles of the period. At Pork Chop Hill, where the American 7th Division met heavy attacks during spring 1953, 'never at Verdun were guns worked at any rate such as this'. In one 24-hour period over 37,000 rounds were fired in support of positions on Arsenal, Dale and Pork Chop.[70] Notably, American and British troops learnt that one effective defensive measure, if a position had to be held, was to shelter in bunkers or tunnels during attacks, while calling down friendly artillery fire on their positions. Under these circumstances the VT (variable time) fuse set to create air bursts was deadly against enemy troops caught in the open. Subsequently, infantry could emerge from these tunnels/bunkers to 'mop up' or launch counter-attacks.[71]

Although both the Marine Corps and US Army were wedded to the concept of having a Main Line of Resistance (MLR) defended by outposts, there were differences in their approaches to static warfare. According to Korean War veteran and historian Lee Ballenger, the former were typically more aggressive than some army units who 'seemed to want to lie back and let the war happen' so that they 'appeared to be strictly defensive with as few offensive actions as possible'.[72] Likewise, there was a difference between what troops had been trained for and what they encountered in Korea. James Brady volunteered for the Marine Corps and had been taught the importance of 'defence in depth, an MLR protected to the front by an outpost line and supported in the rear by various strongpoints wired in, and by counter-attack units'. In theatre he found nothing like this, just the MLR 'that stretched thin' and a reserve unit too far away to assist rapidly against any penetration, while to the front was no man's land and the enemy.[73]

The contrast between American defensive doctrine and that of 1st Commonwealth Division was even starker, although the latter were aided by maintaining a smaller sector of front. British/Commonwealth units sought to hold ground via a series of mutually supporting strong points, capable of all-round defence, and sited on the crests and sides of hills, rather than having an MLR and outposts. As Lee Ballenger remarked, 'the British felt that if a piece of ground was worth fighting for, it should be included in the main defences'.[74] Where required British/Commonwealth units would place small observation posts (OPs) or standing patrols forward of the line, but under pressure these would be withdrawn so as to meet the enemy with massive defensive fire (DF).

American units tended to put their MLR 'at the forward base of the hills' and 'rely on a linear defence, attempting to avoid gaps between localities'. In front of this was the Outpost Line of Resistance (OPLR). Outposts were intended to find, resist and perhaps yield to an enemy assault, or 'roll from the punch', in which case the enemy would have to be halted by the main line. Draftee Sherwin Nagelkirk explained how the US Army defensive layout worked, based on his experience with 25th Division.

> We had a service road behind us and we had a trench where we had our bunkers and the outposts would be on some fingers of that top ridge. Quite often I got duty on them outposts and that's where the trouble usually started as they were the first line of defence.[75]

Author William Berebitsky states that outposts established on important hills as far as 2,000 yards in front of the MLR could help deny ground to the enemy, and because they were well dug-in and covered by artillery and even air support they could serve as rallying points to patrols.[76]

While this system was good in theory, as historian Jeffrey Grey outlined, the MLR was often too shallow, meaning that costly counter-attacks were needed to retake positions penetrated by the enemy. There was a tendency to hold outposts regardless of their tactical significance, causing 'excessive casualties' which 'further weakened the MLR by drawing troops away to retake outposts'.[77] During heavy fighting in August 1952 at the outposts known as Bunker Hill and Siberia in western Korea, the Marines suffered over 700 casualties.[78]

This disparity between tactical doctrines was at times responsible for generating friction between British/Commonwealth units and their American counterparts. During early October 1952 in the Samichon Valley, 1st Battalion Welch Regiment was disconcerted to find that 3rd Battalion, 7th Regiment USMC, appeared to have 'lost control of much of the territory which we had [previously] dominated and considered ours'.[79]

Both American and British units were backed by significant firepower, primarily used to protect UN lines by breaking up enemy attacks, supporting minor operations, and routinely harassing the enemy and providing counter-bombardment (CB) fire. Carl Ballard, a draftee assigned to 9th Infantry Regiment, 2nd Division, spent time on the line at 'Little Gibraltar' during spring 1952 and recounted:

> There was Corps artillery as well as company mortars and regimental artillery. Also quad fifties [half-tracks with machine guns] and tanks in the line, plus air support. It looked as if hills were bombed so not a blade of grass was left and you wondered how anyone could survive.[80]

As well as conventional artillery pieces, like the British 25-pounder field gun, the UNC's arsenal included 4.5-inch rocket batteries, deemed important in Korea for their ability to produce massed fire, which could be especially deadly against enemy troops caught in the open. Self-propelled guns, notably the versatile M-40 that mounted a 155mm gun on an M-4 Sherman tank chassis, were employed to provide either direct or indirect fire. Naval bombardments were even used to assist ground operations. A Marine recalled that the USS *New Jersey* shelled enemy positions opposite his unit, and from considerable distance her sixteen-inch guns punched a hole big enough 'to park two Cadillacs side by side'.[81] However, even though Eighth Army enjoyed increased heavy artillery support by 1952–53, 'a force of around nine hundred guns for one hundred and twenty miles of front was not generous' compared with the world wars. The mountainous terrain masked targets, and hampered many of the methods of target acquisition and spotting then in operation.[82] Military historian Bruce Gudmundsson observed, compared with the ebb and flow of 1950–51, that by the second year of the war 'the emphasis shifted from the massed fire of many battalions responding to a crisis to far fewer guns firing the same sort of missions fired by artillery behind the trenches in the day-to-day fighting of World War One'. Routine tasks, such as interdicting enemy movement, were less spectacular than deploying the massed fire of several batteries, but more demanding on ammunition supply. Consequently, as in the First World War, ammunition rationing was widespread in Korea by winter 1951–52.[83]

Unlike during the First World War, the widespread use of radio ensured that even a comparatively lowly American or British patrol leader could call directly for artillery support, rather than go through the chain of command. This encouraged the view that 'artillery was a sort of utility' that 'could be summoned at will by the customer', an attitude made all the more prevalent during the static phases of the war, because UN infantry operated almost exclusively within easy range of friendly artillery. The situation on the ground facilitated the emplacement of batteries, surveying in of positions and reference markers, and when possible the stockpiling ammunition. Additionally, a communications network developed that was suited to static conditions, which converted 'discrete artillery units into a single artillery system'.[84]

Similarly, throughout the war the system of providing close air support (CAS) was refined and developed to complement artillery. Ground units that employed assistance from 1st Marine Air Wing, whose pilots were dedicated to the ground support role, and the divisions in X Corps that had greater numbers of forward air controllers (FAC), found CAS especially beneficial.[85] The absence of a credible enemy air threat at the battlefront ensured UN air forces could provide more CAS than was normal. Great reliance was placed on Mosquitos, tactical airborne coordinators in 'slow, unarmed, trainer aircraft [usually T-6 Texan]' who contributed 'valiantly to the accomplishment' of CAS in theatre, but were considered unlikely to be as relevant in conflicts elsewhere.[86]

Howard Matthias remembered that during 1952, when expecting an air strike, he and his fellow Marines would lay out coloured air recognition panels on their positions, then 'watch the show'. They were gleeful on hearing the 'slow, regular beat of the motor' that would herald the arrival of prop-driven Marine Corsairs, liable to stay on station for a long time and give a 'target a thorough pasting', but less impressed with US Air Force jets that would rush in to drop their bombs/napalm then 'head home for happy hour'.[87] Yet despite its ready availability, some troops questioned the effectiveness of CAS, because the enemy employed deeply dug defences and most air strikes appeared 'far too slow and deliberate i.e. spotter plane is near the area some time before marking, and often some time elapses between marking and the start of a strike'.[88]

Tanks provided further firepower to frontline units in 1951–53, either from permanent or semi-permanent hill/ridgeline positions. This unorthodox deployment of armour left experienced British tank commanders aghast at 'finding that the role of their tanks was to squat on the top of hills like some prehistoric monster in the British Natural History Museum'.[89] Similarly, an American training bulletin explained how the MLR incorporated steep terrain, so 'special roads have been constructed to enable tank emplacement, mainly in defilade'.[90]

Notably, the American M-46 Patton and British Centurion tanks had good hill-climbing ability and powerful, accurate main armaments that meant they adapted well to this role, where their long-range flat trajectory fire was advantageous. Marine Corps tank crewman Roger Baker recounted that with the '8-power telescope and a 6-power periscope' in his M-46 tank, he was able to snipe individual enemy troops using the 90mm main gun.[91] A report by 5th Royal Inniskilling Dragoon Guards (5DG), the armoured regiment with 1st Commonwealth Division during 1952, explained, 'the Chinese dare not move in daylight within 5,000 yards of the British FDL, except on reverse slopes' because they were easily spotted by tank crews. Centurions were used to harass the enemy at night when they were working on their defences, help repel attacks on infantry positions (sometimes with the aid of specially fitted searchlights), and as 'bunker busters'. In this the Centurion excelled, as with its 20-pounder main gun, 'normally 50 per cent of HE [high explosive] rounds go into the aperture of a bunker at 4,500 yards', while at shorter ranges armoured piercing shot could split bunkers open.[92]

The proximity of tanks to infantry positions was not necessarily welcomed by infantry, however, who caught all sorts of retaliatory shelling meant for the tanks. Marine veteran Lee Ballenger reckoned tanks 'were like magnets for incoming fire', and not just from small mortars but heavy, powerful artillery rounds capable of destroying a tank or caving in entire bunkers.[93]

The enemy's answer to the UNC's firepower was the spade. Although they tended to make less use of barbed wire and minefields compared with UN forces, using the manpower at their disposal the Communists built 'intricate and thorough earthworks'.[94] Some included features such as 'spider holes', a fox hole dug to the depth of a standing man, covered with a well-camouflaged removable lid and enlarged at the base to enable a soldier to hold the position for a prolonged period.[95] Troops from 1st Battalion Royal Norfolk Regiment discovered that the Chinese 'always had extremely deep communications trenches and fire trenches following the contour of a hill'. This enabled them 'to concentrate at any one point to meet a threatened attack. The front of the hill was held lightly and all the bunkers were on the reverse slope' and 'were virtually shell proof'.[96]

A particularly elaborate defensive system was dubbed the 'cartwheel position' by UNC intelligence. From the reverse slope shafts were driven into a hill, forming a personnel chamber at its centre, and from there several other tunnels radiated outwards towards fighting positions on the forward slope. Although labour intensive to construct, these proved difficult to locate on aerial photographs and were virtually impregnable to air attack or shelling. Unsurprisingly, staff officer Hu Seng claimed that 'the tunnel became a great Chinese institution'.[97]

Consequently, by employing such defences the enemy was able 'to live and conduct a vigorous defence for long periods without exposing himself to observation or fire'. Artillery positions were even dug into hillsides as part of the enemy's defences, although this limited the arc of fire of individual guns. Alternatively, individual artillery pieces were sited in gullies or on the reverse slope of steep hills just below the crest, where they were extremely difficult to knock out.[98] Likewise, by 'use of plentiful single-gun roving positions', the enemy was able 'to make good use of observed fire to cause the maximum annoyance to infantry localities'.[99]

A corollary of the enemy's defensive tactics was that counter-bombardment (CB) operations became extremely challenging, despite the UNC having aerial superiority over the battlefront, and being able to employ its firepower more readily than the Communists. To provide information for the CB effort, several methods of locating enemy guns were available, and often more than one was required to verify a position. Methods included deploying air OP-light aircraft that could spot the flashes of enemy guns firing and direct UN heavy artillery against known gun positions. The careful study of aerial photographs could also identify enemy defences and gun positions, along with information gleaned from POWs. Radar was even employed that could track the trajectory of an enemy shell or mortar bomb.

Another method routinely employed by the Americans and British was the 'shellrep' or shell report. American platoon commander John Sullivan remembered that these determined 'the location of enemy artillery from the pattern an exploding shell leaves on the ground'. From this pattern it was possible to discern the gun target line, and a compass bearing taken along this would indicate the likely gun position. As enemy artillery was usually hidden several bearings were needed along that line to acquire an accurate fix by triangulation.[100] American and British troops were encouraged to estimate the calibre of the weapon firing at them (e.g. 122mm howitzer or 120mm mortar) as well. This was done by noting the noise a shell/bomb made on arrival, and when practical collecting shell fragments for analysis at headquarters.[101]

As the war progressed, sound-ranging was employed as a further strand of the CB effort. On the Commonwealth Divisional front a platoon from the American 1st Field Observation Battalion (FOB) operated a long-range base tasked with locating enemy artillery, whereas the Royal Artillery provided short-range bases to deal with mortars and guns firing at closer range.

National Serviceman Alan Causer served with 15th Locating Battery, 61st Light Regiment RA, and was intimately involved with sound-ranging in Korea during 1953. He explained that this:

> method of artillery location was based on measuring the time taken for the sound of the gun to reach a line of four microphones which had been accurately surveyed in position about half a mile behind the forward infantry positions. Each of the microphones was linked by land line to a command post a further half mile behind the microphones where some fairly sophisticated apparatus measured in milliseconds the time differential between the sound hitting each pair of mikes. Using a derivation of the cosine formula the three differentials were then plotted on a grid board and where the lines intersected was the (alleged) location of the gun. It was however necessary for surveyors to be as far forward as possible to start the equipment working when the gun fired and to report on the direction from where the sound emanated, the type of weapon (i.e. gun or mortar), its approximate calibre and the fall of shot.[102]

A distinctive facet of this defensive warfare was that most action occurred at night, when the Communists sought to use the cover of darkness to offset their opponent's advantage in firepower. Consequently, American and British positions had to remain alert in case of attack, especially in areas most likely to be targeted by the enemy. A Marine officer observed that this was incredibly draining, both mentally and physically. Typically, troops were encouraged to throw grenades in defence, because unlike small arms these didn't give their position away at night, and they were under orders to hold their positions and report suspected enemy movements to their superiors.[103]

The night could play tricks on troops' minds, knowing that somewhere out there in the depth of the Korean night was the enemy. Under such conditions wildlife posed a particular problem, as when the movement of animals was mistaken for that of the enemy, it could spark fire-fights. Gordon Butt spent his National Service in Korea with the assault pioneer platoon from 1st Battalion Royal Fusiliers (1 RF) in 1952–53.

> When the Battalion took over their first position I can remember everyone being very apprehensive the first night we manned an observation post, guns were going off in the night where lads were shooting at noises in the bush which were being caused by wild boar, wild cats and rats, this was apparently the norm for new troops. It springs to mind when we lost our first comrade, he trod on a trip flare out on patrol, it brought it home to everyone where we were and what was happening.[104]

Unsurprisingly, soldiers and Marines tended to welcome respite from the tension of night warfare. Generally daylight hours were less frenetic, with time for resting ahead of night patrols and routine tasks to be conducted, such as manning defences so as to observe the enemy. Second Lieutenant Moore experienced action during mid-1952, and discovered during quiet periods it was advisable 'to keep out of sight and ensure that all weapons were in top condition'.[105] However, as the British Official Historian cautioned, the adoption of a purely defensive mindset among UN troops would have encouraged Communist aggression and reduced their ability to resist it. Every effort therefore had to be made to prevent the enemy from dominating no man's land, while simultaneously ensuring a sense of proportion was maintained over operations so as to avoid unnecessary casualties.[106]

Patrolling and Raiding 1952–53

Patrolling and raiding had a sound basis as part of maintaining an 'active defence', provided they were conducted in accordance with the above principle. While patrolling had relevance throughout the war, during the static warfare of 1952–53 it was crucial as the primary means by which American and British infantry engaged the enemy. As the commanding officer of 1st Battalion Durham Light Infantry (DLI) explained, within the overarching intention to dominate no man's land, patrolling had several objectives. Firstly, it enabled UN troops to learn about the enemy's positions and habits, while preventing the enemy from doing likewise and finding out about UN positions. Secondly, active patrolling sought to provide a protective screen in front of the main position, through which the enemy would have to risk passing if he was intent on an attack. Consequently, patrols would provide early warning of any attack that would enable friendly artillery to hit enemy troops as they formed up for an assault, and before they got too close UN positions. These were invariably on steep slopes that offered some protection to the attacker as owing to the topography only mortars could successfully engage them at close range.[107]

Among some American commanders, patrolling was also viewed as a vehicle by which to keep men 'sharp' or alert manning positions on the Jamestown Line. This attitude tended to be resented by the British. As GOC, 1st Commonwealth Division, stressed in January 1953:

> No patrols will be sent out without some specific object. On no account will commanders send out patrols for patrolling sake, nor will they order sub-units to provide so many patrols per so many days. Any form of routine patrolling is dangerous because it invites enemy ambush, it kills initiative, it wearies the men both mentally and physically and it achieves little.[108]

Several types of patrol were employed by the Americans and British. Fighting patrols were intended to make contact with the enemy, and could form firm bases from which to raid enemy positions. As Stanley Maud, a National Serviceman with 1 DWR, recalled, his unit employed numerous 'snatch patrols', an extension of the basic fighting patrol idea. These were specifically tasked with entering enemy positions in order to bring back prisoners, usually a notoriously difficult task to achieve, although damage was often done to enemy defences using explosive charges.[109] An ambitious and highly successful daylight raid on an enemy position was mounted by 1 DWR during 24 January 1953, after thorough preparations and training.[110] On occasion armour was even deployed successfully on raids, notably during Operation Jehu (17 June 1952), when Centurion tanks from 5 DG attacked Point 156, hoping to inflict serious damage and take a prisoner.[111] However, the bulk of the patrolling/raiding operations were conducted by the infantry, almost invariably at night.

Typically, fighting patrols were organised on an ambush basis, and targeted routes or terrain features likely to be used by the enemy. This acted as a means of countering Chinese or North Korean activity in no man's land, and pushed them back towards their own defences. George Brown experienced fighting patrols as a National Serviceman with the King's (Liverpool) Regiment, towards the tail end of the war. He 'felt very comfortable' with this type of activity, despite the anxiety generated by leaving forward positions at night and potentially confronting the enemy. Typically, there were fifteen heavily armed men geared-up for close combat, plus an officer or sergeant leading the patrol. This often included two Bren gunners to provide automatic firepower, and men designated as 'bombers' who carried around 'sixteen grenades, all primed, in extra water bottle holders', unlike anything he'd experienced during training.[112]

Howard Matthias recalled that his Marine platoon was often tasked with setting up ambushes in an effort to hinder enemy patrols and capture prisoners. Simultaneously, the enemy would try to do the same to them, so that the Korean night became dominated by 'a life and death game – who could gather the most information and who would be able to ambush the other'.[113]

In contrast, reconnaissance or listening patrols relied on far fewer troops and were tasked with gathering specific information rather than making contact with the enemy. Draftee Dan Pfeiffer served with 40th Infantry Division during spring 1953, and recounted that in the Punchbowl area:

> Our orders were to go out and recce patrol and try and figure out what the enemy were up to and how many there were. We would try to report how many we thought were there and we did not know. We knew we were outnumbered. But we had far superior firepower, better weapons and more of them. We thought we were outnumbered three to one, later on we found out it was probably more like twenty to one which was the scary thing. This went on for about six and a half months.[114]

A related form of patrolling was to employ standing patrols, consisting of only two to three men, as routinely employed by British/Commonwealth forces in front of their main line instead of outposts. These acted like antennae, were in regular communication by radio or field telephone with the main position, and provided advance warning of any attack. Stanley Maud recounted that on these patrols soldiers were supposed to 'listen and you watch and if you see or hear any of the enemy then the Battalion is willing to sacrifice all three out there to get the rest of the lads standing-to'.[115] However, as the GOC 1st Commonwealth Division emphasised, small patrols (two to three men) stood a good chance of being able to 'fade out' on making contact with the enemy in a way that a section/platoon or larger body of troops probably couldn't achieve.[116]

A sense of the scale of the nightly patrol effort by British units during 1952–53 can be gauged from the records of 1 DLI. Firstly, the battalion maintained a screen of standing patrols in front of its main position and in front of these one to three fighting patrols normally set ambushes. Additionally several reconnaissance patrols usually operated, either independently or employing the ambushes as firm bases. Consequently, as many as 100 men were routinely required to operate ahead of the main position, and this was not uncommon. However, it risked weakening those defences and demanded that all troops constantly remained offensively minded, as well as requiring a high level of leadership and training if such a screen was to be maintained successfully over a prolonged period.[117] A platoon commander from 1 DWR found the situation analogous to 'a game of chess'. Under a patrol master, usually a company commander in a command post, 'the standing patrols were the pawns, the recce patrols the knights, the smaller fighting patrols the bishops and the larger officer-led sorties the queens'.[118]

Patrols and raids required preparation and planning, covering a myriad of issues ranging from their control to administration, as well as debriefing troops upon returning to friendly lines. Major Norman Salmon, Intelligence Officer with 1st Battalion Welch Regiment during 1951–52, recalled:

> All our patrol commanders taking out fighting patrols went out on recce patrols first sometimes more than once. Plans were usually made using up to date air photographs (as I.O. I sometimes went with the Air OP to get a first-hand look). Daylight rehearsals were held, sometimes back in Battalion HQ area or in the reserve company location.[119]

A company commander from the Royal Norfolk Regiment stressed how important it was to make troops 'patrol minded', especially when it might appear that patrolling was 'a routine duty', and that they should never be sent out 'without a complete rehearsal beforehand'.[120] In this regard good communications were vital, and if radio/wireless failed, some form of back-up such as signalling flares had to be available, especially so patrols could call down DF if needed to cover their withdrawal.

Robert James experienced action as a National Service subaltern in Korea, and recalled that before patrols troops were advised to 'take a bath, put on clean clothes and have a hot meal'. Based on long experience the British Army, conditions permitting, sought to 'ensure that troops going into battle would be clean and sterile as possible. This was to minimise wound infection, and have their morale boosted by full stomachs and warm, dry bodies'.[121]

Reflecting on his experience as a draftee with 9th Regiment, 2nd Infantry Division, in 1953, Carl Ballard similarly noted

> We rehearsed patrols in the rear of positions in similar terrain, including the position of the BAR [Browning Automatic Rifle] and riflemen etc. General Clark's son was the Battalion Commander and

very good at getting them out on the ground and trying to be prepared for patrol work.[122]

Martin Russ remembered that during his service with the Marines most
patrols were 'filled by volunteers', and that briefings entailed learning the
relevant nightly password for security, codenames of mortar concentrations,
and studying the route to be taken by a patrol, something of particular
importance for the man on point who would be leading it.[123]

Even so, some soldiers were sceptical about the patrol policy they had to
follow. As a platoon commander with 7th Division, John Sullivan noted his
unit commonly deployed twenty-four-man combat patrols, where six men
acted as an ambush group, and the remainder formed a support group. In theory the ambush group would pin down small enemy reconnaissance patrols
while the support group attacked from a flank. He felt such patrols were too
cumbersome to be effective, and stood little chance of making contact with the
enemy in the expanse of no man's land without giving away their presence.[124]

Most patrols were greeted with a degree of trepidation by participants and
the hours leading up to them were filled with anxiety. National Serviceman
Neville Williams saw action with the Assault Pioneer Platoon (1 Welch), and
as his was the most forward unit in his battalion it was frequently in contact
with patrols.

> This patrol work was very nerve-wracking and sometimes resulted
> in casualties. Going out on one of these patrols the lads would often
> look cheerful, but at the same time were tense. Returning at
> daybreak they looked altogether different. Their eyes had a haunted
> look and their faces almost skeletal, as they plodded back wearily
> to their positions... suffering the after-effects of tension, fear, relief
> and utter weariness.[125]

For some American troops, motivation under the stalemate conditions was
a challenge that overshadowed their overall reaction to patrolling. Many 'felt
useless in the stable situation we were forced to accept. We could die, and the
outcome of the war would not be affected'.[126] As a draftee with 2nd Battalion,
23rd Infantry Regiment, 2nd Division, Rudolph Stephens noted 'whatever they
[the high command] could dream up, we would be the ones paying the price
in blood and guts'.[127] Another factor particularly prevalent in the American
military was the 'body count attitude'. Colonel Robert Kimbrough served with
the Marine Corps in Korea from June 1951–December 1953, and remembered
that it sometimes appeared that his battalion only sent out a patrol so it could
claim to have killed a certain number of enemy troops. That statistic would be

passed up the chain of command from Division to Corps, until Eighth Army had it and the information sat on General Clark's desk in Japan.[128]

Despite every effort to prepare troops, not all patrols/raids went according to plan. Master Sergeant William Schrader described an ambush patrol in his unit (9th Infantry Regiment, 2nd Division) that went tragically awry.

> You'd gotta be out in position before it got dark. This hill we were on we had our defensive positions and a reserve company was to send out the ambush patrol. Finally they got there and it was dark and I talked to this lieutenant and I'll never forget it, he said what the heck happened these guys are late and they'd had trouble getting their trucks – transportation up from the motor pool. It's the little things [like this that could make a difference between success and failure, even life and death]. That man came up there – a West Pointer and six–eight men, and they went out there on our ambush and got there way too late. And about midnight we heard firing all Burp guns etc. Chinese not American and they were all killed. The next morning we went out there to pick up the dead and the Australians [Royal Australian Regiment] provided smoke to cover us in day-light.[129]

Another danger, highlighted by Rudolph Stephens, was when a patrol unwittingly 'bumped' into another friendly patrol, potentially fuelling a fire-fight. Under such conditions troops had to listen out for the identifiable sounds of weapons, as American rifles and carbines wouldn't fire as fast as Chinese Burp guns, so that once they realised they faced friendly troops a patrol would back away quickly. However, such incidents did result in unnecessary casualties in the darkness and confusion of no man's land.[130] Likewise, casualties resulted from clashes between UN patrols and the enemy. One British officer explained how the Chinese attempted to deploy superior numbers, 'to envelop our own patrols by going round both flanks presumably in an attempt to surround them and cut them off from our own lines, and to prevent our own patrols from calling for artillery support'.[131] Alternatively, a ploy used by the enemy was to ambush American or British patrols in proximity to their own lines. In this they were aided by the nature of the UN defences, as minefields ensured there had to be designated gaps for troops to safely exit/enter positions and these could be ruthlessly targeted.[132]

In the close-quarter combat that characterised patrol engagements, grenades and automatic firepower were invaluable, despite the difficulty in being able to distinguish clear targets at night. British soldiers noted that the high rate of fire of the enemy's Burp gun ensured it 'felt that far too many bullets were coming in your direction', plus its 'distinctive noise meant everyone knew the Chinese were in action'.[133] By comparison, the British Sten gun was considered unreliable, although some units experimented with using the Patchett sub-machine gun, deemed to be an improvement. Similarly, American troops had doubts over some of their weapons and equipment. While he respected the accuracy and reliability of the standard issue M-1 rifle, Herm Jongsma from 15th Infantry Regiment, 3rd Division, felt that troops required a weapon like the Burp gun that 'sends a wall of lead at you'. He felt much happier when he obtained an M-3 sub-machine gun or 'Grease gun' of .45 calibre. 'I guarantee you that when a .45 hits you in the arm or hand you are down. It doesn't have to hit you in the arm or chest or anything like that'.[134]

For comparable reasons some Marine patrols experimented with taking several Thompson sub-machine guns with them to provide a rapid, high volume of fire, although these weapons could be hard to control.[135] By contrast, the M-1 Carbine was often considered to lack hitting power, and be mechanically unreliable, which made it unpopular with many troops. However, the BAR was highly valued by most Marines and soldiers because it had 'long range and, with its bipod, extraordinary steadiness'.[136] This, as Carl Ballard, who served as a BAR man on arrival in Korea, discovered, ensured you went 'out first on patrol as you had the most firepower, then you were last back in so as to protect the squad again with the firepower of the BAR'.[137] However, like the British Bren gun, it was a heavy weapon to lug on patrols, often leading new troops to be lumbered with it, and it sometimes malfunctioned in the cold of a Korean winter.

As the war progressed American and British patrols benefited from several innovations. Special microphones were adapted to fit radio sets that enabled the operator to make transmissions with little chance of his voice being detected by the enemy. Despite the rigours of the Korean climate, and dangers in no man's land such as trip wires, successful use was made of dogs in order to provide patrols with advanced warning of the enemy. By 1953 the sniper or 'snooper scope', a first-generation infra-red night sight fitted to an American Carbine, proved useful, despite being cumbersome to deploy as the equipment was powered by a large man-pack battery. A successful British tactic entailed setting up a Bren gun to fire on a fixed line alongside a sniper scope team, who would indicate targets at night.[138] Much use started to be made of flak jackets. Although heavy and uncomfortable, these offered troops significant protection. Howard Matthias reckoned that his saved his life when on patrol he was hit several times, but his torso under his shredded flak jacket remained unscathed.[139]

Troops on patrols or raids faced numerous other hazards. It often took time to acclimatise to the darkness of the Korean night, and new men were potentially a liability as they initially tended to stumble about like drunks.[140] Similarly, noise was a major concern, particularly as the enemy was generally deemed to be stealthy and good at moving about at night. John Sullivan bemoaned that 'GIs made one hell of a racket, what with thermal boots crunching on the frozen ground and weapons and ammo banging together'.[141] Coughing could be a major bug-bear, particularly when trying patiently to lay an ambush. One Marine with a chronic smoker's cough remembered how an irate officer made him chew on a little cigarette tobacco, which seemed to relieve his symptoms.[142] If any Marine or soldier was foolish enough to try and smoke on patrol that could also invite disaster when spotted by the enemy.

Other challenges arose from the vagaries of the Korean climate and the unwelcome attentions of wildlife. Corporal Clark Finks, a National Guardsman, remembered setting up an ambush on the last patrol he went on and being savaged by a large black ant, the ubiquitous insect of Korea.[143] Patrolling/raiding occurred all year round, and winter could be especially severe to deal with. Marine officer James Brady vividly recalled having to wear a parka, field jacket with wool lining, plus an assortment of woollen sweaters, shirts, trousers, mittens, gloves and thermal boots, in order to stay warm while waiting to ambush 'the gooks'.[144]

A corollary of patrolling was that it potentially provided American and British troops scope to foster a live-and-let-live attitude towards the enemy.[145] It would be naïve to think that some patrols didn't resist the temptation to deliberately avoid contact with the enemy, particularly as during part of the overall effort to dominate no man's land patrols did not necessarily always confront the enemy. Some may even have sent back false situation reports by radio, having gone to ground relatively near to their own positions. However, as one former battalion intelligence officer cautioned, this type of behaviour would 'have a habit of becoming known and can't be kept secret'.[146]

According to one account, typically aggressive Marines were baffled by the apparent practice of some US Army units of maintaining 'small, localized truces... along the line', and thereby failing to engage in a thorough patrolling programme.[147] Similarly, it has been alleged that 1 Welch, in theatre during 1951–52, maintained a live-and-let-live arrangement with the Chinese, owing to the socialist inclinations of many of its other ranks.[148] This would seem questionable. As that battalion's former Intelligence Officer expounded:

> The fact that we were not selected for any horrendous attacks... was not because we were all Communists but because we maintained a

wide no man's land between us and the Chinese, which was under constant observation by day and could be dominated by massive fire-power available to us if needed. By night the enemy had to run the gauntlet of our patrols if they wanted to move sufficiently large forces into forming up positions without us knowing, and evidently decided it wasn't worth the risk.[149]

This was entirely in keeping with the defensive principles and patrol philosophy outlined above.

Chapter 7

Coping with Active Service

In Korea personnel faced numerous challenges. Not only did the enemy pose a threat, but the inhospitable terrain, variable climate and fighting miles from home were a burden. Consequently, the morale of American and British troops was important throughout the war, and underpinned their discipline and combat performance. Lieutenant Colonel John H.A. Sparrow (Assistant Adjutant General at the War Office during the Second World War and later Warden of All Souls College, Oxford) was responsible for compiling wartime morale reports on the British Army. He defined morale as the 'attitude of the soldier towards his own employment', and it comprised those factors which made 'the soldier more or less, keen to carry out his job of soldiering, and readier, or less ready to endure the hardships, discomforts, and dangers that it entails'.[1]

This above definition might equally be applied to an awkward theatre like Korea. As during the world wars, the British Army put great faith in the regimental system as a means of maintaining esprit de corps, despite the large amount of 'rebadging' that occurred. Likewise, the Marine Corps was widely seen as a highly motivated, professional force, assisted by having several officers with Second World War experience from the Pacific. Contrastingly, the American army (US Army) found generating esprit de corps more challenging, especially early in the war. Partly this was because the rotation system led to regular losses of experienced personnel in units. Also, as a British veteran observed, 'the distances between places they live [in America] is so vast, they come from different worlds', and this could impact on morale, unless a unit contained several men from the same area.[2]

Surviving on the Battlefield

On the Korean battlefield there was much for troops to appreciate, especially relatively inexperienced draftees and National Servicemen. Handling fear was important. One GI commented that he always experienced a 'gripping fear' under Communist bombardments, and never really acclimatised to shellfire, even when protected in his bunker.[3] Another recounted that it wasn't simply that the hills were physically demanding, but that he also experienced 'constant hunger'. Thirst and fatigue regularly had to be contended with, although humming classical music provided a 'personal stimulus'.[4]

Similarly, religion could help men cope. As 'a good Catholic lad', David Holdsworth, a platoon commander with 1st Battalion Gloucestershire Regiment, 'said his prayers' and found he went into action in a good frame of mind.[5] Both American and British troops were supported by chaplains. As Chaplain to the Glosters, Reverend Sam Davies recalled preaching at outdoor services, including an invitation to one held by the Royal Northumberland Fusiliers, to mark St George's Day (the RNF Regimental Day) in 1951. 'The strong manly singing rose courageously into the blue'.[6]

Humour could prove equally vital in providing moments of relief. A soldier from the Glosters noted during the Battle of the Imjin that an encounter with a unit of Chinese cyclist troops proved highly comical, because when the leaders were engaged by a Vickers MMG, it caused them all to spill 'over one another in a huge pile-up'.[7]

The war of 1950–51 entailed plenty of 'hard, primitive foot slogging' if operations were to be successful, and this kept troops fit.[8] In contrast, under static conditions maintaining fitness was more challenging. Major Gordon, a company commander with 1st Battalion Royal Norfolk Regiment during 1951–52, advised,

> Do everything possible to ensure that all ranks are kept to high state of physical fitness. This requires a certain amount of ingenuity when actually in the line e.g. setting up company field firing in rear of positions, sports, games etc.[9]

A corollary of such activities was that they were also good for maintaining morale and staving off boredom when not in action. Even so, troops throughout the war found Korean conditions awkward. One American Second World War veteran posted there considered that by comparison, it was 'quite a different war'.[10]

Rudolph Stephens, a trained infantryman and combat medic who served with 23rd Infantry Regiment, 2nd Division, during 1952–53, discovered that troops had to recognise the different sounds of battle, so as to 'tell who was firing at any given time'.[11] To the experienced ear, the measured tones of the British Bren gun, or the comparatively slow rate of fire of the American M2 Carbine and M1 Garand rifle, were different from the noisy clatter of the rapid firing Burp gun. Similarly, Soviet-manufactured 120mm mortars used by Communist units 'made an awful noise' so troops knew to take cover, whereas incoming fire from their smaller 81mm mortars couldn't be heard so the 'only warning... was the noise they [rounds/bombs] made as they were leaving the mortar tubes'.[12]

A related issue was the ability to differentiate between incoming (enemy) and outgoing (friendly) artillery and mortar fire. This could spell the difference between life and death. Herm Jongsma was drafted into the army in 1952 and served with 15th Infantry Regiment, 3rd Division, and was posted on liaison duties with the Greek battalion attached to his Division.

> While standing there with 3–5 other individuals I heard this shout 'incoming' and everyone hit the ground and crawled to a ditch and I was no fool and did the same... Then I realised those were incoming shells and the ordnance was going off, and there's one lesson we didn't really get much training in [i.e. the sound of incoming fire]. I'll have to remember that when you hear that boy you've got to hit the ground fast. What also amazed me was how they [veterans] could detect that sound of an incoming shell... that it makes through the air. That ordnance comes flying in at you from as much as two–three miles from the enemy side or maybe a mile behind you, but when it is passing over you still hear that whistle and there's a definite difference in one that's reached its arc and is coming down. There is no whistle like that with mortars which have a different trajectory.[13]

Equally troops had to content with the Korean climate. One British artillery officer recounted how the River Imjin, which flowed across the sector held by 1st Commonwealth Division, 'was around 100 yards wide in the dry season, but after the monsoon in July it could double its width and quadruple its depth', causing flooding and threatening to destroy all the bridging that was essential to the Main Supply Route (MSR) that supported the division. Then there was the Korean winter, when although there were often clear blue skies and sunshine, the temperature could hit as low as -40 degrees Fahrenheit, and 'bitter cold, strong winds from Siberia and Mongolia', were accompanied by 'occasional snow and the harsh frosts... which froze the ground down as much as six feet'. Water sources froze, so what was available had to be used for cooking, drinking and washing clothes/bathing in that order. Vehicles needed to be started regularly or have their radiators drained to avoid 'freeze up' and guards were rotated frequently. 'It was just a case of making the best of things and putting up with it'.[14]

Another officer stressed the morale sapping effect of:

> the icy wind which came down from the north at frequent intervals and blew for four or five days at a time. A wind that made life in the

open absolute hell; a wind that froze one's shaving water on one's face; a wind that froze the oil on automatic weapons and made them quite useless unless very special precautions were taken; a wind that immobilized vehicles in a few hours; a wind that would turn normally even-tempered men into disagreeable beasts; a wind that if it had not died down after a few days would have driven insane all but the very toughest.[15]

Digging slit trenches or fox holes, a constant necessity among combat troops during 1950–51, was frustrating, especially in frozen ground. Sergeant Boris Spiroff observed how young soldiers from 1st Cavalry Division soon learned to act like veterans and dig in so as 'to survive and preserve!'[16] The static warfare of 1951–53 imposed a particular burden on frontline troops as well, given the long hours living in bunkers, and waiting and watching from trenches. Transporting supplies, improving defences and patrolling, often in appalling weather, added to the burden. A soldier from 1st Battalion Welch Regiment described how 'fatigue was clearly etched on the faces of all the men' and 'the relentlessness of the situation' was increasingly harder to deal with the longer his unit remained at the front.[17]

For some new troops orientation programmes organised by their units/ formations were of benefit. John Sullivan commanded a platoon with 17th Infantry Regiment, 7th Division, during 1953, and described how his orientation 'consisted of a series of lectures and situation reports from operations and intelligence staff officers, tours of the front line', and 'visits to many supporting units'. Lectures incorporated topics such as the Chinese preference for concussion grenades. Smaller and less powerful than American fragmentation hand grenades, these usually resulted in stunning and wounding a soldier rather than killing him, unless they exploded very close.[18] In some respects officers were better placed than their men to cope with the strain of combat because, as one British platoon commander found, his duties kept him busy, and he was imbued with a strong sense of duty, plus a 'sense of excitement' allayed fears he might have had.[19]

Confidence in handling weapons was encouraged during training, and boosted morale on the battlefield. During 1953, draftee Carl Ballard from 9th Infantry Regiment, 2nd Division, was transferred from being a BAR man to his unit's heavy weapons platoon, where he became the leader of the squad handling the 57mm recoilless rifle. Recounting the accuracy and punch of the weapon he commented: 'Give me three rounds (3–4,000 yards away) and we could hit a mail box – i.e. fire one, adjustment, then hit the target [normally Chinese defences] and fire for effect.'[20] Similarly, Bob Walding saw action with the Royal Norfolk Regiment as part of his National Service, and learnt to deploy the .30 calibre Browning machine gun. It was 'fairly easy to handle after a little training', not unlike the Bren gun in some respects and used to support frontline companies.[21]

Killing the enemy was a brutal and necessary part of the infantry's war. As a platoon commander from 24th Infantry Regiment observed among his soldiers, some did it easily because they knew they had to, others were motivated by revenge for a fallen comrade, while others became 'almost catatonic' after killing owing to the guilt they suffered.[22] Likewise, Lofty Large (Glosters) found that after action it was disturbing having to search enemy dead for documents because this revealed photographs of the dead men's families 'whose smiles will be wiped away by the war'.[23] The death of Korean civilians was even more difficult to stomach. During the Battle of the Imjin, a British soldier witnessed Korean civilians hit by an American air strike, and was told by a veteran: 'It makes everyone sick, but you have to get used to it', not least because of the North Koreans' tendency to infiltrate UN lines disguised as civilians.[24]

Another form of killing on the battlefield that had implications for morale was friendly fire, which could be especially galling for those involved. A particularly tragic and high-profile case occurred at Hill 282 during 22–23 September 1950, when elements of 1st Battalion Argyll and Sutherland Highlanders (A&SH), tasked with crossing the Naktong River to support the left flank of the American advance, were mistakenly napalmed and rocketed by the USAF, resulting in seventeen dead and over seventy wounded.[25] For his part in the action, Major K. Muir was awarded the Victoria Cross (posthumously).

It would be easy to dismiss Hill 282 as part of the friction/confusion that often happens during wartime, as many have done. However, the airstrike was symptomatic of the low priority that had been given to providing close air support (CAS) by the USAF post-war, which jealously guarded its recently granted identity as a separate armed service, and had become absorbed in providing strategic bombing as part of the Cold War, at the expense of fulfilling the requirement for effective tactical air power over the battlefield.[26]

Troops were also dependent on the quality and quantity of their equipment. The British relied on a wide variety of vehicle types and this 'lack of standardisation' was a challenge, although somewhat ameliorated by the issue of American-built Jeeps.[27] Notably, the British 15cwt 4x2 Bedford truck was a constant bug-bear in the harsh environment of Korea, where it was entirely road-bound.[28] Although new vehicles were employed in Korea, both the Americans and British relied heavily on wartime rebuilds that could be difficult to keep roadworthy.[29] Captain George Warne (194th Engineer Combat Battalion) found the 'Yokohama Rebuilds', as they dubbed equipment / vehicles refurbished in Japan, tended to have a short lifespan.[30] For the British especially, concerns over their lack of mobility, and the poor quality of many vehicles issued, formed a constant refrain in unit war diaries and among respondents to the War Office's Battle Experience Questionnaire programme for 1950–52.

Communications were another important issue if commanders were to remain in touch with their units, and men call upon tank/artillery support. Typically, some adaptation was required and numerous challenges overcome. Both the Americans and British made extensive use of line (field telephone), plus wireless/radio. The latter, as the veteran Lee Ballenger explained, based on the experiences of the Marine Corps during the static 'outpost war' of 1952, 'was subject to the vagaries of age, weather, abuse, battery condition, and other gremlins of war', leading most to prefer the telephone.[31] Similarly, British radios weren't always reliable. A British artillerist observed that 'during the day all sets functioned perfectly, at night though relay procedure had to be used because of heavy atmosphere and disturbances. Line was then used. We found it advisable always to lay three lines for the one job fairly far apart'.[32] Even then there was the danger that lines might be destroyed by shellfire or appropriated for use by other units. Similarly, in 1951 an American artillery officer noted how the infantry radio (SCR-300) was often 'blanked out by the ridges', meaning that in valleys and over longer distances the only effective communication at company level was via the heavier, more cumbersome radio-set carried by the artillery Forward Observer (FO) and his team.[33]

Generally, the American troops were well-equipped. Even so, one rifle-man found he was still cold, despite wearing long johns, two pairs of trousers, two shirts, a polo jacket and a field jacket, plus his personal infantryman's equipment.[34] For British troops the situation was worse, at least initially. Finnish-pattern boots were often regarded as awful, because the insoles of these boots would freeze with sweat from soldiers' feet and risk causing frostbite.[35] Marginally better were the British Army hobnail boots, but even then soldiers found 'the only way to keep feet warm was to stamp them up and down'.[36] Similarly, the savage winter winds cut through greatcoats, battledress trousers and tunics, shirts and string vests 'as a stiff breeze passes through chicken wire', and for officers one of the most demoralising aspects of 1950–51 was hearing their 'men whimpering with pain like infants' owing to the cold.[37]

British troops improved their situation by obtaining items of American uniform, either officially or unofficially.[38] By the second winter of the war, the War Office issued new, improved winter clothing, which according one officer, 'was absolutely first class, warm, windproof and above all light'.[39] Items included various undergarments plus a shirt, jumper, gloves and mittens, together with a middle parka designed to be worn over the combat jacket. Although a vast improvement on what had existed before, the material of the jacket and trousers could tear easily and became grubby under frontline conditions.[40]

Motivational Issues

Troops often wanted to have some idea of what was happening, and why they were in Korea. During 1950–51, there was a palpable sense among many UN troops that they were there to halt the North Korean invasion. Henry O'Kane served with the Royal Ulster Rifles and describes how a War Office pamphlet entitled *Notes on Korea, August 1950*, explained the reason for the deployment of British troops.

> You are going to Korea to help the South Koreans to repel aggression; and, more important still, to uphold the charter of the United Nations and to fight for the principle that the world must be governed by the rule of law and not by force.[41]

Robert Halle, a young member of the Marine Corps who was shipped to Korea from San Diego in early 1951, put it more simply: we were there 'to fight the Communists'.[42]

Officers also bore some responsibility for keeping their troops informed. Colonel Andrew Man commanded 1st Battalion Middlesex Regiment (MX) during 1950–51 and found his soldiers, especially National Servicemen, 'wanted to know what was happening and I used to make it my business to tell them all I knew myself which wasn't a lot'.[43] Similarly, as another British officer found during the static war of 1953, it paid to get to know the men in his platoon by visiting them in their bunkers, talking and passing on any information he had. This reduced the formality of the rank structure, and created an improved understanding between himself and his platoon that was beneficial on active service.[44] In contrast, James Brady, a lieutenant in the Marine Corps, was actively discouraged by his commanding officer from becoming too close to his men. 'Get to know your men too well, too personally, and when you lose one you'll be losing a piece of yourself. A platoon leader can't afford that'.[45]

Typically, troops in combat units were unaware of the wider strategic picture, despite briefings from officers. An American artillery officer found, 'men doing the real fighting seldom know anything except what is within their own sight and hearing'.[46] Although newspapers and magazines were sometimes available, many instead relied on rumours to keep them informed, or what a

Marine termed 'scuttlebutt, the unverified word passed along by marines or, maybe, through listening to local radio stations'.[47]

Almost all combat troops had to cope with the death of comrades, and this was especially difficult for leaders. As many American and British junior officers discovered, they had to suppress their grief for fallen troops, and maintain the morale and integrity of their units by making sure they survived combat intact. To this end, as the American platoon commander Lyle Rishell expounded, men had to have confidence in their officers, and via their leadership 'know that they can get the job done'.[48] Consequently, a good platoon sergeant was a vital asset to many inexperienced junior officers. As one Marine lieutenant remembered, his 'not only quietly carried out his orders but provided me with common sense guidelines for my behaviour', often using subtle hints on what would be an appropriate course of action.[49]

Many troops also became aware of the special type of camaraderie that existed within combat units. According to one National Serviceman, 'comradeship is important in maintaining the morale of any group which was why the fact that we [14th Field Regiment, Royal Artillery] had gone to Korea as a complete unit with relationships already formed was so important'.[50] Another veteran spoke of the 'complete unity of purpose, a sharing of hardships and success, of understanding and forgiveness' that were 'simply a way of life' and unlikely to be experienced elsewhere.[51] However, for others close comradeship was not necessarily deemed an asset. Rudolph Stephens explained how in Korea, 'you didn't want to know someone too well because it hurt to see a buddy die or get wounded real bad'.[52]

A divide existed between those doing the fighting and troops working on the lines of communication that stretched back to Pusan and Japan.[53] In 1951 soldiers from 31st Field Artillery Battalion (FAB) considered that the 'rear' comprised anyone who had a vehicle, access to regular meals, and wasn't required to climb ridgelines. The physical discomfort of living/fighting in the field was often actually viewed as worse than coming under enemy fire. Simultaneously, enduring such conditions, unlike those experienced in relatively safe rear areas, often fuelled a sense of pride in combat units.[54] Likewise, a regular officer who fought with 27th Brigade was 'rather chuffed' on finding his battalion was designated for Korea. 'This was after all what one had joined up to do. And we thought we were very lucky to be selected to go there'.[55]

Initially once in action American morale and motivation nose-dived in face of unexpectedly tough opposition. According to Lieutenant Colonel Charles Bussey, they faced 'a tough, fiercely determined, motivated enemy, who caused casualties never anticipated or even imagined by the US command'.[56]

Consequently, as the war progressed many troops became motivated by the practicalities of coping with their situation, rather than ideas about fighting Communism. For one GI it was the slim hope that you might survive the carnage 'that kept us pushing on day after day'.[57] In January 1951, General Ridgway attempted to improve morale by issuing a communication to Eighth Army entitled: '*Why we are here? What are we fighting for?*' In answer to the first question he stressed it was because troops were to do their duty as they were ordered to be there. He addressed the second question by emphasising the need to thwart Communism so 'individual freedom shall prevail'.[58]

However, by the time that static conditions prevailed during 1951–52, many American soldiers struggled to appreciate why they were in Korea. Harry Van Zandt, a Second World War veteran and officer with 65th Infantry Regiment, a Puerto Rican outfit assigned to 3rd Division, felt the war seemed to lack purpose, leaving soldiers with little belief in the cause they were supposed to be fighting for, and a sense of a lack of accomplishment.[59]

Similarly, writing to a friend in Britain during September 1951, Keith Taylor, a National Service subaltern with the Royal Northumberland Fusiliers, highlighted the frustrations felt by many British troops.

> The trouble with this war is this, there's no object. Everything any-one does is normally done for a reason. In the last war it was Berlin or bust. Out here what is it? To capture the capital Pyongyang? To push the Chinese back to Manchuria? What? No one knows except something vaguely called 'the peace of the world' and what does that mean to the average soldier?[60]

Reflecting on Korea, one 'average soldier', a National Serviceman who had fought with the Royal Artillery during 1951–52, commented:

> I am not sure if we had any sense of purpose of the war on behalf of the UN or the progress of the Peace Talks. It is important to understand that most of us had been conscripted into the forces straight from school with little or no knowledge of world affairs.[61]

Despite these frustrations, however, as the commander of 1st Commonwealth Division outlined during 1952, British/Commonwealth morale remained high, so long as there was hope that something might come from the negotiations with the Communists:

> In spite of a general feeling of frustration and an apparent lack of object in the present fighting the morale of the soldiers is remarkably high. I believe this is partially due to the fact that they

have a faint hope at the back of their minds that something may
eventually come of the Peace Talks and a Cease Fire will be arranged.
If the talks break down and we have to start operations again I feel
there is likely to be a drop in morale and it will take a little time and
considerable effort on the part of all leaders to get things going.

In this connection it is very noticeable that, after about nine
months in Korea, the 'hard core' of a unit (company commanders,
warrant officers etc) lose a lot of their 'sparkle.'[62]

Another issue that affected the morale and motivation of troops was their
exposure to the horrors of war, and Korea was as ghastly as other conflicts
of the twentieth century, if not worse. Stanley Boydell, Medical Officer
attached to 1 MX during 1950–51, questioned the legitimacy of the war after
witnessing scenes of destruction. Was 'liberation' of what was essentially a
peasant society in South Korea morally acceptable? Once a village had been
'done over by the USAF' so that there was little left, 'was it right to go in and
decimate a country where people were probably not bothered whether they
were Communist or not?'[63] Likewise, American artillery officer James Dill
felt 'thoroughly sickened' after having to direct fire to destroy the apparently
peaceful cluster of huts that comprised the village of Mungol-li.[64] Edmund
Ions, a platoon commander with the Royal Ulster Rifles, recalled a horrific
incident during late summer 1951. Mortar fire was requested in the area of
a village where large numbers of suspected enemy troops had been spotted,
despite the widespread understanding that this risked causing civilian casualties. His platoon was ordered through the village, where they discovered a
mother cradling her infant, who was dying from a severe stomach wound,
and the corpse of a young woman with her leg blown off. This made him feel
that he'd 'done with war.'[65]

Integration

For the American armed forces of the Korean War era, racial integration was
a major issue, after the strict policy of segregation enforced during the Second
World War. President Truman's Executive Order 9981, issued on 26 July
1948, stipulated that there was to be equality of treatment and opportunity
for all service personnel, regardless of their race, colour, religion or national
background.

Officially the Marine Corps integrated in 1949. Although there were comparatively few black or African-American Marines, the process was far from
trouble-free. Veteran NCO Bob Smith served in Korea and Vietnam and stated,
'you can't change men's minds with an order, it takes time and lots of it.'[66] In

many ways the racism evident in the military was a wider reflection of the deep divisions in American society, especially in the southern states. During 1951, one Marine platoon commander noted that when a new black sergeant was posted to his unit, there was frequent 'talk about a "nigger"' taking over'.[67] Likewise, as many enlistees in the Marines discovered, the Corps had a rich history that was tied to the south and elitism, the influence of which remained strong, particularly at officer level, well into the early 1950s. Another platoon commander remembered that during his Korean tour in 1952 he had to be careful about how he assigned the limited number of black Marines under his command, because there was still deep distrust between them and white southerners.[68]

In contrast to the Marines, the army entered Korea with segregation still enforced, but by 1951 it fought with a mixture of all-white, all-black and partially integrated units. It was not fully integrated until 1954. Lieutenant Colonel Charles Bussey, a former Tuskegee airman who led 77th Engineer Combat Company in Korea, supporting 24th Regiment, described it as 'a Jim Crow Army' where black soldiers from all branches 'were treated discourteously in military life and mistreated brutally in military courts', and the punishments enforced would invariably be harsher than those given to whites. While there were a few black officers, most black troops 'existed to serve under white officers'.[69]

This did not bode well on active service. According to a study on 24th Infantry Regiment (a notable all-black unit) from 25th Division, segregation was one of the primary reasons behind its poor combat performance during the first year of the Korean War, which led to it being recommended for dissolution. Although some troops performed well, racial prejudice within the regiment had affected leadership 'and destroyed the bonds of mutual trust and reliance that were necessary if the unit was to hold together in combat'.[70] A related and recurring theme of the period, highlighted by military historian Peter Kindsvatter, is that the constant association of poor combat performance with all-black units was extremely detrimental to their morale.[71] Yet one white former platoon commander from 24th Infantry Regiment, with first-hand experience of operations during 1950–51, maintained that all-black units performed no worse than other American units then deployed, and it was unfair to assess troops based on their colour.[72]

During the Korean War era the perception remained among many white soldiers and officers that blacks were unreliable, panicked easily, tended to be negligent and lacked leadership potential.[73] Understandably, many blacks who served in Korea were equally distrustful of white personnel. Many blacks were denied the vote, depending on where they came from in America, and it was extremely bitter to be fighting miles from home to protect the rights of the South Koreans, while those same rights were seemingly being denied to them as African-Americans. As Curtiss Morrow recounted, while they were fighting, their families in America had to endure endless prejudice, such as travelling on segregated public transport, or not even being allowed to enter a restaurant and be treated like a human being. In December 1950, he was especially shocked to hear about a black man being lynched, and find he was from the hometown of a comrade in 24th Regiment. As an 18-year-old north-erner from Illinois, he'd not been exposed to as much racism as his southern comrades, and Korea proved a 'rude awakening to the realities of politics'.[74]

It wasn't only blacks who encountered racism in the army. Mexican-American Octavio Huerta reckoned he was refused promotion several times owing to his background.

> I coped with this by working hard and always trying to do well and rise above the provocation and prejudice. I received discrimination but paid no attention to it. Whatever they were doing I would do even better than they could and they would accept me more.[75]

Similarly, during 1952–53, white Jewish infantryman Arthur May encoun-tered anti-Semitism, as several troops from the Midwest in his unit who had never met Jews before appeared unhappy dealing with him.[76]

Despite the challenges, many white and black soldiers adjusted well to integration or even welcomed it. A white draftee to 32nd Infantry Regiment, 7th Division, in 1951, found that:

> Guys that had been there a while filled you in. I was assigned to Leroy Little from New York and he helped me a lot. We had a coloured lieutenant, two coloured sergeants and Leroy was a corporal. We got along with all of them and those guys would back you up.[77]

Recreation and Welfare

The importance of welfare can be gauged by a British platoon commander, who on return from Korea stressed:

> A man's welfare is your primary duty, never neglect foot, body or weapon inspections and most important of all, the time your men want you with them is not only when the sun is shining and there's no danger, but when everything is at its worst and you feel like looking after yourself first.[78]

Additionally the British were supported by the Navy Army Air Force Institutes (NAAFI) that established road houses, much envied by the Americans, offering troops a chance to buy beer, cups of tea and food. Mobile NAAFI canteens often ventured into forward areas, despite the potential dangers, selling comforts such as toiletries and writing materials. Most British units organised some form of comforts fund for their personnel in Korea. Woollen items were specially knitted for the Argyll and Sutherland Highlanders (A&SH), for example, by organisations established within the regimental area, and sent to their depot for transportation overseas.[79]

Although they had no equivalent of the NAAFI, American troops hoped the Red Cross would provide comforts, especially when 'Doughnut Dollies' offered the chance of food and a hot drink. However, under war conditions this wasn't always the case. A platoon from 24th Infantry Regiment received a large well-intentioned carton from the Red Cross, containing toilet paper, bath towels and toothbrushes: all items that were virtually useless to men on a Korean hillside where there was little water.[80]

Alcohol and smoking provided widespread means of relaxation. In the British Army alcohol was issued officially, including a rum ration, especially in winter. According to Alan Carter, a National Serviceman with the DWR, beer was 'the only thing to spend our bit of money on'.[81] Similarly, British officers normally had access to spirits, and, as one sapper officer found, in Korea alcohol was 'fairly plentiful', with 'gin at 7 shillings a bottle (35p), which meant the NAAFI 'were starting to provide the necessities of life'.[82] By contrast, the American military were technically 'dry', and as many British troops discovered, including Frank Pearson, a corporal with the KOSB, 'we, in the age old custom, bartered with them. ('That's how I got myself a nice rifle, a semi-automatic).'[83] American troops acquired alcohol by other means as well. Members of John Sullivan's platoon routinely obtained a couple of cases of beer from rear echelon troops, and hid these in a bunker in the frontline. When safe, this provided them with a few drinks as a means of release from the static warfare of 1953, a practice he felt wise to let continue.[84]

Both the Americans and British provided men with a cigarette ration, and a Marine Corps doctor noted in the 1950s that it appeared that everyone was a smoker.[85] As during the world wars, many young men were encouraged to pick up the habit as a result of their military experience. GI Arthur May found that non-smokers were usually picked on for details during breaks, and consequently he became a smoker pretty quickly to avoid this.[86] Some British soldiers were even actively encouraged by the authorities to take up smoking in Korea, so as to ward off pests like flies and mosquitoes.[87] Even for non-smokers, cigarettes had value, because they could invariably be traded for other items like chocolate and sweets.[88] In winter pipes proved especially popular, owing to 'the comfort of folding one's stiff hands round the bowl' in an effort to warm them.[89]

For some troops, drugs/narcotics offered further release from the strains of the front line. According to historian Albert Cowdrey, heroin was inexpensive (80–90 cents for 65 milligrams) and the most widely used of the substances available to American troops in Korea, with many using it for 'social indulgence' akin to alcohol, rather than becoming addicts.[90] While serving with the Marines, Martin Russ describes using the drug in this manner while in reserve, and he knew a corpsman (medic) who routinely indulged in opium obtained from locals.[91]

As far as possible, troops sought to make their lives more comfortable. One American commander, visiting his forward units, encountered a two-man foxhole dug deep into a slope so it was cave like, where the occupants had furnished it with generous overhead cover, a rice straw mat, and a stove made from an empty ammunition box and discarded packing tubes for mortar rounds.[92] British soldiers were no slouches either when it came to demonstrating ingenuity and improvisation, as they weren't as lavishly equipped as the Americans. Ronald Orange from Northumberland served with the Royal Artillery during the static warfare of 1951–52. 'We had to build semi-permanent dug outs', he explained, which required heating. Whereas most Americans had purpose-built heaters, the British relied on 'taking an empty ammunition box, and "borrowing" a length or two of radio aerial, and from a drum of diesel oil on the roof' the aerial was fed:

> through to a hole pierced in the top of the ammunition box. The supply of fuel was reduced to a drip by means of a clamp, again taken from empty ammunition boxes, and the amount of heat could then be regulated. Waste gases were vented through empty shell cases with the business ends removed and the series telescoped, issuing from a hole of the required size cut in the roof of the ammunition box.[93]

These were effective, and as well as providing heating could be used to dry clothes and make tea, although as one soldier from the Black Watch cautioned, if the drip 'got out of hand and its flames out of the chimney', the resulting smoke usually 'attracted unwanted attention from the enemy'.[94]

Many British troops improved their dugouts further by fashioning tin cans into candle holders and turning old supply boxes into tables and chairs. One

National Serviceman vividly recalled learning how to use 'old machine-gun belts, woven on steel pickets' to 'make a good bed'.[95] With this type of living rats posed a constant problem. Many were killed using rat poison, or 'skewered on bayonets'.[96]

Under frontline conditions, marking special events provided another opportunity to boost morale. On Coronation Day in 1953, the Commonwealth Division fired red, white and blue smoke onto enemy held features, followed by tanks firing 'an AP [armoured piercing] salvo of one round onto pre-selected targets'. The order to fire was given by the commanding officer of 1st Royal Tank Regiment, who subsequently 'ordered three cheers for Her Majesty over the Regimental Net', while in the rear of the divisional area there was a parade.[97]

For soldiers and Marines throughout the war, mail had a vital morale-boosting effect, and was an important link with home. Not only did letters/parcels provide a glimpse of normality back in America or Britain, but within units men could share items of good news, plus any comestible contents. However, if letters brought bad news they could have the opposite effect. Alan Carter remembered how 'Dear John' letters from girlfriends breaking off relationships would cause men 'to be even more cheesed off than before'.[98]

Various forms of entertainment/recreation were important as well, not least to relieve boredom. Reading offered many troops respite from the conditions and books were obtained privately or distributed to troops by welfare organisations. Other material included periodicals and newspapers, such as *Crown News*, an in-house publication tailored for the various contingents of 1st Commonwealth Division.[99] Similarly, according to a Marine officer, everything from comic books to *Reader's Digest* proved popular, especially overseas editions of *Time*, *Newsweek* and *Life*.[100]

As Howard Matthias observed after serving in the Marines, gambling was synonymous with combat. He found many officers indulged in it, especially poker, while several enlisted Marines played cards in their bunkers, or placed bets on virtually anything, from the contents of unopened C rations, to which platoon might be selected for the next raid. During 1952 this added spice to life in the line, and helped pass the time when not in action.[101] However, gambling could sometimes be taken to extremes. In Rudolph Stephen's unit was a soldier from New York who was passionately fond of Russian Roulette. One day, shortly before going back into the line, his luck ran out and he blew his brains out.[102]

The mobile screening of films was popular, and provided frontline personnel with a break when held in reserve. On the eve of the Battle of the Imjin,

Albert Tyas, a National Serviceman from Yorkshire serving with the Royal Ulster Rifles, 'watched Doris Day and Gordon Macrae in *Tea for Two*'.[103] Music provided relief too, and according to one Black Watch soldier the harmonica was 'the in thing' in the 1950s, especially if you learnt to play contemporary popular tunes, including the theme from the western *High Noon*.[104]

Similarly, for many Americans USO shows provided welcome entertainment behind the lines, even leading one Marine officer to resolve that if he survived the war he would attempt to visit the theatre every week.[105] The British had ENSA-style concert parties that were similarly considered good for morale. National Serviceman Neville Williams recorded attending one close to Christmas 1951, which included performances by famous artists of the day, notably singer Bill Johnson, known for the musical *Annie Get Your Gun*, and actress/comedian Beryl Reid, which brought 'a touch of normality to the troops'.[106]

The presence of characterful individuals within the ranks provided further tonic to many units. The Welch Regiment, for example, comprised several soldiers from Liverpool with natural comedic talents.[107] Despite military regulations, cultivating a particular personal appearance was another method of raising collective spirits. In 3rd Platoon, Able Company, 1st Tank Battalion, 1st Marine Division, men had 'their left earlobe pierced with a string of twine looped through it' much in the manner of pirates.[108]

Sport was another vital form of recreational activity that not only helped troops pass time when held in reserve, but also kept them physically fit for battle and fostered esprit de corps. In the Marine Corps 'endless games of volleyball' proved universally popular, along with betting on the results of matches.[109] For the British football, rugby and boxing were especial favourites. Some of the 'unsung heroes' of the war were the bulldozer drivers from the Royal Engineers who flattened out football/rugby pitches in the Korean terrain.[110]

As the war progressed, both the Americans and British instituted leave arrangements. Men from combat units might be rested in reserve for a few days, as had occurred during the world war wars. Alternatively, R&R (rest and recuperation) trips were organised to Japan, usually lasting five days. Sometimes R&R was even offered as a reward for good performance, especially if units succeeded in taking a prisoner.[111] Soldiers sent to Japan had the opportunity to appreciate a foreign land vastly different from their own. After serving as a medical aid man in Korea with 115th Clearing Company, William Donner was posted to Japan, and assigned to a headquarters unit at Sendai on Honshu, where he was struck by the poverty of the Japanese people and their ingenuity in deploying oxen carts and 'honey pot' wagons to remove human faeces for fertilizer.[112]

As a National Serviceman with the Royal Army Medical Corps (RAMC), Barry Whiting was fortunate enough to be granted two periods of R&R at the Ebisu Commonwealth Rest Camp near Tokyo. From there he took advantage of an organised visit to a museum attached to a local teaching hospital, where there were 'specimens of human skin which were preserved after death from the two atomic explosions... imprinted all over with the shapes and patterns of objects which had obstructed the fall of heat waves'. Another visit took him to see hydroponic farms established by the Americans in an effort to grow clean vegetables, which didn't rely on traditional Japanese and Korean methods of soil fertilisation using human waste. He indulged in watching Japanese artists at work, including a demonstration of wood block printing, a rehearsal of a Japanese play and a trip to 'the Tokyo Opera House to hear *Carmen* sung by the Tokyo Opera Company'.[113]

R&R trips enabled troops to enjoy pleasures that were not available to them when in combat. Sergeant Boris Spiroff greatly appreciated sightseeing, buying souvenirs, eating good food, finding gifts for his wife and the luxury of a hot bath.[114] Recalling a stay in Tokyo organised by the Americans, National Serviceman Brian Hough, from Manchester, was similarly struck by the comforts on offer: 'there were white sheets on the beds! We couldn't believe it. Wonderful'.[115]

Similarly, around the British and Commonwealth base area in Kure were numerous beer halls and clubs for use by troops. On R&R sex was another attraction for some. A National Service NCO with the Black Watch explained that the Japanese were 'decades ahead of Britain, with prostitution legitimate trade and I thoroughly indulged myself with the best window shopping of my life!'[116] In Tokyo the sergeant on duty even gave Brian Hough and 'all the lads a list of all the brothels they could attend' if they wished. These were 'registered hotels with legal prostitutes and the girls working these hotels were inspected every other day and they had a card that was stamped'.[117]

Conversely, according to one Marine officer, when in action it was best to try and think about women as little as possible.[118] Even though civilians were routinely removed or encouraged to vacate frontline areas, there were opportunities for sex in Korea as well. Given the desperate plight of Korean civilians, many were forced into prostitution. Howard Matthias and William Donner both observed girls operating near to their units while on active service.[119] Likewise, an impression of the extent of this problem can be gauged from the records of 1st Commonwealth Division, which reveal that from February–

June 1952 '296 prostitutes were rounded up and removed from the Divisional area.'[120]

For some soldiers homosexuality was an issue as well. One British platoon commander was disturbed to find that two teenage Korean porters attached to his unit were sharing tents with a cook and one of the oldest soldiers in the unit. He was told by another veteran that six months in Korea without contact with women could make a man 'fancy these young boys', so 'either we all bugger them or nobody does'. It was an awkward situation to confront, but he resolved it by putting the Koreans into a tent together.[121]

Food and Rations

Food and rations were inextricably linked to the morale and welfare of troops in Korea. Usually American units were issued combat rations (C rations), which proved popular, as different menus were available, and the cardboard packs contained additional items like coffee, crackers and cigarettes. Usually an amount of trading went on between soldiers, so individuals could vary their diet.[122] For Marines, canned fruit in C rations proved very popular, although other items, notably cocoa discs, proved awkward because they were impossible to crumble or melt adequately in boiling water.[123]

In contrast, during 1950–51 the British Army ration pack, 'the Compo pack (ten men one day) with only three menus was cumbersome and unpopular', whereas when British troops were issued C rations, they not only appreciated the greater variety of menus, but found them 'easier to carry by the individual over the hills'.[124] Once the Commonwealth Division was operational, one British officer reckoned troops 'had the best of all worlds'. Basics such as sugar, butter and tea came from British sources, while American C rations provided tinned food and American fresh rations – meat and vegetables – were shipped in from California or Hawaii on refrigerated vessels. Owing to the Korean climate, especially in winter, the scale of rations issued was often generous and there was access to the NAAFI canteen organisation.[125]

Ideally rations had to be cooked, and the cardboard from ration boxes provided useful kindling. However, under the pressure of combat it could be impractical to light fires to heat canned rations so they were consumed cold, or even half-frozen.[126] At the Chosin Reservoir rations froze in the intense cold. A Marine NCO recalled, 'If you were lucky you had a can of beans. You'd keep it under your armpits all day then warm it up over a fire at night'. They had 'a lot of those Charms candies', plus 'Tootsie Rolls', a type of caramelised confectionery, valued for its high sugar content, which provided rapid energy to help function in the cold.[127]

Alternatively, if conditions allowed, as National Serviceman David Green remembered, forward units might be able to use a cookhouse near to the front that provided them with meals.[128] Marine mortarman C.S. Crawford described how in such cases hot drinks and food were a change from cold C rations and proved a great 'morale booster'.[129] Another method of organising cooking, as employed by 1st Battalion Welch Regiment during 1951–52, was by platoons, which enabled men to have a hot meal with every platoon employing a central fire, rather than potentially hazardous unofficial ones.[130]

Many American and British personnel sought to supplement their rations with local produce when practicable, but there were inherent dangers with this. Members of the A&SH resorted to what an officer termed 'animal living' during the harsh winter of 1950–51, and to compound their misery many 'developed tapeworm through eating local pigs'.[131] Pheasant shooting looms large in Korean War literature, particularly relating to the British Army.[132] By 1952, 'a Stay-Back Line, 10 miles behind the front line' was supposed to bar the presence of civilians, and 'rice fields lay untended with harvests blowing across the ground, to the satisfaction of the pheasant population, who grew fat on the agricultural dereliction'.[133] Unsurprisingly many soldiers, including the commanding officer of 14th Field Regiment, RA, advised officers bound for Korea to 'take a 12 bore shot gun, there are a fair supply of pheasants and quail!'[134]

Medical Matters

Although he questioned how effective doctors could be in the field, one British medical officer in Korea rapidly found his battalion appreciated his presence, because it boosted their spirits.[135] The British had an autonomous medical system up to the level of the American Mobile Army Surgical Hospital (MASH). In March 1953, Barry Whiting (26 Field Ambulance, RAMC) was given charge of Number 4 Section of his unit's Advanced Dressing Station (ADS). As he explained:

> Our sections, Casualty Collection Posts (CCP), were essentially designed to collect casualties from the frontline via their Regimental Aid Posts (RAP), which, of course were sited near the infantry's company's HQ, and where the initial First Aid (FA) posts to deal with wounded, carried in by stretcher or driven in aboard stretcher jeeps.[136]

The most serious cases were rushed to a Field Dressing Station (FDS) or MASH, some miles behind the lines, where dedicated surgeons frequently worked around the clock to save lives and ensure wounded were patched up for evacuation and further treatment away from the front. As a former MASH surgeon recounted, when casualties were heavy, the regular routine was ignored and 'every man [and female army nurses] worked as long as [they] could stay on their feet, think and still function', until they were overcome by tiredness and had to briefly rest before getting back to work.[137]

British casualties sent to a MASH entered the American chain of evacuation, and the most serious were normally flown to the British Commonwealth General Hospital (BCGH) in Kure, Japan. Depending on their condition and treatment required, they might even have been sent for convalescence at a military hospital in Hong Kong or Britain. Similarly, under the American system casualties were typically first treated at a Battalion Aid Station, before being despatched to a Regimental Collecting Station or Divisional Clearing Station, and on to a MASH, prior to being evacuated to a military hospital in Japan, and even back home, depending on the severity of their condition.[138]

During the war numerous MASHs were activated, including one provided by Norway known as NORMASH. Initially all conducted general surgery, but they adopted specialisms as the war progressed. 8076th MASH, for example, became known for treating extreme vascular injuries, and 8055th MASH for head injuries.[139]

Given the awkward topographical nature of Korea, the evacuation of casualties (casevac) was a significant challenge, often depending on 'human muscle and increasingly battered wheeled vehicles'.[140] Communist troops, as William Anderson, a combat medic with 14th Infantry Regiment, 25th Division, during 1951–53 observed, often targeted them, using their distinctive Red Cross helmet badges and armbands as aiming points. This led medics to remove these emblems, and most started carrying weapons for their personal protection.[141]

Robert Mulder, a combat medic with 2nd Infantry Division, accompanied a patrol during 1951 that was ambushed by the enemy:

> There were grenades and bullets flying all over the place. This one kid, he was the youngest on the patrol, got hit by a grenade on the back, causing a serious wound... I put him on my shoulders, grabbed his rifle and got him out of there. We cut a couple of poles [branches] and used jackets as a stretcher and called the aid station as the patrol regrouped.

They continued to carry him on their improvised stretcher, 'until we had reinforcements come and pick him up with a [proper] stretcher. Then we got the hell out of there'.[142]

The casevac process was significantly assisted by the innovative deployment of the helicopter, technologically still in its relative infancy in the early 1950s. One former MASH surgeon reckoned that helicopters 'changed the face of medical care on the battlefield'.[143] According to a report compiled by 1st Commonwealth Division:

> One of the major factors in the very low death rate (1% for abdominal wounds) has been the helicopter evacuation service. The best recorded time is 39 minutes from the time the casualty was hit to his arrival in the pre-operating tent at the Norwegian Mobile Army Surgical Hospital. In many cases helicopter evacuation has been the only practical method of evacuation.[144]

Not only did helicopters transport casualties away from the front, they also brought forward invaluable supplies of blood and medical equipment. However, the Bell H-13D, which was primarily used for casevac, was relatively fragile, leading the official historian to compare their intrepid pilots to those of First World War aviators, given their willingness to push their aircraft to the limit and retrieve casualties virtually under the noses of the enemy.[145]

Unsurprisingly under such conditions, accidents occurred. Draftee Calvin Schutte experienced a heart-rending event in the Punchbowl area during March 1952.

> One night we had soldiers that were wounded and we had a helicopter come in to pick up the wounded. It was about the only way you could get them out. There were no roads or anything, it was rough. It took off and was doing good and then the back spinner wheel hit some branches and it tipped over and blew up and killed everybody, the pilots and the wounded guys. You stood by helpless.[146]

Medical personnel had to deal with various types of wound as contemporary weaponry was capable of causing damage to virtually every part of the human body. Otto Apel, a surgeon with 8076th MASH, noted that shrapnel from tank, artillery and mortar rounds, plus anti-personnel mines, entered all parts of the body, and 'severed arteries, pierced muscles, shattered bones and tendons and ligaments, and destroyed organs'. Abdominal injuries from bullets or edged weapons were pretty common as well, because troops from both sides often resorted to bayonets or knives.[147] One of the first casualties, combat medic Rudolph Stephens, treated near Old Baldy, had a serious chest wound, and as he administered morphine and applied a bandage, the sight of it made him sick.[148]

Dealing with death was another facet of the medic's experience. Corpses had to be tagged, which Robert Mulder from Grand Rapids, Michigan, who was assigned to the Medical Company of 38th Infantry Regiment, 2nd Division, during March 1951, found one of the most traumatic aspects of his entire Korean War service.[149] Another American medic felt you couldn't afford to dwell on the situation, but had to get on and treat the next casualty, while the recently deceased was carried to Graves Registration.[150]

Lamar Bloss, from Munster, Indiana, spent over a year on Graves Registration duty in Korea, leading other soldiers to avoid him and christen him 'Mr Dead'.

> We had a regular truck and bring bodies down by stretcher or in body bags and put them in a morgue. And I was the only one who could go in. And it was very hard for me because I had to take all their personal effects off them and put them in a little bag and hang it on the right side by their head... that was the hardest thing I ever had to do, is take the stuff off the body.[151]

Ultimately, soldiering was potentially hazardous, even when not in contact with the enemy. As in other wars, accidents were another cause of injuries and fatalities in Korea. Although well-trained, disciplined troops tried to keep accidents to a minimum, even they could make mistakes. During 1953 an unfortunate British soldier conducted a striker test on a hand grenade without first removing the detonator. When releasing the safety lever he heard the fuse 'fizzing' and in panic dropped the grenade, which exploded as he and three comrades who had been sharing his bunker dashed for the exit. All four were injured.[152] During his work supporting the surgical team at BCGH, David Oates, a National Service medical orderly with the RAMC, was struck by the fact that in the winter of 1952–53, petrol heaters were responsible for most of the burns cases that they treated.[153]

Malfunctioning ammunition caused other accidents. Barry Whiting never forgot 'a severely injured gunner' who arrived at his ADS

> The victim of a breech-explosion in his 25-pounder field gun. As he lay on our stretcher, in and out of consciousness, I felt for a pulse, but felt my fingers go right into his wrist – all the flesh having blown away. This was also the first time I heard the so-called 'death rattle', during which air is expelled from the collapsing lungs. Fortunately, he died.[154]

Other troops became neuropsychiatric casualties owing to the pressure of combat. American units engaged during the early months of the war notably had many cases of exhaustion, compounded by despair and fear generated by the threat of encirclement as they retreated.[155] Later in the war, as William Anderson discovered, some men reached a 'breaking point' after sustained combat service. This could vary from one individual to another. Symptoms ranged from shell-shock, when men became fearful, sobbing wrecks, unable to function, to those who were suicidal or contemplated a self-inflicted wound (SIW).[156]

As during the world wars, some troops chose the drastic option of maiming themselves deliberately, in an effort to be evacuated from the front line. American infantry officer Herman Bulling, a Second World War veteran, recalled for Korea in December 1950, encountered a lieutenant in his unit who had had enough. He tried to smash his hand against the back of a truck using his rifle, and the medics that treated him and his commanding officer thought he should be court-martialled.[157] However, the standard method of obtaining a SIW was for a man to shoot himself in the hand or foot and pass it off as an accident. Given the unreliability of some weapons, and the fact that accidents can occur owing to mistakes or negligence, this was feasible. The British Sten gun in particular could fire by accident when dropped because it operated on a blowback action. A soldier from the Welch Regiment was widely thought by his comrades to have shot himself in the foot 'accidentally on purpose' by taking advantage of this gun's characteristics on guard one night. Previously he had made it clear 'he didn't rate this Korean War' and in the dark no one could be certain what happened. Consequently, his claim that he had forgotten to apply the safety catch on his Sten, meaning it fired and hit him when he accidentally dropped it, was accepted.[158]

As anyone contemplating an SIW discovered, care had to be taken not to leave powder burns that would indicate a gunshot wound was self-inflicted, or else troops faced punishment. In the front line any soldier who tried it risked bleeding to death before he could receive help. As Curtiss Morrow and his comrades in 24th Infantry Regiment found, these factors tended to persuade most soldiers to reject the idea of SIWs because they wanted to get back home unscathed.[159]

Suspected cases of SIWs were often viewed unsympathetically. One doctor attached to the Marine Corps treated three Marines for deliberate gunshot wounds to their feet during the Chosin Reservoir Campaign, and found they were to be made an example of by being kept with the medics in the field until they could walk, rather than evacuated out of Korea.[160]

Likewise, British medical authorities had to be prepared to contend with what they termed 'battle exhaustion', which covered a multitude of neuropsychiatric conditions. In his study of the Battles for the Hook in 1952–53, Lieutenant Colonel A.J. Barker cites the example of a courageous, experienced Yorkshire NCO who found 'he could no longer face another patrol' and 'had cracked under the strain'. However, shortly afterward he was able to conduct himself bravely in battle, where the circumstances were different and 'he knew how to control himself'.[161]

Disease was another potential threat. During Operation Killer in early 1951, it was discovered that cases of typhus, smallpox and typhoid were rife in Communist-held areas, affecting civilians and enemy combatants alike, as their medical services were not up to the same standard as those of Western armies.[162] According to official records, the entire British force 'was immunised against Enteric Typhus, Cholera and Tetanus and was vaccinated against Smallpox'. Malaria, Japanese encephalitis, infective hepatitis, typhoid and para-typhoid all posed a serious threat, as well as parasites such as hook-worm.[163]

Of all the diseases encountered, haemorrhagic fever caused the greatest alarm, particularly as it proved resistant to the range of antibiotics available in the early 1950s. American and British medics were initially baffled as to how to deal with it. It was thought to be spread by mites living on rodents in the field, and experience demonstrated that rapid evacuation, ideally by helicopter, and 'minimal interference and maintenance of electrolytic balance of body fluids' were critical to a patient's chances of survival.[164] While serving with 115th Clearing Company, William Donner recalled:

> We had a fever from rats or mice and the death rate from that was about 6%. And so we had some guys come in and we rushed them down to the hospital quick as we could... then they were sending in rats in cans that were alive and mice, that had to be tested to see if they had this fever.[165]

Obviously preventative measures were important in combating disease throughout the war. In late 1950, troops from 45th Field Regiment, Royal Artillery, were ordered to always dig deep latrines, use water purification tablets and maintain high standards when it came to personal hygiene and preparing/cooking food.[166] A soldier from 1 MX recalled that improvised baths consisted of 'two jeep trailers with wheels dug into the ground, large oil drums washed out and top cut off with water in and a fire underneath... and you'd bucket water from the oil drum into the trailer and four men went through the baths at a time.'[167] Once the front was stable during 1952 and 1953, preventative measures were in some respects easier to implement than under fluid conditions. Soldiers from 1 DWR, for example, were ordered 'to smear items of clothing in repellent' to counter the threat of haemorrhagic fever. Anti-malaria precautions included using mosquito nets, taking paludrine daily, ensuring trousers were worn and 'shirt sleeves rolled down from sun set to sun rise and collars buttoned'.[168] Both the Americans and British also employed DDT spray and powder to combat malaria-carrying mosquitoes.

Most troops received lectures on the potential dangers of illicit sex, and VD clinics were established at divisional level.[169] By the 1950s, the availability of penicillin made the treatment of such conditions easier than had previously been the case. A British report noted 'Venereal Diseases… were common' with around 10,000 recorded cases during 1952, although 'improvement was obtained by reducing the time that reinforcements en route to Korea spent in the Base areas'.[170]

Even so, rates of VD among American and British Commonwealth troops remained high, especially once the war headed towards static mode, providing troops with greater opportunity to interact with local women. Poor hygiene, lack of alternative female companions or other forms of recreation might have contributed to the problem. Ironically, the availability of drugs, such as penicillin, might have encouraged some men to be more cavalier in their attitudes towards sex, knowing modern treatments were available.[171]

The cold weather encountered in Korea was another significant cause of injury, despite the numerous precautions troops were encouraged to take against it. According to William Donner, 'guys would slip on the steep hills and lose gloves' so that 'a lot of them came in with frozen hands all puffed up and that'.[172] Notably, during the Chosin Reservoir campaign, eventually 'everyone… complained about the cold' of the North Korean winter.[173] Even performing basic bodily functions was difficult. Artillery Sergeant John Saddic (11th Marines) noted:

> The worst thing was trying to take a leak. You're trying to find your pecker through six inches of clothing… It shrinks so it feels like it's gone into your belly. That's tough. And when you take a crap – well, you don't read any newspapers. Boom, boom, it's over. You try to clean yourself off and get your pants back on'.[174]

Temperatures at Chosin could reach as low as twenty below zero, frequently worsened by the wind, which many troops dubbed the 'Siberian Express'.[175] A US Navy surgeon attached to the Marine Corps identified several cases 'of what appeared to be shock… the shock of a terrific cold spell they weren't ready for'.[176] Symptoms were similar to men who had endured an extreme artillery bombardment and included 'a marked tremor' and sometimes 'suppression of the breathing rate'.[177] A major method of combating this was the provision of warming tents, where men who had been out in the cold could be revived with hot drinks, thaw out their boots and dry their socks before going back on duty. These were also places where the wounded could be sheltered. Marine Robert Samuels was evacuated with frostbitten feet and eventually hospitalised in America, where 'lots of guys lost… their legs or feet' because of it.[178]

However, treating frostbite didn't necessarily have to involve amputation. Lieutenant Colonel J.C. Watts, a surgeon at BCGH, considered such injuries similar to those from burns. After injecting a patient with penicillin, he removed the dead skin and swabbed the affected areas with detergent. Patients were then returned to their wards to dry out their blackened extremities and continue taking penicillin. After several weeks healthy skin began to break through the blackened crust, obviating the requirement for amputation and the patient could be prepared for a skin graft.[179]

Chapter 8

Prisoner of War Experiences

Official statistics state that 1,060 British servicemen were captured during the Korean War, a relatively small number when compared with the world wars.[1] Most soldiers and Royal Marines who became POWs were unprepared for what capture by Communist forces might entail. Cyril Cunningham, who worked for A19 (the POW Intelligence organisation) during the Korean War, emphasised that Whitehall was initially uncertain how the North Koreans and Chinese would treat prisoners. It was feared (rightly, as it transpired) that the former would prove as brutal as those Koreans that had served with the Imperial Japanese Army during the Second World War, and been responsible for helping run notorious POW camps in the Far East. Likewise, it was unclear to what extent Russia held influence above the 38th Parallel and would influence POW policy. Another important complication was that neither North Korea nor China were signatories to the Geneva Convention, which generated further uncertainty over how POWs would be treated.[2] Consequently, these countries didn't recognise the Red Cross either, which was deemed a 'capitalist organisation'.

As the British Official Historian noted, when compared with the NKPA the CPV tended to be 'better disciplined' and provided 'more humane' treatment, especially on marches to POW camps. Yet this was in relative terms, and anyone who stepped out of line with the Chinese could generally expect punishment. Both the NKPA and CPV held the opinion that 'military forces fighting against the Communist cause were, by definition, war criminals, political sinners'. As such they were allowed the chance to repent and via political education take up the fight against imperialism and capitalism.[3] Significantly, this was attempted by concerted efforts at political indoctrination or subversion, as part of what the Chinese termed their 'Lenient Policy'.

The popular view is that British POWs were highly resistant to this indoctrination, but as historian S.P. Mackenzie demonstrates in his book *British Prisoners of the Korean War* (2012), the truth was rather more nuanced, and varied over time and from location to location. While some prisoners were openly hostile and branded as 'reactionaries', to use Communist or Marxist terminology, others proved willing to collaborate or cooperate on various levels, leading them to be viewed as 'progressives'. However, the vast majority were simply desperate to make the best of the situation and survive until they were released.[4]

Over 7,000 American personnel were captured from 1950–53, and at least 2,583 died in captivity.[5] Notably, those taken prisoner by the North Koreans during the early phases of the war endured particularly barbarous treatment, several even being executed shortly after capture. Others died in camps under appalling conditions, not helped by suffering from 'giving-up-it is', a negative mental outlook that was detrimental to their chances of survival, and looms large in the literature on the Korean War.

Like their British counterparts, American POWs were subjected to Communist indoctrination, and, as Max Hastings observed, this was successful in turning several men into progressives or collaborators, even at officer level. At times American soldiers proved unwilling to cooperate with one another in captivity as well, because they tended to lack the esprit de corps that was a characteristic of the British regimental system. This was advantageous to their Communist captors, who sought to isolate them as part of their political re-education.[6] In the aftermath of the war, 'disturbing charges of collaboration and moral and physical softness' were levelled against many former American POWs, although few were actually convicted.[7] According to figures released by the US Department of Defence in 1955, of 3,973 army prisoners repatriated, 426 required 'further investigation' for alleged or suspected misconduct in captivity, along with fifty-two of the 200 repatriated POWs from the Marine Corps.[8] The situation was so serious that in August 1955 President Eisenhower was forced to issue Executive Order 10631, 'Code of Conduct for Members of the Armed Forces of the United States', regarding the behaviour expectedof personnel taken prisoner in the future.[9] Similarly, the fact that twenty-oneAmericansandoneRoyalMarinechosenottoberepatriatedafterthe ceasefire was an immense embarrassment to the West, and at the height of the Cold War generated hysteria over the threat of Communist 'brainwashing'.

However, several Americans became reactionaries and, like their British counterparts, were involved in escape attempts or other means of active resistance. Equally, many simply wanted to stay alive until their release and neither sought to collaborate with their captors nor openly resist them. Albert Biderman studied the behaviour of American POWs, and in the early 1960s questioned many of the findings made by earlier investigations on Korea. Despite the widespread allegations of collaboration, he maintained that one of the greatest lessons of 'Korean prisoner-of-war history' is that 'the ordinary man, when in a large mass of men, does not rush forth to be either a spectacular hero or a notorious traitor'.[10]

The Point of Capture or Surrender

If they were captured American and British troops were, in accordance with the Geneva Convention, expected to give their name, rank and number to the enemy and this was fostered during training. Gordon Lantz, an army NCO, former National Guardsman and farm boy from Leslie, Michigan, was captured in Korea. He recalled how he and his comrades had been told 'to act dumb' if they became POWs.[11] However, in the early 1950s the majority of personnel from both countries had not received any specialist training in escape and evasion or methods of countering political subversion by an enemy.

Although most men ended up in some form of camp, so long as they survived being captured, the actual circumstances of becoming a prisoner could vary from one individual or group to another. During the fighting at 'Happy Valley' in January 1951, the British lost around 200 men, mainly from 8th King's Royal Irish Hussars (8H) and 1st Battalion Royal Ulster rifles (RUR). Second World War veteran Edward (Ted) Beckerley served as a Cromwell tank driver with 8H and during the action discovered that the road they were on was blocked, so his tank would have to be abandoned and destroyed before he and the rest of the crew escaped on foot. Pursued by Chinese infantry, they climbed a nearby hill, where they came under fire from a Chinese machine gun, forcing them back the way they'd come. On taking cover the soldiers decided to pretend to be dead in an effort to fool the Chinese, a ruse employed by numerous UN soldiers during the war in an effort to evade capture. Unfortunately on this occasion it failed, and they were seized by a Chinese soldier at gun point and brought to join men who'd been captured in other parts of the valley.[12]

Other soldiers were forced into a position where their only choice was to surrender or risk being annihilated. At the Chosin Reservoir on 2 December 1950, PFC Lawrence Bailey from C Company, 32nd Infantry Regiment, recounted how they'd been surrounded by the Chinese for three weeks, and with supplies running out had no means of continuing the fight, so there 'wasn't much else we could do but surrender, and that's what we did'.[13] Similarly, in April 1951 towards the end of the Battle of the Imjin, where 1st Battalion Gloucestershire Regiment (Glosters) made its famous stand, with the gun lines under attack and unable to furnish effective support, 'every man' was ordered 'to make his own way back'. The adjutant of that battalion recorded how he and a large body of troops attempted to seek safety on foot, when from the hill sides around them they realised they were exposed to Chinese machine-gunners, who could have despatched them with ease if they'd desired. Their only credible option, despite all the determination with which they'd fought, was to lay down their arms and surrender to the enemy, something that was considered especially shameful by professional soldiers.[14]

Ambushes were another common means by which troops were taken prisoner, especially during the confused fighting of 1950–51, and later during the patrol warfare that characterised the static conditions at the front. Dale King enlisted in 1948 and was posted to Korea with 555th Field Artillery Battalion (FAB) or 'The Triple Nickels', part of 5th Regimental Combat Team (5th RCT), which saw heavy action early in the war. While his battery was moving southwards by road Chinese troops infiltrated to their rear and established roadblocks, forcing them into a trap. Eventually Dale King, with about fourteen others from his unit, found shelter in a drainage ditch, from where they engaged in a lengthy firefight with the Chinese on the road to their front. This lasted until night-time, when the Chinese surrounded them and closed in, leading the American lieutenant in charge to order his men to put down their weapons and surrender.[15]

Similarly, Corporal Billy Gaddy from A Company, 9th Infantry Regiment, 2nd Division, was ambushed while employed leading a small team laying telephone wire at Heartbreak Ridge during September 1951. Suddenly, bullets whizzed around them and he was hit in the leg, unable to walk. As he lay wounded, alone and afraid, North Korean soldiers 'moved in like lions closing on their prey' and he was dragged away, stripped of most of his uniform and put in 'a dug-out place, sort of like a cellar, for the night'.[16]

Sometimes troops were simply overrun during combat, and taken prisoner that way. Such a fate befell Sergeant Kenneth Nevill from 7th Marines on 7 July 1953, as he held an outpost known as East Berlin. His BAR jammed at a critical moment, enabling Chinese infantry to swarm towards the position. As they drew closer he threw as many grenades at them as he could, before being confronted by a Chinese soldier. Briefly they stared at one another 'eyeball to eyeball', before the enemy soldier leapt backwards as several of his comrades appeared. They bound the sergeant's hands, searched him and led him away as their attack continued.[17]

On being captured soldiers tended to experience a gamut of emotions, compounded by the fact that many were often still dazed and/or drained by recently experiencing combat. As a soldier from 'The Triple Nickels', who was captured in April 1951, found, it could take time for it to register that you really were a POW.[18] Other soldiers felt a sense of failure and conviction that they'd not only let themselves down, but also their country, unit and even family. One of the 600 other ranks from the Glosters, captured at the Battle of the Imjin in April 1951, started reviewing the circumstances of his capture in his mind and questioning events. 'Was I a coward? If I had done this differently, or that faster, or something else another way-would it have made any difference?'[19]

Ultimately, becoming a POW was degrading, frightening and clouded by uncertainty as to how the North Koreans or Chinese might behave. When John Erickson from 23rd Infantry Regiment, 2nd Division, was captured by the Chinese, he and his comrades had been forced to surrender, or else the enemy were going to rake the Korean hut in which they'd been sheltering with machine-gun fire. Subsequently, they were hauled off into a pig pen for the night. Initially he:

> didn't know what was going to happen. I didn't know if we were gonna go down the road and they were trying to open up on us. There was probably 15–25 of us right there. I didn't know if they was gonna open up and fire on us and kill us all or nothing. I had no idea what they were going to do.[20]

In contrast, David Green, a National Serviceman from the Glosters, taken prisoner at the Imjin, was bewildered to be confronted by the sight of 'lightly leather-belted men in sand-coloured uniforms' who were 'hugging and shaking hands with our blokes who, like me were in a state of shock'.[21] Typically, shortly after this most troops were searched and relieved of their equipment and personal kit, plus 'such items as fountain pens and watches'.[22] Many captured at the Imjin, including Rifleman Leonard Jones (RUR), also remembered being gathered together with others captured during the fighting, and initially the wounded didn't receive any medical treatment.[23] Under such conditions Bill Fox, a young National Serviceman from Manchester with the Glosters, feared that they might be shot 'a bullet in the back of the head'.[24] He was justified to fear such brutality, as numerous atrocities had been committed by the Communists, and as a soldier from the RUR recounted most UN troops were aware of this or had even witnessed them.[25] During October 1950, for example, American troops from 5th Cavalry Regiment, captured near Waeg-wan, had been led into a ravine and shot by North Korean personnel.[26]

Unsurprisingly, as he sat smoking his last cigarette shortly after capture in April 1951, feeling like a condemned man, Henry O'Kane, a regular soldier with the RUR, 'did not feel assured by the safe conduct pass that had been given to me earlier in the day'.[27] However, even amid the fear and confusion of being captured like this, the situation was sometimes ameliorated by moments of humour. The adjutant of the Glosters witnessed Chinese soldiers rifling through their former HQ area in search of loot. One little Chinaman stumbled upon a tin of peaches, which he ate, and then with relish proceeded to tackle another tin of what turned out to be solid fuel. He 'dropped writhing to the ground' and was violently sick, 'an incident which kept me fairly cheerful for the rest of the day'.[28]

Journey to the Camps

Having been captured, prisoners had to be transported away from the battle area, and if they survived long enough most would spend months or years in POW camps in North Korea. In this regard those captured from 1951 onwards tended to be at an advantage because by then overall responsibility for running the POW camps had passed from the notoriously cruel North Koreans to the Chinese. Even so, most POWs still endured gruelling marches to camps on the border between North Korea and Manchuria.

After being captured near Taejon in July 1950, Corporal Jack Browning from M Company, 34th Infantry Regiment, was marched to a railhead with around 700–750 other bedraggled POWs. Here they were forced into boxcars for a journey to Pyongyang, the North Korean capital, all the while fervently hoping that the train would not be targeted by UN fighter-bombers. Subsequently, he was made to embark on a brutal march, under a North Korean Security Police officer dubbed 'The Tiger', during which many POWs died from malnutrition, dysentery, sheer exhaustion or being shot as a lesson to others. Veterans of the Pacific Campaign, who'd survived the infamous Bataan Death March, reckoned the conditions were even worse than those they'd endured under the Japanese during the Second World War.[29]

Another POW from 34th Regiment who experienced this event during autumn/winter 1950 remembered that men had to eat and defecate in their uniforms as they marched, and often as they plodded along a rifle shot would signify that 'some American would not see home again'. During the night a GI would sometimes lean on him, only to be found dead from exposure in the morning. Under such dire conditions men did try to support one another when possible, inspired by the presence of a Catholic priest who was part of a small band of civilian captives held by the North Koreans and forced onto the march. However, this was not always the case. A badly wounded American airman had one of his crutches stolen by a GI for firewood, and because of this he was later forced out of the column for being too slow and a shot was heard, so he was assumed to have been killed.[30]

Jack Chapman, an NCO from D Company, 31st RCT, was captured at the Chosin Reservoir in late November 1950, after suffering multiple wounds, and endured a similarly tough experience. After being stripped of personal possessions, together with captured Marines, and a small number of Royal Marines from 41 Independent Commando, he was marched for around nineteen days in freezing conditions towards Kangyee, and never received treatment for his wounds. Anyone who fell out of the column was shot and left to freeze by the roadside, and he witnessed a Marine with a bad leg wound being murdered by a Chinese soldier under exactly these circumstances.[31]

Frostbite, dysentery caused by drinking snow/water from fields fertilized by human waste, and constant hunger added to the miseries of the prisoners captured during the Chosin Reservoir campaign. Notably, Royal Marines attempted to buck each other up by telling themselves that conditions had been 'far worse on the Commando course'. It was also during this early phase of captivity that they first became aware of the cultural gulf between themselves and the Chinese. After one day's march the Royal Marines in the group were shepherded into a building to hide during the day, when a Chinese soldier brought in a bowl of hot water. Desperate to clean up they assumed this was meant for their ablutions and queued to wash their face and hands, only to be confronted by livid Chinese guards brandishing their rifles. As an irate Chinese officer explained, the guards had specially heated the water so they could have a hot drink, and their actions were an insult, as only snow was for washing.[32] Likewise, once in captivity many British soldiers found the Chinese practice of 'walking hand-in-hand' or with their 'arms round one another' strange, and even wondered if they were all 'poofters'.[33]

Those members of 29th Brigade captured in January 1951, including Ted Beckerley, endured a torrid march northwards into captivity, typically covering about fifteen miles per night and sheltering by day in Korean villages so as to avoid the attentions of UN aircraft. Initially the Chinese guards were not too bad and insisted that the POWs were to be taken somewhere 'where they would see the light'. However, during the latter stages North Korean guards took over, and proved only too happy to loot prisoners or lash out with their rifle butts at the merest provocation. For men who were becoming increasingly weak as a result of their captivity and limited rations, the Korean terrain and climate were further significant challenges.[34]

According to the historian S.P. Mackenzie, when compared with the North Koreans some of the Chinese troops guarding British POWs after the Battle of the Imjin behaved relatively well, particularly those supervising able-bodied prisoners who were able to march unaided as opposed to stretcher-bound wounded. As he put it 'the nasty ones were often balanced out by those with a sense of common humanity'.[35] David Green vividly remembered an old Chinese guard who would sometimes slip him tobacco that he had scrounged especially for the prisoners.[36] Even so, another POW from the RUR found there were times when the Chinese guards were only too ready to 'use their rifle butts on us'.[37]

The POWs were split up so that officers marched at the head of columns and junior NCOs and private soldiers stayed further back. This was part of the Communists' efforts to break down the existing rank structure, organize men into squads, and so make them more malleable to indoctrination. Typically, they were fed on sorghum and soya beans, plus limited amounts of hot water, and often housed en route to North Korea in village huts or bunkers, where they became infested with body lice. Some troops' plight was made even worse as their boots had worn out on active service, so they had to wear their 'best boots', which had been polished to perfection, but under the strain of marching the leather cracked and cut severely into men's feet.[38] On the plus side, those captured in April 1951 were at least aided by the warmer spring weather when compared with troops captured earlier in the war.

Lofty Large, a regular soldier with the Glosters, was badly wounded during the Imjin Battle, but still went on to have a distinguished career with the SAS. He recalled that for him, the march was a 'grinding, stumbling trek through the dark mountains and hills of Korea'. It was a relief to hear a shout 'like Sueselah-Ah', broadly meaning 'taking five', and even better when the guards shouted 'Sweejo-Ah', the signal that a column had reached its destination and would be laying up after a night's march.[39]

Despite the conditions, many British POWs seem to have been able to maintain their morale and support each other. On reflection one reckoned that often 'the irrepressible British soldier's spirit was well to the fore'.[40] One way in which this was demonstrated was via singing, including calypso-style songs such as *Stone Cold Dead in de Market*, *Brown Skin Girl* and *The Blue Tail Fly*, as the Glosters had been stationed in the West Indies during the late 1940s, and there were still sufficient regulars around in Korea who remembered these.[41] Given the paucity of their rations, fantasising about food provided another method of raising their spirits. According to Albert Tyas, who spent most of his National Service with the RUR:

> My favourite pastime was with a couple of Leeds lads who would describe a walk through Leeds Market, talk about each stall, describe its delicious contents, then finally we would come to the stall that sold wonderful teacakes and opposite there was a sausage

stall, 'Wonderful Paul Thorpes'. We would purchase a sausage and a teacake, cook them and put them together.[42]

However, as Derek Kinne, who served with the Royal Northumberland Fusiliers (RNF) and was notably awarded the George Cross for his resistance to the Communists while in captivity, noted, simultaneously he sensed a divide between how well British officers stood up to becoming prisoners when compared with other ranks. On the marches he appreciated that despite the difficulties encountered, such as lack of food and exhaustion, 'all the fancy ways an officer had gave him something worthwhile to keep him going', whereas BORs seemed to lose much of 'the old "mucking-in" spirit', and didn't help each other unless they were good friends, and some even attempted to get 'food at the expense of other men'.[43]

Various camps were used to house American and British POWs. These didn't conform to the stereotypical image of a POW camp, as reinforced by Second World War experience, especially in Europe. Typically, there were no guard towers, barrack blocks/huts, or elaborate wire fences. When David Green entered Camp 1 at Chongsong, which housed most of those taken at the Imjin, he founded it 'entirely different' to the popular image of a POW camp, as it was based around that village in a picturesque valley near the Manchurian border deep into North Korea, where the 'chances of making a successful escape were remote'.[44] According to the Communists, the guards at this and other camps were there to keep the POWs safe from the North Korean locals, rather than keep them in, and there was a core of truth in this, especially as the country was regularly being bombed, thus stoking up hatred against the American-led UN forces.

The 'Bean or Mining Camp', forty-five miles southeast of Pyongyang, was used as a transit camp for POWs being taken further north towards the Yalu, and based on accommodation originally employed by a mine located in a ravine surrounded by high ridges. Darrell Krenz served with 24th Infantry Division and was captured near Taejon on 20 July 1950. When he finally arrived at a camp in North Korea, he was put in a small mud hut with twenty other men, before being moved to an old school house.[45]

During 1950–51, Camp 10 near Kangyee, about ninety miles northwest of Hungnam, was used as a temporary indoctrination centre for UN troops captured in northeast Korea, including members of 41 Independent Commando RM. It comprised a series of huts either side of track that ran along a valley floor, about ten miles north of Kangyee. Here POWs were split up into companies, each of three platoons of five squads, with one guard for every two prisoners. Although the huts provided some protection from the weather, they were bare, save for straw mats, and there were no washing facilities of any kind. Crammed together prisoners soon 'found themselves crawling with lice and other parasites', which added to their misery.[46]

At Camp 12 at Pyongyang a group of Americans were initially held who had been selected for propaganda work. The establishment went on to form what was termed the 'Peace Fighters School' and as the war continued, here and at Camp 5 POWs could generally expect better treatment so long as they cooperated. Anyone who refused risked being sent to Camp 9, better known as the Kandong Caves, which consisted of a few huts and tunnels dug deep into the hillside. Here hundreds of UN prisoners and countless Koreans died from neglect in appalling conditions, characterized by overcrowding and lack of sanitation and medical treatment.[47]

Interrogation, Indoctrination, and the Chinese Lenient Policy

Shortly after capture, many troops underwent some form of interrogation by the Communists, and often the process was continued later in their captivity as well. While the Chinese and their Russian allies in particular were interested in gathering potentially useful military intelligence from POWs, simultaneously a major thrust of interrogations was initiating the process of identifying prisoners who might be most susceptible to political indoctrination. Henry O'Kane's experience was fairly typical of a great many BORs who were captured, and were not privy to specialist military information. He recounted that after asking for his name, rank and number, his interrogator:

> appeared uninterested in military matters, but he demanded the names of three British officers who I was on familiar terms with. I had to reply that I was, as a private soldier, not personally acquainted with any of the officers in my unit. His main theme then seemed to be how and what I was doing in Korea.[48]

This was a common theme of numerous interrogations endured by American and British troops. Several Royal Marines found that rather than being grilled for military information, the Chinese wanted them to provide details that would provide a socio-economic impression of their lives. Under these conditions one Cockney Royal Marine caused immense amusement among British POWs, as when questioned about the amount of land belonging to his family, he 'vividly described his window box'.[49]

Nick Tosques remembered that he and his fellow American prisoners endured numerous initial interrogation sessions, but didn't feel they ever divulged any worthwhile military information. When asked if he had belonged to an artillery unit, he simply replied 'yeah' without going into further details and that seemed to satisfy his captors.[50] At other times the conditions were more threatening. Shortly after his capture, Billy Gaddy was questioned throughout the night and repeatedly threatened by a North Korean officer brandishing a pistol, before eventually being told he would be sent to a POW camp, where he was led to believe he would be adequately fed and receive medical treatment.[51] Anyone identified as possessing specialist/technical training also feared that the enemy might single them out for particularly tough treatment in order to extract information. A Japanese-American NCO from 163rd Military Intelligence (US Army) was attached to 41 Independent Commando RM as an interpreter and POW interrogator. When captured in December 1950, he was mightily relieved that no one revealed his background.[52]

Typically, the Communists were only interested in viewing the world from their perspective, and proved masters at manipulating the facts, regardless of the evidence and the rank/status of the prisoner they were dealing with. During an early interrogation, Derek Kinne, who was branded a 'reactionary', was harangued by an English-speaking North Korean officer who said that he was a: 'Capitalist! Imperialist aggressor! Tool of Wall Street! Raper of Korean national aspirations!' All these terms he found difficult to comprehend, like many British troops.[53] Major General William Dean, who had commanded the American 24th Infantry Division, spent his entire captivity in the hands of the North Koreans. His interrogators spent hours attempting to convince him that the South Koreans were responsible for starting the war, and that the North Korean invasion of June 1950 was simply a 'counterattack' launched in self-defence.[54] Similarly, another 'reactionary', the adjutant of the Glosters, was instructed by a Chinese political officer how capitalist states, in fear of 'oppressed working people' worldwide, 'had engineered the war in Korea to whip up feeling against the "democratic" states of the Cominform block'.[55]

Most American and British POWs were exposed to what the CPV termed their 'Lenient Policy', forged during the Chinese Civil War (1945–49) that saw the Communists under Mao Tse-tung rise to power. The essential tenet of the policy was that the Korean War was unjust, and that UN prisoners were 'war criminals', who deserved to be killed, but as 'ordinary working men' they had been misled by their 'reactionary rulers' and would not be executed (hence the 'leniency') but instead given a chance at 'repentance for their crimes'.[56] As Reverend Sam Davies, chaplain to the Glosters, discovered shortly after his capture in April 1951, the Chinese considered them to be 'duped by the American imperialists' and 'fighting against the righteous cause of the Korean people', but they would be given an opportunity 'to learn the truth through study', and correct their errors. They were told not to be afraid and that 'at home your loved ones await you. Obey our rules and regulations and you will not be shot'.[57]

While at transit camps, many POWs, including the 200-odd British troops captured at 'Happy Valley', were interviewed about their political affiliations and issued an autobiographical form to complete. Some were hesitant about this as the form went beyond merely giving 'name, rank and number', whereas others felt it wouldn't do any harm to provide truthful details about their age, politics, educational and family backgrounds or even military function. The Chinese hoped that this would identify men potentially sympathetic to their beliefs, while the North Koreans desired that such individuals might be employed in propaganda efforts.[58] Conversely, there were those who felt it wise to provide facetious answers, sometimes aided by the language barrier, which could make it difficult for the Chinese to spot deliberate mistakes. However, even when information was given correctly during interrogations, many POWs found the truth antagonised their Communist captors. Dale King recalled that the Chinese who questioned him refused to believe that in the 1950s car ownership was widespread in America. The disparity between what the average American had compared with the Chinese made them 'mad', and consistently they seemed unable to grasp what conditions were really like in the West.[59]

Closely linked to interrogation was indoctrination or 'political re-education'. Having started this shortly after capture, the Communists persisted with it in some form or other at the various POW camps. According to Reverend Davies, as prisoners of the Chinese they were to be deemed 'fellow students – that is of Marxist Leninism'.[60] This process of 're-education' encompassed all facets of camp life, and was designed to make POWs 'more receptive to the Communist way of thinking'. Even something as simple as 'a sing-song' by prisoners required censorship by the Chinese, if it were not to be branded as a hostile act and therefore worthy of punishment. As an official British booklet from 1955 outlined, such conditions ensured that many prisoners began to say what the Chinese wanted them to hear, so as to avoid being branded a 'reactionary' and suffer punishment. While this didn't mean they actively collaborated with the Chinese, it did entail a willingness to put their names to 'peace' petitions/broadcasts, or insert 'Communist jargon' into letters home.[61] Another motivation behind such limited cooperation was that it did raise the possibility for men to let the outside world know that they'd been captured and were still alive.

Indoctrination for prisoners captured during 1950–51 also took the form of lengthy lectures and discussion periods. Typical topics included: 'The

Democratic Reformation and Democratic structure in North Korea and the Peaceful Unification Policy of the North Korean Government.'[62] Prisoners were issued with notebooks and expected to take the compulsory study seriously, something that was sometimes reinforced by written examinations, designed to test whether they had understood the points made. At Camp 1, Henry O'Kane noted:

> we spent hours on the square attending long lectures on the manifesto of the Communist Party, political economics, the writings of Marx, Engels, Lenin and the thoughts of Mao. We then had lectures at company level, then at platoon level and later, after discussion in our rooms we had to make notes on paper which we had to submit to our political instructors.

Alongside this often went further interrogations from Chinese political staff, primarily aimed at establishing POW's backgrounds, and sounding out their views on questions such as: 'Who started the Korean War?'[63] Another common theme was: 'Capitalist society needs a war every two years. Why?' Only the Communist/Marxist viewpoint was accepted as being correct.

The effectiveness of 'compulsory study' was open to question, and it is noteworthy that by mid-1952 the Chinese dropped such efforts in favour of 'voluntary study groups'. Those who didn't attend these were frequently submitted to personal indoctrination, a potentially formidable weapon, as although during a lecture a man might doze or not pay attention, when face-to-face with an instructor, 'he was forced to listen to talk when it was directed at him personally'.[64] Several BORs, including Albert Tyas, found that the constant barrage of Marxist Leninism was 'over their heads' and they were confused by the seemingly impenetrable terminology. 'We didn't know what Proletariat meant or what they were on about'.[65] For Derek Kinne, the lectures and study became extremely boring, and he was put off cooperating when he heard the 'slanderous' comments instructors made in relation to Britain, which he knew to be inaccurate.[66] Another POW observed that 'the British Army is a non-political organisation. Loyalty is to the Crown, representing the Country, irrespective of political parties. Hardly any of us knew anything of politics in those days'.[67]

In contrast, Bill Fox found that he 'listened intently to the education', and as a Manchester lad was fascinated to hear about the work of Friedrich Engels and his observations on nineteenth-century working conditions and slums in that city, plus mention of the *Manchester Guardian*, all of which were new to him.[68] After the war, work by personnel from A19 established that the small numbers of Royal Marines held at Kangyee comprised the greatest numbers of collaborators among British POWs.[69] Notably, Marine Andrew Condron from West Lothian 'converted to Communism' and chose not to be repatriated in 1953, although he did later return home from China. The material he was exposed to at Kangyee apparently sparked his interest, and later at Camp 5, Pyoktong, he was able to continue with his political interests, and as part of the camp's committee, endorsed by the Chinese, he managed to negotiate some improvement in living conditions on behalf of the POWs, so remained popular.[70] According to Max Hastings, with hindsight his actions might 'owe far less to the wiles of his Communist captors than to his own wilfulness', as he was something of a 'maverick', deeply infatuated with Marxism, as opposed to Communism, including a self-confessed fascination about whether it worked in practice.[71]

American POWs were exposed to comparable levels of indoctrination, or what they often termed 'brainwashing', and similarly risked suffering punishment, particularly if they were deemed to have exhibited 'reactionary' behaviour. Although he admitted that some American POWs were receptive to Communism, Nick Tosques felt it was all 'baloney', and most men in his camp tried to appear as if they agreed with their captors, while inwardly they were desperately thinking about home, being free and getting on with their lives.[72] Similarly, PFC Charles Quiring (USMC) was captured at the Chosin Reservoir in December 1950 and taken to a camp near Kangdong, before being selected for repatriation during 1951. The Communists hoped that he would continue the class struggle once released. He described being subjected to numerous interviews on his home life, political lectures, Communist reading material, and being taught a song about the Proletariat to the tune of *Glory, Glory, Hallelujah*. Later he confided that 'most didn't have a clue what these terms meant', but went along with the 'charade', as the enemy sought to re-educate them along Communist lines.[73]

Another strand to the experience of indoctrination came during spring 1952, when the Communists accused the Americans of mounting a 'germ warfare' campaign against North Korea by dropping bombs containing insects infected with anthrax, cholera and encephalitis. This was supported by confessions drawn from captured American airmen, and numerous propaganda materials of questionable validity such as highly inconclusive photographs, but had it been true it would have constituted a war crime. This had a knock-on effect on many POWs, and as one British soldier recounted at his camp a massive 'hygiene campaign' ensued during this period. Simultaneously, they were berated by the Chinese commandant about this alleged use of 'germ warfare' by the Americans, which unfortunately from their captors' viewpoint lost its impact in translation, as they were informed the 'Capitalist, Imperialist Aggressors' had initiated 'Black Treacle Warfare!'[74]

Life in the Camps

Clearly coping with indoctrination formed a large part of the American and British POWs' experience in Korea. Officers and NCOs from the British Army, for example, appear to have been better at resisting it than reservists and other ranks split up from their leaders.[75] While some men proved susceptible to it, owing to holding left-wing political views prior to captivity, many others were coerced into cooperating with their captors simply in order to survive. Derek Kinne vividly remembered a visit to his camp by a couple of dedicated progressives, a British lance corporal accompanied by an American sergeant, who among other things exhorted them 'to strike a blow against capitalism for world peace!'[76] In contrast, a British sergeant at Camp 12 who questioned the propaganda activities conducted by prisoners was told by an American soldier that: 'We all want to stay alive and the way we're playing it now will keep us that way'.[77]

Like their American counterparts, many British prisoners, especially at Camp 10, developed an ability to appear attentive during lectures as the instructors roamed among them, when in fact they were dreaming of other things or switched off altogether. Similarly, during study periods discussions could often be turned onto subjects such as football, provided suitable Marxist phrases were thrown in when appropriate, as most Chinese who came to observe spoke little or no English. To many the constant questioning was regarded as 'a big joke', particularly as the alternative was to become embroiled in an argument with their instructors, which the Chinese welcomed, especially as they tended to demonstrate the knack of repeatedly twisting the facts to fit with their Communist outlook.[78]

Related to this was the expectation that prisoners would conduct Marxist-style self-criticism when they'd infringed the rules, usually after having faced some form of punishment, such as a spell of solitary confinement. This was delivered in front of the rest of the prisoners and taken seriously by their captors. To some POWs the whole process 'generated a feeling of distaste', and was further evidence of a clash of cultures and ideologies.[79] However, they often provided moments of much-needed humour for prisoners, especially if gags were able to be slipped past their captors, while still subscribing to the necessary use of Marxist phrases. On some occasions recaptured escapees were even able to impart useful information to other would be escapees during self-confessions, again hidden among the Marxist terminology.

As one former POW observed, soon 'prisoners became aware that political expediency lay at the heart of everything required of them'.[80] It wasn't just the efforts at indoctrination, but also subjects such as mail, food and access to medical treatment effectively became political weapons. As indicated above, the opportunity to let friends and family know that they were alive was a motivating force for many POWs, and one eagerly exploited by the Communists. In 1952 POWs were given 'the choice of using airmail stationary decorated with the Communist "peace dove" and with propaganda slogans such as "Unite for Peace", or of not writing at all'. Likewise, for anyone wishing to reply, the designated return address ultimately became 'POW Camp, Democratic People's Republic of Korea, c/o the Chinese People's Committee for World Peace, Peking China', so that any prisoner sending a letter was forced into disseminating propaganda material.[81] Prisoners were also forced to put suitable Communist slogans into their letters, if they were to stand any chance of being delivered.

Some POWs (usually progressives) were also interviewed by a handful of journalists, including Alan Winnington of the *Daily Worker* and the violently anti-American Michael Shapiro, plus British Communists, notably Monica Felton (chair of the British National Assembly of Women). Potentially, these individuals could have done something to improve camp conditions, but this wasn't in the Communists' interests as they didn't wish to raise the morale of prisoners. Instead, they typically spread numerous false stories about the 'idyllic life' led by POWs held in North Korea, and were supportive of Communist propaganda efforts against the West.[82]

Food was grossly inadequate for most prisoners, especially during 1950–51. Initially Darrell Krenz and his fellow POWs received a little millet and sip of water from the North Koreans once a day and that was all.[83] Similarly, a Hawaiian NCO held in transit at the 'Mining Camp' found that he could manage the daily meal 'of soupy rice or millet', but many of his fellow prisoners couldn't and starved to death.[84] Captured a little later in the war by the Chinese, Albert Tyas survived much of his captivity on a soya bean breakfast, and 'a meal' of sorghum (like pearl barley) later on, plus rice was issued about every ten days.[85]

The threat of starvation was one way in which the Communists induced men to cooperate with them, even if on a comparatively minor level such as signing a peace petition, as those who signed would be given better food. Similarly, progressives such as those at Camp 5 tended to receive better rations as they were deemed to 'study well' by their Chinese captors. According to one report, as the war progressed the food in most camps improved enough to reduce the incidence of malnutrition and problems related to vitamin deficiency.[86] Even so, like their counterparts during the Second World War, hunger was routinely experienced by most POWs in Korea.

Medical provision was initially non-existent, leading to numerous deaths among POWs, and doctors taken prisoner were prevented from working unless they 'learnt the truth'.[87] The Intelligence Officer from 1 RNF was wounded in the leg when a Centurion tank fired on his group shortly after their capture at the Imjin, and he found the Chinese 'did not like our own doctors looking after us'.[88] An American doctor captured early in the war commented that in his camp, 'a patient had to be almost dead or have an obscure medical problem before the Chinese would allow him to go to the hospital'.[89]

Like Far East Prisoners of War (FEPOWs) during the Second World War, troops captured in Korea suffered from a range of problems and diseases owing to neglect and/or deliberate mistreatment by their captors, as well as the harsh environment of North Korea. At the 'Mining Camp' during 1950–51, it was recorded by an American doctor that 100 per cent of POWs had dysentery and suffered from severe weight loss, and a similar number were affected by cold injuries, of whom 15 per cent suffered tissue loss. Some POWs contracted pneumonia or developed infectious hepatitis, and by late February 'nutritional edema began to develop'.[90] A British POW at Camp 1 remembered that most suffered from a type of scabies caused by lice that infested their bodies and the remains of their uniforms, and later the clothes they were given by the Chinese. Typically, these could be crushed between thumb and forefinger until men's fingernails turned black with their encrusted blood. Malnutrition 'caused our tongues and mouths to become red and raw', plus many suffered from dysentery, and 'what was known as "bone pains", …mostly in the thigh bones and legs which occurred at night or when resting'. He also contracted 'a type of jaundice fever that kept reoccurring', and although the Chinese offered no help, Filipino prisoners fed him specially cooked rice, and gave him a herbal remedy made from leaves gathered in the hills when out foraging wood for the camp.[91]

For early American POWs, who had previously been used to a daily US Army combat ration of 3,500 calories, the change in diet, such as that endured by Darrel Krenz, was especially difficult to cope with. It was 'devoid of vegetables, almost barren of proteins, minerals or vitamins'.[92] Men became embroiled in a desperate battle for survival, and in numerous cases discipline broke down when a 'dog-eat-dog' attitude developed among groups of prisoners. Others tried to help one another, but there were still numerous cases of 'give-up-itis' where men fell into a state of utter despair, refused any help or to eat and died. This was a shock to the many British POWs who came into contact with Americans, especially at Camp 1, where, as Albert Tyas witnessed, 'Boot Hill [the burial ground] claimed its victims'. Routinely he watched as around thirty American corpses per day were taken there, when he first arrived at the camp.[93]

As the war continued some medical treatment was provided in many camps, including for intestinal worms, which along with tapeworms were arguably the most unpleasant of the many parasites that bedevilled POWs, and when left untreated contributed to men's deaths. They tended to look like earth worms, but were white and would often spatter out in a ball when a prisoner defecated or even be coughed up. John Erickson was given some garlic by the Chinese, and 'next day I could feel my stomach really acting up. And I could see the worms coming out and I gotta hold of it in my hand and pulled on it and I gotta load of blood and everything and I had to take a third lot of garlic. That's the reason I am alive today'.[94]

Similarly, many POWs endured primitive dentistry, such as at Camp 1 where the only tool available for extractions was 'a pair of rusty pliers with padded handles'. In the absence of anaesthetic, patients often found that 'a smoke of the weed' that grew plentifully nearby was welcome. Alternatively, being made to bend over and touch their toes and stretch a few times, before being rapidly bear-hugged, could induce a brief spell of unconsciousness, hopefully just long enough to pull a tooth.[95] Likewise, many POWs found that smoking marijuana could relieve the pain they suffered from wounds, and provide recreational relief from the daily grind of their captivity.

Many POWs found mechanisms that could help them better cope mentally with captivity. Captain Carl Dain had commanded a radar troop with 45th Field Regiment, Royal Artillery, intended for counter-bombardment work, and was held at the separate officers' camp established near Chongsong, where his speciality remained a secret from the Chinese. A fellow prisoner remembered how he appeared 'to keep sane' by reciting various logarithms and gunnery data to himself.[96] Another method employed by all ranks was to embark on so called 'crazy activity' or even a 'Crazy Week', as notably conducted by American officer POWs. Prisoners of the Axis powers during the Second World War had undertaken similar activity, sometimes dubbed 'goon baiting', and there were several troops taken prisoner in Korea who had been wartime captives, so were already familiar with this type of behaviour. Essentially the aim was to employ 'schoolboy prankishness' in order to rile and bewilder their captors while boosting their own morale. This could include activities such as walking invisible dogs on invisible leads, or football matches with an invisible ball. Alternatively, men might walk around their camp fondling imaginary ladies, or riding imaginary horses, motorcycles and bicycles. Large crowds would gather to watch enthusiastic games of ping-pong, their heads moving from side to side, except there was no bat or ball, 'merely a mime show to needle the Chinese'.[97]

Although less dramatic, another factor that helped buoy prisoner's spirits was giving their guards and instructors nicknames. One instructor demanded that all British officers hand over any 'erotic pictures' he believed they owned, and was forever after known as 'Dirty Picture' or 'DP Wong'.[98] Dave Green remembered one Chinese instructor at Camp 1 who proved more likeable than most, appeared less fanatical, and was keen to improve his English. On account of being tall with fair skin and a possessing a large head, he was christened 'Maggot'.[99]

Like their counterparts during the Second World War, American and British POWs in Korea engaged in a variety of entertainments when possible, although these were carefully censored by the Chinese. Until it was banned, darts was popular in Camp 1. Prisoners employed home-made boards and darts, and established their own league, often with teams of soldiers from the same part of Britain. Similarly, old cardboard was used to make sets of playing cards. Novel haircuts provided another form of amusement, as the soldiers who set themselves up as camp barbers were able to produce a variety of designs, including 'Mohicans', 'hot cross buns' and 'Friar Tucks'.[100]

Reading was allowed, and some POWs enjoyed it, but they were only able to consult material approved by their captors for its Marxist-Leninist content. This included old copies of the *Daily Worker*, an English-language newspaper, or books such as *Das Kapital*, and certain novels by the likes of George Eliot and Charles Dickens. The *Daily Worker* was especially appreciated by many British POWs, not for its political content, but because it contained the cricket scores.[101] Likewise, smoking offered relief to many when POWs tobacco was issued, and any scraps of paper from the walls in huts to pages from books were liable to be rolled into cigarettes. Another relatively benign occupation, but one which reminded prisoners that they were not alone and the war was still being fought, was watching aerial combat from their camps, as high-flying American Sabre jets slugged it out with Communist Mig-15s.

Potentially plays and films provided another avenue of entertainment. Henry O'Kane remembered being herded together with a large group of tired, hungry prisoners during late summer 1951, to watch a production of *The Whitehaired Girl* put on by a travelling Chinese opera/theatre group. They 'applauded joyfully every time the girl got raped by the landlord and hissed at the wrong places much to the disgust' of their captors. Films usually consisted of Communist propaganda material covering subjects such as 'food production', which many POWs found boring.[102] In contrast, another British soldier reckoned that the shows POWs were allowed to produce themselves reflected, 'the ingenuity of the talented men who ran them'.[103]

According to one account of POW experience in Korea, there was 'virtually no homosexuality' and soon after being captured men lost interest in sex.[104] Certainly, as for FEPOWs, the diet and conditions prisoners endured in Korea probably did reduce the male sex drive, plus survival might have seemed a more important issue. However, as David Green explains in his memoirs, there were plenty of instances when they talked about girls/sex, and he and some of the other POWs at Camp 1 found one of their female Chinese instructors/interrogators attractive. Similarly, one of his hut mates maintained an active interest in masturbation, even knocking a hole in the hut wall from which he could see a Korean girl doing her laundry. Other POWs were open about being homosexuals, and 'some of the "leading ladies" from theatrical productions had to watch their step in camp', although 'there were a couple who seemed to enjoy the attention'.[105]

As with other aspects of camp life, religion was closely monitored by the Chinese. Reverend Davies (the only UN chaplain to survive captivity) explained how he encountered a 'degree of religious toleration' in that it was possible to hold services in the officers' camp where he was held. However, matters were so encumbered with 'prohibitions, warnings, accusations, mental harassment, censorings, punishments', that to term this 'Religious Freedom' was laughable.[106] Even so, the services he was able to hold provided succour to many, and from Christmas 1951 involved the stone cross that the commanding officer of the Glosters had carved in captivity, using only two nails, a primitive hammer and concrete steps to smooth the sides.[107] Likewise, an American sergeant and committed Christian incarcerated at Camp 4 was relieved to receive reluctant permission from the Chinese to hold religious services with the men, where *The Old Rugged Cross* written on cigarette paper, the only paper available, proved popular.[108]

Escape was a difficult proposition, as while breaking out of the camps was often practicable, potential escapees were then faced with numerous difficulties if they were to reach the safety of UN lines from North Korea. This was more onerous than the challenge faced by escapees in occupied Europe during the Second World War, and had more in common with the experience of FEPOWs. Along with the hostile terrain and climate, potential escapees faced the almost insurmountable problems of language, lack of knowledge about Korean life and their vastly different physical appearance. Inevitably these made it more difficult to evade encounters with enemy soldiers or civilians. Nor could escapees reach a neutral country or even a port where there might be neutral shipping, because they were 'bottled up on a narrow peninsula'.[109]

Generally, one of the best times to mount an escape was shortly after capture, before the enemy had fully processed prisoners, but often troops were dazed from recent combat at this stage and not necessarily attuned to escape. They also often lacked the necessary 'hero-like mentality' to pull this sort of venture off successfully. Even General Sir Anthony Farrar-Hockley and Fusilier Derek Kinne, who notably made several escape attempts during their captivity, as described in their books *The Edge of the Sword* (1955) and *The Wooden Boxes* (1955) respectively, were ultimately unsuccessful and brutally tortured when recaptured. Notably, the former was subjected to a prolonged water torture, better known in the twenty-first century as 'water boarding', while the latter's 'punishment' included numerous beatings, being severely manacled, and confined to a stinking, bug-infested wooden box, around 5 feet 9 inches long, by 4 feet 6 inches high, and 2 feet in width. Both were highly courageous, intelligent soldiers and the former, as adjutant to the Glosters, had the advantage of possessing a better understanding of Korea than most POWs.

However, there were some successful escape efforts by soldiers, under certain conditions, especially early in the war.[110] Former Second World War POW Private Paul Smith was captured again in July 1950, when serving with 24th Division in Korea. He was briefly held at Camps 4 and 5 in Pyoktong, North Korea. The fighting was particularly confused at this stage, and he was captured long before the Chinese entry into the war. Having been taken to work on a farm by North Korean guards, he and other prisoners spotted some trucks that appeared unguarded. They stole one, and hurtled southwards despite coming under fire. Eventually they had to abandon their bullet-riddled vehicle and continue on foot. After about 24 hours they contacted an American unit, thus making it to freedom.[111]

Release and Repatriation

The resumption of the Peace Talks in late 1951 was a catalyst for a gradual improvement in the living conditions of most POWs from the UNC, such as better sanitary arrangements and clothing being issued to replace their old uniforms. Having boasted of capturing 65,000 prisoners, the Chinese found that in reality they only held around 12,000, and realized that as part of the negotiations accurate figures for an exchange would be required. To let too many more die from disease or neglect would cause embarrassment.[112] One American study noted how, during summer 1952, 'the fattening process got under way' as wheat flour began to reach camp kitchens. By the following year the 'cracked corn and kaoliang' familiar to many American POWs disappeared and 'the staple was either a bowl of steamed rice or a couple of four inch loaves of steamed white bread', plus a small bowl of vegetables and 'a little fat in the soup'.[113] PFC Donald Elliot, captured in May 1951 and held at the 'Mining Camp', then Camp 1, confirmed this, as he remembered the diet improving later in the war, along with better living conditions and the chance to play baseball, something that had been denied to them earlier.[114] Likewise, at this stage a British POW recorded that meat (mainly pork) appeared more often, and for the first time they were issued toiletries and a towel.[115]

During March–April 1953, the Chinese agreed to exchange sick and wounded POW before the actual ceasefire was signed. In what was known as Operation 'Little Switch' 684 UN prisoners (including 149 Americans and thirty-two British) were transported from camps to Panmunjom, to be met by a reception committee that included a contingent from the Women's Voluntary Service, as well as military personnel, interrogators and medical staff. Many seemed surprisingly healthy, and as many accounts have indicated, later interrogations revealed that some were progressives who had responded to Communist indoctrination and were being released for propaganda purposes, leaving many other wounded or sick POWs in North Korea.[116] According to PFC Shinagawa, who was one of those released, the Chinese wanted to create a good impression, and his group were held in Pyongyang for a few days so that they could be better fed and clean themselves up. After this he exited North Korea via the famous 'Bridge of No Return' at Panmunjom to be met by American military personnel, and like many released prisoners in his situation became embroiled in a heady mix of medical tests, interrogations, press conferences, and trying food stuffs like milk shakes, chewing gum and coffee, which had seemed unimaginable luxuries when in captivity, and were not necessarily the best sort of thing for someone in his condition to consume so soon after release.[117]

The exchange of other prisoners began after the armistice was signed in July 1953, when as part of 'Operation Big Switch' during August and September, 3,597 American and 945 British POWs were released. Despite having found some of the Communist teaching stimulating, Bill Fox of the Glosters was desperate to get home as rapidly as possible, especially as his parents had originally feared he had been killed, although they had been able to exchange a couple of letters with him during 1951–53, which confirmed he was actually a prisoner.[118] Many Americans, including Donald Elliot, understandably cried on first seeing the Stars and Stripes flying, and like many other recently released

POWs he began a batch of medical examinations/interviews, including with a psychiatrist, as part of a programme to help him adjust to civilian life.[119]

Many returning POWs were profoundly affected by their experience. While Albert Tyas, who later became a plumber in his native Yorkshire, reckoned plenty of leave and home cooking restored his body weight, 'mentally we were never the same again'. After years sleeping on the floor in primitive conditions, it also took several months to learn how to sleep in a bed. For prisoners who were National Servicemen, like him, another frustration was that despite their war service and period in captivity, many still had to complete a period of liability with the Territorial Army on return to Britain.[120] Similarly, an officer who'd served with 29th Brigade, and survived the Imjin Battle without being captured, after the war encountered fellow officers who had been captured, many of whom were close friends, and found them 'somehow different men'.[121]

Aside from the mental impact, many also developed physical health problems. Dan Johnson, a former NCO with the US Army, was afflicted by problems with his nerves, arthritis, heart disease, and issues relating to having suffered frostbite, all stemming from his 27 months of captivity on a starvation diet without adequate medical care.[122]

Chapter 9

From Ceasefire to Returning Home

At 22:00 hours on 27 July 1953 a ceasefire came into effect in Korea, rapidly followed by an armistice agreement that brought the brutal war to a halt. In one sense the war was a 'victory' for the American-led UN forces, in that blatant Communist aggression against South Korea ultimately had not succeeded. However, over the three years of war, the Communists, especially the Chinese military, gained invaluable experience against Western armies, while remaining undefeated in the stalemate that had developed.[1] The war had been costly, not only in human terms, but also, as author Donald Knox stated, because 'the uncertain victory was purchased dearly'. America alone spent $67,000,000,000 on the war, and during it property valued at around $1,000,000,000 was obliterated in South Korea.[2] The path towards the armistice was decidedly turbulent. As General Mark Clark (UN Commander-in-Chief, 1952–53) ruefully commented, 'never it seemed to me, was it more thoroughly demonstrated that winning a satisfactory peace, even a temporary one, is more difficult than winning a war'.[3]

One of the major stumbling blocks between the two sides was the handling of POWs, an issue complicated by political and ideological differences. In July 1951, not long after peace talks had been initiated, the Communists denied the UNC request that the International Committee of the Red Cross should inspect POW camps in North Korea. However, the exchange and repatriation of POWs remained one of the main topics on the agenda as the talks progressed in a haphazard manner during 1951–53. Notably, the UNC were keen that POWs should be given the right to determine whether they wanted to be repatriated, given that many of the prisoners they held were Chinese Nationalist soldiers who had been impressed by the Communists. Voluntary repatriation was greeted unenthusiastically by the Chinese and disagreement over the exact number of POWs that each side held caused further problems. Eventually, under the terms of the armistice all POWs who wished to be repatriated were to be handed over within sixty days, under the auspices of a 'Committee for Repatriation of POWs' comprised of three officers from each side, supervised by a 'Neutral Nations Repatriation Commission'. The latter was made up of officers from Czechoslovakia, India, Poland, Sweden and Switzerland, and India also provided the necessary 'Custodial Force'.

Other vital aspects of the armistice included the establishment of a 'Demarcation Line', which ran roughly along the frontlines of the opposing forces. Again this had been a contentious issue, as the Communists originally wished to see it drawn along the 38th Parallel, whereas the UNC were happy for it to reflect the actual battlefield position.[4] Both sides had to withdraw two kilometres from this in order to form a Demilitarised Zone (DMZ), intended to act as a buffer that would prevent further hostilities between North and South Korea. It remains in place today, and as a by-product of the political situation has become a haven for wildlife. Within 72 hours of signing the armistice, both sides were to withdraw all their forces from the DMZ, and were to be prevented from moving in reinforcements, although routine rotations/reliefs could occur. Under the armistice agreement various 'Commissions and Inspecting Teams' were set up, and to be offered assistance and protection by both sides. At the time it was hoped that the armistice might lead to a formal Korean Peace Treaty being drawn up between the respective governments of North and South Korea, an event which over six decades later has never been realised.[5]

Shortly before the ceasefire, there was what one GI on the line with 40th Division termed a 'Turkey Shoot', an artillery barrage intended either as 'one last threat to the enemy in case they decided to overrun us after the ceasefire', or as a means of 'expending our ammo... Everything opened up and they retaliated. There were casualties. That was probably the fiercest fighting I experienced – the last two hours of the Korean War'.[6] Likewise, according to another soldier from 3rd Division it '...was wild. All this artillery was gathered and it was as if they were saying we're not carrying this stuff back with us. The sky was full'.[7]

At the time of the ceasefire, Norman Spring was serving with 31st Infantry Regiment, part of 7th Division, repairing trenches near Old Baldy and Pork Chop Hill in the area known as the 'Iron Triangle'. His commanding officer warned that, 'the next 12 hours would probably be dangerous since the North Koreans might throw their remaining ammunition at us before the truce went into effect', as this 'happened in the last hours of World War Two'. His unit was moved back into a blocking position, where:

> we sat on the back of a steep hill. As predicted the shelling went on all day. Someone right next to me got shrapnel in his leg from a cannon shell. No one in our company fired back. We just sat waiting. Finally at 10 that night the firing stopped as if someone had

turned off a water tap. Then we saw lights coming on both sides of the frontline – truck lights, flashlights, candles and lanterns. It was a strange experience because we had worked in the dark for so many months.

Later, 'North Korean loudspeakers invited our soldiers to cross the line and join in a party. A few of our men did go over. They came back, but were court martialled afterward for fraternizing with the enemy.'[8]

By July 1953, Carl Ballard was a squad leader on a 57mm recoilless rifle with 9th Infantry Regiment from 2nd Division, and similarly remembered greeting the ceasefire with a mixture of fear and trepidation because 'we didn't believe the CCF [Chinese Communist Forces] would obey it'. Once the firing ceased 'you heard these night sounds, you just hadn't heard before', such as frogs and crickets. Soon the comparative quiet:

> was very eerie, but there was a relief. And next morning the sun came out and the Chinese were out… they were sunning themselves and washing their clothes and waving back and forth, when the night before we'd have been shooting at them. Some guys went over and gave them some cigarettes. It just shows you, you're not fighting the people, it's the governments – governments are doing this. You had no personal feelings against that Chinese man over there or that North Korean, but you're doing your job and their doing theirs. That was it.[9]

British soldier Alan Causer experienced the ceasefire while completing his National Service with a sound-ranging troop from the Royal Artillery. He had been only too aware that as it approached, the Chinese had constantly been 'trying to win a bit more territory' and savage fighting had occurred at the Hook 'about three miles to our left'. They were elated when it was announced and fired off their only flare with 'our one little three-inch mortar… to celebrate 10 o'clock', before embarking on the process of moving equipment back to the Kansas Line and demolishing bunkers as part of establishing the DMZ. While most troops were relieved the fighting was over, one regular who had been awarded the Military Medal couldn't cope with the prospect of living without action, and soon 'chucked all his kit into the Imjin', necessitating his evacuation as a psychiatric casualty.[10]

Despite the ceasefire, American and British troops still had to be prepared to resume hostilities should it break down, or somehow be violated. Under Operation 'Swanlake' for example, 1st Commonwealth Division withdrew to positions near the Imjin River, which it had held earlier in the war, and maintained a presence in the country until the mid-1950s. Newly arrived units, including 1st Battalion Royal Scots, discovered that a 'hard and monotonous' routine awaited them, devoid of the drama or professional satisfaction that demonstrating their prowess under fire would have offered, although troops were pleased not 'to undergo the fears and tragedies of war'. Intensive training was conducted for offensive and defensive operations, which for infantry had an accent on patrolling, given the combat experienced during 1952–53. Defensive works and accommodation were established, in case of enemy attack, and materials had to be salvaged from the DMZ. All this had to be completed prior to winter, which would make such work more difficult. Simultaneously, all units were expected to maintain a high level of readiness, morale and discipline.[11]

As a National Serviceman with the Royal Irish Fusiliers, Ron Hawkes served in Korea after the armistice and remembered maintaining 'trenches' on the Kansas Line. In fact their positions were more 'like the old pillboxes but much bigger. They were criss-crossed all across Korea… the idea was that if they [the Chinese or North Koreans] tried to come forward again, the cross fire would wipe them out'. Extensive use continued to be made of minefields, and often the trip flares that were part of these defences would be set off by wild animals, causing panic, as 'we didn't know if it was the real thing'. Although fairly well equipped by this stage, troops still had to contend with the Korean winter, and always wear gloves 'because …bare fingers would stick to the metal of your rifle'.[12]

Just as most American and British personnel had been shipped to the Far East, it was also the primary means by which many were transported back home after Korean tours, or on to other postings. Often these voyages were more relaxed than those previously undertaken. A soldier from 1st Battalion Black Watch, which was sent to counter the Mau-Mau insurgency in Kenya after completing its Korean tour, recounted that a stopover in Singapore 'was grand', especially 'after that traumatic year'.[13] Another advantageous aspect of these voyages was that mentally they tended to provide a period of decompression for those who had recently endured the pressures of active service. A soldier from the Royal Artillery aboard homeward-bound HMT *Empire Fowey* welcomed being excused duties on the four-week voyage, as they were 'all very jumpy' and it provided time 'to cool off'.[14]

Even so, voyages were not necessarily without incident, especially those carrying recently repatriated POWs back home, who invariably were kept segregated from other troops. PFC Donald Elliott vividly recorded how he and other repatriated prisoners were kept on a separate part of his troopship, prevented from mixing with other personnel, complete with their own mess hall, which provided a specific diet after their ordeal, and that they had fun acting up in front of the other troops who would constantly watch them from their decks.[15] Likewise, one National Serviceman described how he left Korea aboard HMT *Dunera* with a group of repatriated British POWs, and 'there was mayhem'. Four of the former POWs tragically committed suicide, and many were frantically spending their back pay, drinking too much and 'doing all sorts of things'.[16]

After service in Korea, troops' experiences of homecoming varied. Manchester lad Brian Hough ended up doing his National Service with the King's (Liverpool) Regiment in Korea during 1952–53, before returning to the New Territories (Hong Kong). In December 1953 they sailed into South-ampton, feeling like 'heroes' wearing their campaign medal ribbons, and those who lived south of London were allowed to leave straight away, whereas northerners like him had to wait. He was then issued a cheese sandwich, half a crown and a rail ticket for Manchester, and expected to make his own way home.[17] In contrast, Calvin Schutte, who'd been drafted to Korea in late 1951 and served there for 11 months with 25th Infantry Division, encountered 'fire boats firing columns of water in different colours and bands playing to welcome us home' when he returned home via Seattle, Washington, on the *Marine Adder*.[18]

The war affected men and women returning from Korea in different ways, partly depending on the nature of their service. Some were maimed for life owing to serious injuries, such as those caused by mines or frostbite, and/ or required medical treatment for health problems long after they were discharged. Many others were mentally scarred by their experiences, and the suicide rate among American veterans in percentage terms is thought to be even worse than that for Vietnam.[19] Yet others remained relatively unscathed, although they had a mixture of unpleasant and pleasant memories of their Korean tours. One National Serviceman in theatre with 5th Royal Inniskilling Dragoon Guards, while conditions headed towards stalemate, had a comparatively benign experience. As he remembered,

> I led a fairly mundane life, our losses were thankfully low, and tended to be replaced by members of the Australian Armoured Corps so I never served as a tank gunner [for which he'd been trained], I was attached to Tac HQ security, and sometimes rode shotgun on supply lorries up the line, took part in patrols hunting guerrillas and various odd jobs.[20]

In contrast, those who had undergone traumatic experiences, such as being a POW or witnessing close combat, were liable to show particular signs of strain. According to an NCO from the Middlesex Regiment:

> War turns a decent human being into an animal, cold, dirty, hungry and sometimes scared, your only way to survive is to become like a wolf… Yet, the day comes when it all ends and the animal you have become has now to return to society and become a decent human being once again. The army cannot prepare you for this, the transition is something that you have to do alone, some turn to drink, others become sullen and silent, while the majority try desperately to put it all behind them and start life anew. But you will never be the person you were before you went to war, you are scarred, some of us physically through wounds, others mentally.[21]

Walter Adelmann was drafted in December 1950, and spent most of his time in Korea as a POW, something that led him to drink heavily once repatriated in order to forget his past. Diagnosed with 'battle fatigue', he continued to drink until the early 1960s when Alcoholics Anonymous helped him change his life.[22]

Another soldier from the Middlesex Regiment remembered how a few years after being demobbed on return from Korea, he awoke in the middle of the night thinking he was being shelled and flung himself on top of his wife to protect her.[23] He was possibly suffering from what today might be better recognised as a sign of Post-Traumatic Stress disorder (PTSD). In this he was far from alone. Having been discharged from the US Army in 1952, Glen Bailey returned to Grand Rapids, Michigan and recalled, 'the Korean conflict got to me a lot and I almost got a divorce. Three years after the war I woke up and was nearly choking my wife'. On reflection he reckoned he was probably suffering from PTSD or something similar, but didn't find help until later in his sixties, when as a member of a veteran's association it proved easier to talk about the past. As he put it post-war, 'you don't want to tell people you shot somebody or whatever. People don't really believe what you went through anyway'.[24]

Other veterans found that returning to civilian life was extremely unsettling. Former Marine Robert Samuels held a succession of jobs, before eventually managing to get established with a company that manufactured baking equipment in Michigan, where he worked until his retirement.[25] Barry Whiting, who had completed his National Service with the Royal Army Medical Corps, found that initially on returning from Korea friends found him 'an absolute sod' owing to a delayed stress reaction and the frustration caused by his civilian routine, which was tedious and dull compared with his military existence.[26]

After Korea, some draftees and National Servicemen went on to re-enlist, but most were happy to put their military service behind them. A veteran from 7th Division recounted how at Fort Custer, Michigan:

> I walked in a room and the supply sergeant I had in Korea and a lieutenant were sitting there and the sergeant knew what we went through the last couple of months up there and he said to the lieutenant I don't think he's going to re-enlist. So we just sat there, just shooting the bull you know, having a good time.[27]

However, many regular personnel from both America and Britain went on to have long and distinguished careers after cutting their teeth as young soldiers or Marines in Korea. Having joined the Territorial Army in 1948, Joni Johnston was subsequently commissioned into the King's Own Scottish Borderers as a regular officer and served as a platoon commander with 1 KOSB in Korea in 1951–52. He went on to see active service in Kenya (1954–57); Malaya (1957–58); Borneo (Sarawak) during 1965–66; and Operation Vantage Kuwait (1961) before retiring as a lieutenant colonel in 1985.[28]

For some veterans government incentives offered a means via which to adapt to life after Korea and forge a civilian life. By 1956, approximately 8.8 million American Second World War and Korean veterans had received financial assistance provided under the terms of the 'GI Bill' (Servicemen's Readjustment Act, 1944). This covered issues such as the cost of tuition and living expenses for high school, college or vocational/technical training. After his experience working in graves registration in Korea, Lamar Bloss retrained as an X-ray technician.[29] Similarly, the GI Bill enabled Carl Ballard to 'improve himself by gaining an education' after demobilisation.[30]

In contrast, British veterans returning home were not always as well supported. Having completed his National Service with the Royal Artillery, John Robottom attended college to study pharmacy, which proved a miserable experience.

> Although my mother owned the house we lived in we were quite poor, the more so since I was refused a grant of any form of assistance towards the cost of my studies. The attitude of Birmingham Education Committee was that I had broken my educational thread by not going straight from school, in spite of the fact that I had been conscripted, and indeed risked my life in Korea on behalf of the government.[31]

Korean War veterans' opinions of being drafted or conscripted also varied. Former GI Norman Spring reckoned the draft was a good thing and that everyone, out of appreciation for their country, should spend two years in the military. As he points out, not everyone has to serve in a direct combat role, as there are 'all kinds of service jobs'.[32] Likewise, National Service other ranks, including Gordon Butt who served with the Royal Fusiliers, often found that they left the army wiser and more mature than when they were called up.[33] Despite having been called up straight from school and having led 'a very sheltered life due to parental restrictions', John Robottom came to regard National Service 'as totally beneficial'.[34]

Reflecting on his experiences as a National Service subaltern with the Royal Northumberland Fusiliers (RNF), Keith Taylor discovered it:

> gave me self-confidence, leadership experience, gratitude to Eaton Hall Officer Cadet School and a certain undeserved admiration from contemporaries that I had done some 'real' soldiering [in Korea] not ceremonial duties in Germany or the UK![35]

However, another former officer and Korean veteran considered:

> those who suggest that, as a general principle, universal military service was a good thing and turned out a better sort of young person seem to me grossly mistaken, usually motivated by malice or envy towards the young.[36]

After their Korean tour personnel of all ranks were eligible for various medals, although at least one American sergeant considered that, 'the ones doing the fighting ain't the ones getting the medals; rather it was personnel in rear areas doing all the paperwork that tended to receive most awards, whether deserved or not.[37] Sometimes medals were not issued until years later. In 1997 Walter Adelmann, a former NCO with 1st Cavalry Division, proudly received two Purple Hearts, the National Defence Medal, the Korean Service Medal (with four battle stars), the POW Medal and the UN Service Medal.[38] As one British veteran recalled, they received two campaign medals, 'one had the new Queen's head on, like any decent British medal', whereas 'the other was a lightweight, anodised job suitable for armies that do not believe in Brasso' emblazoned with the statement: 'For service in defence of the principles of the charter of the United Nations'.[39] The former was known as the 'Korea Medal' and soldiers could qualify for it by serving for a day or more on the posted strength of a unit formation in theatre. Similarly, one day's service in theatre under UN command entitled troops to the UN Service Medal for Korea, with its distinctive blue and white striped ribbon, leading some to dub it 'MacArthur's pyjamas'.[40]

For many veterans and the public in both America and Britain, Korea has often been viewed as 'the Forgotten War'. There are numerous reasons for this, including its geographical remoteness, particularly from Britain, and the fact that the British contribution was dwarfed by that of the Americans. It was fought in an era when widespread media coverage was impracticable. Although people in the 1950s could read about it in the newspapers and glean information from radio broadcasts, television was in its infancy so 'folks back home' couldn't easily watch what was happening in the way they could during later conflicts such as Vietnam, the Falklands or the First and Second Gulf Wars. Apart from artillery barrages and major battles like those at the Hook during 1952 and 1953, the latter static phase of the war tended to lack the drama associated with the first year of the war, making it appear as if nothing was happening. Likewise, the proximity of Korea to the ending of the Second World War ensured that by mid-1951 the American and British public were not always interested in the conflict, unless they had relatives or friends serving there. In Britain too, people were still contending with rationing and post-war austerity, so were not necessarily keen to take an interest in a war on the other side of the world.

The involvement of American and British forces in later conflicts has arguably served to shroud the memory of Korea. Glen Bailey, who had seen action with 1st Cavalry Division in Korea:

> felt for the guys [Vietnam veterans] because they had tough going too. I gotta bad attitude about it and I hate to say it but I do. Anything you hear today is Vietnam, Vietnam or Afghanistan but you don't hear a damn word about the Korean vets.[41]

On returning home many veterans, including Glen Bailey, found that when Korea came up in conversation 'you changed the subject'.[42] Likewise, a former British infantryman confessed years later that he simply 'didn't talk about Korea' on coming home, and 'there was absolutely no one to discuss it with', although following Chelsea Football Club with other ex-soldiers at regular home fixtures provided an emotional release.[43] For many troops, especially at other rank level, a lack of understanding of the war, the fact it appeared to lack purpose, and that many viewed Korea as 'a barren, horrible place; just ranges of hills, paddy fields and a few villages' further encouraged them to try and forget it.[44]

Even so, there are plenty of memorials to the Korean War, including one dedicated on Victoria Embankment, Westminster, London, on 13 December 2014, given by the people of South Korea to the people of Britain. Perhaps the war is best recognised among the wider public via the popular film and television series *M*A*S*H*. While these were set in Korea, and based on real-life experiences, as a former MASH surgeon highlights, 'the irreverence and the social attitudes' evident in these works were more reflective of part of the American population during the Vietnam War, a decade and a half later.[45]

Not all veterans were negative about the war or their involvement in it. American soldier Carl Ballard found his war experience strengthened his faith as a Christian, and was proud to have played a role in saving South Korea from the North.[46] Other soldiers took pride in the performance of their units. According to a veteran from 1st Battalion Middlesex Regiment, it was his 'profound belief that we [27th Brigade] did the British Army proud while serving in Korea, despite the paucity of supporting arms that did not arrive until January 1951'.[47] Likewise, Barry Whiting stressed that 'National Servicemen, on the whole, were quite amazing in terms of their contribution to the conflict and well deserved the medals which we all proudly wear'.[48]

At officer level in particular, there was sometimes a better understanding of the war, and a sense that it had been an attempt to stem Communism. One former British artillery officer reflected:

> the war was authorised by, and fought on behalf of, the UN – it was a just war. It was not another ex-colonial war. It seemed the right thing to do, and a challenge for which you would volunteer. I count myself very lucky not to have been killed or wounded. I worked with some incredible individuals and I saw some amazing and some horrific sights. I would not have missed it for the world. It was probably the best part of my education.[49]

Similarly, Keith Taylor considered that,

> The macro view has to be that the invasion of South Korea at that time was a very serious threat to world peace and had to be resisted. The personal micro view was that I felt a very small cog in a massive event involving 21 countries and knew next to nothing!

However, it was a hugely beneficial experience to him personally, assisting him with his civilian career, and later on he was honoured to serve as 'a Patron of the British Korean Veterans Association (BKVA) to represent the significant number of National Serviceman who served in the Korean War'.[50]

For some veterans revisiting South Korea either formally or informally in postwar years, has generated 'the deepest admiration and respect for the Korean people – and Government – to have risen from the ashes of a bitter war in which over 1 million civilian refugees died'.[51] British veteran Jim Lucock, like many others, had at the time felt that Korea was an awful country in which to fight a war, and that it had all been a wasted effort. This was until he went back to South Korea years later, and found a country where the population was well-educated and everyone seemed adequately fed and clothed. People were keen to shake veterans by the hand, leading him to feel that the war was worthwhile after all.[52] A former British Army nurse, who revisited Seoul in 1990 as a member of the BKVA, discovered, 'a vast conglomeration of sky-scrapers and broad tree-lined streets, in stark contrast to the war-torn, barren and mutilated landscape from which I had flown out in 1953'.[53] Such positivity when viewing contemporary South Korea has led some veterans, including ex-Marine Art Braatz, to hope that there will one day be a peace accord, and that the North Korean regime will collapse under the strain of the economic pressures upon it.[54]

So far this has not happened. Since 1953 North Korea has remained a potential threat to regional and global stability. With a standing army of around 1.2 million soldiers, supported by a reserve of over 7 million, and a sizeable well-trained paramilitary force, North Korea's conventional military capability remains impressive, at least in numerical terms, even if some of its equipment is dated. If any renewed confrontation erupted, the artillery at the disposal of the North could easily target Seoul, posing a significant threat.

For decades the North Koreans have been pursuing a nuclear weapons programme, which was fully realised in 2006, in conjunction with stockpiling an arsenal of missiles. Most commentators and analysts agree that it is only a matter of time before the two are married to form a fully functioning or 'weaponized' ICBM (Inter-Continental Ballistic Missile). Perhaps less well publicised is the fact that North Korea has developed a potentially formidable chemical warfare capability. A report in the *Sunday Telegraph* as far back as 2004 noted that human experimentation conducted at a prison camp was designed to test liquid gas for chemical weapons. Over the decades numerous incidents have occurred that have ratcheted up the tension between the two Koreas, and the threat of further confrontation remains.[55]

During 2017-18 an intense war-like atmosphere developed between America and North Korea in large part owing to the latter's missile test programme. While the international community has imposed economic sanctions on North Korea, in order to encourage her to eliminate her nuclear weapons, these have been flouted by the Chinese and the Russians. In January 2018 the Americans put in place contingency plans for a second Korean War, and held the largest logistical and troop movement exercises witnessed for decades. Yet, the Pyeongchang Winter Olympics in February, during which among other things the two Koreas agreed to compete under a united flag, have presented the North Koreans with a golden propaganda opportunity by seemingly stepping back from the brink, and so enhancing their image.

Notes

Introduction

1. For an overview of air and naval warfare in Korea see: Stanley Sandler, *The Korean War: No Victors No Vanquished* (London: UCL Press, 1999), esp. Ch. 10, pp. 171–196.

2. Although the Communists built up their air strength during the war, their efforts were geared towards the interception of UN bombers and fighters over North Korea, primarily in what became known as 'Mig Alley'. Over the actual battlefront there was little Communist air activity, except for the actions of 'Bed Check Charlie's', antiquated bi-planes that undertook primitive night bombing runs against UN positions. Although one such raider did knock out several F-86 Sabre jets parked at Pyongyang when the city was held by the UNC, these usually did little damage other than to disrupt the sleep of personnel. See for example, Boris R. Spiroff, *Korea: Frozen Hell on Earth: A Platoon Sergeants's Diary Korean War 1950–1951* (Baltimore, Maryland: American Literary Press Inc., 1998), p. 54.

Chapter 1

1. Michael Carver, *War Since 1945* (London: Weidenfeld & Nicolson, 1980), p. 151.

2. Alan R. Millett, 'Introduction to the Korean War', The Journal of Military History Volume 65 (October 2001) , p. 921.

3. William E Berry, Jr. *Global Security Watch: A Reference Handbook: KOREA* (Westport, CT, Praeger Security International, 2008), p. 5.

4. Millett, 'Introduction to the Korean War', The Journal of Military History Vol. 65 (Oct 2001) , p. 922.

5. Robert Leckie, *Conflict: The History of the Korean War* (New York: Da Capo Press, 1996), p. 25.

6. Peter Lowe, *The Origins of the Korean War* (London: Longman, 1997), p. 7.

7. Crawford F. Sams, *'Medic' The Mission of an American Military Doctor in Occupied Japan and Wartorn Korea* (New York: M.E. Sharpe, 1998), p. 203.

8. Figures from: Berry, Jr. *Global Security Watch: A Reference Handbook: KOREA*, p. 7.

9. Carter J. Eckert, Ki-baik Lee, Young Ick Lew, Michael Robinson, Edward W. Wagner, *Korea Old and New A* History (Seoul: Korea Institute, Harvard University, 1990) , p. 327.

10. Lowe, *The Origins of the Korean War*, p. 47.

11. Ibid, p. 49.

12. William F. Dean, *General Dean's Story* (London: Weidenfeld & Nicolson, 1954), p. 6.

13. Anthony Farrar-Hockley, *The British Part in the Korean War, Volume I: A Distant Obligation* (London: HMSO, 1990), p. 22.

14. Berry, Jr. *Global Security Watch: A Reference Handbook: KOREA*, p. 3.

15. Steven Zaloga & Jim Kinnear, *T-34/85 Medium Tank, 1944–1994* (London: Osprey, 1996), p. 34.

16. Matthew B. Ridgway, *The Korean War* (New York: Da Capo Press, 1967), p. 15.

17. Jeffrey Grey, *The Commonwealth armies and the Korean War* (Manchester: Manchester University Press, 1988), p. 22.

18. Farrar-Hockley, *A Distant Obligation*, p. 29.

19. Alan R. Millett, 'The Korean War: A 50-Year Critical Historiography', The Journal of Strategic Studies, Volume 24, Number 1 (March 2001), p. 190.
20. Grey, *The Commonwealth armies and the Korean Wars*, p. 23.
21. Dean, *General Dean's Story*, p. 8.
22. Albert J. McAdoo & James E. Marshall, The 5th RCT in Korea: The Pusan Perimeter Battles, 1950 (Privately Published, 2012), p. 72.
23. Colin McInnes, *Hot War Cold War: The British Army's Way in Warfare 1945–95* (London: Brassey's, 1996), p. 34.
24. Casualty figures from: Berry, Jr. *Global Security Watch. A Reference Handbook: KOREA*, pp. 14–15; Carter Malkasian, *The Korean War 1950–1953* (Botley, Ox: Osprey Publishing, 2001), p. 88; Leckie, *Conflict: The History of the Korean War*, Appendix: 'Estimated Casualties of the Korean War' p. 429; Author's Correspondence with Mr. Keith Taylor (Patron of the British Korean Veterans Association), 11 December 2016.
25. Anthony Farrar-Hockley, *The British Part in the Korean War, Volume II: An Honourable Discharge* (London: HMSO, 1995), App. P British Casualties in the Korean War, p. 491.
26. Charles R. Shrader, Communist Logistics in the Korean War (Westport: Greenwood Press, 1995), p. 7.
27. Ibid, p. 8.
28. James Hamilton Dill, *Sixteen Days at Mungol-li* (Fayetteville: M & M Press, 1993), p. 228.
29. The National Archives (TNA), WO 308/96, 1st Commonwealth Division Booklet: 'Conquer the Korean Winter 1952–53: Simple Rules for All,' Introduction, Paragraph 1 Characteristics, p. 1.
30. Darrell Thornley Interview, Grand Valley State University (GVSU) Veterans History Project.
31. Brig C.N. Barclay, *The First Commonwealth Division, The Story of British Commonwealth Land Forces in Korea, 1950-53* (Aldershot: Gale and Polden, 1954), p. 3.
32. C. S. Crawford, *The Four Deuces: A Korean War Story* (New York: Ballatine Books, 1989), p. 42.
33. Dan Raschen, *Send Port & Pyjamas!* (London: Buckland Pub. Ltd, 1987), pp. 48–49.
34. Rudolph W. Stephens, *Old Ugly Hill: A G.I.'s Fourteen Months in the Korean Trenches, 1952–1953* Jefferson: McFarland & Company, 1995), p. 89.
35. Ridgway, *The Korean War*, p. 2.
36. Shrader, *Communist Logistics in the Korean War*, p. 18.
37. George Cooper, *Fight, Dig and Live: The Story of the Royal Engineers in the Korean War* (Barnsley: Pen and Sword, 2011), pp. 75–76.
38. Ridgway, *The Korean War*, p. 4.

Chapter 2

1. Roy E. Appleman, *South to the Naktong, North to the Yalu* (Washington, D. C: Centre of Military History United States Army, 1992), p. 46.
2. Lt Col Charles Olsen Interview: Grand Valley State University (Veterans History Project).
3. Clay Blair, *The Forgotten War: America in Korea 1950–1953* (New York: Times Books, 1987), p. 91.
4. Appleman, *South to the Naktong, North to the Yalu*, pp. 49–50.
5. Glen Bailey Interview: GVSU (VHP).
6. Darrell Thornley Interview: GVSU (VHP).
7. Ibid.
8. Blair, *The Forgotten War: America in Korea 1950–1953*, p. 89.
9. Lyle Gibbs Interview: GVSU (VHP).
10. Tanjore Splan Interview: GVSU (VHP).
11. Boris R. Spiroff, *Korea: Frozen Hell on Earth: A Platoon Sergeant's Diary Korean War 1950–1951* (Baltimore, American Literary Press, 1998), pp. 8–9.
12. Lacey Barnett, in Donald Knox, *The Korean War: Pusan to Chosin, An Oral History* (New York: Harcourt Brace and Co., 1985)

13. Charles M. Bussey, *Firefight at Yechon: Courage and Racism in the Korean War* (London: Bison Books, 2002), p.73.
14. William Berebitsky, *A Very Long Weekend: The Army National Guard in Korea, 1950–1953* (Shippensburg, PA: White Mane Publishing Co., 1996), p. 3.
15. First Lieutenant Dave Matteson, 'A' Coy, 378th Eng Combat Bn (N. Carolina) in *A Very Long Weekend*, p. 17.
16. Lynn Montross and Capt. Nicholas A. Canzona, *U. S. Marine Operations in Korea Volume 1: The Pusan Perimeter* (Historical Branch, G-3 Head Quarters, U.S. Marine Corps: Washington, D.C., 1954), p. 49.
17. Ibid, p.50.
18. Ray 'Highpockets' Murray in Henry Berry, *Hey, Mac, Where Ya Been? Living Memories of the U.S Marines in the Korean War* (New York: St. Martin's Press, 1990), pp. 50–51.
19. Ed Simons Interview in Rudy Tomedi, *No Bugles, No Drums: An Oral History of the Korean War* (New York: John Wiley & Sons, 1994), p. 31.
20. Robert Smith in *Hey, Mac, Where Ya Been?*, p. 170.
21. Harold Roise in *Hey, Mac, Where Ya Been?*, p. 64.
22. Robert Samuels Interview: GVSU (VHP).
23. Eddy McCabe in *Hey, Mac, Where Ya Been?*, p. 93.
24. Robert C. Shoemaker, *A Surgeon Remembers Korea 1950–1951 and the Marines* (Victoria, BC: Trafford, 2005), p. 8.
25. J.A. Williams, '*Korea and the Malayan Emergency-the Strategic Priorities*' Royal United Services Institute Journal, Volume 118, Number 2 (June 1973), pp. 61–62.
26. Eric Linklater, *Our Men in Korea* (London: HMSO, 1952), p. 16.
27. Anthony Farrar-Hockley, *The British Part in the Korean War, Volume I: A Distant Obligation* (London: HMSO, 1990), p. 128.
28. The National Archives (Kew), WO 281/1166, War Diary 1st Battalion Argyll & Sutherland Highlanders, 20 August 1950, Appendix A: Operation Graduate Establishment of an Infantry Battalion.
29. Author's Correspondence with Mr. D. F. Barrett (Korean veteran and former NCO 1st Battalion Middlesex Regiment), 10 December 2002.
30. Tim Carew, Korea: *The Commonwealth at War* (London: Cassell, 1967), p. 139; Charles Whiting, *Battleground Korea: The British in Korea* (Stroud, Gloucestershire: Sutton Publishing, 1999), p. 80.
31. Author's Correspondence with Mr. Robert Yerby (Korean veteran and former NCO 1st Battalion Middlesex Regiment), 18 July 2003.
32. Author's Correspondence with Mr. D. F. Barrett, 22 December 2002.
33. Ibid, 10 December 2002.
34. Carew, *Korea: The Commonwealth at War*, p. 41.
35. TNA, WO 308/45, 27th British Commonwealth Brigade Report on Operations, Part I, p. 2.
36. IWM, Sound Archive 9537, Reel 1, Colonel Andrew Morrice Man (CO 1 MX).
37. IWM, Sound Archive 18625, Reel 1, Dr. Stanley Boydell (RAMC 1949–1951, attached as MO to 1 MX).
38. Author's Correspondence with General Sir Anthony Farrar-Hockley, 29 May 2002.
39. 1st Battalion Middlesex Regiment served as Medium Machine Gun (MMG) Battalion during the Second World War. Consequently, Regular Officers and NCOs who were wartime veterans were not necessarily as experienced in direct infantry action as they would have been had their unit acted as standard infantry. I am grateful to Mr. Don Barrett (former NCO 1 MX and Korean War veteran) for highlighting this in his correspondence with me.
40. National Army Museum (NAM) 8905–159, Oral History Interview with Michael Eastap (Sgt No. 1 Platoon, A Company, 1 MX, Korea 1950–1951).
41. IWM, Sound Archive 18003, Reel 1, Ronald Yetman (NCO 5 Platoon B Company 1 A&SH).

42. Lieutenant-Colonel G. I. Malcolm of Poltalloch, *The Argylls in Korea* (Edinburgh: Thomas Nelson and Sons Ltd, 1952), p. 2.
43. Carew, *Korea: The Commonwealth at War*, p. 49.
44. Whiting, *Battleground Korea: The British in Korea*, p. 61.
45. This overview of 29th Brigade was based on information in: TNA, WO 308/ 42, A Brief History of 29th Independent Infantry Brigade Group from September 1949 to October 1951 "ACCELARAMUS," p. 1.
46. Michael Hickey, 'The Chinese are in. World War Three has begun' Royal United Services Institute Journal, Volume 144, Number 3 (June 1999), p. 104.
47. NA, WO 308/ 42, A Brief History of 29th Independent Infantry Brigade Group from September 1949 to October 1951, p. 2.
48. TNA, WO231/89, Battle Experience Questionnaire (BEQ): Major J. C. S. G. De Longueuil, (1RUR), 24 November 1951.
49. TNA, WO231/89, BEQ: Lt. L. J. Beavis (West Yorkshire Regiment attached 1 RNF), 15 January 1952.
50. Digby Grist, *Remembered with Advantage: A Personal Account of Service with the Glosters during the Korean War* (Gloucester: The Gloucestershire Regiment, 1976), p. 7.
51. Major H. J. Winn letter to his Mother, Straits of el Mandeb, 26 October 1950 in Anthony Perrins (ed), *'a Pretty rough do altogether' The Fifth Fusiliers in Korea 1950–51* (Alnwick: The Trustees of the Fusiliers Museum of Northumberland, 2004), p. 9.
52. RSM Jack Hobbs quoted in Carew, *Korea: The Commonwealth at War*, p. 140.
53. Perrins (ed), *'a Pretty rough do altogether'*, pp. 6 -7, Author's correspondence with Mr. A. R. D. Perrins, 7 December 2015.
54. Michael Hickey, 'Have We Learnt the Lessons of Readiness from Korea?' Royal United Services Institute Journal, June 2000, p. 64.
55. Grist, *Remembered with Advantage*, pp. 7–8.
56. TNA, WO231/89, BEQ: Major J. W. H. Mulligan, (1st Battalion Royal Ulster Rifles), 5 May 1951.
57. Author's conversations with Mr. S.A.S. Phillips (Platoon Commander: 9 Platoon and later 7 Platoon, Y Company, 1 RNF, Korea 1950- 51).
58. Hickey, 'Have We Learnt the Lessons of Readiness from Korea?', pp. 63–64.
59. TNA, WO231/89, BEQ: Capt. Henry John Bergin (attached 1 Glosters), 11 September 1951.
60. Carl Ballard Interview: GVSU (VHP).
61. Kindsvatter, *American Soldiers: Ground Combat in the World Wars, Korea, & Vietnam*, pp. 259–260.
62. Ron Larby, *Signals to the Right Armoured Corps to the Left* (Royal Leamington Spa: Korvet Publishing, 1993), p. 2.
63. Tom Hickman, *The Call-Up: A History of National Service* (London: Headline, 2004), p. 228.
64. These statistics regarding 1st Battalion Durham light Infantry are taken from the following sources: Durham County Record Office, DLI 195/8, 1st Bn DLI Commanding Officer's Report, Korea 1952–53, Paragraph 4: National Service Officers & Other Ranks, p. 3 & Bryan Tonkinson, *Subalterns Serving with the 1st Battalion Durham Light Infantry in Korea September 1952–September 1953* (Privately Published, 2003), pp. 15–16.
65. Hickman, *The Call-Up: A History of National Service*, p. 223; George Younger in Adrian Walker, *A Barren Place: National Servicemen in Korea 1950–1954* (London: Leo Cooper, 1994), pp. 34–41.
66. Kindsvatter, *American Soldiers: Ground Combat in the World Wars, Korea, & Vietnam*, p. 17.
67. Richard Holmes, *Firing Line* (London: Jonathon Cape, 1995), p. 36.
68. Ibid.
69. George C. Pagan, *A National Serviceman in Korea: The Royal Signals Regiment at War 1950–1953* (Swanage: Finial Publishing, 2003), p. 1.
70. Walter Adams in *A Barren Place: National Servicemen in Korea 1950–1954*, p. 19.
71. Glen Bailey Interview: GVSU (VHP).

72. Dan Pfeiffer Interview: GVSU (VHP).
73. Alan Carter, *Korea: We Lived... They Died: Diary of a Forgotten War* (Bognor Regis: Woodfield Publishing, 1999), p. 10.
74. Michael Caine, *What's it all about? The Autobiography* (London: Century, 1992), p. 54.
75. D. E. Whatmore, *One Road to Imjin: A National Service Experience* (Cheltenham: Dew Line Publications, undated), pp. 7–8.
76. Carl Ballard Interview: GVSU (VHP).
77. Larby, *Signals to the Right Armoured Corps to the Left*, p. 9.
78. 22405019 Pte. Taylor, K, X Platoon, Hut 35, 'B'Coy Budbrooke Barracks, Warwick, Letter to a friend, Thursday 28 September 1950 in Keith M. Taylor, *Wither the Fates Call: A Personal Account of National Service in the British Army 1950-1952* (Privately Published, 2009), p. 11.
79. Dan Pfeiffer Interview: GVSU (VHP).
80. Pagan, *A National Serviceman in Korea*, p. 1.
81. Derek Halley, *The Iron Claw: A Conscript's tale* (Privately Published, 1998), pp. 28–29.
82. 22405091 Rct. Taylor, K, L/Cpl Jackson's Squad, 13th Company, Coldstream Guards, Guards Depot, Caterham, Surrey, 15 September 1950 letter to friend in Taylor, *Wither the Fates Call*, p. 4.
83. Keith Taylor & Brian Stewart CMG, *Call to Arms: Officer Cadet Training at Eaton Hall 1943-1958* (Privately Published, 2006), p. 204.
84. Carl Ballard Interview: GVSU (VHP).
85. Ibid.
86. Author's Correspondence with Mr. G. Butt (Re: his National Service with the Queen's Regiment 1951 and 1st Battalion Royal Fusiliers, Korea 1952–1953), 25 February 2003.
87. Dan Pfeiffer Interview: GVSU (VHP).
88. William Schrader Interview: GVSU (VHP).
89. Robert Halle Interview: GVSU (VHP).
90. Reuben Holroyd, *Moving On* (Privately Published, 1964), p. 1.
91. Howard Matthias, *The Korean War: Reflections of a Young Combat Platoon Leader* (Tallahassee: Father & Son, 1993), p. 3.
92. Robert Samuels Interview: GVSU (VHP).
93. Hew Strachan, 'Training, Morale and Modern War' Journal of Contemporary History, Volume 41, Number 2 (2006), p. 216.
94. War Office Manual Code: 8510, Drill (All Arms) 1951, Introduction, p. xi.
95. War Office Pamphlet Code: WO 8369, Infantry Training Volume 1, Infantry Platoon Weapons Pamphlet No. 1 General (All Arms), Chapter 1 Introduction to Infantry Training, Weapons paragraph 7, p. 1.
96. Author's correspondence with Mr. H. A. Lotherington (Re: his National Service training and Korean War experience with 1st Battalion KSLI, 1951–1953), undated.
97. Rod Chapman Interview: GVSU (VHP).
98. Glendle Callahan Interview: GVSU (VHP).
99. Robert Samuels Interview: GVSU (VHP).
100. Caine, *What's it all about?*, p. 56.
101. Lamar Bloss Interview: GVSU (VHP).
102. Sherwin Nagelkirk Interview: GVSU (VHP).
103. Colonel Michaelis quoted in Marguerite Higgins, *War in Korea: The Report of a Woman War Correspondent* (New York: Doubleday, 1951), p. 221.
104. Ibid, p. 220.
105. Martin Russ, *The Last Parallel* (New York: Zebra Books, 1985), pp. 9–10.
106. Dan Pfeiffer Interview: GVSU (VHP).
107. George Hyslop Interview: GVSU (VHP).
108. TNA, WO231/89, BEQ: 2/Lt. (later Col. Sir) James Stirling (1 A&SH), 27 February 1951.

109. For discussion on wartime battle schools see: Timothy Harrison Place, Military *Training in the British Army, 1940–1944 From Dunkirk to D-Day* (London: Frank Cass, 2000), esp. Ch. 4-5: James Goulty, *The Second World War Through Soldiers' Eyes* (Barnsley: Pen and Sword, 2016), pp. 32–35.
110. War Office Manual Code: WO 8508, Training for War 1950, Ch. 1 Organisation of Training, Section 4 Divisions and Brigades, Paragraph 5, p. 13.
111. Summary based on information contained in: TNA, WO 308/23, Notes on the History of 1st Commonwealth Div Battle School, Development of the Units Organisation, paragraph 1–4, p. 1.
112. Ibid, paragraph 5 and 10.
113. Author's conversations with Mr. Tom Hennessy (Second Lieutenant 1 DLI, Korea 1952–1953 and Battle School Instructor, Japan).
114. Author's conversations with Major John Maclean (Royal Welsh Fusiliers att 1st Bn Welch Regiment, Korea and Battle School Instructor, 1951–1953).
115. Whatmore, *One Road to Imjin*, p. 31.
116. Brigadier M. R. Lonsdale (Mike) DSO, OBE late North Staffords (b. 1907–d. 1989), Obituary in *The Stafford Knot* (Early 1990 Edition), p. 15.
117. Keith Taylor, Friday 24 August 1951 Letter to Friend from Hara Mura, in Taylor, *Wither the Fates Call*, p. 165.
118. Edmund Ions, *A Call to Arms: Interlude with the Military* (Newton Abbot: David & Charles, 1972), p.155.
119. Lofty Large, *One Man's War in Korea* (Wellingborough: William Kimber, 1988), p. 35.
120. Ibid, p. 36.
121. General Sir Peter de la Billière, *Looking for Trouble: SAS to Gulf Command: The Autobiography* (London: Harper Collins, 1994), p. 62.
122. Author's correspondence: Mr K. M. Taylor (OC MMG Section, Fifth Fusiliers and 2i/c Y Company for Operation Commando, Korea 1951) 5 November 2002.
123. Author's correspondence: Mr. Joe Bailes (Sniper Corporal 1 DWR and Battle School Instructor, 1952–1953), 2 May and 29 November 2002.
124. Jim Lucock, in Stephen F. Kelly, *British Soldiers of the Korean War: In Their Own Words* (Stroud: The History Press, 2013), p. 51.
125. Keith Taylor, Friday 24 August 1951 Letter to Friend from Hara Mura, in Taylor, *Wither the Fates Call*, p. 161.
126. Author's correspondence: Mr. J. C. Hall (National Service 1 RTR and 5th RIDG, BAOR and Korea 1952–1953), 8 May 2002.
127. TNA, WO 308/23, Notes on the History of 1st Commonwealth Div Battle School, Conclusion, paragraph 15, p. 3.
128. Carter, *Korea: We Lived... They Died: Diary of a Forgotten War*, p. 42.
129. Author's correspondence: Mr. Malcolm Frost (National Service Royal Norfolk Regiment and Cpl. 1st Bn Royal Fusiliers, Korea 1952–1953) 2 November 2002.
130. General Sir Peter de la Billière: Author's Interview Re: the General's service with 1 DLI, Japan and Korea, 1952–1953 and experience at the Battle School, 7 September 2002.
131. Ibid.

Chapter 3

1. George Cooper, *Fight, Dig And Live: The Story of the Royal Engineers in the Korean War* (Barnsley: Pen and Sword, 2011), p. 115.
2. Peter S. Kindsvatter, *American Soldiers: Ground Combat in the World Wars, Korea, & Vietnam* (Kansas: University of Kansas Press, 2003), p. 121.
3. Paul Dunning Interview: Grand Valley State University (Veterans History Project).
4. Rudolph W. Stephens, *Old Ugly Hill: A G.I.'s Fourteen Months in the Korean Trenches, 1952–1953* (Jefferson, NC: McFarland & Co, 1995), p. 87.
5. Lt James Brady quoted in Kindsvatter, *American Soldiers*, p. 121.

6. C.S. Crawford, *The Four Deuces: A Korean War Story* (New York: Ballantine Books, 1989), p. 135.
7. Details of James B. Carlaw's Second World War and Korean War service can be found at Rutgers Oral History Archives: http://oralhistory.rutgers.edu.
8. Paul Dunning Interview: GVSU (VHP).
9. William Schrader Interview: GVSU (VHP).
10. Rod Chapman Interview: GVSU (VHP).
11. Kindsvatter, *American Soldiers*, p. 91.
12. Lyle Rishell, *With a Black Platoon in Combat: A Year in Korea* (Texas A & M University Press, 1993), p.163.
13. Howard Matthias, *The Korean War: Reflections of a Young Combat Platoon Leader* (Tallahassee: Father & Son, 1993), pp. 163–164.
14. Cpl. Robert Hall in Donald Knox, *The Korean War: Uncertain Victory* (New York: Harcourt Brace Jovanovich, 1988), p. 462
15. David French, *Military Identities: The Regimental System, The British Army and The British People c.1870-2000* (Oxford: OUP, 2008), pp. 294-295.
16. Author's correspondence with Colonel Michael Hickey, 8 July 2002.
17. Ibid.
18. Author's correspondence: Lieutenant-Colonel David M. C. Rose, undated.
19. Dan Raschen, *Send Port & Pyjamas!* (London: Buckland Publications Ltd, 1987), p. 32.
20. Derek Kinne, *The Wooden Boxes* (London: Frederick Muller Ltd, 1955), p. 12.
21. General Sir Peter de la Billière: Author's Interview Re: the General's service with 1 DLI, Japan and Korea, 1952–1953 and experience at the Battle School, 7 September 2002.
22. Robert C. Shoemaker, *A Surgeon Remembers: Korea 1950–1951 and the Marines* (Victoria BC: Trafford, 2005), p. 14.
23. Crawford, *The Four Deuces*, pp. 28–29.
24. Dave Reeg Interview: GVSU (VHP).
25. Author's Correspondence: Mr. Barry Tunnicliffe (National Service subaltern Royal Artillery, Korea 1952–1953), 21 December 2015.
26. IWM, Sound Archive 9537, Reel 1, Colonel Andrew Morrice Man (CO 1 MX); Tim Carew, *Korea: The Commonwealth at War* (London: Cassell, 1967), pp. 53–54.
27. Anon, *The Royal Ulster Rifles in Korea* (Belfast: Wm. Mullan & Son Ltd, 1953), p. 10.
28. Noel Trigg, *A Different Kind of Fighting: Memories of National Service* (Privately Published, undated) , p. 80.
29. 2/Lt K. M. Taylor letter to a friend, Saturday, 14 July 1951 in Keith M. Taylor, *Wither the Fates Call: A Personal Account of National Service in the British Army 1950-1952* (Privately Published, 2009), p. 114.
30. Martin Russ, *The Last Parallel* (New York: Zebra Books, 1985), p. 55.
31. John Martin, *K Force to the Sharp-End* (Leamington Spa: Korvet Publishing, 1999), p. 14.
32. Robert Halle Interview: GVSU (VHP).
33. Calvin Schutte Interview: GVSU (VHP).
34. Derek Halley, *The Iron Claw: A Conscript's tale* (Privately Published, 1998), p. 39.
35. Anon, *The Royal Ulster Rifles in Korea*, p. 11.
36. General Sir Peter de la Billière, *Looking for Trouble: SAS to Gulf Command: The Autobiography* (London: Harper Collins, 1994), p. 56.
37. 2/Lt. Taylor letter to a friend, Saturday, 14 July 1951 in Taylor, *Wither the Fates Call*, p. 113.
38. Author's Correspondence: Mr. Barry Tunnicliffe (61st Light Regt, RA, Korea 1952–1953), 21 December 2015.
39. Shoemaker, *A Surgeon Remembers*, p. 12.
40. Sgt. Robert Jamieson (HQ Company, 1st Battalion, 5th RCT) Letter home, 29 July 1950 in Louis Baldovi (ed), *A Foxhole View: Personal Accounts of Hawaii's Korean War Veterans* (Honolulu: University of Hawai'i Press, 2002), pp. 28–29.
41. de la Billière, *Looking for Trouble*, p. 56.

42. Geoff Holland, in Stephen F. Kelly, *British Soldiers of the Korean War: In Their Own Words* (Stroud: The History Press, 2013), p. 76.
43. Whatmore, *One Road to Imjin*, p. 24.
44. Michael Caine, *What's it all about? The Autobiography* (London: Century, 1992), p. 58.
45. Richard Newman, in Henry Berry, *Hey, Mac, Where Ya Been? Living Memories of the U.S. Marines in the Korean War* (New York: St. Martin's Press, 1990), p. 264.
46. Russ, *The Last Parallel*, p. 54.
47. Carl Ballard Interview: GVSU (VHP)
48. Octavio Huerta Interview: GVSU (VHP).
49. Kinne, *The Wooden Boxes*, p. 11.
50. Lofty Large, *One Man's War in Korea* (Wellingborough: William Kimber, 1988), p. 26.
51. Alan Carter, *Korea: We Lived... They Died: Diary of a Forgotten War* (Bognor Regis: Woodfield Publishing, 1999), p. 21.
52. Major H. J. Winn MC (OC 'Z' Company, 1 RNF), Letter to his mother, Port Said, 21 October 1950 in Anthony Perrins (ed), 'a pretty rough do altogether' *The Fifth Fusiliers in Korea, 1950–1951* (Alnwick: The Trustees of the Fusiliers Museum of Northumberland, 2004), p. 5.
53. Russ, *The Last Parallel*, p. 53.
54. Halley, *The Iron Claw*, p. 39.
55. John Erickson Interview: GVSU (VHP).
56. Author's correspondence: Mr. Bob Walding (National Service 1st R. Norfolk Regt, Korea 1951–1952), undated.
57. Author's correspondence: Mr. Alan Causer (National Service, Royal Artillery, Korea 1953), 30 October 2002.
58. Warrant Officer Bill Norman (1st DWR, Korea 1952–1953): Conversation with author.
59. Author's Interview: Lt. Col. J. C. M. Johnston (1st KOSB, Korea 1951–1952), 18 December 2001.
60. Author's correspondence: Mr. Malcolm Frost (National Service Royal Norfolk Regiment and Cpl. 1st Bn Royal Fusiliers, Korea 1952–1953), 2 November 2002.
61. PFC Pedro Behasa (Item Company, 5th RCT), July 1950 in Baldovi (ed), *A Foxhole View*, p. 28.
62. Author's correspondence: Major Norman Salmon (1st Welch Regt, Korea 1951–1952), May 2007.
63. Brigadier M. G. Harvey, *The War in Korea: The Battle Decides All* (Eggleston, Co Durham: Raby Books, 2002), pp. 20–22.
64. Russ, *The Last Parallel*, p. 53.
65. Carter, *Korea: We Lived... They Died: Diary of a Forgotten War*, p. 21.
66. Martin, *K Force to the Sharp-End*, p. 18.
67. F. J. McNair, *A British Army Nurse in the Korean War: Shadows of the Forgotten War* (Stroud: Tempus Publishing, 2007), p. 24.
68. Author's Correspondence: Mr. Barry Tunnicliffe, 21 December 2015.
69. Harvey, *The War in Korea: The Battle Decides All*, p. 22.
70. Trigg, *A Different Kind of Fighting*, p. 96.
71. George Pagan, *A National Serviceman in Korea: The Royal Signals Regiment at War 1950–1953* (Swanage: Finial Publishing, 2003), p. 14.
72. Carter, *Korea: We Lived... They Died: Diary of a Forgotten War*, p. 21.
73. Caine, *What's it all about?*, p. 58.
74. George Sarros Interview: GVSU (VHP).
75. David Torrance, *George Younger: A Life Well Lived* (Edinburgh: Birlinn, 2008), p. 23.
76. John Shipster, *Mist Over the Rice Fields: A Soldier's Story of the Burma Campaign 1943–45 and Korea 1950–51* (Barnsley: Leo Cooper, 2000), p. 119.
77. Edmund Ions, *A Call to Arms: Interlude with the Military* (Newton Abbot: David & Charles, 1972), pp. 152–153.
78. Matthias, *The Korean War: Reflections of a Young Combat Platoon Leader*, pp. 16–17.
79. Ibid, p. 16.

80. David Wilson, *The Sum of Things* (Spellmount: Staplehurst, 2001), p. 159.
81. Matthias, *The Korean War: Reflections of a Young Combat Platoon Leader*, p. 17.
82. Boris R. Spiroff, *Korea: Frozen Hell on Earth: A Platoon Sergeant's Diary Korean War 1950–1951* (Baltimore: American Literary Press, 1998), pp. 11–12.
83. William Schrader Interview: GVSU (VHP).
84. National Army Museum (NAM) 8905-160, Oral History Interview: Jarleth Donellan (1st RTR).
85. Alfie Fowler in Walker, *A Barren Place*, p. 61
86. Rishell, *With a Black Platoon in Combat*, p.19.
87. George Hyslop Interview: GVSU (VHP).
88. Sherwin Nagelkirk Interview: GVSU (VHP).
89. Calvin Schutte Interview: GVSU (VHP).
90. NAM 8905-261, Oral History Interview: Sam Mercer (Gloucestershire Regt).
91. Sherwin Nagelkirk Interview: GVSU (VHP).

Chapter 4

1. Michael Hickey, *Korean War: The West Confronts Communism 1950–1953* (London: John Murray, 2000), p. 46. (Another origin of the term 'Gook' might stem from the fact that South Koreans would greet English-speaking UN soldiers with something sounding like 'Me Gook,' leading them to think 'he says he's a Gook so we'll call him one.' However, it rapidly became the term for the NK enemy.
2. Clay Blair, *The Forgotten War: America in Korea 1950–1953* (New York: Times Books, 1987), p. 88.
3. '*Editorial: Korea Retrospect*' British Army Journal Volume 5 (January 1951), p. 2.
4. Charles M. Bussey, *Firefight at Yechon: Courage and Racism in the Korean War* (Lincoln, Nebraska: Bison Books, 2002), p. 159.
5. Major (later Brig.) A.D R. G. Wilson MBE (1 A&SH), 'A *Company in Korea*' British Army Journal Volume 6 (July 1951), p. 12.
6. The National Archives (Kew): WO 208/3081, War Office Booklet: Weapons and Equipment of the North Korean Army, August 1950; WO 208/3214, Notes on Armed Forces Operating in Korea, Pt. II: NKPA Tactics and Training, 22 August 1950, pp. 10–11; WO 308/96, 26/GS Trg Publications 1952: Korea Notes No.1 (Reactions to the First Part of the Korean Campaign Prior to the Inchon Landings), Prepared under the Direction of the CIGS, March 1951, pp. 1–2; '*Editorial: Korea Retrospect*' BAJ Vol. 5 (Jan 1951), pp. 2–3.
7. Darrell Thornley Interview: Grand Valley State University (Veterans History Project).
8. Matthew B. Ridgway, *The Korean War* (New York: Da Capo, 1967), p. 26.
9. Anonymous American sergeant quoted in Marguerite Higgins, *War in Korea: The Report of a Woman Combat Correspondent* (New York: Doubleday & Co, 1951), p. 63.
10. Roy E. Appleman, *South to the Nakltong, North to the Yalu* (Washington DC: Centre of Military History United States Army, 1992), p. 180.
11. Hickey, *Korean War: The West Confronts Communism 1950–1953*, p. 47.
12. Al Burnett quoted in Uzal Ent, *Fighting on the Brink: Defence of the Pusan Perimeter* (Paducah KY, Turner Publishing Co, 1996), p. 96.
13. Lyle Gibbs Interview: GVSU (VHP).
14. Max Hastings, *The Korean War* (London: Michael Joseph, 1987), p. 82.
15. C. W. 'Bill' Menninger in Donald Knox, *The Korean War Pusan to Chosin: An Oral History* (San Diego: Harcourt Brace & Co, 1985), p. 44.
16. Leroy Wirth quoted in Ent, *Fighting on the Brink: Defence of the Pusan Perimeter*, p. 141.
17. Appleman, *South to the Nakltong, North to the Yalu*, p. 180.
18. Charles Menninger quoted in Blair, *The Forgotten War: America in Korea 1950–1953*, p. 110.
19. Higgins, *War in Korea*, p. 71.
20. William F. Dean, *General Dean's Story* (London: Weidenfeld and Nicolson, 1954), p. 24.
21. John Shipster, *Mist Over the Rice Fields: A Soldier's Story of the Burma Campaign 1943–45 and Korean War 1950–51* (Barnsley: Leo Cooper, 2000), p. 120.

22. Russel A. Guegler, *Combat Actions in Korea* (Washington DC: Office of the Chief of Military History United Stated Army, 1970), p. 37.
23. Events regarding the massacre at No Gun Ri (25–29 July 1950) started to emerge more widely in the 1990s. A good overview can be found online via Wikipedia. This includes information on the investigations into this tragic event, plus comments from veterans. Evidence from declassified documents suggests that it became official American policy to shoot on refugees in frontline areas at this time, owing to the fear of NKPA infiltration tactics.
24. Charles Payne in Knox, *The Korean War Pusan to Chosin*, p. 52.
25. Darrell Thornley Interview: GVSU (VHP).
26. Glen Bailey Interview: GVSU (VHP).
27. Darrell Thornley Interview: GVSU (VHP).
28. Blair, *The Forgotten War: America in Korea 1950–1953*, p. 131.
29. This figure is taken from Ent, *Fighting on the Brink: Defence of the Pusan Perimeter*, p. 123.
30. Appleman, *South to the Nakltong, North to the Yalu*, p. 251.
31. Joseph C. Goulden, *Korea: The Untold Story of the War* (New York: McGraw Hill Inc., 1982), p. 165.
32. Uzal Ent in Rudy Tomedi, *No Bugles, No Drums: An Oral history of the Korean War* (New York: John Wiley & Sons, 1994), p. 20.
33. Edwin P. Hoyt, *The Pusan Perimeter* (New York: Stein and Day, 1984), p. 139.
34. Ent, *Fighting on the Brink: Defence of the Pusan Perimeter*, pp. 134, 161.
35. Addison Terry, *The Battle for Pusan: A Korean War Memoir* (Novato, CA: Presidio, 2000), p. 53.
36. Bussey, *Firefight at Yechon*, p. 136.
37. Appleman, *South to the Nakltong, North to the Yalu*, p. 255.
38. Ent in Tomedi, *No Bugles, No Drums. An Oral history of the Korean War*, p. 18.
39. Glen Bailey Interview: GVSU (VHP).
40. George Sarros Interview: GVSU (VHP).
41. Figure for 9th Regiment's frontage is taken from: Ent, *Fighting on the Brink: Defence of the Pusan Perimeter*, p. 282.
42. The National Archives (Kew), WO 308/45, 27th British Commonwealth Brigade Report on Operations, Aug 1950–March 1951, p. 2.
43. Lieutenant-Colonel G. I. Malcolm of Poltalloch, *The Argylls in Korea* (Edinburgh: Thomas Nelson and Sons Ltd, 1952), pp. 10–11.
44. David Wilson, *The Sum of Things* (Staplehurst: Spellmount, 2001), pp. 160–161.
45. Albert J. McAdoo & James E. Marshall, *The 5th RCT in Korea: The Pusan Perimeter Battles, 1950* (Privately published, 2012), p. 80.
46. Tanjore Splan Interview: GVSU (VHP).
47. TNA, WO 231/89, Battle Experience Questionnaires (BEQ): T/Maj. Penman (1 A&SH), 30 March 1951; Major James Blair Gillies (1 A&SH), 5 April 1951.
48. TNA, WO 231/89, BEQ: Major A. S. J. de S. Clayton (1 MX), 14 September 1951.
49. Tony Kingsford in Adrian Walker, *A Barren Place: National Servicemen in Korea 1950–1954* (London: Leo Cooper, 1994), p. 4.
50. TNA, WO 231/89, BEQ: 2/Lt. James Stirling (1 A&SH), 27 February 1951; Author's Conversation with Col. Sir James Stirling, 27 September 2003.
51. Wilson, 'A Company in Korea' BAJ Vol. 6 (July 1951), pp. 14–17.
52. TNA, WO 231/89, BEQ: T/Maj. Penman (1 A&SH), 30 March 1951.
53. TNA, WO 231/89, BEQ: Lt. P. M. K. Mackellar (1 A&SH), 20 February 1951.
54. Lyle Rishell, *With a Black Platoon in Combat: A Year in Korea* (Texas A&M University Press, 1993), p. 85.
55. J.B.A. Bailey, *Field Artillery and Firepower* (Annapolis, Naval Institute Press, 2004), p. 367.
56. Terry, *The Battle for Pusan: A Korean War Memoir*, p. 59.
57. TNA, WO 308/88, BM 1319 (MT2) British Information from Korea, Paragraph 7(a) Difficulties Encountered by the British in Defence, 5 February 1951, p. 2

58. Ibid.
59. Glen Bailey Interview: GVSU (VHP).
60. Ent, *Fighting on the Brink: Defence of the Pusan Perimeter*, p. 178.
61. Ibid, p. 263.
62. Ent in Tomedi, *No Bugles, No Drums: An Oral history of the Korean War*, p. 17.
63. TNA, WO 308/88, BM 1319 (MT2) British Information from Korea, Paragraph 6 (b) Enemy Tactics Employed, 5 February 1951, p. 2
64. Rishell, *With a Black Platoon in Combat*, p. 89.
65. Lynn Montross and Capt. Nicholas A. Canzona, *US Marine Operations in Korea 1950–1953, Volume I: The Pusan Perimeter* (Washington DC, Historical Branch, G-3 HQ USMC, 1954), p. 191.
66. Arnold Winter (5th Marines, 1st Provisional Marine Brigade, Korea 1950) in Tomedi, *No Bugles, No Drums: An Oral history of the Korean War*, pp. 26–27.
67. NKPA POW quoted in McAdoo & Marshall, *The 5th RCT in Korea: The Pusan Perimeter Battles, 1950*, p. 42.
68. The Naktong River 'D' Company, 1st Middlesex [D.C.O.], Naktong River, Korea, September 1950, Sergeant E. J. Bermingham, No. 12 Platoon, p. 4 (Kindly provided by Mr. D. F. Barrett former NCO with 1 MX).
69. Edward F. Balbi in Ent, *Fighting on the Brink: Defence of the Pusan Perimeter*, p. 113.
70. Lt. Cols Ray Murray and Harold Roise (USMC) quoted in Henry Berry, *Hey, Mac, Where Ya Been? Living Memories of the U.S. Marines in the Korean War* (New York: St. Martin's Press, 1988), pp. 53, 67.
71. Blair, *The Forgotten War: America in Korea 1950–1953*, p. 87.
72. Michael Schaller, *Douglas MacArthur: The Far Eastern General* (Oxford: OUP, 1989), p. 198.
73. Max Hastings, *The Korean War* (London: Michael Joseph, 1987), p. 116.
74. Robert Bohn in Knox, *The Korean War Pusan to Chosin: An Oral History*, p. 223.
75. Francis 'Ike' Fenton, Jr. in Knox, *The Korean War Pusan to Chosin: An Oral History*, p. 214.
76. Robert Debs Heinl, Jr. (Col. USMC retd), *Victory at High Tide: The Inchon Seoul Campaign* (Annapolis: The Nautical and Aviation Publishing Co of America, 1979), p. 108.
77. Inchon casualty figures from: Michael Langley, *Inchon: MacArthur's Last Triumph* (London: Batsford, 1979), p. 96.
78. Colonel (later General) Ellis Williamson quoted in Hastings, *The Korean War*, p.129.
79. Reginald Thompson, *Cry Korea* (London: MacDonald & Co. Ltd, 1952), p. 77.
80. Leroy Schuff in Sarah A. Larsen and Jenifer M. Miller, *Wisconsin Korean War Stories: Veterans Tell Their Stories from the Forgotten War* (Wisconsin Historical Society Press, 2008), pp. 27, 32–33.
81. W.O. Wood in Larsen and Miller, *Wisconsin Korean War Stories: Veterans Tell Their Stories from the Forgotten War*, p. 92.
82. Victor Fox quoted in Blair, *The Forgotten War: America in Korea 1950–1953*, p. 285.
83. Goulden, *Korea: The Untold Story of the War*, p. 232.
84. Heinl, *Victory at High Tide: The Inchon Seoul Campaign*, p. 267.
85. NAM, 8905–159, Oral History Interview Michael Eastap (Sgt No. 1 Pl, 'A' Coy, 1 MX).
86. Guegler, *Combat Actions in Korea*, p. 26.
87. TNA, WO 231/89, BEQ: Major C. W. A. Bath (1 Glosters), 2 April 1951.
88. Anon, 'Korea' in St. George's Gazette, 30th December 1950, p. 230.
89. Wilson, 'A Company in Korea' BAJ Vol. 6 (July 1951), pp. 16–17.
90. Colonel Andrew M. Man, 'The Naktong River and "Middlesex Hill," September 1950' in Ashley Cunningham-Boothe and PeterFarrar (Eds), *British Forces in the Korean War* (British Korean Veteran's Association, 1997), p. 21.
91. Boris R. Spiroff, *Korea: Frozen Hell on Earth: A Platoon Sergeant's Diary Korean War 1950–1951* (Baltimore, American Literary Press, 1998), p. 46.

92. Colin Mitchell, *Having Been a Soldier* (London: Hamish Hamilton, 1969), p. 80.
93. TNA, WO 231/89, Battle Notes from Korea by Capt. M. G. Harvey MC (1st Battalion, The Gloucestershire Regiment), Section headed 'Our Attack', undated, p. 2.
94. TNA, WO 231/89, BEQ: Capt. A. P. H. B. Fowle, MC (170th Ind Mor Btty, RA), September 1951.
95. Curtis James Morrow, *What's a Commie Ever Done to Black People? A Korean War Memoir* (Jefferson, NC: McFarland & Co Inc, 1997), p. 30.
96. Imperial War Museum, Dept. of Sound 18003, Oral History Interview: Ronald Yetman (NCO No 5 Pl, 'B' Coy, 1 A&SH), Reel 2.
97. TNA, WO 231/89, BEQ: Major C. W. A. Bath (1 Glosters), 2 April 1951.
98. Spiroff, *Korea: Frozen Hell on Earth: A Platoon Sergeant's Diary Korean War 1950–1951*, p. 28.
99. Glen Bailey Interview: GVSU (VHP).
100. Samuel B. Griffith II, *The Chinese People's Liberation Army* (New York: McGraw-Hill, 1967), p. 143.
101. Hickey, *Korean War: The West Confronts Communism 1950–1953*, p.143.
102. Sherman Pratt in Tomedi, *No Bugles, No Drums: An Oral History of the Korean War*, p. 65.
103. Charles Payne in Knox, *The Korean War Pusan to Chosin*, pp. 438–439.
104. Marshall, *Infantry Operations and Weapons Usage in Korea*, pp. 5–6.
105. TNA, WO 231/89, Battle Notes from Korea by Capt. Harvey, Section headed 'Chinese Attack', p. 1.
106. Griffith, *The Chinese People's Liberation Army*, p 142.
107. TNA, WO 231/89, BEQ: Major Sir C. J. Nixon Bart, MC (1 RUR), 29 September 1951.
108. TNA, WO 231/89, BEQ: Major J. C. S. G. De Longueil (1 RUR), 24 November 1951.
109. TNA, WO 231/89, BEQ: Major R. Leith-Macgregor (1 RNF), 26 November 1951.
110. Bertram Sehreeos in Baldovi (Ed), *A Foxhole View: Personal Accounts of Hawaii's Korean War Veterans* (Honolulu: University of Hawai'i Press, 2002), p. 107.
111. TNA, WO 231/90, BEQ: Capt. P. L. D. Weldon (45th Field Regiment, RA), 7 July 1952.
112. Gerald H. Corr, *The Chinese Red Army: Campaigns and Politics Since 1949* (London: Purnell, 1972), p. 89.
113. NAM, 8905-261, Oral History Interview: Sam Mercer (1 Glosters, Korea 1950–1951).
114. Anonymous American NCO quoted in Marshall, *Infantry Operations and Weapons Usage in Korea*, p. 14.
115. M.G. Harvey, *The War in Korea: The Battle Decides All* (Eggleston: Raby Books, 2002), p. 49.
116. T NA, WO 231/89, BEQ: Lt. L. C. Sharpe (1 MX), 24 July 1951.
117. TNA, WO 231/89, Battle Notes from Korea by Capt. Harvey, Section headed 'Chinese Attack', p. 1.
118. Harvey, *The War in Korea*, p. 21.
119. TNA, WO 231/89, Battle Notes from Korea by Capt. Harvey, Section headed 'Chinese Attack', p. 1.
120. Ibid.
121. Ibid, p. 2.
122. Ibid, Section headed 'Our Attack', p. 2.
123. TNA, WO 231/89, BEQ: Capt. John Henry Bergin (Royal Fusiliers att. 1 Glosters), 11 September 1951.
124. TNA, WO 231/89, BEQ: Lt. J. M. Cubiss (West Yorkshire Regt att. 1 RNF), 18 September 1951.
125. Herbert Ikeda in Baldovi (Ed), *A Foxhole View: Personal Accounts of Hawaii's Korean War Veterans*, p. 131.
126. TNA, WO 231/89, BEQ: Major R. Leith-Macgregor (1 RNF), 26 November 1951.

Chapter 5

1. Clay Blair, *The Forgotten War: America in Korea 1950–1953* (New York: Times Books, 1987), pp. 332–333.
2. Roy E. Appleman, *Escaping the Trap: The US Army X Corps in Northeast Korea, 1950* (Texas A &M University Press, 1990), p. 26.

3. Joseph R. Owen, *Colder than Hell: A Marine Rifle Company at Chosin Reservoir* (Annapolis: Naval Institute Press, 2000), p. 90.
4. Chet Kesy in Sarah A. Larsen & Jennifer M. Miller, *Wisconsin War Stories: Veteran's Tell Their Stories from the Forgotten War* (Wisconsin Historical Society Press, 2008), p. 55.
5. Ibid, p. 56.
6. Richard Gruenther quoted in Blair, *The Forgotten War: America in Korea 1950–1953*, pp. 367–368.
7. Appleman, *Escaping the Trap: The US Army X Corps in Northeast Korea, 1950*, p. 82.
8. Russel Gugeler, *Combat Actions in Korea* (Washington, DC: Office of the Chief of Military History U.S. Army, 1970), p. 55.
9. General Almond's communique to Major-General Barr quoted in Appleman, *South to the Naktong, North to the Yalu*, pp. 736–737.
10. Blair, *The Forgotten War: America in Korea 1950–1953*, p. 418.
11. Col. Charles Olsen Interview: Grand Valley State University (Veterans History Project). In the official History there is a photograph of Brig. Gen. Homer Kiefer (7th Division's artillery commander), Generals Hodes (Assistant 7th Division commander), Almond (X Corps commander) and Barr (7th Division commander), plus Colonel Powell (OC 17th Regiment) 'looking across the Yalu'- see Appleman, *South to the Naktong, North to the Yalu*, p. 735.
12. William O. Wood in Larsen & Miller, *Wisconsin War Stories: Veteran's Tell Their Stories from the Forgotten War*, p. 95.
13. Appleman, *Escaping the Trap: The US Army X Corps in Northeast Korea, 1950*, p. 82.
14. Don McAlister quoted in Max Hastings, *The Korean War* (London: Michael Joseph, 1987), p. 183.
15. James Ransone, Jr in Donald Knox, *The Korean War Pusan to Chosin: An Oral History* (New York: Harcourt Brace & Co., 1985), p. 551.
16. Figures taken from Gugeler, *Combat Actions in Korea*, p. 78.
17. James Ransone, Jr in Knox, *The Korean War Pusan to Chosin: An Oral History*, p. 552.
18. Chester Bair in Knox, *The Korean War Pusan to Chosin*, p. 558.
19. William B. Hopkins, *One Bugle No Drums: The Marines at Chosin Reservoir* (Chapel Hill NC: Algonquin Books, 1986), p. 133.
20. Colonel Alpha L. Bowser quoted in Martin Russ, *Breakout: The Chosin Reservoir Campaign, Korea 1950* (New York: Penguin Books, 1999), p. 52.
21. Yu Bin, 'What China Learned from Its "Forgotten War" in Korea' in Mark A. Ryan, David M. Finkelstein, & Michael A. Mc Devitt, *Chinese War Fighting: The PLA Experience Since 1949* (Armonk NY: M. E. Sharpe, 2003), p. 127.
22. Appleman, *Escaping the Trap: The US Army X Corps in Northeast Korea, 1950*, pp. 362–363.
23. Robert Samuels Interview: Grand Valley State University (Veterans History Project).
24. Patrick Stingley quoted in Russ, *Breakout: The Chosin Reservoir Campaign, Korea 1950*, p. 127.
25. Dave Brady, *One of the Chosin Few: A Royal Marine Commando's Fight for Survival Behind Enemy Lines in Korea* (Stanford Rivers, Essex: Neat Books, 2004), p. 94.
26. Lt. Patrick Roe quoted in Russ, *Breakout: The Chosin Reservoir Campaign, Korea 1950*, p. 320.
27. General Smith quoted in Hastings, *The Korean War*, pp. 187–188.
28. Russ, *Breakout: The Chosin Reservoir Campaign, Korea 1950*, p. 292.
29. Appleman, *Escaping the Trap: The US Army X Corps in Northeast Korea, 1950*, p. 211.
30. Hopkins, *One Bugle No Drums: The Marines at Chosin Reservoir*, p. 73.
31. Owen, *Colder than Hell: A Marine Rifle Company at Chosin Reservoir*, pp. 152, 158.
32. Appleman, *South to the Naktong, North to the Yalu*, p. 739.
33. Ibid, p. 740.
34. George Zonge in Rudy Tomedi, *No Bugles, No Drums: An Oral History of the Korean War* (New York: Wiley,1994), p. 100.
35. Cpl. Bertram Sebresos in Louis Baldovi (ed) *A Fox Hole View: Personnel Accounts of Hawaii's Korean War Veterans* (Honolulu: University of Hawai'i Press, 2002), p. 108.

36. Billy C. Mossman, *United States Army in the Korean War: Ebb and Flow November 1950-July 1951* (Honolulu: University Press of the Pacific, 2005), p. 165.
37. Figures from: Hopkins, *One Bugle No Drums: The Marines at Chosin Reservoir*, p. 214.
38. John W. Connor, *Let Slip the Dogs of War: A Memoir of the GHQ 1st Raider Company (8245th Army Unit) a.k.a. Special Operations Company Korea 1950-51* (Bennington VT: Merriam Press, 2008), p. 134
39. Joseph Owen quoted in in Russ, *Breakout: The Chosin Reservoir Campaign, Korea 1950*, p. 133.
40. Thomas Fleming, 'The Man Who Saved Korea' MHQ The Quarterly Journal of Military History Volume 5, Number 2 (Winter 1993), p. 59.
41. Roy E. Appleman, *Ridgway Duels for Korea* (Texas A&M University Press, 1990), p. 17.
42. Matthew B. Ridgway, *The Korean War* (New York: Da Capo, 1967), p. 86.
43. Ibid, pp. 88–89.
44. Harry Summers in Rudy Tomedi, *No Bugles, No Drums: An Oral History of the Korean War* (New York: John Wiley & Sons, Inc, 1994), p. 106.
45. Ridgway, *The Korean War*, p. 89.
46. Gen. Ridgway's Address to elements of 29th Bde, near Suwon late Jan 1951, quoted in Anthony Farrar-Hockley, *The British Part in the Korean War Volume II* (London: HMSO, 1995), p .31.
47. Anon, *General Matthew B. Ridgway and Army Design Methodology during the Korean War* (privately published, undated), p. 30.
48. Ibid.
49. David Green, *Captured at the Imjin River: The Korean War Memories of a Gloster 1950–1953* (Barnsley: Leo Cooper, 2003), p. 69.
50. Harry Summers in Tomedi, *No Bugles, No Drums*, p. 108.
51. General Ridgway quoted in Appleman, *Ridgway Duels for Korea*, p. 51.
52. The National Archives (TNA), Kew, WO 308/45, 27th British Commonwealth Brigade Report on Operations, August 1950-March 1951, p. 23.
53. Author's Correspondence: Mr. Bob Yerby (1 MX, Korea 1950–1951), 6 July 2003.
54. Appleman, *Ridgway Duels for Korea*, p. 65.
55. TNA, WO 231/89, Battle Experience Questionnaire (BEQ): Major J. W. II. Mulligan (1 RUR), 5 May 1951.
56. Royal Northumberland Fusiliers Museum, Alnwick, RNF Box 1/2, The Battle of Koyang: Fought by 29 Indep Inf Bde Gp North of Seoul on 3 Jan 51, p. 2.
57. TNA, WO 281/1143, C Sqn, 7th RTR (RAC) War Diary, Korea: Entry 3 January 1951.
58. Anon, *The Royal Ulster Rifles in Korea* (Belfast: Wm. Mullan & Sons, 1953), p. 31.
59. TNA, WO 281/1165, 1 RUR War Diary, Korea: Entry 21.30 hours, 3 January 1951.
60. Imperial War Museum (IWM), 99/31/1: E. G. Beckerley Papers: Memoir re: his service as a tank driver with 8th Hussars & POW Experience, Korea 1950–1953.
61. Extracts from: TNA, WO 281/1142, War Diary Korea, 8th King's Royal Irish Hussars, Jan 1951: App D: Cooper Force 3/4. Jan 1951, Personal Testimony of Maj. Howe (45 Fd Regt RA).
62. Anon, *The Royal Ulster Rifles in Korea*, p. 32.
63. Gen, Ridgway communications with Gen. Collins quoted in Billy C. Mossman, *Ebb and Flow November 1950-July 1951* (Honolulu: University Press of the Pacific, 2005), p. 209.
64. S/Sgt. W.B. Woodruff, Jr. in Donald Knox, *The Korean War: Uncertain Victory* (New York: Harcourt Brace Jovanovich, 1988), pp. 28–29.
65. Pfc. Jerry Emer in Knox, *The Korean War: Uncertain Victory*, p. 84.
66. TNA, WO 231/89, BEQ: Lt. R. M. Cain (1 MX), 2 June 1951.
67. TNA, WO 231/89, BEQ: Lt. L. C. Sharpe (1 MX), 24 July 1951.
68. 2/Lt. Edmund Krekorian in Knox, *The Korean War: Uncertain Victory*, p. 139.
69. TNA, WO 231/89, BEQ: 2/Lt. A. C. Gilmour (The Black Watch (RHR) att. 1 A&SH), 30 July 1951.
70. J. D. Coleman, *Wonju: The Gettysburg of the Korean War* (Washington, DC: Brassey's Inc, 2000), p. 184.

71. Unidentified American Soldier quoted in Kenneth E. Hamburger, *Leadership in the Crucible: The Korean War Battles of Twin tunnels & Chipyong-ni* (Texas A & M University, 2003), p. 190.
72. Pfc. Ben Judd in Knox, *The Korean War: Uncertain Victory*, p. 68.
73. Hamburger, *Leadership in the Crucible: The Korean War Battles of Twin tunnels & Chipyong-*ni, pp. 219–220.
74. Casualty figures from: Coleman, *Wonju: The Gettysburg of the Korean* War, p. 225.
75. Hamburger, *Leadership in the Crucible: The Korean War Battles of Twin tunnels & Chipyong-*ni, p. 192.
76. René Cutforth, *Korean Reporter* (London: Allan Wingate, 1952), p. 167.
77. R.C.W. Thomas, *The War in Korea: A military study of the war in Korea up to the signing of the Cease Fire* (New Dehli: J. D. Chowdhry, 1968), p. 60.
78. TNA, WO 308/42, A Brief History of 29 Independent Infantry Brigade Group from September 1949 to October 1951, paragraph 10: 1 -21 April, p. 4.
79. P.J. Kavanagh, *The Perfect Stranger* (London: Quartet Books, 1974), p. 93.
80. Major John Winn Letter Home, Korea 22 April 1951 in Anthony Perrins (ed) 'a *pretty rough do altogether*' *The Fifth Fusiliers in Korea 1950-1951* (Alnwick: The Trustees of the Fusiliers Museum, 2004), p. 113.
81. Tim Carew, *Korea: The Commonwealth at War* (London: Cassel, 1967), p. 175.
82. Green, *Captured at the Imjin River*, p. 96.
83. IWM, Sound Archive Oral History Interview (19387): A. R. D. Perrins, Reel 3.
84. 'Action on 22nd-25th April, 1951' in *St. George's Gazette, 31st May 1951*, p. 100.
85. TNA, WO 308/49, Operations of the 1st Belgian Contingent in Korea by Col. Crahay (Originally published In Revue de Documentation Militaire), Entry: 21 April 1951.
86. Digby Grist, *Remembered with Advantage: A Personal Account of Service with the Glosters during the Korean War* (The Gloucestershire Regiment, 1976), p. 41.
87. S.J. Davies, *In Spite of Dungeons* (London: Hodder and Stoughton, 1964), p. 15.
88. IWM, Sound Archive 15428, Reel 2, David James Holdsworth.
89. 'Y Company Notes' in *St. George's Gazette, 31st May, 1951*, p. 105.
90. Derek Kinne, *The Wooden Boxes* (London: Frederick Muller Ltd, 1955), p. 15.
91. IWM, Sound Archive 19387, Reel 3, A.R.D. Perrins.
92. TNA, WO 231/89, BEQ: Major Sir C. J. Nixon Bart MC, (1 RUR), 29 September 1951.
93. TNA, WO 231/89, BEQ: Major (later Lt. Col.) R. Leith-Macgregor MC, DFC (1 RNF), 26 November 1951.
94. For widely available published narratives on the Battle of the Imjin see: Anthony Farrar-Hockley, *The British Part in the Korean War Volume II* (London: HMSO, 1995), pp. 111–136 and *The Edge of the Sword* (London: The Companion Book Club, 1955), pp. 15–70; Anon, *The Royal Ulster Rifles in Korea*, pp. 62–84; Brian Catchpole, *The Korean War* (London: Constable, 2000), pp. 122–128; Tim Carew, *The Glorious Glosters: A Short History of the Gloucestershire Regiment 1945-1970* (London: Leo Cooper, 1970), pp. 68–91 and *Korea: The Commonwealth at War*, pp. 173–222; Cutforth, *Korean Reporter*, pp. 182–188; Hastings, *The Korean War*, pp. 249–271; Michael Hickey, *Korean War: The West Confronts Communism 1950-1953* (London: John Murray, 2000), pp. 220–233; Andrew Salmon, *To the Last Round: The Epic British Stand on the Imjin River, Korea 1951*(London: Aurum, 2009), pp. 136–233.
95. Figures for ammunition expenditure from: TNA, WO 308/50, Extracts from DO report dated 24 July 1951 By Lt Col M.T. Young, DSO, RA Commanding 45 Field Regiment RA, p. 1.
96. Tactical Doctrine Retrieval Cell (MOD), 8408, Korean Episode: The Story of the 45th Field Regiment, Royal Artillery in the Korean War by Brig. M. Young, Ch. 10 The Imjin River Battle, p. 4.
97. TNA, WO 281/1146, 45th Field Regt RA, War Diary, Korea, Entries for 22–25 April 1951.
98. Ridgway, *The Korean War*, p. 172.
99. Author's Correspondence: Col. Michael Hickey, 16 October 2001.

100. Farrar-Hockley, *The British Part in the Korean War Volume II*, p. 136.
101. Salmon, *To the Last Round*, p. 318.
102. TNA, WO 32/14417, Report on Centurion in Korea Period 25 Oct-6 Dec 1951, 8th KRIH, 8H/Sec/T/21, 29 Dec 51: Appendix 'B' Para. 2 a: The Imjin Battle 23–25 April 1951.
103. TNA, WO 231/89, BEQ: Lt. Lennard (1 Glosters), 19 January 1952.
104. TNA, WO 231/89, BEQ: Major C. H. Mitchell (1 RNF), 14 July 1951.
105. Farrar-Hockley, *The Edge of the Sword*, pp. 43–45.
106. Salmon, *To the Last Round*, p. 4.
107. Lofty Large, *One Man's War in Korea* (Wellingborough: William Kimber, 1988), pp. 51–52; I am also deeply grateful to Mr Lofty Large for recounting this episode and other aspects of his Korean War service, 3 December 2003.
108. Large, *One Man's War in Korea*, pp. 56, 58.
109. IWM, Sound Archive 18474, Reel 3, John Dyer.
110. Davies, *In Spite of Dungeons*, p. 24.
111. Kinne, *The Wooden Boxes*, p. 20.
112. Farrar-Hockley, *The Edge of the Sword*, p. 62.
113. Bruce I. Gudmundsson, *On Artillery* (Westport, CT: Praeger, 1993), p. 145.
114. National Army Museum (NAM), Acc. No. 8009-79-104, Papers and Maps of Lt. Col. C. J. G. Meade, 1940–1967, Document entitled: 8th K.R.I. Hussars in Korea, p. 2.
115. TNA, WO 32/14417, Report on Centurion in Korea Period 25 Oct-6 Dec 1951, 8th KRIH, 8H/Sec/T/21, 29 Dec 51: Appendix 'B' Para. 2 a: The Imjin Battle 23–25 April 1951.
116. William Johnston, *A War of Patrols: Canadian Army Operations in Korea* (Vancouver: UBC Press, 2003), p. 93.
117. Farrar-Hockley, *The British Part in the Korean War Volume II*, p. 138.
118. NAM Oral History Tape: Transcript of Major Barry Reed's Interview, pp. 50–51. (I am deeply grateful to Major Reed for supplying a copy of this document, and for sharing his memories of the Korean War, 22 November 2002).
119. Ian McGibbon, *New Zealand and the Korean War Volume II: Combat Operations* (Auckland: OUP New Zealand, 1996), p. 139.

Chapter 6

1. James Hamilton Dill, *Sixteen Days at Mungo-li* (Fayettville, Arkansas: m & m Press, 1993), pp. 179–180.
2. TNA, WO231/89, Battle Experience Questionnaires (BEQs): Major John Lancelot Bromhead (1st Battalion Royal Leicestershire Regiment), 27 April 1952 and T/Capt. Bettington (1 KSLI), 24 September 1951.
3. Mark Clark, *From the Danube to the Yalu* (London: George G. Harrap & Co. Ltd, 1954), p. 72.
4. Billy C. Mossman, *Ebb and Flow November 1950–July 1951* (Honolulu: University Press of the Pacific, 1990), pp. 502–504.
5. Boris R. Spiroff, *Korea: Frozen Hell on Earth: A Platoon Sergeant's Diary Korean War 1950–1951* (Baltimore: American Literary Press Inc, 1998), p. 64.
6. Anonymous soldier from 1st KSLI quoted in H. B. Eaton, *Something Extra: 28th Commonwealth Brigade 1951–1974* (Durham: The Pentland Press Ltd, 1993), p. 19.
7. Brig. George Taylor, 'The 28th British Commonwealth Brigade, in the Battle of Kowang San and Maryang San' British Army Journal Volume 9, January 1953, p. 45; C. N. Barclay, *The First Commonwealth Division: The Story of British Land Forces in Korea, 1950–1953* (Aldershot: Gale & Polden, 1954), p. 92.
8. Walter G. Hermes, *Truce Tent and Fighting Front* (Honolulu: University Press of the Pacific, 2005), p. 81.

9. J. Lawton Collins, *War in Peacetime: The History and Lessons of Korea* (Boston: Houghton Mifflin Co, 1969), p. 309.
10. Calvin Schutte Interview: Grand Valley State University (Veterans History Project).
11. Sherwin Nagelkirk Interview: GVSU (VHP).
12. Hermes, *Truce Tent and Fighting Front*, p. 311.
13. Bevin Alexander, *Korea: The First War We Lost* (New York: Hippocrene Books, 2000), p. 439.
14. Sherman Pratt in Rudy Tomedi, *No Bugles, No Drums: An Oral History of the Korean War* (New York: John Wiley & Sons, 1994), p. 144.
15. D. Clayton James with Anne Sharp Wells, *Refighting the Last War: Command and Crisis in Korea 1950–1953* (New York: The Free Press, 1993), p. 74.
16. Hermes, *Truce Tent and Fighting Front*, p. 89.
17. Alexander, *Korea: The First War We Lost*, p. 440.
18. John Iwatomo in Louis Baldovi (ed), *A Fox Hole View: Personal Accounts of Hawaii's Korean War Veterans* (Honolulu: University of Hawai'I Press, 2002), p. 163.
19. Ben Judd in Donald Knox, *The Korean War Uncertain Victory* (New York: Harcourt Brace Jovanovich, 1988), p. 310.
20. Elroy Roeder in Sarah A. Larsen and Jenifer M. Miller, *Wisconsin War Stories: Veterans Tell Their Stories from the Forgotten War* (Wisconsin Historical Society Press, 2008), p. 106.
21. Russel Gugler, *Combat Actions in Korea*, (Washington, DC: Office of the Chief of Military History, US Army, 1970), p. 213.
22. Alan R. Millett, *Their War for Korea: American, Asian, and European Combatants and Civilians, 1945–53* (Washington, DC: Brassey's, 2002), pp. 221–225.
23. Letter home from Brigadier W. G. H. Pike (Commander Royal Artillery, 1st Commonwealth Div), 5 October 1951 in Hew Pike, *From the Frontline: Family Letters & Diaries 1900 to the Falklands and Afghanistan* (Barnsley: Pen and Sword, 2008), p. 112.
24. Taylor, 'The 28th British Commonwealth Brigade, in the Battle of Kowang San and Maryang San' BAJ Vol. 9, Jan 1953, p. 45.
25. Ibid, p. 48.
26. TNA, WO 231/89, BEQ: T/Capt. R.G. Handley (1 KSLI), 3 March 1952.
27. Major Heard (OC 'A' Coy, 1 KSLI) quoted in Eaton, *Something Extra: 28th Commonwealth Brigade*, p. 47.
28. Tactical Doctrine Retrieval Cell (TDRC, MOD) Serial No. 6280, Operations in Korea Bulletin No. 1 Operation Commando 5–8 Oct 51, Para 2 (b): Arty Support, Jan 1952, p.1.
29. J.F.M. MacDonald, *The Borderers in Korea* (Berwick-upon-Tweed, 1954), p. 31; Taylor, 'The 28th British Commonwealth Brigade, in the Battle of Kowang San and Maryang San' BAJ Vol. 9, Jan 1953, p. 49.
30. TDRC (MOD) Serial No. 6280, Operations in Korea Bulletin No. 1 Operation Commando 5–8 Oct 51, Para 2 (a): Arty Support, Jan 1952, p.1.
31. TNA, WO 32/14417, 8th Hussars Report on the Centurion in Korea, November 1951, App. 'A' Operation Commando, Paragraph 5: 'The Going', p. 1.
32. Ibid, Para 8 d (i): On D+1 'A' Sqn with KSLI, pp. 4–5.
33. Wilson, *Tempting the Fates*, p. 171.
34. TNA, WO 281/452, 1 RNF War Diary: Korea, October 1951, App. 'K' Action Fought for Point 217, 5–8 Oct' 51, pp. 1–3.
35. Author's Interview with Mr. K.M. Taylor (re: National Service with 1 RNF, Korea, 1951), 6 February 2003.
36. Farrar-Hockley, *The British Part in the Korean War Volume II*, p. 231.
37. Hermes, *Truce Tent and Fighting Front*, p. 176.
38. Collins, *War in Peacetime: The History and Lessons of Korea*, p. 311.
39. Zhang Shu-guang, *Mao's Military Romanticism: China and the Korean War, 1950–1953* (Lawrence, KS: University Press of Kansas, 1995), p. 186.

40. TNA, WO 231/90, BEQ: Capt. W. N. A. Axworthy (1 KSLI), 13 September 1952.

41. TNA, WO 231/89, BEQ: T/Capt. R. G. Handley (1 KSLI), 3 March 1952.

42. Michael Hickey, *Korean War: The West Confronts Communism 1950–1953* (London: John Murray, 1999), p. 265.

43. MacDonald, *The Borderers in Korea*, p. 34.

44. TNA, WO 231/90, BEQ: Major H. R. Holden (1 R. Norfolk Regt), 21 June 1952.

45. Hickey, *Korean War: The West Confronts Communism 1950–1953*, p. 266.

46. MacDonald, *The Borderers in Korea*, p. 35.

47. Max Hastings, *The Korean War* (London: Michael Joseph, 1987), p. 358. (A copy of Pte. Speakman's citation from the *London Gazette* of 28 Dec 1951 is reproduced in MacDonald, *The Borderers in Korea*, p. 37). Notably, for his actions at the Knoll, 2/Lt. William Purves was awarded the DSO, a unique distinction for a National Service officer-see MacDonald, *The Borderers in Korea*, p. 36.

48. TNA, WO231/89, BEQ: Lt. G. H. Benson (1 KSLI), 20 January 1952.

49. Hickey, *Korean War: The West Confronts Communism 1950–1953*, p. 266.

50. W.E. Underhill, *The History of the Royal Leicestershire Regiment 1928–1956*, pp. 251–254 (I am grateful to Leicester Record Office for providing a photocopy of Brig. Underhill's chapter on Korea); TNA, WO 281/1162, 1 R. Leicestershire Regt War Diary Korea, Nov 51, App. G: An Account of the actions of the 1st Bn The Royal Leicestershire Regiment in Korea from 4 Nov to 22 Nov 1951, pp. 2–4.

51. TNA, WO 231/89, BEQ: T/Capt. Handley (1 KSLI), 3 March 1952.

52. Hastings, *The Korean War*, p. 358.

53. Hermes, *Truce Tent and Fighting Front*, p. 178.

54. John Breske in Larsen and Miller, *Wisconsin War Stories*, p. 187.

55. Tom Clawson in Tomedi, *No Bugles, No Drums*, pp. 147–148.

56. Sherman Pratt in Tomedi, *No Bugles, No Drums*, pp. 145–146.

57. Rod Chapman Interview: GVSU (VHP).

58. Author's correspondence with Mr. Barry Tunnicliffe: (A Mortar Man's Memories), Dec 2015.

59. TNA, WO 231/90, BEQ: Capt. J De Gray (14th Field Regt, RA). Capt. J. De Gray served in theatre c. April 1951– July 1952.

60. Baldovi (ed), *A Fox Hole View*, p. 197.

61. Rudolph W. Stephens, *Old Ugly Hill: A G.I.'s Fourteen Months in the Korean Trenches, 1952–1953* (Jefferson, NC: McFarland & Co, 1995), p. 49.

62. TNA, WO231/89, BEQ: Major Bromhead (1st R. Leicestershire Regt), 27 April 1952.

63. TNA, WO 231/90, BEQ: Maj. C. W. Woods (28th Fd Regt, RE), 31 August 1952.

64. Second Lieutenant Don Stafford ('B' Company, 578th Engineer Combat Battalion) in William Berebitsky, *A Very Long Weekend: The Army National Guard in Korea, 1950–1953* (Shippensburg, PA: White Mane Publishing Co, 1996), p. 225.

65. Howard Matthias, *The Korean War: Reflections of a Combat Platoon Leader* (Tallahassee, Florida: Father & Son, 1993), p. 82.

66. Widely available sources on the Hook battles include: Lt. Col. Pat Meid and Maj. James M. Yingling, *U.S. Marine Operations in Korea 1950–1953: Vol. 5 Operations in West Korea* (Washington D.C.: Historical Division Headquarters, USMC, 1972), esp. Ch 5; Bernard C. Nalty, *Stalemate U.S. Marines from Bunker Hill to the Hook: Marines in the Korean War Commemorative Series* (Produced in Great Britain by Amazon.co.uk, Lee Ballenger, *The Outpost War: U.S. Marines in Korea, Vol.1: 1952* (Washington, DC: Potomac Books, 2005), pp. 198–218; Farrar-Hockley, *The British Part in the Korean War Volume II*, pp. 368–372, 379–383; A. J. Barker, *Fortune Favours the Brave: The Battles of the Hook Korea 1952–1953* (London: Leo Cooper, 2002). Personal accounts by veterans are included within: Derek Halley, *The Iron Claw: A Conscript's tale* (Privately Published, 2000); Tom Nowell, MM, *The Intrepid Observers: Notes on My Experiences in Korea 1952–1953* (Privately Published, 1995): Alan Carter, *Korea we lived…they died: Diary of a Forgotten War* (Bognor Regis: Woodfield Publishing, 1999); Brig. Brian Parritt, *Chinese*

Hordes and Human Waves: A Personal Perspective of the Korean War 1950–1953 (Barnsley: Pen and Sword, 2011); James Jacobs, *From the Imjin to the Hook: A National Service Gunner in the Korean War* (Barnsley: Pen and Sword, 2013).

67. Nowell, *The Intrepid Observers*, p. 88.
68. Barker, *Fortune Favours the Braver*, pp. 126–127.
69. Parritt, *Chinese Hordes and Human Waves*, p. 73.
70. S.L.A. Marshall, *Pork Chop Hill: The American Fighting Man in Action Korea, Spring 1953* (New York: Berkley Books, 2000), p. 146. Marshall's account remains a classic. For further coverage of actions at Pork Chop Hill (Hill 255) see: Bill McWilliams, *On Hallowed Ground: The Last Battle for Pork Chop Hill* (New York: Berkley Calibre Books, 2004); U.S. Army Official History: Hermes, *Truce Tent and Fighting Front*, pp. 287–289, 379, 392–395, 473–474. Oral history material can be found in Baldovi (ed), *A Fox Hole View*, pp. 216–219 and Knox, *The Korean War Uncertain Victory*, pp. 489–491.
71. A good discussion of this technique is contained in: TNA, WO 281/837, 1st Bn Black Watch: War Diary, March 1953, App.'F' The Tunnel Technique and Allied Problems, pp. 1–5.
72. Lee Ballenger, *The Final Crucible: U.S. Marines in Korea, Vol. 2: 1953* (Washington, DC: Potomac Books, 2006), p. 206.
73. James Brady, *The Coldest War: A Memoir of Korea* (New York: Thomas Dunne Books, 2000), p. 22.
74. Ballenger, *The Outpost War: U.S. Marines in Korea, Vol.1: 1952*, p. 47.
75. Sherwin Nagelkirk Interview: GVSU (VHP).
76. Berebitsky, *A Very Long Weekend*, p. 216.
77. Grey, *The Commonwealth armies and the Korean War*, pp. 143–144.
78. See: Ballenger, *The Outpost War*, pp. 106–136.
79. Bryn Owen and Norman Salmon (eds) *An Account of the Services of 1st Battalion The Welch Regiment in Korea 1951–1952* (The Welch Regiment, 2005), p. 103.
80. Carl Ballard Interview: GVSU (VHP).
81. Crawford, *The Four Deuces: A Korean War Story*, p. 120.
82. Alan R. Millett, 'Korea, 1950–1953' in Benjamin Franklin Cooling (ed) *Case Studies in the Development of Close Air Support* (Washington, DC: Office of Air Force History USAF, 1990), pp. 386–387.
83. Bruce I. Gudmundsson, *On Artillery* (Westport, Connecticut: Praeger, 1993), pp. 146–147.
84. Ibid, pp. 146–147.
85. Millett, 'Korea, 1950–1953' in Cooling (ed) *Case Studies in the Development of Close Air Support*, p. 396.
86. Robert Frank Futrell, *The United States Air Force in Korea 1950–1953* (New York: Duell, Sloan and Pearce, 1961), p. 662.
87. Matthias, *The Korean War: Reflections of a Combat Platoon Leader*, p. 124.
88. TNA, WO 231/90, BEQ: Maj. A. L. Gordon (1 R. Norfolk), 11 September 1952.
89. R.C.W. Thomas, *The War in Korea 1950–1953: A military study of the war in Korea up to the signing of the Cease Fire* (London: Gale and Polden, 1968), p. 97.
90. Training Bulletin No. 4: Armor Employment in Korea reproduced in Knox, *The Korean War Uncertain Victory*, p. 408.
91. Roger 'Rog' G. Baker, *USMC Tanker's War in Korea: The War in Photos, Sketches and Letters Home* (Oakland, Oregon: Elderberry Press, 2001), p. 120.
92. TDRC (MOD) Serial 6281, Lessons from Korea (Operations in Korea-Bulletin No. 3), Tac Emp of Armd Regt (5 DG) SP 1 Commonwealth Div, Tasks of Armour Para 3–6, p. 1, 1952.
93. Ballenger, *The Outpost War*, p. 161.
94. TNA, WO 231/90, BEQ: Lt. K. A. R. Cleaver (N. Staffs att 1 KSLI), 8 July 1952.
95. Ballenger, *The Outpost War*, p. 74.
96. TNA, WO 231/90, BEQ: Maj. I. A. Haycraft (1 R. Norfolk), 3 May 1952.
97. Hu Seng quoted in Hastings, *The Korean War*, p. 359.

98. Prepared by the CRE 1 CW Div from information available up to May 1952, 'Enemy *Field Defences in Korea'* BAJ Vol. 9 Jan 1953, esp. pp. 56–60; Imperial War Museum (IWM) 84/13/1, Capt N.H. Phillips (RA) Papers: Notes on Military Interpretation in Korea, Dec 1952, esp. p. 3, 7–8.

99. Major E. V. Thomas *'Counter-Bombardment in Korea'* The Journal of the Royal Artillery Volume LXXX, No. 2, April 1953, p. 103.

100. John A. Sullivan, *Toy Soldiers: Memoir of a Platoon Leader in Korea* (Jefferson, NC: McFarland & Co, 1991), p. 51.

101. NA, WO 281/251, 61st Light Regt RA, War Diary: Korea, RA 1 Comwel Div Periodical CB Summary No. 5, 2 March 1952, Para 4 Shellreps & Para 5 Identification from Fragments, pp. 2–3.

102. Author's correspondence: Mr. Alan Causer (National Service RA, 1952–1954), 30 October 2002.

103. Matthias, *The Korean War: Reflections of a Combat Platoon Leader*, pp. 109–111.

104. Author's correspondence: Mr. Gordon Butt (National Service 1 RF, Korea 1952–1953), 25 February 2003.

105. TNA, WO 231/90, BEQ: 2/Lt. B. Moore (RUR att. 1 R. Norfolk), 5 October 1952.

106. Farrar-Hockley, *The British Part in the Korean War Volume II*, pp. 356–357.

107. Durham County Record Office (DCRO), Durham Light Infantry Archives, DLI 195/8, Commanding Officer's End of Tour Report, 1st DLI Korea 1952–1953, Section 8 Patrolling, p. 5.

108. TNA, WO 308/94, GOC Personal Memorandum No. 9: Patrol Policy, 1st Comwel Div 23 January 1953, paragraph 4, p. 1.

109. Stanley Maud in Adrian Walker, *A Barren Place: National Servicemen in Korea 1950–1954* (London: Leo Cooper, 1994), p. 109.

110. See for example, 'A Daylight Raid in Korea' in The Iron Duke Volume 29, No. 88, April 1953, pp. 72–74. This highly successful raid was based on thorough preparations, including organising co-ordination with supporting fire from tanks and artillery, and resulted in the destruction of enemy defences. Code-named 'Full Moon,' it in fact took advantage of the early morning sun to dazzle the defenders.

111. For further details on Operation Jehu see: Gen. Sir Cecil Blacker and Maj. Gen. H. G. Woods, *Change and Challenge: The 5th Royal Inniskilling Dragoon Guards, 1928–1957* (Colchester, 1978), pp. 105–108.

112. George Brown in Adrian Walker, *Six Campaigns: National Servicemen at War 1948–1960* (London: Leo Cooper, 1993) p. 22.

113. Matthias, *The Korean War: Reflections of a Combat Platoon Leader*, p. 95.

114. Dan Pfeiffer Interview: GVSU (VHP).

115. Stanley Maud in Walker, *A Barren Place*, p. 109.

116. TNA, WO 308/94, GOC Personal Memorandum No. 9: Patrol Policy, 1st Comwel Div 23 January 1953, paragraph 6, p. 2.

117. DCRO, DLI 195/8, Commanding Officer's End of Tour Report, 1st DLI Korea 1952–1953, Section 8 Patrolling, p. 7.

118. 2/Lt. John Stacpole in Barker, *Fortune Favours the Brave*, p. 47.

119. Author's Correspondence: Major Norman Salmon (I.O. 1st Battalion Welch Regt, Korea 1951–1952), May 2007.

120. TNA, WO 231/90, BEQ: Major A. L. Gordon (1 R. Norfolk), 11 September 1952.

121. Robert James, *Tales from a Kitbag* (Enstone, Ox: Writersworld, 2004), p. 39.

122. Carl Ballard Interview: GVSU (VHP).

123. Russ, *The Last Parallel*, pp. 299–300, 320–322.

124. Sullivan, *Toy Soldiers*, pp. 48–49.

125. Neville Williams, *A Conscript in Korea* (Barnsley: Pen and Sword, 2009), p. 109.

126. Sullivan, *Toy Soldiers*, p. 101.

127. Stephens, *Old Ugly Hill*, p. 95.

128. Robert Kimbrough in Larsen and Miller, *Wisconsin Korean War Stories*, p. 160.

129. William Schrader Interview: GVSU (VHP).
130. Stephens, *Old Ugly Hill,* pp. 152–153.
131. TNA, WO 231/90, BEQ: T/Major B. Aikens (1 R Norfolk), 1952.
132. Nicholas Harman (Subaltern with 1 RF) in B. S. Johnson (ed), *All Bull: The National Servicemen* (London: Quartet Books, 1973), pp. 250–251; Cpl. Elgen Fujimoto (Item Company, 179th Infantry) in Baldovi (ed), *A Fox Hole View,* pp. 275–276.
133. TNA, WO 231/90, BEQs: 2/Lt. B. Moore (RUR att. 1 R. Norfolk), 5 October 1952 and 2/Lt M.F. Reynolds (The Queen's Royal Regt att. 1 R Norfolk), 11 November 1952.
134. Herm Jongsma Interview: GVSU (VHP).
135. Matthias, *The Korean War: Reflections of a Combat Platoon Leader*, p. 101.
136. Brady, *The Coldest War*, p. 47.
137. Carl Ballard Interview: GVSU (VHP).
138. IWM P.125, General Sir Michael M. A. R. West Papers (GOC 1st Commonwealth Division, 1952–1953): File MW1: Notes entitled Patrol Dogs: Uses and Limitations, 6 Sept 1953; 1st Commonwealth Division Infantry Liaison Letter-KOREA No. 1, July 1953.
139. Matthias, *The Korean War: Reflections of a Combat Platoon Leader*, pp. 173–174.
140. Ibid, p. 96.
141. Sullivan, *Toy Soldiers*, p. 45.
142. Anonymous Marine in Ballenger, *The Final Crucible*, p. 90.
143. Corporal Clark Finks ('L' Company, 223rd Infantry Regiment) in Berebitsky, *A Very Long Weekend*, pp. 231–232.
144. Brady, *The Coldest War*, pp. 93–94.
145. For a brilliant discussion on live-and-let-live see: Tony Ashworth, *Trench Warfare 1914–1918: The Live and Let Live System* (London: Pan Books, 2000).
146. Author's Correspondence: Major N. Salmon, May 2007.
147. Ballenger, *The Final Crucible*, p. 205.
148. Brent Byron Watson, *Far Eastern Tour: The Canadian Infantry in Korea 1950–1953*, (Montreal: McGill Queen's University Press, 2002), p. 95.
149. Author's Correspondence: Major N. Salmon, May 2007.

Chapter 7

1. Lt. Col. J.H.A. Sparrow quoted in Jonathan Fennell, *Combat and Morale in the North African Campaign: The Eighth Army and the Path to El Alamein* (Cambridge University Press, 2011), pp. 8–9.
2. Albert Tyas in Adrian Walker, *A Barren Place National Servicemen in Korea 1950–1954* (London: Leo Cooper, 1994), p. 31.
3. Rudolph W. Stephens, *Old Ugly Hill: A G.I.'s Fourteen Months in the Korean Trenches, 1952–1953* (Jefferson, NC: McFarland & Company, 1995), p. 77.
4. Morrow, Curtis James, *What's a Commie Ever Done to Black People? A Korean War Memoir* (Jefferson, NC: McFarland & Co., 1997), p. 36.
5. Imperial War Museum, Sound Archieve 15428, Reel 3, David James Holdsworth (OC 12 Platoon, D. Coy 1 Glosters).
6. S.J. Davies, *In Spite of Dungeons: The Experiences as a Prisoner-of-War in North Korea of the Chaplain to the First Battalion, the Gloucester Regiment* (London: Hodder and Stoughton, 1964), p. 16.
7. Green, David, *Captured at the Imjin River: The Korean War Memoirs of a Gloster 1950–1953* (Barnsley: Pen & Sword, 2003), p. 102.
8. Lt. Col. Kingsley Foster (OC 1 RNF, Korea 1950–1951) in René Cutforth, *Korean Reporter* (London: Allan Wingate, 1952), p. 172.
9. The National Archives, WO 231/90, BEQ: Maj. A. L. Gordon (1 R Norfolk Regt), 11 September 1952.

10. Boris R. Spiroff, *Korea: Frozen Hell on Earth: A Platoon Sergeant's Diary Korean War 1950–1951* (Baltimore, Maryland: American Literary Press, 1998), p. 16.
11. Stephens, *Old Ugly Hill*, p. 62.
12. Ibid, p. 51.
13. Herm Jongsma Interview: Grand Valley State University (Veterans History Project).
14. Author's Correspondence: Mr. Barry Tunnicliffe (Re: his National Service with 61st Light Regt, RA, Korea 1952–1953), 21 December 2015.
15. Major C.E.B. Walwyn, 'Limited Offensive' British Army Journal Volume 7 (January 1952), pp. 36–37.
16. Spiroff, *Korea: Frozen Hell on Earth*, p. 25.
17. Neville Williams, *A Conscript in Korea* (Barnsley: Pen and Sword, 2009), p. 100.
18. John A. Sullivan, *Toy Soldiers: Memoir of a Combat Platoon Leader in Korea* (Jefferson, NC: McFarland & Company, 1991), pp. 18–22.
19. IWM, Sound Archive 15428: Reel 3, David James Holdsworth.
20. Carl Ballard Interview: GVSU (VHP).
21. Author's Correspondence: Mr. Bob Walding (Re: National Service with 1 Royal Norfolk Regt, Korea 1951–1952), 2003.
22. Lyle Rishell, *With a Black Platoon in Combat: A Year in Korea* (Texas A&M University Press, 1993), pp. 83–84.
23. Lofty Large, *One Man's War in Korea* (Wellingborough, Northamptonshire: William Kimber, 1988), p. 53.
24. Ibid, p. 51.
25. For narratives of events surrounding Hill 282 see: TNA, WO 281/1166, War Diary (Korea) 1 A&SH, Entries 22–23 Sept 1950; *The Thin Red Line* Volume 5 No. 1, January 1951, pp. 23–25; Lt Col G.I. Malcolm of Potalloch, *The Argylls in Korea* (Edinburgh: Thomas Nelson and Sons Ltd, 1952), pp. 16–25.
26. Jeffrey Grey, *The Commonwealth armies and the Korean War* (Manchester: MUP, 1988), pp. 70–73.
27. TNA, WO 231/90, BEQ: Maj. J. W. H. Mulligan (1 RUR), 5 May 1951.
28. TNA, WO 231/90, BEQ: Maj. L. G. Wilkes (61st Light Regt RA), 14 September 1952.
29. See for example, James A. Huston, *Guns and Butter, Powder and Rice: U.S. Army Logistics in the Korean War* (London: Associated University Press, 1989), pp. 179–181.
30. Captain George Warne [S-4, 194th Engineer Combat Battalion (Tennessee)] in William Berebitsky, *A Very Long Weekend: The Army National Guard in Korea, 1950–1953* (Shippensburg, PA: White Mane Publishing Company, 1996), p. 93.
31. Lee Ballenger, *The Outpost War: U.S. Marines in Korea, Vol. 1: 1952* (Washington, DC: Potomac Books, Inc, 2005), pp. 52–53.
32. The National Archives, WO 231/90, BEQ: Lt. John R. Moffat (14th Field Regt RA), 15 September 1952.
33. Dill, James Hamilton, Sixteen Days at Mungol-li (Fayetteville, Arkansas: M&M Press, 1993) pp. 44–45.
34. Morrow, *What's a Commie Ever Done to black People*, p. 17. Note: for specifics on American uniforms of the Korean War era see-Shelby Stanton, *U.S. Army Uniforms of the Korean War* (Harrisburg, PA: Stackpole Books, 1992).
35. M.G. Harvey, *The War in Korea: The Battle Decides All* (Eggleston, Co Durham: Raby Books, 2002), pp. 58–59.
36. National Army Museum (NAM), Acc No. 8905-261, Oral History Interview: Sam Mercer (1st Battalion Gloucestershire Regiment), Tape 1.
37. Edmund Ions, *A Call to Arms: Interlude with the Military* (Newton Abbot: David & Charles, 1972), p. 175.

38. See for example, TNA, WO 281/1146, 45th Field Regt, RA: War Diary, Korea, December 1950: Entry for 4/12/50.
39. TNA, WO 231/89, BEQ: Maj. G. M. Strachan, MC (8 KRIH), 5 March 1952.
40. Details of this improved winter clothing can be found in: Maj. R. E. Austin, 'Winter Clothing in Korea' in The Iron Duke, Volume 29 Number 88, April 1953, pp. 62–63, 65–66.
41. Henry O'Kane, O'Kane's Korea: A Soldier's tale of three years of Combat and Captivity in Korea 1950–1953 (Privately Published, 1988), p. 9.
42. Robert Halle Interview: GVSU (VHP).
43. IWM Sound Archive 9537, Reel 4: Col. Andrew Morrice Man (OC 1 MX, Korea 1950–51).
44. General Sir Peter de la Billière, Looking for Trouble: SAS to Gulf Command: The Autobiography (London: Harper Collins, 1995), p. 78.
45. James Brady, The Coldest War: A Memoir of Korea (New York: Thomas Dunne Books, 2000), p. 69.
46. Dill, Sixteen Days at Mungoli-li, p. 21.
47. C.S. Crawford, The Four Deuces: A Korean War Story (New York: Ballantine Books, 1989), p. 24.
48. Rishell, With a Black Platoon in Combat: A Year in Korea, p. 83.
49. Howard Matthias, The Korean War: Reflections of a Young Combat Leader (Tallahassee, Florida: Father & Son, 1993), pp. 42–43.
50. Author's correspondence: Mr. John Robottom (Re: his National Service as a Technical Assistant RA with 13th Battery HQ, 14th Field Regt, RA, Korea Nov 1951–July 1952), 16 November 2015.
51. Rishell, With a Black Platoon in Combat: A Year in Korea, p. 137.
52. Stephens, Old Ugly Hill, p. 126.
53. For discussion on the logistics organisation during the Korean War see: Huston, Guns and Butter, Powder and Rice U.S. Army Logistics in the Korean War, esp. pp. 314–321 and Grey, The Commonwealth armies and the Korean War, esp. Ch. 9 Finance and Logistics, pp. 167–181.
54. Dill, Sixteen Days at Mungoli-li, pp. 87–88.
55. IWM, Sound Archive 18699, Reel 1, Brig. A. D. R. G. Wilson (OC 'A' Company 1 A&SH, 27th Brigade, Korea 1950–51).
56. Charles M. Bussey, Firefight at Yechon: Courage and Racism in the Korean War (London: Bison Books, 2002), p. 91.
57. Morrow, What's a Commie Ever Done to black People?, p. 21.
58. For a full draft of this communique see: Matthew B. Ridgway, The Korean War (New York, Da Capo Press, Inc, 1967), Appendix 4: Why we are here? What are we fighting for? pp. 264–265.
59. www.oralhistory.rutgers: Harry Van Zandt (Infantry Officer ETO and Korea) Online Oral History Interview, c. August 1998, Transcript, p. 37.
60. Letter to a friend in UK from: 2/Lt K. M. Taylor (RNF) British Commonwealth Transit Camp, Pusan, Korea, Sunday 2 September 1951, republished in Keith M. Taylor, Wither the Fates Call: A Personal Account of National Service in the British Army 1950–1952 (Privately Published, 2009), p. 179.
61. Author's correspondence: Mr. John Robottom (Re: his National Service as a TARA with 13th Battery HQ, 14th Field Regt, RA, Korea Nov 1951–July 1952), 16 November 2015.
62. TNA (Kew), WO 308/28, 1st Commonwealth Div Periodic Report 15 October 1951–15 February 1952, Section 7: Morale, p, 4.
63. IWM, Sound Archive 18699, Reel 2, Dr Stanley Boydell (MO att. 1 MX, Korea 1950-51).
64. Dill, Sixteen Days at Mungoli-li, p. 354.
65. Ions, A Call to Arms: Interlude with the Military, pp. 188–192.
66. Bob Smith quoted in Henry Berry, Hey, Mac, Where Ya Been? Living Memories of the U.S. Marines in the Korean War (New York: St. Martin's Press, 1988), p. 167.
67. Brady, The Coldest War: A Memoir of Korea, p. 99.
68. Howard Matthias, The Korean War: Reflections of a Young Combat Platoon Leader, p. 104.
69. Bussey, Firefight at Yechon: Courage and Racism in the Korean War, pp. 44, 116–118.

70. William T. Bowers, William M. Hammond and George L. MacGarrigle, *Black Soldier White Army: The 24th Infantry Regiment in Korea* (Washington, DC: Centre of Military History United States Army, 1996), p. 263.

71. Peter S. Kindsvatter, *American Soldiers: Ground Combat in the World Wars, Korea, & Vietnam* (University Press of Kansas, 2003), p. 271.

72. Rishell, *With a Black Platoon in Combat: A Year in Korea*, p. 47.

73. Kindsvatter, *American Soldiers: Ground Combat in the World Wars, Korea, & Vietnam* , p. 271.

74. Morrow, *What's a Commie Ever Done to Black People?*, pp. 8–9, 11, 34–35 .

75. Octavio Huerta Interview: GVSU (VHP).

76. www.oralhistory.rutgers: Arthur R. May (Korean War Draftee), Online Oral History Interview, c. 2003–04, Transcript, p. 14.

77. Rod Chapman Interview: GVSU (VHP).

78. TNA, WO 231/90, 2/Lt. M. F. Reynolds (The Queen's Royal Regt att. 1st Bn Royal Norfolk Regt), 11 November 1952.

79. Headquarters and Depot Notes in 'The Thin Red Line,' Volume 5 Number 1, January 1951, p. 29.

80. Rishell, *With a Black Platoon in Combat: A Year in Korea*, p. 66.

81. Alan Carter, *Korea: we lived…they died: Diary of a Forgotten War* (Bognor Regis: Woodfield Publishing, 1999), p. 66.

82. Dan Raschen, *Send Port and Pyjamas!* (London: Buckland Publications Ltd, 1987) , p. 46.

83. Author's Correspondence: Mr. Frank Pearson (Corporal and driver/escort to the CO 1 KOSB, Korea 1951–1952), 23/12/03.

84. Sullivan, *Toy Soldiers: Memoir of a Combat Platoon Leader in Korea*, pp. 99–100.

85. Robert C. Shoemaker, *A Surgeon Remembers: Korea 1950–1951 and the Marines* (Victoria BC: Trafford, 2005), p. 93.

86. www.oralhistory.rutgers: Arthur R. May (Korean War Draftee), Online Oral History Interview, c. 2003–04, Transcript, p. 28.

87. I am grateful to Major General A. C. Birtwhistle (President of the British Korean Veterans Association, which has now laid up its standard) for bringing this to my attention.

88. Carter, *Korea: we lived…they died: Diary of a Forgotten War*, p. 66.

89. Harry Miller, Services to the Services: The Story of NAAFI (London: Newman Neame, 1971), p. 99.

90. Cowdrey, *The Medics' War*, p. 250.

91. Martin Russ, *The Last Parallel* (New York: Zebra Books, 1985), pp. 345, 400.

92. Dill, *Sixteen Days at Mungoli-li*, p. 87.

93. Author's Correspondence: Mr. Ronald V. Orange (42 Ind, Mortar Btty, RA, Korea 1951–1952), 24 April 2002.

94. Derek Halley, *The Iron Claw: A Conscript's Tale* (privately published, 1998), p. 69.

95. Williams, *A Conscript in Korea*, p. 68.

96. Ibid.

97. TNA, WO 32/14418, First Royal Tank Regiment: Korean Report for June 1953, Coronation Day, Paragraph 21–23, p. 5.

98. Carter, *Korea: we lived…they died: Diary of a Forgotten War*, p. 72..

99. TNA, WO 308/28, 1st Commonwealth Division Periodic Report 16 October 1951–15 February 1952, Welfare, Paragraph 12, p. 10.

100. Hopkins, William B., *One Bugle No Drums: The Marines at Chosin Reservoir* (Chapel Hill, NC: Algonquin Books, 1986), p. 67.

101. Matthias, *The Korean War: Reflections of a Young Combat Platoon Leader*, pp. 84–86.

102. Stephens, *Old Ugly Hill*, p. 140.

103. Albert Tyas in Walker, *A Barren Place*, p. 29.

104. Halley, *The Iron Claw*, p. 85.

105. Brady, *The Coldest War: A Memoir of Kore*a, p. 63.

106. Williams, *A Conscript in Korea*, pp. 94–95.

107. Ibid, pp. 96–97.
108. Roger 'Rog' G. Baker, *USMC Tanker's Korea: The War in Photos, Sketches and Letters Home* (Oakland, Oregon: Elderberry Press, 2001), p. 69.
109. Brady, *The Coldest War: A Memoir of Korea*, p. 221.
110. I am grateful to Mr. Tony Perrins (Intelligence Officer, 1st RNF 1950–1951 and POW 1951–1953) for drawing my attention to this.
111. Stephens, *Old Ugly Hill*, p. 73.
112. William Donner Interview: GVSU (VHP).
113. Barry Whiting in Adrian Walker, *A Barren Place: National Servicemen in Korea 1950–1954* (London: Leo Cooper, 1994), pp. 129–130.
114. Spiroff, *Korea: Frozen Hell on Earth*, p. 66.
115. Brian Hough in Stephen F. Kelly, *British Soldiers of the Korean War: In Their Own Words* (Stroud, Gloucestershire: The History Press, 2013), pp. 83–84.
116. Derek Halley, *The Iron Claw: A Conscript's Tale* (privately published, 1998), p. 55–56.
117. Brian Hough in Kelly, *British Soldiers of the Korean War: In Their Own Words*, pp. 83–84.
118. Brady, *The Coldest War: A Memoir of Korea*, p. 200.
119. Matthias, *The Korean War: Reflections of a Young Combat Platoon Leader*, pp. 107–108; William Donner Interview: GVSU (VHP).
120. TNA, WO 308/29, 1st Commonwealth Division Periodic Report, Feb–June 1952, Section 7: Provost, Paragraph (d), p. 8.
121. Ions, *A Call to Arms: Interlude with the Military*, pp. 168–169.
122. Ibid, p. 65; Russ, *The Last Parallel*, p. 360.
123. Joseph R. Owen, *Colder than Hell: A Marine Rifle Company at Chosin Reservoir* (Annapolis, Maryland: Bluejacket Books, 1996), p. 137; Crawford, *The Four Deuces: A Korean War Story*, p. 138.
124. TNA WO 231/89, BEQ: Maj. J. C. S. G. De Longuieuil (1 RUR), 24 November 1951.
125. Raschen, *Send Port and Pyjamas!*, pp.117–118.
126. Morrow, *What's a Commie Ever Done to black People?*, p. 37.
127. Joseph Demonaco in *Hey Mac, Where Ya Been? Living Memories of the U.S. Marines in the Korean War*, p. 160.
128. David Green, *Captured at the Imjin River: The Korean War Memoirs of a Gloster 1950–1953* (Barnsley: Leo Cooper, 2003), p. 95.
129. Crawford, *The Four Deuces: A Korean War Story*, pp. 106–109.
130. Welch Regiment Museum Archives, Cardiff Castle: Box 16 Cabinet No. 1 (Red File 1993), Document entitled: 'Keeping Alive in a Korean Winter,' p. 1.
131. Colin Mitchell, *Having Been a Soldier* (London: Hamish Hamilton, 1969), p. 85.
132. Particularly good coverage of this can be found in: Raschen, *Send Port and Pyjamas!*, esp. pp. 11, 23, 117, 142, 170 and 238–239; 'Pheasant Shooting in Korea' in DLI Regimental Journal, Volume 7, pp. 161–162.
133. Author's Correspondence: Mr. Barry Tunnicliffe (Re: his National Service with 61st Light Regt, RA, Korea 1952–1953), 21 December 2015.
134. TNA WO 231/90, BEQ: Lt. Col. J. H. Slade Powell (OC 14th Field Regt, RA), c. Autumn/Winter 1952.
135. National Army Museum (NAM), Acc. No. 2001–02–398–1–3, Oral History Interview: Dr Stanley Boydell (RAMC att.1 MX, 1949–1951), Tape 3.
136. Author's Correspondence: Mr. Barry Whiting (26 Field Ambulance, RAMC), 7 November 2015.
137. Richard Hooker, M*A*S*H (London: Cassell, 2004), pp. 35–36. (Richard Hooker was the pseudonym of Capt. H. Richard Hornberger, 8055th MASH).
138. Cowdrey, *The Medics' War*, p. 151.
139. Otto F. Apel Jr & Pat Apel, *MASH: An Army Surgeon in Korea* (Lexington: The University Press of Kentucky, 1998), p. 80.

140. Cowdrey, *The Medics' War*, p. 163.
141. William J. 'Doc' Anderson, *Battlefield Doc: Memoirs of A Korean War Combat Medic* (St. Louis, Missouri: Moonbridge Publications, 2015), esp. pp. 4, 57, 71–72.
142. Robert Mulder Interview: GVSU (VHP).
143. Apel, *MASH: An Army Surgeon in Korea*, p. 68.
144. TNA, WO 308/27, 1st Commonwealth Division Periodic Report 2 May–15 October 1951: App. D The Administrative Organisation: Medical: Paragraph 7 (a) Evacuation, p. 4.
145. See: Cowdrey, *The Medics' War*, pp. 163–167.
146. Calvin Schutte Interview: GVSU (VHP).
147. Apel, *MASH: An Army Surgeon in Korea*, p. 130.
148. Stephens, *Old Ugly Hill*, p. 129.
149. Robert Mulder Interview: GVSU (VHP).
150. Anderson, *Battlefield Doc*, p. 47.
151. Lamar Bloss Interview: GVSU (VHP).
152. De la Billière, *Looking for Trouble*, p. 73.
153. IWM 01/10/1, TS manuscript compiled by David Oates: *Memories of the British Commonwealth General Hospital, Kure, Japan, during the Korean War 1950–1953*, p. 5.
154. Author's Correspondence: Mr. Barry Whiting (26 Field Ambulance, RAMC), 7 November 2015.
155. Cowdrey, *The Medics' War*, pp. 91–92.
156. Anderson, *Battlefield Doc*, p. 40.
157. www.oralhistory.rutgers: Herman E. Bulling (Second World War & Korean War Infantry Officer), Online Oral History Interview, 27 June 2003, Transcript, p. 30.
158. Williams, *A Conscript in Korea*, p. 79.
159. Morrow, *What's a Commie Ever Done to black People?*, pp. 27, 40.
160. Robert C. Shoemaker, *A Surgeon Remembers: Korea 1950–1951 and the Marines* (Victoria BC: Trafford, 2005), p. 48.
161. A.J. Barker, *Fortune Favours the Brave: The Battles of the Hook, Korea 1952–53* (Barnsley: Leo Cooper, 2002), pp. 49–50.
162. Crawford F. Sams (Ed by Zabelle Zakarian), *'Medic' The Mission of an American Military Doctor in Occupied Japan and Wartorn Korea* (New York: M. E. Sharpe, 1998), p. 246.
163. TNA, WO 308/21, Historical Notes: Medical Services, Sept 1950–June 1953, Part III Army Health, pp. 1–2.
164. Ibid, p. 1.
165. William Donner Interview: GVSU (VHP).
166. TNA, WO 281/1146, 45th Fd Regt RA War Diary: Korea 17 November 1950, SO for War No. 4 Hygiene and Medical.
167. NAM Oral History Interview, Acc. No. 8905–159, Michael Eastap (Sgt, No. 1 Platoon, 'A' Company, 1 MX, Korea 1950–1951).
168. TNA, WO 281/830, 1 DWR War Diary: Korea April–May 1953, Notes re: Prevention of Malaria, 14 April 1953.
169. Cowdrey, *The Medics' War*, p. 183.
170. TNA, WO 308/21, Historical Notes: Medical Services, pp. 1–2.
171. For further details see: K. Meghan Fitzpatrick, 'Prostitutes, penicillin and prophylaxis: Fighting Venereal Disease in the Commonweath Division During The Korean War (1950-1953)', *Social History of Medicine* Vol.28, Issue 3, August 2015, pp. 555-575
172. Willam Donner interview: GVSU (VHP).
173. Hopkins, *One Bugle No Drums: The Marines at Chosin Reservoir*, p. 77.

174. John Saddic in *Hey Mac, Where Ya Been? Living Memories of the U.S. Marines in the Korean War,* p. 185.
175. Russ, *Breakout: The Chosin Reservoir Campaign, Korea 1950,* p. 116.
176. Lt. Henry Litvin (U.S. Navy, battalion surgeon att USMC) quoted in Russ, *Breakout: The Chosin Reservoir Campaign, Korea 1950,* p. 63.
177. S.L.A. Marshall, 'A Study based on the Operations of 1st Marine Division in the Koto-ri, Hagaru-ri, Yudam-ni Area, 20 November-10 December 1950: Section on Shock and Fatigue' reproduced in Hopkins, *One Bugle No Drums: The Marines at Chosin Reservoir,* p. 262.
178. Robert Samuels Interview: GVSU (VHP).
179. J.C. Watts, *Surgeon at War* (London: Digit Books, 1955), pp. 141–143.

Chapter 8

1. Anthony Farrar-Hockley, *The British Part in the Korean War Volume II: An Honourable Discharge* (London: HMSO, 1995), Appendix 'M' British Prisoners of War in Korea, p. 486.
2. Cyril Cunningham, *No Mercy, No Leniency: Communist Mistreatment of British & Allied Prisoners of War in Korea* (Barnsley: Leo Cooper, 2000), p. 8.
3. Farrar-Hockley, *The British Part in the Korean War Volume II,* p. 266.
4. See: S.P. Mackenzie, *British Prisoners of the Korean War* (Oxford: OUP, 2012), passim.
5. Billy C. Mossman, *United States Army in the Korean War: Ebb and Flow November 1950-July 1951* (Honolulu: University Press of the Pacific, 2005), p. 503.
6. Max Hastings, *The Korean War* (London: Michael Joseph, 1987), pp. 347–348.
7. Walter G. Hermes, *United States Army in the Korean War: Truce Tent and Fighting Font* (Honolulu: University Press of the Pacific, 2005), pp. 496–497.
8. Albert D Biderman, *March to Calumny: The Story of American POWs in the Korean War* (New York: The Macmillan Company, 1963), p. 30.
9. Ibid, Appendix B: Executive Order 10631: '*Code of Conduct for Members of the Armed Forces of the United States,*' Signed Dwight D Eisenhower, The White House, August 17, 1955, pp. 278–282.
10. Ibid, p. 43.
11. Gordon Lantz Interview: Grand Valley State University, Veterans History Project.
12. Imperial War Museum (IWM), Department of Documents, Acc. No. 99/31/1, Booklet In Memory of E.G. Beckerley (Compiled by Michael White), pp. 4–5.
13. Lawrence Bailey in Donald Knox, *The Korean War: Uncertain Victory* (New York: Hardcourt Brace Jovanovich, 1988), pp. 327–328.
14. Anthony Farrar-Hockley, *The Edge of the Sword* (London: The Companion Book Club, 1955), pp. 68–70.
15. Dale King in Sarah A. Larsen and Jenifer M. Miller, *Wisconsin Korean War Stories: Veterans Tell Their Stories from the Forgotten War* (Wisconsin Historical Society Press, 2008), pp. 39–41.
16. Billy N. Gaddy in Harry Spiller (ed), *American POWs in Korea: Sixteen Personal Accounts* (Jefferson, NC: McFarland & Co, Inc, 1998), pp. 76–77.
17. Kenneth Nevill (Sgt. 1st Platoon, F Coy, 2nd Battalion, 7th Marines, 1st Marine Div) in Spiller (ed), *American POWs in Korea,* p. 125.
18. Nick Tosques in Rudy Tomedi, *No Bugles, No Drums: An Oral History of the Korean War* (New York: John Wiley & Sons, Inc, 1994), p. 223.
19. Lofty Large, *One Man's War in Korea* (Wellingborough, Northamptonshire: William Kimber, 1988), p. 71.
20. John Erickson Interview: GVSU (VHP).
21. David Green, *Captured at the Imjin River: The Korean War Memoirs of A Gloster 1950–1953* (Barsley: Leo Cooper, 2003), pp. 104–105.
22. Henry O'Kane, *A Soldier's Tale of Three Years of Combat and Captivity in Korea 1950–53* (Privately published, 1988), p. 32.

23. Leonard Jones in Knox, *The Korean War: Uncertain Victory*, p. 334.
24. Bill Fox in Stephen F. Kelly, *British Soldiers of the Korean War: In Their Own Words* (Stroud, Gloucs: The History Press, 2013), p. 183.
25. O'Kane, *A Soldier's Tale of Three Years of Combat and Captivity in Korea 1950–53*, p. 33.
26. Phillip D. Chinnery, *Korean Atrocity! Forgotten War Crimes 1950–1953* (Barnsley: Pen and Sword, 2009), pp. 23–24.
27. O'Kane, *A Soldier's Tale of Three Years of Combat and Captivity in Korea 1950–53*, p. 33.
28. Farrar-Hockley, *The Edge of the Sword*, pp. 79–80.
29. Jack Browning in Knox, *The Korean War: Uncertain Victory*, pp. 330–333.
30. Susumu Shinagawa in Louis Baldovi (ed) *A Foxhole View: Personal Accounts of Hawaii's Korean War Veterans* (Honolulu: University of Hawai'i Press, 2002), pp. 73–90.
31. Jack Chapman in Knox, *The Korean War: Uncertain Victory*, p. 340.
32. Fred Hayhurst, *Green Berets in Korea: The Story of 41 Independent Commando Royal Marines* (Cambridge: Vanguard Press, 2001), pp. 157–159.
33. Green, *Captured at the Imjin River*, p. 139.
34. See for example, Mackenzie, *British Prisoners of the Korean War*, pp. 32–33.
35. Ibid, p. 78.
36. Green, *Captured at the Imjin River*, p. 111.
37. O'Kane, *A Soldier's Tale of Three Years of Combat and Captivity in Korea 1950–53*, p. 34.
38. Large, *One Man's War in Korea*, p. 83.
39. Ibid, pp. 82–83.
40. Green, *Captured at the Imjin River*, p. 111.
41. Large, *One Man's War in Korea*, p. 82.
42. Albert Tyas in Adrian Walker, *A Barren Place: National Servicemen in Korea 1950–1953* (London: Leo Cooper, 1994), p. 30.
43. Derek Kinne, *The Wooden Boxes* (London: Frederick Muller Ltd, 1955), pp. 56–57.
44. Green, *Captured at the Imjin River*, pp. 114–115.
45. Darrell Krenz in Larsen and Miller, *Wisconsin Korean War Stories*, pp. 41–42.
46. Mackenzie, *British Prisoners of the Korean War*, p. 24.
47. MOD, *Treatment of British Prisoners of War in Korea* (London: HMSO, 1955), *Appendix 1 Main Camps in North Korea in which British Troops were held Prisoner, pp. 37–38*; Mackenzie, British Prisoners of the Korean War, pp. 58. (NB. The MOD booklet contains App. II 'Citations for Gallantry in Captivity' covering the following: Fus. Derek Kinne, George Cross; Lt. Terence Waters, George Cross (Posthumous); Capt. Acton Gibbon, George Medal)–see pp.38–41.
48. O'Kane, *A Soldier's Tale of Three Years of Combat and Captivity in Korea 1950–53*, p. 36.
49. Hastings, *The Korean War*, pp. 333–334.
50. Nick Tosques in Tomedi, *No Bugles, No Drums*, p. 224.
51. Billy N. Gaddy in Spiller (ed), *American POWs in Korea: Sixteen Personal Accounts*, p. 77.
52. Hayhurst, *Green Berets in Korea*, p. 158.
53. Kinne, *The Wooden Boxes*, p. 36.
54. William F. Dean, *General Dean's Story* (London: Weidenfeld and Nicolson, 1954), p. 110.
55. Farrar-Hockley, *The Edge of the Sword*, p. 114.
56. MOD, *Treatment of British Prisoners of War in Korea*, p. 1.
57. S.J. Davies, *In Spite of Dungeons* (London: Hodder & Stoughton, 1964), pp. 30–31.
58. See for example, Mackenzie, *British Prisoners of the Korean War*, p. 34.
59. Dale King in Larsen and Miller, *Wisconsin Korean War Stories*, p. 203.
60. Davies, *In Spite of Dungeons*, p. 31.
61. MOD, *Treatment of British Prisoners of War in Korea*, p. 4.
62. Ibid, p. 5.
63. O'Kane, *A Soldier's Tale of Three Years of Combat and Captivity in Korea 1950–53*, p. 44.
64. MOD, *Treatment of British Prisoners of War in Korea*, pp. 6, 8.

65. Author's Conversations with Mr. Albert Tyas (1 RUR and Korean War POW, 1951–1953).
66. Kinne, *The Wooden Boxes*, p. 76.
67. Large, *One Man's War in Korea*, p. 99.
68. Bill Fox in Kelly, *British Soldiers of the Korean War*, pp. 192–193.
69. Cunningham, *No Mercy, No Leniency*, p. 48.
70. Mackenzie, *British Prisoners of the Korean War*, pp. 28, 43.
71. Hastings, *The Korean War*, pp. 350, 406–407.
72. Nick Tosques in Tomedi, *No Bugles, No Drums*, p. 227.
73. Charles Quiring (I Company, 3rd Battalion, 5th Marines, 1st Marine Division) in Spiller (ed), *American POWs in Korea*, p. 148.
74. Large, *One Man's War in Korea*, pp. 123–124.
75. For detailed discussion on this point see Mackenzie, *British Prisoners of the Korean War*, esp. Ch. 4.
76. Kinne, *The Wooden Boxes*, p. 92.
77. Sgt. P.J. Hoper quoted in Farrar-Hockley, *The British Part in the Korean War Volume II*, p. 277.
78. See for example, Large, *One Man's War in Korea*, pp. 100–101; Green, *Captured at the Imjin River*, p. 122.
79. Farrar-Hockley, *The Edge of the Sword*, p. 123.
80. Farrar-Hockley, *The British Part in the Korean War Volume II*, p. 269.
81. Biderman, *March to Calumny*, p. 47.
82. See for example, Brian Catchpole, *The Korean War* (London: Constable, 2000), pp. 217–219; Hastings, *The Korean War*, p. 344.
83. Darrell Krenz in Larsen and Miller, *Wisconsin Korean War Stories*, pp. 41–42.
84. Clarence Young in Baldovi (ed) *A Foxhole View*, p. 146.
85. Author's Conversations with Mr Albert Tyas (1 RUR and Korean War POW, 1951–1953).
86. MOD, *Treatment of British Prisoners of War in Korea*, p. 21.
87. Ibid, p. 22.
88. IWM, Sound Archive 19387, Reel 5, A.R.D. Perrins (I.O. 1 RNF 1950–1951 and Korean War POW 1951–1953.
89. Appendix E: A Medical Officer's Experiences: From Capture Through to the Early Period in Permanent Camps in Biderman, *March to Calumny*, p. 294.
90. Ibid, p. 292.
91. O'Kane, *A Soldier's Tale of Three Years of Combat and Captivity in Korea 1950–53*, p. 40.
92. Hastings, *The Korean War*, p. 336.
93. Albert Tyas in Walker, *A Barren Place*, p. 31.
94. John Erickson Interview: GVSU (VHP).
95. Green, *Captured at the Imjin River*, p. 149.
96. Author's conversation with Mr. Tony Perrins (I.O. 1 RNF 1950–1951 and Korean War POW 1951–1953).
97. Biderman, *March to Calumny*, pp. 59–60; Hastings, *The Korean War*, p. 346; Large, *One Man's War in Korea*, pp. 120–121.
98. Farrar–Hockley, *The Edge of the Sword*, p. 221.
99. Green, *Captured at the Imjin River*, p. 126.
100. See for example, Large, *One Man's War in Korea*, pp. 119–122.
    101. Catchpole, *The Korean War*, p. 217.
102. O'Kane, *A Soldier's Tale of Three Years of Combat and Captivity in Korea 1950–53*, pp. 46–47.
103. Green, *Captured at the Imjin River*, p. 151.
104. Hastings, *The Korean War*, p. 345.
105. Green, *Captured at the Imjin River*, esp. pp. 129, 139, 149, 151.
106. Davies, *In Spite of Dungeons*, p. 82.

107. The Carne Cross: Carved by Lt. Col. J. P. Carne VC, DSO (OC 1st Battalion Gloucestershire Regiment) during his captivity in North Korea, today resides in Gloucester Cathedral, where it is on public display by the Regimental Chapel.
108. Eugene L. Inman (9th Infantry Regt, 2nd Division) in Spiller (ed), *American POWs in Korea*, p. 89.
109. Biderman, *March to Calumny*, pp. 87–88.
110. Detail of escape efforts by U.S. Marines and Royal Marines can be found in: Pat Meid and James M. Yingling, *U.S. Marine operations in Korea, 1950–1953 Volume 5 Operations in West Korea* (Washington, D.C.: Historical Division, Headquarters, USMC, 1972), pp. 435–440.
111. Paul H. Smith (19th Regiment, 24th Division) in Spiller (ed), *American POWs in Korea*, p. 99.
112. Farrar-Hockley, *The British Part in the Korean War Volume II*, p. 268.
113. William Lindsay White, *The Captives of Korea: An Unofficial White Paper On the Treatment of War Prisoners* (New York: Charles Scribner's Sons, 1957), p. 220.
114. Donald M. Elliott (HQ Coy, 38th Infantry Regt, 2nd Division) in Spiller (ed), *American POWs in Korea*, p. 11.
115. Large, *One Man's War in Korea*, p. 135.
116. See for example, Catchpole, *The Korean War*, p. 226.
117. Susumu Shinagawa in Baldovi (ed) *A Foxhole View*, pp. 273–275.
118. Bill Fox in Kelly, *British Soldiers of the Korean War*, pp. 190, 193.
119. Donald Elliott in Spiller (ed), *American POWs in Korea*, pp. 15–16.
120. Albert Tyas in Walker, *A Barren Place*, p. 33; Author's Conversations with Mr. Albert Tyas (1 RUR and Korean War POW, 1951–1953).
121. Author's Conversations with Mr. Sam Phillips (9 and 7 Platoon Commander, Y Coy, 1 RNF, Korea, 1950–1951).
122. Daniel L. Johnson, Sr. (1st Battalion, Coy B, 38th Infantry Regt, 2nd Division) in Spiller (ed), *American POWs in Korea*, p. 30.

Chapter 9

1. For lessons China took from the Korean War see: Yu Bin 'What China Learned from Its "Forgotten War" in Korea' in Mark A. Ryan, David M. Finkelstein, & Michael A. McDevitt, *Chinese War Fighting: The PLA Experience Since 1949* (New York: M. E. Sharpe, 2003), pp. 123–142; Shu-guang Zhang, *Mao's Military Romanticism: China and the Korean War, 1950–1953* (Lawrence: University of Kansas Press, 1995).
2. Donald Knox (with additional text by Alfred Coppel), *The Korean War: Uncertain Victory* (New York: Harcourt Brace Jovanovich, 1988), p. 507.
3. Mark Clark, *From the Danube to the Yalu* (London: George G. Harrap & Co. Ltd, 1954), p. 243.
4. See for example, Michael Hickey, *Korean War: The West Confronts Communism 1950–1953* (London: John Murray, 1999), pp. 242, 275.
5. For further details on issues surrounding the armistice and copies of the agreement see: Clark, *From the Danube to the Yalu*, esp. Appendix, pp. 311–351; C. N. Barclay, *The First Commonwealth Division: The Story of British Land Forces in Korea, 1950–1953* (Aldershot: Gale and Polden,1954), pp. 155–163; Walter G. Hermes, *Truce Tent and Fighting Front* (Honolulu: University of Hawaii Press, 2005), esp. 479–497 and Appendix C: Armistice Agreement, pp. 516–538.
6. Dan Pfeiffer Interview: Grand Valley State University (Veterans History Project).
7. Herm Jongsma Interview: GVSU (VHP).
8. *2003 50th Anniversary Korean Truce Remembered*, pp. 1–2, Attached to Norman Spring Interview: GVSU (VHP).
9. Carl Ballard Interview: GVSU (VHP).
10. Alan Causer in Adrian Walker, *A Barren Place: National Servicemen in Korea 1950–1954* (London: Leo Cooper, 1994), pp. 143–144.

11. See for example, Barclay, *The First Commonwealth Division*, p.159; Robert H. Paterson, *Pontius Pilate's Bodyguard: A History of the First or Royal Regiment of Foot The Royal Scots (The Royal Regiment) Volume Two, 1919–2000* (Edinburgh, 2001), pp. 302–304.
12. Ron Hawkes in Adrian Walker, *Six Campaigns: National Servicemen at War 1948–1960* (London: Leo Cooper, 1993), p. 86.
13. Derek Halley, *The Iron Claw: A Conscript's Tale* (Privately Published, 2000), p. 126.
14. Ivan Williams in Stephen F. Kelly, *British Soldiers of the Korean War: In Their Own Words* (Stroud, Gloucs: The History Press, 2013), pp. 204–205.
15. Donald M. Elliott (HQ Coy, 38th Infantry Regt, 2nd Div and POW May 1951–August 1953) in Harry Spiller (ed), *American POWs in Korea: Sixteen Personal Accounts* (Jefferson, NC: McFarland & Company, Inc, 1998), pp. 15–16.
16. Walter Smith in Walker, *Six Campaigns*, p. 154.
17. Brian Hough in Kelly, *British Soldiers of the Korean War*, pp. 207–208.
18. Calvin Schutte Interview: GVSU (VHP).
19. Author's Correspondence: Mr. Keith M. Taylor (ABF The Soldiers Charity, Chairman of Trustees), 11 December 2016.
20. Author's Correspondence: Mr. J. C. Hall (re: National Service with 1st RTR and 5th RIDG, Germany and Korea, 1952–1953), 8 May 2002.
21. Author's Correspondence: Mr. Bob Yerby (NCO, 1st Battalion Middlesex Regiment, Korea 1950–1951 and Honorary Chairman Essex No. 1 Colchester Branch British Korean Veterans Association), 18 July 2003.
22. Walter G. Adelmann (Sgt. 7th Regt, 1st Cav Div, Korea and POW Nov 1951–August 1953) in Spiller (ed) *American POWs in Korea*, pp. 37–38.
23. Tony Kingsford in Walker, *A Barren Place*, p. 9.
24. Glen Bailey Interview: GVSU (VHP).
25. Robert Samuels Interview: GVSU (VHP).
26. Barry Whiting in Walker, *A Barren Place*, p. 131.
27. Rod Chapman Interview: GVSU (VHP).
28. *Biographical Notes J.C.M. Johnston* (Kindly supplied to the author by Col. Johnston, Dec 2001).
29. Lamar Bloss Interview: GVSU (VHP).
30. Carl Ballard Interview: GVSU (VHP).
31. Author's Correspondence: Mr. John Robottom (Technical Assistant Royal Artillery 13th Battery HQ, 14th Field Regiment, RA, Korea Nov 1951–July 1952), 18 November 2015.
32. Norman Spring Interview: GVSU (VHP).
33. Gordon Butt in Walker, *Six Campaigns*, p. 34; Author's Correspondence: Mr Gordon Butt (re his National Service with 1 RF, Korea 1952–53), 25 February 2003.
34. Author's Correspondence: Mr. John Robottom, 18 November 2015.
35. Author's Correspondence: Mr. Keith Taylor (OC MMG Section 1 RNF, and assistant to 2 i/c Y Coy for Operation Commando), 11 December 2016.
36. Nicholas Harman in B. S. Johnson (ed) *All Bull: The National Servicemen* (London: Quartet Books, 1973), p. 254.
37. Lyle Gibbs Interview: GVSU (VHP).
38. Walter G. Adelmann in Spiller (ed) *American POWs in Korea*, p. 39.
39. Nicholas Harman in Johnson (ed) *All Bull*, p 253.
40. See for example, H. Taprell Dorling, *Ribbons and Medals* (London: Osprey, 1983), pp. 73, 148.
41. Glen Bailey Interview: GVSU (VHP).
42. Ibid.
43. Tony Lovell in Walker, *A Barren Place*, p. 85.
44. See for example, George Brown and Gordon Butt in Walker, *Six Campaigns*, pp. 26, 34.
45. Otto F. Apel, *MASH: An Army Surgeon in Korea* (The University Press of Kentucky, 1998), p. 94.
46. Carl Ballard Interview: GVSU (VHP).

47. Author's Correspondence: Mr Don F. Barrett (Re: his National Service as a Junior NCO with 1 MX, Korea 1950–51), 30 January 2009.
48. Author's Correspondence: Mr Barry Whiting (Re: his National Service with RAMC, Korea 1952–53), 7 November 2015.
49. Author's Correspondence: Mr Barry Tunnicliffe (Re: his Korean tour as a National Service officer with the Royal Artillery, 1952–53), 21 December 2015.
50. Author's Correspondence: Mr Keith Taylor (OC MMG Section 1 RNF, and assistant to 2 i/c Y Coy for Operation Commando), 11 December 2016.
51. Ibid.
52. Jim Lucock in. Kelly, *British Soldiers of the Korean War,* p. 200.
53. E.J. McNair, *A British Army Nurse in the Korean War: Shadows of the Far Forgotten* (Stroud, Gloucs: Tempus Publishing, 2007), p. 218.
54. Art Braatz in Sarah A. Larsen and Jennifer M. Miller, *Wisconsin War Stories: Veterans Tell Their Stories From the Forgotten War* (Wisconsin Historical Society Press, 2008), pp. 219–220.
55. For information on Korea post–1953 see for example: William E. Berry, Jr., *Global Security Watch: A Reference Handbook Korea* (Westport, Connecticut: Praeger Security International, 2008); *The Sunday Telegraph,* 1 February 2004, p. 27; *The Saturday Times,* 15 April 2015, pp. 6–7, 29, 31; For information on the North Korean People's Army see the following websites: globalfirepower.com and Korean People's Army -Wikipedia.

Bibliography

Primary Sources

Imperial War Museum, London
Documents
91/8/1 Major P.A. Angier, 'Account of a Regular Officer in the Gloucestershire Regiment, 1941–1951'
(Unpublished Memoir Compiled by his Widow using his Letters)
99/31/1 Trooper E.G. Beckerley, Unfinished Memoir Re: Service with 8th KRIH, Korea 1950–51 &
Subsequent Experience as POW
66/78/1 Major General B.A. Coad Papers:
Report on Operations of 27th British Infantry Brigade (later 27th British Commonwealth Infantry
Brigade) in Korea, 29/8/50–31/3/51
Korean War Scrap Book/Press Cuttings
01/01/01 David Oates, 'Memories of the British Commonwealth General Hospital Kure, Japan Dur-
ing the Korean War 1950–1953 (Unpublished Memoir, January 2001)
92/40/1 Lt. Col. G.A. Phelps, DSO (Royal Sussex Regiment and OC Troopships c. 1949–51):
Voyage Reports: HMT *Empire Medway* Southampton to Kure, 23/11/50
HMT *Empire Orwell* Southampton to Kure, c. Sept–Oct 1951 (inc. Training Officer's Report re: 1st
Battalion The Royal Norfolk Regiment, 29/9/51)
84/13/1 Capt. N.H. Phillips (RA):
Notes on CCF Camouflage in Korea, 1952
Notes on Military Interpretation in Korea, Compiled Dec 1952
Leaflet: Study of Enemy Gun Positions in Korea (Compiled by HQ 25th Canadian Infantry Brigade)
Notes Re: Army Photographic Interpretation Unit
97/19/1 2/Lt. J.J. Potter (RA), Letters to his Parents from Korea, 1950–1951
99/77/1 Brig. D.F. Ryan OBE (RA), 'The Korean Chapter' (Unofficial Draft History and Memoir Ser-
vice with 74th Medium Battery RA in Korea February 1953–April 1954)
86/61/1 Lt. L.G.G. Smith (5 RIDG), Letters to Parents from Korea, 1951–1952
IWM P.125, File MW 1, General Sir Michael West Papers:
1st Commonwealth Division Notes on Chinese Communist Tactics in Korea, 20/9/53
GOC 1st Commonwealth Div Personal Memo No.7 Defence Policy, 26/10/52, No.8 Defence Policy,
7/12/52, No.9 Patrol Policy, 23/1/53, No.11 Defence Policy, 29/8/53, No.12 Patrolling, 16/9/53
Revised Notes Substitute for CRE LO Letter No 7 App 'D:' Patrol Dogs, 6/9/53
Artillery Methods (Compiled by CRA Brig. P. Gregson, c. Sept 1953)
1st Commonwealth Div Infantry LO Letter: Korea No. 1, July 1953
1st Commonwealth Div Infantry LO Letter: Korea No. 2, October 1953
Notes on Patrolling in Korea (Compiled by HQ 28th British Commonwealth Infantry Brigade)
File MW 2, Transcript of Talk Compiled for NZ Radio, c. July 1953

Sound Archive (Oral History Interviews)
10982: Edward Beckerley
18022: Kenneth Black
9395: Colin Bower
18262: Francis Carter
9693: Andrew Condron
9158: Gen. Sir George Cooper
19040: Peter Duckworth
18474: John Dyer
12783: Anthony Eagles

15428: James Holdsworth
9537: Col. Andrew Man
12729: Dennis Matthews
13522: Michael O'Brien
19387: Anthony Perrins
18668: Eric Peters
17688: Samuel Phillips
18443: Col. John Shipster
18439: Albert Tyas
18669: Brig. David Wilson
18003: Ronald Yetman

National Army Museum (NAM), London
Documents
APFS1996-11-22 (TS) History 'Korean Episode:' The Story of 45th Field Regiment RA in the Korean War
APFS1995-01-164 Cpl. Robert Gomme, Unpublished Memoir Relating his Experiences as a National Service NCO with Battalion Intelligence Section, 1st Bn Royal Norfolk Regiment
APFS2000-05-87 Transcript of an Account by 14187910 Sgt. E. Bermingham, 'D' Coy 1 MX, of Service during the Korean War, Aug 1950-May 1951 (ed. Mr. D. F. Barrett 1997–99)
APFS2000-05-08 Bound Copies & Extracts from 'The Die Hard' Regimental Magazine of The Middlesex Regiment, Covering Korea Aug 1950-May 1951(Compiled by Mr D.F. Barrett)
7903-16 Miscellaneous Documents Colonel J.L. Maxwell, DSO, (Royal Scots Fusiliers) 1921–1959 (Sub Area Commander British Commonwealth, Japan 1952–53)
8009-79 Papers and Maps of Lieutenant-Colonel C.J.G. Meade, MBE, 1940–1967

Oral History Interviews
2001-02-398-1-3 Dr Stanley Boydell
8905-160 Jarleth Donellan
8905-159 Major Michael P. Eastap
8905-261 Sam Mercer
8905-259 D.R. Millbery
APFS2001-02-397: Major Barry Reed

National Archives (NA), Kew, Surrey
WO 231 Directorate of Military Training Papers
WO 281 British Commonwealth Division of UN Force: War Diaries, Korean War
WO 291 Operational Research Papers
WO 308 British and Commonwealth Forces: Historical Records/Reports, Korean War

Tactical Doctrine Retrieval Cell (MOD), Pewsey, Wiltshire
6280 Lessons from Korea (Operations in Korea-Bulletins Nos. 1 & 2), 1952
6281 Lessons from Korea (Operations in Korea-Bulletin No. 3), 1952
6282 Lessons from Korea (Operations in Korea-Bulletin No. 4), 1952
6283 Lessons from Korea (Operations in Korea-Bulletin No. 5), 1952
6284 Lessons from Korea (Operations in Korea-Bulletin No. 6), 1952
6285 Exercise Babel: Additional DS Notes re: Staff College Exercise based on Logistical Information for 29th Independent Infantry Brigade Group, Korea 1950

8500 Battle of the Imjin River (22-25 April 1951) Notes of Presentation by Lt Col G.D.S. Truell TDRC, The Staff College

Regimental Museums

Regimental journals and other documents regarding the Korean War were consulted via the following British regimental museums/archives.

The Royal Dragoon Guards Museum, York
Firepower! Royal Artillery Museum, Woolwich, London
The Royal Scots (The Royal Regiment), The Castle, Edinburgh
The Fusiliers of Northumberland Museum, Alnwick
The Royal Regiment of Fusiliers (City of London) Museum
The King's Regiment (Archives Held by Museum of Liverpool Life)
Royal Leicestershire Regiment (Leicester City Museums Service)
Durham Light Infantry (Archives held by Durham County Record Office)
The Welch Regiment Museum (41st/69th Foot) of the Royal Regiment of Wales (24th/41st Foot), Cardiff
RHQ of The King's Own Scottish Borderers, The Barracks, Berwick-upon-Tweed
Duke of Wellington's Regimental Museum, Halifax
The Black Watch Museum (Royal Highland Regiment), Perth
Regimental Museum Argyll & Sutherland Highlanders, Stirling

Grand Valley State University: Veterans History Project (Oral History Interviews)

Glen Bailey
Carl Ballard
Lamar Bloss
Murl Bogert
Glendle Gene Callahan
Rod Chapman
William Donner
Paul Dunning
John Erickson
Lyle Gibbs
Robert A. Halle
Octavio Huerta
George Hyslop
Herm Jongsma
Gordon Lantz
Robert W. Lewis
Fred Litty
Greg Melonas
Leslie Meyering
Robert P. Mulder
Sherwin J. Nagelkirk
Lt Col Charles Olsen
Dan Pfeiffer
Dave Reeg
Robert Samuels
George Sarros

William Schrader
Calvin Schutte
Tanjore Splan
Norman Spring
Richard Swanson
Darrell Thornley
Isabelino Vazquez

Rutgers Oral History Archives (Korean War)
Lt Col Howard K. Alberts
Frank Ambrosy
Raymond Bodnar
Francis J. Brennan Jr.
Herman E. Bulling
James B. Carlaw
Sidney Cohn
Leonard Dabundo
Lawrence Downey
Walter B. English
Richard M. George
Allen Gordon
Richard M. Hale
John A. Holdorf
Bernard A. Kannen
Col. Vincent Kramer
Robert Krugh
Dr Frederick R. Lapides
Dr Dominic Mauriello
Arthur R. May
Raymond B. Morgan
Col. William L. Prout
Joseph T. Salerno
Theodore E. Symanski
Eileen Witte Treash
Col. William G. Van Allen
Harry Van Zandt
Irving Verosloff

Author's Correspondence/Interviewees
Joe Bailes (NCO, 1 DWR and 1st Commonwealth Div Battle School Staff, 1952–53)
Don F. Barrett (National Service NCO, 1 MX 1949–51)
Major-General A. C. Birtwistle (1st Commonwealth Signal Regiment HQ, 1951–52)
Terrence Brierley (National Service, 1RNF & R. Leics, 1951–52)
George Brown (National Service, 1 King's Regt, 1953)
Gordon Butt (National Service, 1 RF, 1952–53)
Alan Causer (61st Light Regt RA, 1953–54)
General Sir Peter de la Billière (2/Lt. with 1 DLI, Korea 1953 and Battle School Trainee)
John Dutton (REME)
General Sir Anthony Farrar-Hockley (former Adjutant 1 Glosters & POW, Korea 1950–1953)
Alfie Fowler (National Service, 1 Welch, 1952)

Malcolm Frost (National Service NCO, 1 RF, Korea 1952–53)
John Grey (National Service, 8 H, 1950–51)
J.C. Hall (National Service, 5 DG, 1952)
Derek Halley (National Service, 1 BW, 1952–53)
T.M. Hennessy (National Service Officer att. 1 DLI & Battle School Instructor, 1952–53)
Col Michael Hickey (RASC)
Reuben Holroyd (National Service, 1 DWR, 1952–53)
Prof Edmund Ions (Platoon Comd 1 RUR, Korea 1951)
Lt Col J.C.M. Johnston (Platoon Comd 1 KOSB & Battle School Trainee, 1951–52)
WO II Lofty Large (Pte 1 Glosters & POW, Korea 1950–53)
Donald Lloyd (National Service Gunner, RHQ Troop 20th Field Regt RA, 1952–53)
Harold Arthur Lotherington (National Service, 1 KSLI, 1951–52)
C. Luger (REME)
John MacLean (National Service Officer att. 1 Welch & Battle School Instructor, 1951–53)
RSM James Dirom Murdoch (1 KOSB)
CSM Bill Norman (Sgt 1 DWR, Korea 1952–53)
Tom Nowell, (Sgt. att. 1 DWR, Korea 1952–53)
Ronald V. Orange (National Service, 42nd Ind Mortar Battery, RA, 1951–52)
Frank Pearson (NCO, 1 KOSB, 1951–52)
Tony Perrins (I.O. I RNF & POW, Korea 1950–53)
Sam Phillips (Platoon Comd 1 RNF, Korea 1950–51)
Major Barry Reed (National Service Officer 1 MX, 1950–51)
John Robottom (National Service, 14th Field Regt, RA, 1951–1952)
Lt Col David Rose (OC 1 BW, Korea 1952–53)
Major N. Salmon (I.O. 1 Welch, Korea 1951–52)
Lt Col Sir James Stirling of Garden (National Service Officer 1 A&SH Korea, 1950–51)
Keith M. Taylor (National Service Officer 1 RNF, Korea 1951: OC MMG Sec & Assistant to 2i/c 'Y'
    Coy for Operation COMMANDO)
Major J.B. Tonkinson, (Signals Officer 1 DLI, Korea 1952–53)
Joe Thompson (NCO, 1 RNF, 1950–51)
Barry Tunnicliffe (National Service Officer, 61st Light Regt RA, 1952–53)
Albert Tyas (National Service, 1 RUR & POW, Korea 1950–53)
Bob Walding (National Service, Royal Norfolk Regt, 1951–52)
Barry Whiting (National Service, RAMC, 1952–53)
Robert Yerby (NCO, 1 MX, 1950–51).

Secondary Sources
Books

Alexander, Bevin, *Korea: The First War We Lost* (New York: Hippocrene Books, 2000)
Anon, *The Royal Ulster Rifles in Korea* (Belfast: Wm. Mullan & Son Ltd, 1953)
Appleman, Roy E., *Escaping the Trap: The U.S. Army X Corps in North East Korea, 1950* (Texas A &
    M University Press, 1990)
———— *Ridgway Duels for Korea* (Texas, A+M University Press, 1990)
Anderson, J. *Battlefield Doc: Memoirs of a Korean War Combat Medic* (St Louis, Missouri: Moon-
    bridge Publications, 2015)
———— *United States Army in the Korean War: South to the Naktong, North to the Yalu, June–Novem-
    ber 1950* (Washington, DC: Center of Military History, U.S. Army, 1992)
Apel, Otto F. Jr and Pat Apel, *MASH An Army Surgeon in Korea* (The University Press of Kentucky,
    1998).

Bailey, J.B.A., *Field Artillery and Firepower* (Annapolis, Maryland: Naval Institute Press, 2004)

Baker, Roger G., *USMC Tanker's Korea: The War in Photos, Sketches and Letters Home* (Oakland, Oregon: Elderberry Press, 2001)

Baldovi, Louis (ed.), A Foxhole View: Personal Accounts of Hawaii's Korean War Veterans (Honolulu: University of Hawaii Press, 2000)

Ballenger, Lee, *The Outpost War: U.S. Marines in Korea, Vol.1: 1952* (Washington, DC: Potomac Books, 2005

Barclay, Brigadier C.N., The *First Commonwealth Division: The Story of British Commonwealth Land Forces in Korea, 1950-1953* (Delhi: Army Publishers, 1965)

Barker, Lt Col A.J., *Fortune Favours The Brave: The Battles Of The Hook Korea 1952-53* (Barnsley: Pen & Sword, 2002)

———— *The Final Crucible: U.S. Marines in Korea, Vol. 2: 1953* (Washington, DC: Potomac Books, 2006)

Berebitsky, William, *A Very Long Weekend: The National Guard in Korea, 1950-1953* (Shippensburg, PA: White Mane Publishing Co., 1996)

Berry, Henry, *Hey, Mac, Where Ya Been? Living Memories of the U.S. Marines in the Korean War* (New York: St. Martin's Press, 1990)

Biderman, Albert, D., *March to Calumny: The Story of American POWs in the Korean War* (New York: Macmillan, 1963)

Blacker, Gen. Sir Cecil and Maj Gen H.G. Woods, *Change and Challenge: 5th Royal Inniskilling Dragoon Guards, 1928-57* (Colchester, 1978)

Blair, Clay, *The Forgotten War: America in Korea 1950-1953* (New York: Times Books, 1987)

Boose, Donald W., Jr., *US Army Field Forces in the Korean War 1950-1953* (Oxford: Osprey Publishing, 2005)

Bowers, William T., Hammond, William M. & MacGarrigle George L., *Black Soldier White Army: The 24th Infantry Regiment in Korea* (Washington, D.C.: Center of Military History U.S. Army, 1996)

Brady, David *One of the Chosin Few: A Royal Marine Commando's Fight For Survival Behind Enemy lines In Korea* (Stanford Rivers, Essex, Neat Books, 2004)

Brady, James, *The Coldest War: A Memoir of Korea* (New York: Thomas Dunne, 2000)

Brune, Lester H., *The Korean War: Handbook of the Literature and Research* (London: Greenwood Press, 1996)

Bussey, Charles M., *Fire Fight at Yechon: Courage and Racism in the Korea War* (London: Bison Books, 2002)

Caine, Michael, *What's It All About?* (London: Random House UK, 1992)

Catchpole, Brian, *The Korean War 1950-53* (London: Constable & Robinson Ltd, 2000)

Carter, Alan, *Korea we lived... they died: Diary of a Forgotten War* (Bognor Regis, West Sussex, Woodfield Publishing, 1999)

Carew, Tim, *Korea: The Commonwealth at War* (London: Cassell & Co Ltd, 1967)

———— *The Glorious Glosters: A Short History of the Gloucestershire Regiment 1945-1970* (London: Leo Cooper Ltd, 1970)

Carver, Michael, *War Since 1945* (London: Weidenfeld and Nicolson, 1980)

Chandler, David and Ian Becket (eds), *The Oxford History of the British Army* (Oxford: Oxford University Press, 1994)

Chinnery, Phillip D., *Korean Atrocity! Forgotten War Crimes 1950-1953* (Barnsley: Pen and Sword, 2009)

Clark, Mark, *From the Danube to the Yalu* (London: George G. Harrap & Co Ltd, 1954)

Clayton James, D., *Re-fighting the Last War: Command and Crisis in Korea 1950-1953* (New York: The Free Press, 1993)

Cooling, Benjamin, Franklin (ed.), *Case Studies in the Development of Close Air Support* (Washington, DC: Office of Air Force History USAF, 1990)

Coleman, J.D., *Wonju: The Gettysburg of the Korean War* (Washington, DC: Brassey's, 2000)

Connor, John W., *Let Slip the Dogs of War: A Memoir of the GHQ 1st Raider Company (8245th Army Unit) a.k.a Special Operations Company Korea 1950–1951* (Bennington, Vermont, Merriam Press, 2012)

Corr, Gerald, H., *The Chinese Red Army: Campaigns and Politics Since 1949* (London: Purnell Boook Services Ltd, 1973)

Collins, J. Lawton, *War in Peacetime: The History and Lessons of Korea* (Boston: Houghton Mifflin Company, 1969)

Crawford, C.S., *The Four Deuces: A Korean War Story* (New York: Ballantine Books, 1989)

Cowdrey, Albert E., *The Medics' War: United States Army in the Korean War,* (Honolulu: University Press of the Pacific, 2005)

Cunningham, Cyril, *No Mercy, No Leniency: Communist Mistreatment of British & Allied Prisoners of War in Korea* (Barnsley: Leo Cooper, 2000)

Cunninghan-Boothe, Ashley & Peter Farrar (eds), *British Forces in the Korean War* (Halifax: British Korean Veterans Association, 1997)

Cutforth, René, *Korean Reporter* (London: Allan Wingate Ltd, 1952)

Davies, S.J., *In Spite of Dungeons: The Experiences as Prisoner-of-War in North Korea of the Chaplain to the First Battalion, the Gloucestershire Regiment* (London: Hodder and Stoughton, 1964)

Dean, William F., General Dean's Story (London: Weidenfeld & Nicolson, 1954)

de la Billière, General Sir Peter, *Looking for Trouble: SAS To Gulf Command The Autobiography* (London: Harper Collins, 1995)

Dill, James Hamilton, Sixteen Days at Mungol-li (Fayetteville, Arkansas: M&M Press, 1993)

Eaton, H.B., *Something Extra: 28th British Commonwealth Brigade 1951–1974* (Durham: The Pentland Press Ltd, 1993)

Eckert, Carter, J. and Ki-baik Lee, *Korea Old and New A History* (Seoul: Ilchokak, 1990)

English, John, A., *On Infantry* (New York: Praeger, 1981)

Ent, Uzal W., *Fighting on the Brink: Defense of the Pusan Perimeter* (Paducah, KY: Turner Publishing Co., 1996)

Farrar-Hockley, General Sir Anthony, The Edge of the Sword (London: The Companion Book Club, 1955)

———*The British Part in the Korean War Vol. I: A Distant Obligation* (London: HMSO, 1990)

———*The British Part in the Korean War Vol. II: An Honourable Discharge* (London: HMSO, 1995)

Fehrenbach, T.R., *This Kind of War* (Washington, DC: Brassey's, 1998)

Forty, George, *At War in Korea* (London: Arms and Armour, 1997)

French, David, *Military Identities: The Regimental System, the British Army, & the British People c. 1870–2000* (Oxford: OUP, 2008)

George, Alexander, L., *The Communist Army In Action: The Korean War and its Aftermath* (New York: Columbia University Press, 1967)

Gittings, John, *The Role of the Chinese Army* (Oxford: OUP, 1967)

Goulden, Joseph C., *Korea: The Untold Story of the War* (New York: McGraw-Hill, 1983)

Green, David, *Captured at the Imjin River: The Korean War Memoirs of a Gloster 1950–1953* (Barnsley: Pen & Sword, 2003)

Grey, Jeffrey, *The Commonwealth armies and the Korean War* (Manchester: MUP, 1988)

Griffith, Samuel, B., *The Chinese People's Liberation Army* (New York: McGraw Hill Book Co, 1967)

Gudmundsson, Bruce, I., *On Artillery* (Westport, Connecticut, Praeger, 1993)

Gugeler, Russell A., *Combat Actions in Korea* (Washington, DC: Office of the Chief of Military History United States Army, 1970)

Halley, Derek, *The Iron Claw: A Conscript's tale* (Privately published: 2000)

Hamburger, Kenneth, E., *Leadership in the Crucible: The Korean War Battles of Twin Tunnels & Chipyong-Ni* (College Station: Texas A&M University Press, 2003)

Harvey, M.G., *The War In Korea: The Battle Decides All* (Eggleston, Co. Durham: Raby Books, 2002)

Hastings, Max, *The Korean War* (London: Michael Joseph Ltd, 1987)

Hayhurst, Fred, *Green Berets in Korea: The Story of 41 Independent Commando Royal Marines* (Cambridge: Vanguard Press, 2001)

Heinl, Robert, Debs Jr., *Victory at High Tide: The Inchon-Seoul Campaign* (Annapolis, Maryland: The Nautical and Aviation Publishing Co of America, 1979)

Hermes, Walter, G., *United States Army in the Korean War: Truce Tent & Fighting Front* (Honolulu: University Press of the Pacific, 2005)

Hickey, Michael, *The Korean War: The West Confronts Communism 1950–1953* (London: John Murray, 1999)

Hickman, Tom, *The Call Up: A History of National Service* (London: Headline, 2004)

Hooker, Richard, *MASH* (London: Cassell, 2004)

Hopkins, William B., *One Bugle No Drums: The Marines at Chosin Reservoir* (Chapel Hill, NC: Algonquin Books, 1986)

Hoyt, Edwin P., *The Pusan Perimeter* (New York: Stein & Day, 1984)

Ions, Edmund, *A Call to Arms: Interlude with the Military* (Newton Abbot, Devon: David & Charles, 1972)

Jacobs, James, *From the Imjin to the Hook: A National Service Gunner in the Korean War* (Barnsley: Pen and Sword, 2013)

James, Robert, *Tales from a Kitbag* (Enstone, Ox: Writersworld, 2004)

Johnson, B.S. (ed.), *All Bull: The National Servicemen* (London: Quartet Books Ltd, 1973)

Johnston, William, *A War of Patrols: Canadian Army Operations in Korea* (Toronto: UBC Press, 2003)

Kelly, Stephen F., *British Soldiers of the Korean War: In Their Own Words* (Stroud, Gloucestershire: The History Press, 2013)

Kindsvatter, Peter S., *American Soldiers: Ground Combat in the World Wars, Korea, and Vietnam* (Lawrence, Kansas: University of Kansas Press, 2003)

Kinne, Derek, *The Wooden Boxes* (London: Corgi Books, 1955)

Knox, Donald, *The Korean War: An Oral History: Pusan to Chosin* (New York: Harcourt Brace & Co., 1985)

——— *The Korean War. Uncertain Victory* (New York: Harcourt Brace & Co., 1988)

Larby, Ron, *Signals to the Right... Armoured Corps to the Left* (Privately published, 1993)

Large, Lofty, *One Man's War in Korea* (Wellingborough, Northamptonshire: William Kimber & Co Ltd, 1988)

Larsen, Sarah A , & Miller, Jennifer M , *Wisconsin Korean War Stories: Veterans Tell Their Stories from the Forgotten War* (Wisconsin Historical Society Press, 2008)

Lawton Collins, J., *War In Peacetime: The History and Lessons of Korea* (Boston: Houghton Mifflin Company, 1969)

Leckie, Robert, *Conflict: The History of the Korean War* (New York: Da Capo Press, 1996)

——— *March To Glory* (New York: ibooks inc, 2001)

Linklater, Eric, *Our Men in Korea* (London: HMSO, 1952)

Lowe, Peter, *The Origins of the Korean War Second Edition* (London: Longman, 1997)

Macadoo, Albert J. & Marshall, James E., *The 5th RCT in Korea: The Pusan Perimeter Battles, 1950* (Privately published, 2012)

MacDonald, C.A., *Korea: The War Before Vietnam* (London: Macmillan Press, 1986)

Macdonald, J.F.M., *The Borderers in Korea* (Berwick-upon-Tweed: Martins Print Works Ltd, 1954)

Mackenzie, S. P., *British Prisoners of the Korean War* (Oxford: OUP, 2012)

Macksey, Kenneth, *The Tanks: The History of the Royal Tank Regiment, 1945–1975* (London: Arms and Armour Press, 1979)

Malcolm, G.I., *The Argylls in Korea* (Edinburgh: Thomas Nelson And Sons Ltd, 1952)

Malkasian, Carter, *Essential Histories: The Korean War 1950–1953* (Oxford: Osprey Publishing Ltd, 2001)

Marshall, S.L.A., *Infantry Operations and Weapons Usage in Korea* (London: Greenhill Books, 1988)

————— *Pork Chop Hill: The American Fighting Man in Action Korea, Spring, 1953* (New York: Berkley Books, 2000)

Martin, John, *K Force to the Sharp-End* (Leamington Spar: Korvet Publishing, 1999)

Matthias, Howard, *The Korean War: Reflections of a Combat Platoon Leader* (Tallahassee, Florida: Father & Son, 1993)

McCutcheon, Campbell (ed.), *Infantry Training: The National Service Handbook* (Stroud, Gloucestershire: Tempus Publishing, 2007)

McInnes, Colin, *Hot War, Cold War: The British Army's Way in Warfare 1945–95* (London: Brassey's, 1996)

McNair, E.J., *A British Army Nurse in the Korean War: Shadows of the Far Forgotten* (Stroud, Gloucestershire: Tempus Publishing, 2007)

McWilliams, Bill, *On Hallowed Ground: The Last Battle for Por k Chop Hill* (New York: Berkley Calibre Books, 2004)

Meid, Pat & Yingling, James M., *U.S. Marine Operations in Korea 1950–1953: Volume 5 Operations in West Korea* (Washington D.C.: Historical Division, Headquarters U.S. Marine Corps, 1972)

Millet, A.R., *Essential Bibliography Series: The Korean War* (Washington, DC: Potomac Books, 2007)

Mitchell, Colin, *Having Been A Soldier* (London: Hamish Hamilton Ltd, 1969)

MOD, Treatment of British Prisoners of War in Korea (London: HMSO, 1955)

Montross, Lynn & Canzona, Nicholas A., *U.S. Marine Operations in Korea 1950–1953: Volume 1 The Pusan Perimeter* (Washington D.C.: Historical Branch, G-3 Headquarters, U.S. Marine Corps, 1954)

Morrow, Curtis James, *What's a Commie Ever Done to Black People? A Korean War Memoir* (Jefferson, NC: McFarland & Co., 1997)

Mossman, Billy C., *United States Army in the Korean War: Ebb and Flow, November 1950–July 1951* (Honolulu: University Press of the Pacific, 2005)

Nowell, Tom, *The Intrepid Observers: Notes On My Experiences in Korea 1952–1953* (Privately published, 1995)

O'Kane, Henry *O'Kane's Korea: A Soldier's tale of three years of Combat and Captivity in Korea 1950–1953* (Compiled: 1988)

Owen, Bryn and Salmon, Norman (eds), *An Account of the Services of 1st Battalion The Welch Regiment in Korea 1951–1952* (Cardiff: The Trustees of The Welch Regiment Museum, 2005)

Owen, Joseph R., *Colder than Hell: A Marine Rifle Company at Chosin Reservoir* (Annapolis, Maryland: Naval Institute Press, 1996)

Pagan, George, C., *A National Serviceman in Korea: The Royal Signals Regiment at War 1950–1953* (Swanage, Dorset: Finial Publishing, 2003)

Parritt, Brian, *Chinese Hordes and Human Waves: A Personal Account of the Korean War 1950–1953* (Barnsley: Pen and Sword, 2011)

Perrins, Anthony (ed.), *'A pretty rough do altogether': The Fifth Fusiliers in Korea 1950–1951* (Alnwick, Northumberland: The Trustees of the Fusiliers Museum of Northumberland, 2004)

Raschen, Dan, *Send Port & Pyjamas!* (London: Buckland Publications Ltd., 1987)

Rees, David, *Korea: The Limited War* (New York: Macmillan, 1964)

————— (ed.) *The Korean War History and Tactics* (London: Orbis Publishing, 1984)

————— *Korea: An Illustrated History from Ancient Times to 1945* (New York: Hippocrene Books, 2001)

Ridgway, Matthew B., *The Korean War* (New York: Da Capo Press, 1967)

Rishell, Lyle, *With a Black Platoon in Combat: A Year in Korea* (Texas A&M University Press, 1993)

Rose, David, *Off the Record: The Life and Letters of a Black Watch Officer* (Staplehurst, Kent: Spellmount Ltd, 1996)

Russ, Martin, *Breakout: The Chosin Reservoir Campaign, Korea 1950* (London: Penguin, 1999)

————— *The Last Parallel* (New York: Zebra Books, 1985)

Ryan, Mark A. and David M. Finklestein, *Chinese Warfighting: The PLA Experience Since 1949* (New York: M. E. Sharpe, 2003)

Sandler, Stanley, *The Korean War: No victors, No Vanquished* (London: UCL Press, 1999)

Shipster, John, *Mist Over the Rice-Fields: A Soldier's Story of the Burma Campaign 1943–45 and Korean War 1950–51* (Barnsley: Leo Cooper, 2000)

Shrader, Charles R., *Communist Logistics in the Korean War* (Westport, CT: Greenwood Press, 1995)

Spiller, Harry (ed), American POWs in Korea: Sixteen Personal Accounts (Jefferson, NC: McFarland & Co., 1998)

Sullivan, John A., *Toy Soldiers: Memoir of a Platoon Leader in Korea* (Jefferson, NC: McFarland & Co., 1991)

Sutton, Brig. D.J. (ed.), *The Story of the RASC and RCT 1945–1982* (London, 1983)

Taylor, Keith and Stewart, Brian (eds), *Call to Arms: Officer Cadet Training at Eaton Hall 1948–1958* (Privately published, 2006)

Taylor Keith M., *Wither the Fates Call: A Personal Account of National Service in the British Army 1950–1952* (Privately Published, 2009)

Terry, Addison, *The Battle for Pusan: A Korean War Memoir* (Novato, CA: Presidio Press Inc., 2000)

Thomas, R.C.W., *The War in Korea 1950–1953: A military Study of the War in Korea up to the Signing of the Cease Fire* (New Delhi: The English Book Store, 1968)

Thomas, Nigel and Peter Abbot, *The Korean War 1950–53* (London: Osprey, 1993)

Thompson, Julian, *The Royal Marines: From Sea Soldiers to a Special Force* (London: Pan Books, 2001)

Thompson, Reginald, *Cry Korea* (London: MacDonald & Co Ltd, 1952)

Tomedi, Rudy, *No Bugles, No Drums: An Oral History of the Korean War* (New York: John Wiley & Sons, 1994)

Tonkinson, Major Bryan, *Subalterns Serving with the 1st Battalion Durham Light Infantry in Korea September 1952–September 1953* (Privately published, 2003)

Torrance, David, *George Younger: A Life Well Lived* (Edinburgh: Birlinn, 2008)

Trigg, Noel, *A Different Kind of Fighting: From Copra to Korea, Memories of National Service* (Privately published, undated)

Walker, Adrian, *Six Campaigns: National Servicemen at War 1948–1960* (London: Leo Cooper, 1993)

——— *A Barren Place: National Servicemen in Korea 1950–1954* (London: Leo Cooper, 1994)

Watson, Brent Byron, *Far Eastern Tour: The Canadian Infantry in Korea 1950–1953* (Montreal: McGill-Queen's University Press, 2002)

Watts, J.C, *Surgeon at War* (London: Digit Books, 1955)

Westover, John G., *Combat Support in Korea* (Washington, DC: Centre of Military History United States Army, 1987)

Whatmore, D,E., *One Road to Imjin: A National Service Experience 1949–1951* (Cheltenham, Gloucestershire: Dew Line Publications, 1997)

Whelan, Richard, *Drawing the Line: The Korean War 1950–53* (London: Faber & Faber, 1990)

Williams, Neville, *A Conscript in Korea* (Barnsley: Pen and Sword, 2009)

Wilson, Dare, *Tempting the Fates: A Memoir of Service in the Second World War Palestine Korea Kenya-Aden* (Barnsley: Pen & Sword, 2006)

Wilson, David, *The Sum of Things* (Staplehurst, Kent: Spellmount, 2001)

Younger, Tony, *Blowing Our Bridges: A Memoir From Dunkirk to Korea Via Normandy* (Barnsley: Pen & Sword, 2004)

Zhang Shu Gang, *Mao's Military Romanticism: China and the Korean War, 1950–1953* (Lawrence: University Press of Kansas, 1995)

Articles

Anon, 'Editorial Korea Retrospect,' *British Army Journal,* No. 5, January 1951, pp. 2–5

——— 'Where there's a will there's a way,' *British Army Journal,* No. 7, January 1952, pp. 80–81

——— 'Operation Snatch: An account of a night operation by 2 RCR, Korea Sept 1951,' *British Army Journal,* No. 8, July 1952, pp. 51–53

Butler, Major R.S., 'The Glosters in Korea: Anti-Guerrilla Action,' *British Army Journal,* No. 7, January 1952, pp. 28–33

Cassels, Lieutenant General Sir A. James H., 'The Commonwealth Division in Korea,' *Journal of the Royal United Service Institution* Vol. XCVII, No. 591, April 1953, pp. 362–372

Coad, Major General B.A., 'The Land Campaign in Korea,' *Journal of the Royal United Service Institution* Vol. XCVII, No. 585, February 1952, pp. 2–15

Cook, Glen Steven, 'Korea: No Longer the Forgotten War' *Journal of Military History* Vol. 56, No. 3, July 1992, pp. 489–494

Courtenay, William, 'The Campaign in Korea,' *Army Quarterly* Vol. LXII, No. 2, July 1951, pp. 185–189

CRE 1 Commonwealth Div, 'Enemy Field Defences in Korea,' *British Army Journal* No. 9, January 1953, pp. 56–62

De Las Casas, Captain B., 'Irishmen over the Imjin,' *British Army Journal*, No. 7, January 1952, pp. 88–90

De Longueuil, Major J.C.S.G., 'The Daily Round,' *British Army Journal*, No. 8, July 1952, pp. 54–58

Farrar-Hockley, General Sir Anthony, 'A Reminiscence of the Chinese People's Volunteers in the Korean War,' *The China Quarterly* Vol. 98, June 1984, pp. 287–304

Fitzpatrick, Meghan K., 'Prostitutes, Penicillin and Prophylaxis: Fighting Venereal Disease in the Commonweath Division During The Korean War, 1950-1953' *Social History of Medicine*, Vol.28, Issue 3, August 2015 pp. 555-575

Gale, Lieutenant General Sir Richard N., 'Lessons of Korea,' *British Army Journal*, No. 7, January 1952, pp. 6–7

Grey, Jeffrey, 'Commonwealth Prisoners of War and British Policy during the Korean War,' *Journal of the Royal United Service Institution* Vol. 133, No. 1, 1988, pp. 71–77

Henderson, Lieutenant J.B., 'Defence of the Knoll' *British Army Journal*, No. 10, July 1953, pp. 20–24

Hickey, Colonel Michael, 'The Chinese are in. World War Three has begun,' *Journal of the Royal United Service Institution* Vol. 144, No. 3, June 1999, pp. 102–106

––––––– 'Westminster Medal Presentation: Have We Learnt the Lessons of Readiness from Korea?' *Journal of the Royal United Service Institution*, June 2000, pp. 63–69

Lowther, Lt Col Sir William G., 'Tanks in Support of Infantry' *British Army Journal*, No. 8, July 1952, pp. 48–50

Mackenzie, Major A.D., 'Letter from Chunchon' *British Army Journal*, No. 7, January 1952, pp. 86–88

Millett, Allan R., 'The Korean War: A 50–Year Critical Historiography,' in *Journal of Strategic Studies*, Vol. 24, No. 1 (March, 2001), pp. 188–224

––––––– 'The George C. Marshall Lecture in Military History: Introduction to the Korean War' *Journal of Military History* Vol. 65, October 2001, pp. 921–936

Pike, Brigadier W.G.H., 'Artillery and Other Matters' *British Army Journal*, No. 8, July 1952, pp. 59–62

'Sheldrake,' 'Bats from a Korean Belfry,' *British Army Journal*, No.8, July 1952, pp. 43–48

Taylor, Brig. G., 'The 28th British Commonwealth Brigade in the Battle of Kowang San and Maryang San,' *British Army Journal*, No. 9, January 1953, pp. 45–54

Thomas, Major E.V., 'Counter-Bombardment in Korea' *The Journal of the Royal Artillery* Vol. LXXX, No. 2, April 1953, pp. 96–106

Thomas, Major R.C.W., 'The First Commonwealth Division in Korea' *Army Quarterly* Vol. LXIV, No. 1, April 1952, pp. 41–47

––––––– 'The Chinese Communist Forces in Korea' *Army Quarterly* Vol. LXV No. 1, October 1952, pp. 35–41

Walwyn, Major C.E.B., 'Ambush,' *British Army Journal*, No. 7, January 1952, pp. 33–35

––––––– 'Limited Offensive,' *British Army Journal*, No. 7, January 1952, pp. 35–39

Willoughby, Lt Col J.E.F., 'Pont 112,' *British Army Journal*, No. 7, January 1952, pp. 76–79

Williams, J.A., 'Korea and the Malayan Emergency-the Strategic Priorities,' *Journal of the Royal United Service Institution* Vol. 118, No. 2, June 1973, pp. 56–62

Wilson, Major A.D.R.G., 'A Company in Korea,' *British Army Journal*, No. 6, July 1951, pp. 12–18

_____ 'Vanguard in Action,' *British Army Journal*, No. 7, January 1952, pp. 90–93

Wilz, John Edward, 'Korea: The Forgotten War' *Journal of Military History* Vol. 53, January 1989, pp. 95–100

Unpublished Dissertations

Dealtry, Tom, *Compare the integration of 41 Commando Royal Marines with the United States Marine Corps and that of 27th and 29th Infantry Brigade with the United States Army during the Korean War,* University of Salford, BA thesis, undated

Goulty, James H.R., *Training, Preparations and Combat Experience of the British Army during the Korean War, 1950–1953,* University of Leeds, PhD thesis, 2009.

Index

A

ABCA (Army Bureau of Current Affairs), 60
Adams, Walter, 35, 212
Adelmann, Walter, 203, 205
Almond, Gen. Edward M., 82, 93-95, 98, 221
Anderson, William, 168, 171, 246
Apel, Dr. Otto, 169, 233, 239, 245
Appleman, Lt. Col. Roy E., 94, 99, 210, 217-218, 220-222, 246
Astley-Cooper, Capt. D., 106

B

BAR (Browning Automatic Rifle), 59, 72, 99, 125, 143
BAOR (British Army of the Rhine), 25, 214
Bair, Chester, 97, 221
Bailes, Joe, 46, 214, 244
Bailey, Glen, 20, 35, 72, 75, 87, 203, 206, 210, 212, 218, 220, 239, 243
Bailey, Lawrence, 177, 235
Baldovi, Louis, 132, 215-216, 220-221, 225-229, 235, 237, 246
Ballard, Carl, 33, 36-37, 58, 134, 143, 146, 152, 200, 204, 207, 212-213, 216, 227-230, 238- 239
Ballenger, Lee, 134, 137, 154, 226,-227, 229-230, 246
Barr, Maj-Gen. David, 95, 221
Barclay, Brig. C. N., 16, 210, 224, 238, 246
Barker, Lt. Col. A. J., 226, 228, 234, 246
Barrett, Don, 26, 211, 219, 239, 242, 244
Bazooka, 12, 21, 68-70, 119

BCGH (British Commonwealth General Hospital), 168, 170, 174
Beavis, Lt. J., 30, 212
Beckerley, Edward (Ted), 107, 177, 181, 222, 235, 241-242
Benson, Lt. G. H., 129, 226
Benedict, Richard, 78
Berebitsky, William, 134, 210, 226-227, 229-230, 246
Biderman, Albert, 176, 235-237, 246
Blair, Clay, 21, 67, 80, 93, 210, 217-221, 246
Bloody Gulch, 74
Bloody Ridge, 123-125
Bloss, Lamar, 41, 170, 204, 213, 234, 239, 243
Bowser, Col. Alpha, 98, 221
Boydell, Dr. Stanley, 27, 158, 211, 231, 233, 242
Brady, Dave, 99, 221, 246
Brady, Lt. James, 50, 134, 147, 155, 214, 227, 229-233 246
Bren gun, 40, 44, 47, 91, 107, 116, 129, 142, 146, 150, 153
Breske, John, 130, 226
Brodie, Maj-Gen. Tom, 112
Brown, George, 141, 228, 239, 245
Browning, Jack, 180, 235
Browning Medium Machine Gun, 116, 153
Budbrooke Barracks, 35-36, 213
Bulling, Herman, 171, 234, 244
Bussey, Lt. Col. Charles, 22, 67, 156, 159, 210, 217-218, 231, 246
Butt, Gordon, 38, 140, 205, 228, 239, 245
'Burp gun,' 67, 77, 145-146, 150
Burnett, Capt. Al, 69, 217

C

C Rations, 163, 166-167
CAS (close air support), 1, 100, 110, 136, 153, 227, 246
Cain, Lt. R. M., 109, 222
Caine, Michael, 36, 41, 57, 62, 212-213, 215-216, 246
California, 23, 42, 55, 63-64, 73, 166
Callahan, Glendle, 41, 213, 243
Camps:
  Breckenridge, 36-37
  Catterick, 35-36
  Lejeune, 24
  Pendleton, 23, 42
Carew, Tim, 26, 28, 31, 211-212, 215, 223, 246
Carlaw, Maj. James, 50, 214, 244
Carter, Alan, 35, 47, 58, 61-62, 161, 163, 212, 214, 216, 226, 232, 246
Carter, Francis, 242
Caterham (Surrey), 37, 213
Causer, Alan, 139, 200, 216, 228, 238, 245
Chapman, Jack, 181, 235
Chapman, Rod , 41, 51, 131, 213, 215, 226, 232, 239, 243
Chipyong-ni, 109-110, 222-223, 247
Chogam-ni, 114
Chongsong (Camp 1), 183, 192, 247
Chorwon, 111, 122
Chosin Reservoir, 14, 94-102, 171, 173, 177, 181, 188, 220-222, 232-234, 248-249
Chungdam-ni, 74
Clark, Commander Eugene, 80
Clark, Gen. Mark, 121, 143, 145, 198, 224, 238, 246
Clawson, Tom, 131, 226
Coad, Brig. (later Maj-Gen.) B. A., 105, 241, 251
Colchester (Essex), 29-30, 238, 246
Condron, Andrew, 188, 242
Connor, John, 102, 221, 247
Cooper, Gen. Sir George, 18, 49, 210, 214, 242
Craig, Brig-Gen. Edward A., 23
Crawford, C. S., 50, 167, 210, 214-215, 227, 230, 233, 247
Crombez, Col. Marcel G., 110
Coulter, Lt. Gen. John B., 83
Cubiss, Lt. (later Brig.) J. M., 91, 220
Cunningham, Cyril, 175, 234, 236 247

D

Davies, Rev. Sam, 150, 185-186, 194, 223-224, 229, 236-237, 247
Dean, Maj. Gen. William F., 9, 12, 71, 185, 209-210, 217, 236, 247
De la Billière, Gen. Sir Peter, 46, 48, 53, 56, 58, 214-215, 230, 234, 245, 247
Dill, Lt. Col. James H., 158, 210, 224, 230-232, 247
DMZ (Demilitarised Zone), 3, 199-201
Donnellan, Jarleth, 64, 217, 242
Donner, William, 164-165, 172-173, 232-234, 243
Drysdale, Lt. Col. D. B., 99
Dunning, Paul, 50, 214, 243
Dyer, John, 117, 224, 242

E

Eaton Hall OCS, 34, 36, 43, 127, 205, 213, 250
Eastap, (Sgt. later Maj.) Michael, 28, 84, 211, 219, 234, 242
Ebisu (Japan), 165
Eckert, Carter J., 8, 247
Eisenhower, President D., 176, 235
Elliot, Donald (Don), 196, 201, 237-238
Emer, Jerry, 108, 222
Ent, Brig-Gen. Uzal, 217-218, 247
Erickson, John, 59, 179, 192, 216, 235, 237, 243

F

FAC (Forward Air Controller), 136
Faith, Lt. Col. Don C., 96-97
Farrar-Hockley, Gen. Sir Anthony, 10, 27, 114, 116-117, 195, 210-211, 222-226, 228, 234-237, 245, 247, 251
FEC (Far East Command), 12
Felton, Monica, 190
Fenton, Capt. Francis, 81, 219
Finks, Clark, 147, 229
Finland, 30
Forts:
George , 36
Leonard, 41
Riley, 35-36, 41, 43
Formosa (Taiwan), 19
France, 15, 25, 123
Freeman, Col. Paul, 109
French, David, 52, 247

G

Gaddy, Billy, 178, 185, 235-236
Geneva Convention, 175, 177
Gibbs, Lyle, 21, 70, 210, 217, 239, 243
Gordon, Maj. A. L., 150, 227-229
Goulden, Joseph, 73, 83, 218-219, 247
Grey, Prof. Jeffrey, 11, 135, 210, 227, 230-231, 245, 247, 251
Green, David, 112, 167, 179, 182-183, 193-194, 222-223, 229, 233, 235-237, 247
Graves Registration, 170, 204
Grist, Lt. Col. Digby, 30-31, 113, 212, 223
Gruenther, Lt. Richard, 95, 221
Gugeler, Russel, 71, 84, 221, 247
Gudmundsson, Bruce, 117, 136, 224, 227, 247

H

Hagaru-ri, 97-100, 234
Hall, J. C., 47, 214, 238, 245
Halle, Robert, 39, 55, 155, 213, 215, 230, 243
Halley, Derek, 37, 55, 59, 213, 215-216, 226, 232-233, 238, 245, 247
Hamhung, 96, 101
Hara Mura (Japan), 44-46, 48, 51, 214
Harding, Gen. Sir John, 54
Harvey (Capt. later Brig.) M. G., 85, 88, 90-91, 216, 219-220, 230, 247
Hastings, Max, 81, 130, 176, 188, 217, 219, 221, 223, 226-227, 235-237, 247
Hawaii, 20, 56, 73, 132, 166, 215, 220-221, 225, 235, 238, 246
Hawkes, Ron, 201, 238
Heinl, Col. Robert, 83, 219, 248
Heartbreak Ridge, 14, 123-125, 131, 178
Henderson, Lt. J. B., 251
Hill 174, 83
Hill 227, 126, 129-130
Hill 282, 153, 230
Hill 347, 132
Hickey, Col. Michael, 29, 31-32, 52, 87, 115, 130, 212, 215, 217, 220, 223, 225-226, 238, 245, 248, 251
Hickman, Tom, 34, 212, 248
Higgins, Marguerite, 69, 71, 213, 217
Hobbs, RSM Jack, 31, 212
Holmes, Richard, 35, 212
Holdsworth, Lt. David, 113, 150, 223, 230, 242

Holland, 25
Holland, Geoff, 57, 215
Holroyd, Reuben, 39, 213, 245
Hong Kong, 19, 25-28, 49, 52, 54, 62-63, 73, 122, 168, 202
Hook (The), 14, 133, 172, 200, 206
Hough, Brian, 165, 202, 232-233, 238
Howe, Maj., 107
Huerta, Octavio, 58, 160, 216, 231, 243
Hungnam, 94, 98, 101-102, 183
Hyslop, George, 43, 64, 213, 217, 243

I

IJA (Imperial Japanese Army), 66, 76
Ikeda, Lt. Herbert, 91, 220
Imjin River, 111-113, 115-116, 118, 123, 125, 150-151, 153, 163, 177, 179, 181-183, 191, 197, 200
Inchon, 1, 13, 31, 58, 64, 67, 80-84, 93, 217, 219, 248
Ions, Lt. Edmund, 63, 158, 214, 216, 230, 245
'Iron Triangle,' 122, 199
Italy, 66-67, 78, 80
Iwon, 94-95

J

Japan, 5-7, 12, 17, 19-22, 44, 46-47, 49, 51, 53, 56, 59, 61-63, 65, 69, 73, 145, 154, 156, 164, 168
James, Robert, 143, 228, 248
Jamestown Line, 125, 128, 130, 141
Jamieson, Robert, 56, 215
JCS (Joint Chiefs of Staff), 12-13, 93, 128
Johnston Island, 63-64
Johnston, Lt. Col. J. C. M., 59, 204, 216, 239, 245
Johnston, William, 224
Jongsma, Herm, 146, 151, 229, 238, 243
JRBD (Joint Reinforcement Base Depot), 51
Judd, Ben, 110, 124, 222, 225

K

K Volunteers, 52
Kap'yong, 105, 222
Kansas Line, 112, 122, 200-201
Kesy, Chet, 94, 220
Kimpo Airfield, 82
Kimbrough, Col. Robert, 144, 228

King, Dale, 178, 186, 235-236
Kingsford, Tony, 76, 218, 239
Kinne, Derek, 58, 113, 117, 183, 185, 187, 189, 195, 215-216, 223-224, 236, 248
Kindsvatter, Lt. Col. Peter S., 20, 33-34, 51, 159, 212, 214-215, 231, 248
KMAG (Korea Military Advisory Group), 11
Knox, Donald, 198, 210, 215, 217-222, 225, 227, 235, 238, 248
Koch, Lt. Kenneth W., 118
Koto-ri, 98-100, 234
Kowang-sang (Point 355), 125-126
Koyang, 105, 222
Krenz, Darrell, 183, 190-191, 236-237

L

Larby, Ron, 33, 36, 212-213, 248
Large, Lofty, 45, 116-117, 153, 182, 214, 216, 224, 230, 235- 237, 245, 248
Lantz, Gordon, 177, 235, 243
Lee Enfield Rifle, 89, 116
Leith-Macgregor, Lt. Col. Robert, 92, 114, 220
Linklater, Eric, 25, 211, 248
Lonsdale, Brig. M. R. (Mike) 45, 214
Lowe, Peter 7, 9, 210, 248
Lucock, Jim 47, 208, 214, 239

M

M-1 Rifle, 42, 146
MacArthur, Gen. Douglas, 12-14, 19, 23, 25, 66, 80, 83, 93-94, 121, 206, 219
MacDonald, Maj-Gen. J. F. M., 225-226, 248
MacDonald, Malcolm, 54
Mackellar, Lt. P., 77, 218
MacLean, Col. Allan D., 96
MacLean, Maj. John, 214, 245
Man, Col. Andrew M., 27, 155, 242
Manchester, 165, 179, 187, 202
Manchuria, 5, 7-8, 19, 157, 180
Marshall, S. L. A., 88-89, 220, 226, 234, 248
MASH (Mobile Army Surgical Hospital), 167-169, 207, 233, 239, 248
Masan, 74
Matteson, Dave, 23, 211
Matthias, Lt. Howard, 39, 51, 63-64, 136, 142, 146, 163, 165, 213, 215-216, 226-229, 231-233, 249
Maud, Stanley, 141-142, 228

May, Arthur, 160-161
McAlister, Don, 96, 221
McCabe, Eddy , 24, 211
McInnes, Colin, 15, 210, 249,
Menninger, Charles, 70-71, 217
Mercer, Sam, 65, 89, 217, 220, 230, 242
Michaelis, Lt. Col. J. H., 42, 213
Mig-15, 193
Milburn, Maj-Gen. Frank W., 83
Millett, Alan R., 5, 8, 11, 209, 225, 227, 251
Moore, 2/Lt., 140, 228
Monclar, Gen. Ralph, 110
Morrow, Curtiss, 86, 160, 171, 220, 229-231, 233-234, 249
MLR (Main Line of Resistance), 133-135, 137
Mulder, Robert, 54, 168, 170, 233, 244
Mulligan, Maj. J. W. H., 32, 212, 222,230
Murray, Lt. Col. Ray, 23, 80, 211, 219

N

NAAFI (Navy Army and Air Force Institutes), 161, 166, 232
Nagelkirk, Sherwin, 41, 65, 123, 134, 213, 217, 224,227, 244
Naktong River, 13, 16, 73-75, 79, 84, 153
Napalm, 97, 110, 129, 132, 136, 153
NATO (North Atlantic Treaty Organisation), 24
National Guard, 20, 22-23, 133, 147, 177, 210, 226, 230
National Service (Act), 33
Nevill, Kenneth, 178, 235
Newman, Richard, 57, 215
NKPA (North Korean People's Army), 10, 13, 66-68, 71-72, 75-80, 83-84, 86, 90, 93-94, 101, 122, 175, 217-219
Normandy, 30, 250
North Korea, 10-13, 15, 19, 42, 53, 71, 86-87, 93, 97, 114, 175, 180, 182-183, 187-188, 190-191, 194-196, 198, 208-209, 229, 236-237, 247

O

Oates, David, 170, 234, 241
Obong-ni Ridge, 79
O'Kane, Henry, 155, 179, 184, 187, 193, 230, 235-237, 249
Okinawa, 12, 20
Old Baldy, 131, 169, 199

O'Leary, Lloyd, 100
Olsen, Lt. Col. Charles, 19, 95, 210, 221, 244
OP (Outposts), 98, 128, 133-135, 142
OPLR (Outpost Line of Resistance), 134
Operations:
Big Switch, 196
Bluehearts, 66, 80
Chromite, 13, 80-81
Commando, 125, 127-128, 214, 225,
    239, 245
Full Moon, 228
Graduate, 26, 211
Jehu, 141, 228
Killer, 108-109, 172
Little Switch, 196
Piledriver, 122
Swanlake, 200
Thunderbolt, 108
Ripper, 108-109
Roundup, 108
Osan, 68
Orange, Ronald V., 162, 245
Owen, Lt. Joseph, 94, 220-222, 233, 249

P

Panmunjom, 128, 130, 196
38th Parallel, 8, 13-15, 22, 24, 50, 83, 92-93,
    108, 111-113, 120-122, 175, 199
Parris Island, 39
Peace Talks, 122, 128, 130, 157-158, 195, 198
Pearson, Frank, 161, 232, 245
Penman, Major, 76, 218
Perrins, Capt. Tony, 31, 212, 216, 223, 232,
    237, 241-242, 245, 249
Phillips, Capt. Sam A. S., 32, 212, 238, 242,
    245
Pililaau, Herbert K., 125
Point 187, 125
Point 210, 125-126
Pork Chop Hill (Hill 255), 14, 133, 199, 226-
    227, 248-249
Port Arthur, 5, 7
PTSD (Post Traumatic Stress Disorder), 203
Punchbowl, 123, 142, 169
Pusan Perimeter, 1, 13, 25, 43, 63, 73-74, 78-
    81, 83, 92, 210-211, 217-219, 247-249
Pyoktong (Camp 5), 188, 195
Pyongyang, 13-14, 17, 122, 157, 180, 183-
    184, 196, 209

Q

Quiring, Charles, 188, 236

R

RAF Lyneham , 62
Raschen, Col. Dan, 53, 210, 215, 232-233,
    249
Red Cross, 161, 175, 198
R&R (Rest & Recuperation), 164-165
Rhee, Syngman, 9-11
Ridgway, Gen. Matthew B., 10, 14, 17-18,
    68, 92, 102-104, 108, 111, 121, 128, 157,
    209-210, 217, 222-223, 231, 249
Rishell, Lt. Lyle, 51, 64, 156, 215, 217-219,
    230-232, 249
Robertson, Sgt., 77
Robottom, John, 204-205, 231, 239, 245
Roeder, Elroy, 124, 225
Roise, Lt. Col. Harold, 24, 80, 211, 219
Russia, 6, 8-10, 19, 175
Russo-Japanese War, 6-7

S

Sachon Pass, 74
Sarros, George , 62, 75, 216, 218, 244
Saddic, John, 173, 234
San Francisco, 55, 58
Sams, Brig. Gen. Crawford F., 7, 209, 234
Sandhurst (Royal Military Academy) , 31, 59
Samuels, Robert, 24, 40-41, 99, 174, 203, 211,
    213, 221, 234, 239, 244
Salmon, Maj. Norman, 60, 143, 216, 227-229,
    245, 249
Samichon Valley, 133, 135
San Diego, 39, 53, 55, 99, 155
Schuff, Leroy, 82, 219
Schrader, William, 39, 50, 64, 145, 213-214,
    216, 228, 244
Schutte, Calvin, 55, 65, 169, 202, 215, 217,
    224, 233, 238, 244
Seoul, 6, 12-14, 17, 48-49, 64, 68, 72, 80-83,
    93, 104- 108, 111, 208
Sebresos, Bertram, 89, 220-221
Seattle, 22, 202
Selective Service Act, 32-33
Sharpe, Lt. L. C., 90, 220, 222
Shipster, Col. John, 62, 71, 216-217, 242, 250

Shrader, Charles R., 16, 210, 250
Shoemaker, Dr. Robert, 24, 56, 211, 215, 232, 234, 250
Shinagawa, Susumu, 196, 235, 237
Sibyon-ni, 84
Singapore, 62, 201
Simons, Brig. Gen. Ed, 23, 211
SIW (Self Inflicted Wounds), 3, 171
Smith, Lt. Col. C. B., 68
Smith, Maj-Gen. O. P., 98
Smith, Paul, 195
Smith, Robert (Bob), 24, 158, 211, 231
Spring, Norman, 199, 205, 238-239, 244
Spiroff, Boris, 22, 64, 85-86, 122, 152, 165, 209-210, 216, 219- 220, 224, 229, 232
Speakman, Bill, 129, 226
Sparrow, Lt. Col. John H. A., 149, 229
Splan, Tanjore, 22, 75, 210, 218, 244
Stanford Point, 30
Stafford, Don, 133, 226
Sten gun, 40, 47, 146, 171
Stingley, Patrick, 99, 221
Stirling, Col. Sir James 43, 77, 213, 218, 245
Suez 62
Sullivan, Lt. John, 138, 144, 147, 152, 161, 227-230, 232, 250
Summers, Harry, 103-104, 222
Sumatra, 53

T

Taylor, Brig. George, 123, 224
Taylor, Lt. Keith M., 36-37, 46-47, 55-56, 127, 157, 205, 207, 210, 213-214, 239
Terry, Maj. Addison, 74, 78, 218, 250
Thomas, Maj. E. V., 227
Thomas, Maj. R. C. W., 223, 227
Thornley, Darrell, 16, 21-22, 68, 72, 210, 217-218, 244
Tokyo, 21, 23, 93, 165
Triangle Hill, 51
Trigg, Noel, 54, 62, 215-216, 250
Truman, President Harry, 14, 19, 22, 24, 66, 108, 158
Tunnicliffe, Lt. Barry, 54, 56, 61, 131, 215-216, 226, 229, 233, 239, 245

Tyas, Albert, 164, 182, 187, 190, 192, 197, 229, 232, 236-237, 242, 245

U

Universal Military Training Act, 33

V

Van Fleet, Gen. James A., 14, 111, 121, 128
Van Zandt, Lt. Harry, 157, 231, 244
VD (Venereal Disease), 173, 251
Vickers Medium Machine Gun, 40, 44, 126, 150
Vietnam, 1, 33, 50, 62, 158, 202, 206-207, 212, 214, 231, 248

W

Waegwan, 179
Walker, Gen. Walton H., 14, 73, 81, 83, 92, 102
Washington D. C., 14, 22-23, 73, 202
Watts, Lt. Col. J. C., 174, 234, 250
Wellesley Barracks, 39
Whatmore, Col. Denys F., 36, 45, 213-215, 250
Whiting, Barry, 165, 167, 170, 203, 207, 232-234, 239, 245
Williams, J. A., 25, 211
Williams, Neville, 144, 164
Wilson, Brig. David, 63, 75, 78, 216-219, 250-251, 232, 242
Wirth, Leroy, 70, 217
Winn, Maj. John, 112, 212, 216, 223
Winnington, Alan, 190
Wood, William, 82, 96
Wyoming Line 122

Y

Yalu River, 5-7, 13, 15, 87, 94-96, 108, 183
Yerby, Bob, 26, 105, 2111, 222, 238, 245
Yudam-ni, 98

Z

Zonge, George, 101, 221